COMPASSION IN EARLY MODERN LITERATURE AND CULTURE

This collection is an enquiry into compassion as an early modern emotional phenomenon, situating it within the complexity of European economic, social, cultural and religious tensions. Drawing on recent work in the history of emotions, leading scholars consider the particularities of early modern compassion, demonstrating its entanglements with diverse genres and geographies. Chapters on canonical and less familiar works explore tragedy, comedy, sermons, philosophy, treatises on consolation, medical writing, and dramatic theory, showing how early modern compassion shaped attitudes and social structures that remain central to the way we imagine our response to suffering today, and suggesting how such investigations can ultimately provoke new ways of thinking about community in contemporary Europe.

KRISTINE STEENBERGH is Associate Professor of English Literature at Vrije Universiteit, Amsterdam.

KATHERINE IBBETT is Professor of French at the University of Oxford. She is the author of *Compassion's Edge: Fellow-Feeling and Its Limits in Early Modern France* (2018).

COMPASSION IN EARLY MODERN LITERATURE AND CULTURE

Feeling and Practice

EDITED BY

KRISTINE STEENBERGH

Vrije Universiteit Amsterdam

KATHERINE IBBETT

University of Oxford

CAMBRIDGE
UNIVERSITY PRESS

University Printing House, Cambridge CB2 8BS, United Kingdom

One Liberty Plaza, 20th Floor, New York, NY 10006, USA

477 Williamstown Road, Port Melbourne, VIC 3207, Australia

314–321, 3rd Floor, Plot 3, Splendor Forum, Jasola District Centre, New Delhi – 110025, India

79 Anson Road, #06–04/06, Singapore 079906

Cambridge University Press is part of the University of Cambridge.

It furthers the University's mission by disseminating knowledge in the pursuit of education, learning, and research at the highest international levels of excellence.

www.cambridge.org
Information on this title: www.cambridge.org/9781108495394
DOI: 10.1017/9781108862172

© Cambridge University Press 2021

This publication is in copyright. Subject to statutory exception and to the provisions of relevant collective licensing agreements, no reproduction of any part may take place without the written permission of Cambridge University Press.

First published 2021

A catalogue record for this publication is available from the British Library.

Library of Congress Cataloging-in-Publication Data
NAMES: Ibbett, Katherine, editor. | Steenbergh, Kristine, editor.
TITLE: Compassion in early modern literature and culture : feeling and practice / edited by Katherine Ibbett, Kristine Steenbergh.
DESCRIPTION: Cambridge, United Kingdom ; New York, NY : Cambridge University Press, 2021. | Includes bibliographical references and index.
IDENTIFIERS: LCCN 2020058206 (print) | LCCN 2020058207 (ebook) | ISBN 9781108495394 (hardback) | ISBN 9781108818025 (paperback) | ISBN 9781108862172 (epub)
SUBJECTS: LCSH: English literature–Early modern, 1500-1700–History and criticism. | Compassion in literature. | Christianity and literature–England–History–16th century. | Christianity and literature–England–History–17th century. | Literature and society–England–History–16th century. | Literature and society–England–History–17th century.
CLASSIFICATION: LCC PR408.C618 C66 2021 (print) | LCC PR408.C618 (ebook) | DDC 820.9/353–dc23
LC record available at https://lccn.loc.gov/2020058206
LC ebook record available at https://lccn.loc.gov/2020058207

ISBN 978-1-108-49539-4 Hardback

Cambridge University Press has no responsibility for the persistence or accuracy of URLs for external or third-party internet websites referred to in this publication and does not guarantee that any content on such websites is, or will remain, accurate or appropriate.

Contents

Acknowledgements	*page* viii
List of Contributors	ix

Introduction   1
Kristine Steenbergh and Katherine Ibbett

PART I THEORISING

1   The Ethics of Compassion in Early Modern England   25
Bruce R. Smith

2   The Compassionate Self of the Catholic Reformation   44
Katherine Ibbett

PART II CONSOLING

3   'Hee Left Them Not Comfortlesse By the Way': Grief and Compassion in Early Modern English Consolatory Culture   63
Paula Barros

4   Friendship, Counsel and Compassion in Early Modern Medical Thought   82
Stephen Pender

PART III EXHORTING

5   'Compassion and Mercie Draw Teares from the Godlyfull Often': The Rhetoric of Sympathy in the Early Modern Sermon   103
Richard Meek

v

Contents

6 Mollified Hearts and Enlarged Bowels: Practising Compassion in Reformation England 121
Kristine Steenbergh

PART IV PERFORMING

7 Civic Liberties and Community Compassion: The Jesuit Drama of Poland-Lithuania 141
Clarinda E. Calma and Jolanta Rzegocka

8 Compassion, Contingency and Conversion in James Shirley's *The Sisters* 159
Alison Searle

PART V RESPONDING

9 Mountainish Inhumanity in Illyria: Compassion in *Twelfth Night* as Social Luxury and Political Duty 179
Elisabetta Tarantino

10 Standing on a Beach: Shakespeare and the Sympathetic Imagination 197
Eric Langley

PART VI GIVING

11 'To Feel What Wretches Feel': Reformation and the Re-naming of English Compassion 219
Toria Johnson

12 Alms Petitions and Compassion in Sixteenth-Century London 237
Rebecca Tomlin

PART VII RACIALISING

13 Pity and Empire in the *Brevísima relación de la destrucción de las Indias* (1552) 257
Matthew Goldmark

14 'Our Black Hero': Compassion for Friends and Others
in Aphra Behn's *Oroonoko* 273
John D. Staines

PART VIII CONTEMPORARY COMPASSIONS

15 Contemporary Compassions: Interrelating in
the Anthropocene 293
Kristine Steenbergh

Index 302

Acknowledgements

Kristine would like to thank all participants in the conference "Compassion in Early Modern Culture 1500–1700," at Vrije Universiteit Amsterdam, which inspired this volume. The conference was part of the research programme "Moving Scenes" (project number 275-30-021) financed by the Dutch Research Council (NWO). She is also grateful to all contributors to the volume, to Emily Hockley and Natasha Burton at Cambridge University Press for seeing the book through the publication process, and to Beth Morel for her thoughtful copy-editing. Finally, warm thanks to Katherine Ibbett for being such a generous and compassionate co-editor.

Katherine, too, would like to thank the contributors and editors, but most of all she thanks Kristine: for including her, and for exemplifying compassionate care for prose and people alike.

Contributors

PAULA BARROS is *maître de conférences* in the English Department at Université Paul-Valéry, Montpellier 3. She is a member of the Institute for Research on the Renaissance, the Neo-classical Age and the Enlightenment (IRCL), a joint research centre of the CNRS. Her research focuses on religion and emotion in early modern England. Her recent publications include articles on mourning and consolation in the letters of Sir Kenelm Digby and the emotions of God in Protestant spirituality. With Claudie Martin-Ulrich and Inès Kirschleger, she has co-edited *Prêcher la mort à l'époque moderne: regards croisés sur la France et l'Angleterre* (Classiques Garnier, 2020).

CLARINDA E. CALMA is Associate Professor at Tischner European University in Kraków. Recent articles include "Mikołaj Krzysztof Radziwiłł: Prince, Patron and Printer" (Brill, 2016) and "Edmund Campion's Prague Homilies: The Concionale ex concionibus a R.P. Edmundo Campiano" (Brill, 2019). She co-edited *Publishing Subversive Texts in Elizabeth England and the Polish-Lithuanian Commonwealth* (Brill, 2016) with Teresa Bela and Jolanta Rzegocka. Her current book project explores the reception of the English Jesuit Edmund Campion (1540–1581) in the Polish-Lithuanian Commonwealth and Central Europe.

MATTHEW GOLDMARK is Assistant Professor of Spanish at Florida State University. He is a specialist in colonial Latin American literature and culture and in gender and sexuality studies. His current book project, *Forms of Relation: Composition and Kinship in Colonial Spanish America*, studies the reproduction of empire in the early modern Atlantic. He has published on topics including transgender studies, the indigenous Andes, and colonial intimacy.

List of Contributors

KATHERINE IBBETT is Professor of French at Oxford University and Caroline de Jager Fellow at Trinity College, Oxford. She is the author of *The Style of the State in French Theater 1630–1660: Neoclassicism and Government* (Ashgate, 2009) and *Compassion's Edge: Fellow-Feeling and Its Limits in Early Modern France* (University of Pennsylvania Press, 2018); her work on compassion has been supported by the Australian Research Council Centre for the History of the Emotions and the Radcliffe Institute of Advanced Studies. She's now working on a book about water in early modern France and New France.

TORIA JOHNSON is Lecturer in Early Modern Literature at the University of Birmingham. She has recently published work on the intersections of law and emotion in early modern Europe, and cultures of fear in *Macbeth* and *Othello*. Her book, which explores early modern understandings of emotion as a social construct, and considers how dramatic portrayals of pity reflect and contribute to early modern English notions of selfhood, is forthcoming with Boydell & Brewer.

ERIC LANGLEY is Associate Professor in Shakespeare and Renaissance Literature at UCL. His first monograph – *Narcissism and Suicide in the Works of Shakespeare and His Contemporaries* – was published by Oxford University Press in 2009; in 2018, Oxford published a second monograph entitled *Shakespeare's Contagious Sympathies: Ill Communications*. He has written articles on a range of topics including Renaissance erotica, friendship essays, atomism, and Montaigne's digressive tendencies, and his first poetry collection – *Raking Light* (Carcanet, 2017) – was nominated for the Felix Dennis award at that year's Forward Prizes. He is currently researching a monograph on early modern conceptions of causality.

RICHARD MEEK is Lecturer in English at the University of Hull. He is the author of *Narrating the Visual in Shakespeare* (Ashgate, 2009), and co-editor of *Shakespeare's Book: Essays in Reading, Writing and Reception* (Manchester University Press, 2008), *The Renaissance of Emotion: Understanding Affect in Shakespeare and His Contemporaries* (Manchester University Press, 2015), and *Ekphrastic Encounters: New Interdisciplinary Essays on Literature and the Visual Arts* (Manchester University Press, 2019). He is currently completing a study of sympathy in early modern literature and culture.

STEPHEN PENDER is Associate Professor of English at the University of Windsor (Canada) and specialist in early modern literature and intellectual history, the history of rhetoric, and the history of medicine. With Nancy J. Struever he is the co-editor of *Rhetoric and Medicine in Early Modern Europe 1500 to 1700* (Ashgate, 2012). He is currently at work on the relationship between rhetoric, medicine, and the passions in early modern England, to be published in a monograph, *Therapy and the Passions in Early Modern England: Rhetoric, Medicine, Moral Philosophy*, which was supported by an SSHRC grant in intellectual history.

JOLANTA RZEGOCKA is Honorary Lecturer at the Department of English Language and Drama (UCL), and Associate Professor of Anglo-American Literature at the Jesuit University Ignatianum in Kraków, Poland. She is currently working on playbills from the school theatres of the Jesuit Province of Poland-Lithuania in the context of civic virtues. Her research is funded by the National Science Centre of Poland. With Teresa Bela and Clarinda Calma she coedited *Publishing Subversive Texts in Elizabeth England and the Polish-Lithuanian Commonwealth* (2016), and with Paweł Kaźmierczak *Moral Upbringing Through the Arts and Literature* (2018).

ALISON SEARLE is Associate Professor of Textual Studies at the University of Leeds. Her monograph entitled *'The Eyes of Your Heart': Literary and Theological Trajectories of Imagining Biblically* was published in 2008. She is co-general editor (with Johanna Harris) of a complete edition of Richard Baxter's correspondence forthcoming with Oxford University Press. She is currently writing her second book *Pastoral Care Through Letters in the British Atlantic* under contract with Cambridge University Press.

BRUCE R. SMITH is Dean's Professor of English and Theatre at the University of Southern California. He studies the literature and culture of early modern England, including Shakespeare, gender, sexuality, acoustic ecology and historical phenomenology. Among his books are *The Acoustic World of Early Modern England: Attending to the O-Factor* (1999); *The Key of Green: Passion and Perception in Renaissance Culture* (2008); *Phenomenal Shakespeare* (2010); and *Shakespeare | Cut: Rethinking Cutwork in an Age of Distraction* (2016). He is also the editor of the two-volume *Cambridge Guide to the Worlds of Shakespeare* (2016 and online in the Cambridge Shakespeare database, 2020).

JOHN D. STAINES is Associate Professor of English at John Jay College of Criminal Justice, CUNY, New York. He is the author of *The Tragic*

Histories of Mary Queen of Scots, 1560–1690: Rhetoric, Passions, and Political Literature (Ashgate, 2009). Among his many articles, in 2004 he published an essay on early modern compassion which lies behind the interests of many of us in this volume ("Compassion in the Public Sphere of Milton and King Charles," in *Reading the Early Modern Passions: Essays in the Cultural History of Emotion*, ed. Gail Kern Paster et al., University of Pennsylvania Press, 2004). His current research explores early modern responses to religious violence.

KRISTINE STEENBERGH is Associate Professor in English Literature at Vrije Universiteit Amsterdam. Her research interests include early modern English literature, the cultural history of emotions, and the environmental humanities. Her current book project, supported by the Netherlands Organisation for Scientific Research, focuses on the practice of compassion in early modern English theatres. She co-edited *Sexed Sentiments: Interdisciplinary Perspectives on Gender and Emotion* (2011). Among her recent publications are "Cognition and Affect" in the *Cambridge Guide to the Worlds of Shakespeare* (2016) and "Weeping Verse" on the role of compassion in Jasper Heywood's translation of Seneca's *Troades* in *Renaissance Studies* (2016).

ELISABETTA TARANTINO studied English literature at postgraduate level in Strasbourg and Rome, and then went on to teach in Italian departments in the UK. She is currently an independent scholar and an honorary research fellow of the Faculty of Medieval and Modern Languages, University of Oxford. She has published on both English and Italian literature, and her specialism is in early modern English drama. Her latest publication is a co-edited volume on *Imitative Series and Clusters from Classical to Early Modern Literature* (2020).

REBECCA TOMLIN is Research Associate on the ERC-funded project *Crossroads of Knowledge in Early Modern England: The Place of Literature* co-hosted by CRASSH and the Faculty of English at the University of Cambridge. Rebecca recently completed her Ph.D. on *Narratives of Exchange in Early Modern London, 1580–1600* at Birkbeck College, University of London. Her research takes an inter-disciplinary approach to explore ways in which early modern Londoners used narratives presented on stage and in church to think about the rapidly changing nature of their city, with a particular emphasis on commerce and charity.

Introduction

Kristine Steenbergh and Katherine Ibbett

Compassion is a response to suffering, be it before our eyes or imagined at a distance: in seeing an afflicted person, hurt physically or otherwise, we are moved to suffer with the sufferer, whether or not we act on that feeling. It slides on various scales: it can figure the response of an individual or of a nation. This emotional sharing, variously hailed or rebuffed throughout history, provides an extraordinary prism through which to see at similarly multiple perspectives. It is sometimes hailed, even pushed on us, as an anti-politics: we should show *compassion*, voters in both Britain and the United States were told in 2016, for those who voted in ways that displeased us. In this exhortation's figuring of the emotion, compassion knows no borders: it erodes the distance between us. But compassion also provides a way to read or sometimes reinforce social and political fault lines, as 2020's response to the pandemic suggests: in asking us to attend to suffering, it also draws attention to inequities, including our unequal capacities for response.

We write at a time when public capacity for compassion appears to be severely reduced; in writing of emotion in an early modern world riven by crises over religious and racial difference and facing the large-scale migrations that stemmed from them, it is hard not to think of our own response to such scenarios today. Perhaps the study of historical compassion always invites such comparisons: for Lauren Berlant, scholarly work on compassion will always be a history of the present because 'the word *compassion* carries the weight of ongoing debates about the ethics of privilege'.[1] One of compassion's latter-day privileges has been to regard itself as a private and sentimental response. In our contemporary culture compassion is universally and often facilely hailed as a good, a cheap shot for politicians looking to buffer their image but often failing to bring about any substantive relief. In response to that trumpeting of public emotion, scholars have proffered critiques of contemporary compassion, tracing the compassionate vocabularies that veil and sustain immigration's repressions[2] or censuring what

Lauren Berlant calls the 'reparative compassion' that allows US liberalism to tune out a violently racist history: 'Compassionate liberalism is, at best, a kind of sandpaper on the surface of the racist monument whose structural and economic solidity endures.'[3] Berlant's rejection of compassion recalls that of Hannah Arendt, who thought compassion's attention to the singular case or contingent sufferer made compassion ungeneralisable, and no fit basis for political action: 'Because compassion abolishes the distance, the worldly space between men where political matters, the whole realm of human affairs, are located, it remains, politically speaking, irrelevant and without consequence.'[4]

Early modern texts can throw a different light on these concerns. For seventeenth-century theorists of the emotions, compassion could be surprisingly akin to anger: Nicolas Coeffeteau, for example, defines mercy as 'a Griefe or feeling which we have of another mans miseries, whom we hold worthy of a better fortune' and views it as the flip-side of indignation, which 'proceeds from the discontent we receive to see the wicked flourish'.[5] Compassion's capacity for judgement, that is, partakes of a fiercer quality than that usually imagined. If Arendt worried that compassion, in attending to singular cases, shut down any larger political capacity, many texts from other traditions and times suggest that compassion can multi-task: it makes room for *both* an attention to individual pain and a larger reading of social structures. Taking compassion seriously means taking seriously its capacity for change.[6]

Modern views of compassion often draw on eighteenth-century secular views on the social roles of compassion. Eighteenth-century debates about compassion were central to larger considerations of the social sphere, and they rewrote the classical and Christianised vocabulary of the early modern period into a new and seemingly transparent lexicon: the term 'sympathy' takes precedence in this period, referring not only to the sharing of misery but to the larger sharing of any sort of emotional state. Many Enlightenment deliberations considered the emotion's role as a building block in larger relational structures, be they private or public: for David Hume in the *Treatise on Human Nature* (1739–40), the tracing of sympathy's structural relations allows for an appraisal of the ways different selves relate spontaneously to one another; for Jean-Jacques Rousseau in the *Discourse on Inequality* (1755), a spontaneous and natural pity cancels out our human tendency to self-regard, and is thus central to political community (although in his *Letter to D'Alembert* he worried that such an emotion could be displaced by the false emotion we feel at the theatre); in the *Theory of Moral Sentiments* (1759), Adam Smith similarly imagined compassion at the heart of human society. These eighteenth-century discussions are often drawn on in discussion of compassion today – see, for example, Luc Boltanski's discussion on media and emotion in *Distant Suffering*, which takes its model of compassion from Rousseau – but their secular structures of sympathy look quite different from the forms we trace in this book. Instead of drawing on an Enlightenment intellectual history to understand compassion's power, we suggest that digging into compassion's early modern entanglements provides a different way for thinking through emotion today.

Compassion: A History

Before we turn to these early modern entanglements, we look briefly at compassion's shapes and practices in the classical and medieval periods. Compassion was a contested concept in classical literature and philosophy. In ancient Greece and Rome, the capacity for compassion – principally known by the Greek *eleos* and *oiktos* and the Latin *misericordia* – was often considered necessary to humanity. Across such diverse texts as Homeric epic, Roman tragedy and the treatises of Aristotle, pity appears as a morally right response to another person's suffering, while a lack of pity is a sign of a base character.[7] In Stoic philosophy, however, pity is seen as a dangerous passion considered irrational, painful and as incompatible with justice.

These contrasting judgements on the value of compassion in society are shaped, in part, by a difference in definitions. Aristotelian pity is more objective, cognitive and less overwhelming. Although he describes pity (*eleos*) as 'a kind of pain', Aristotle does not envisage it as involving shared suffering.[8] As David Konstan explains, 'the subject and object of pity do not merge but rather maintain distinct emotions – that of the pitier is precisely pity'. The observer is not a participant in the feelings of the other, but regards the pain of others from the outside.[9] Perhaps influenced by the rhetorical context in which he wrote, Aristotle sees pity as a strongly cognitive emotion. It is preceded by an evaluation: only when the suffering person did nothing to warrant their grief does the observer experience pity. And lastly, Aristotelian pity is kept within bounds because it is initially a self-directed feeling. The person perceiving the suffering needs to recognise him or herself in the sufferer in order to be able to feel pity. The emotion hinges on a similarity: of age, character, disposition, social status and family. For this reason, pity and fear are coupled in Aristotle's description of catharsis: we pity the other's suffering precisely because we fear that such a situation might also befall us.[10] An Aristotelian audience would for example not experience pity for the suffering of slaves, since they didn't share their social situation.[11]

The Stoics, on the other hand, viewed compassion as a dangerous feeling. They made a fierce moral distinction between *misericordia* and *clementia* (clemency), seeing the former as 'the vice of a petty mind that collapses at the sight of the misfortune of others'. (These distinctions return throughout the history of philosophy: like the Stoics, Kant too made the distinction between a rational and necessary emotion that he called sympathy, and what he saw as a more worrying contagious compassion.) Pity is, in this analysis, a disturbance of the mind, and Seneca gendered it as feminine, considering it a passion typical of old women. Whereas clemency is considered a virtue, *misericordia* is dangerous because it does not involve a cognitive judgement: 'pity looks to the condition, not the reason, whereas clemency assents to reason'.[12] This does not mean the Stoics would not respond to the suffering of another person: they would endeavour to remove the cause of suffering, and could thus be said to act compassionately, but these actions would not spring from a sense of shared suffering. This Stoic resistance to compassion lies firmly behind the many early modern authors who worried about compassion as infection or contagion, and behind the figure of the judicious male compassionate, apportioning emotion reasonably, who so often figures in their texts.

If Greek and Latin philosophers urged emotional distance and decorum, early Christian authors in the fourth to the seventh century reassessed the need for positive emotions such as love and compassion. Susan Wessel argues that the beginnings of 'an affective compassion – of deeply sympathizing with another person's suffering' can be traced to the early Christians.[13] The first uses of the word *compassio* also date from this period.[14] Early Church fathers used the Latin *compassio* to translate the Greek *sympatheia*: both these words literally mean 'feeling or suffering with'.[15] In the Gospels, compassion was central to Jesus' ministry, and figured as an embodied experience often referred to as '*splanchnizomai*', deriving from '*splanchna*', meaning 'guts' or 'entrails'. Even more central than Christ's compassion with the sick and the poor in this reassessment of the moral and ethical function of compassion was the idea that the Son of God became human and suffered in the flesh.[16] Compassion in early Christianity became a mode of mediation between human beings and their God. As Karl Morrison notes, 'in the developing humanist tradition represented by Aristotle and Cicero, fellow feeling had been a human affair, closed at the highest ranges, as Aristotle observed, since gods did not have friends'.[17] In Christian doctrine, compassion and mercy were central to the relation between the believer and God, through the mediation of Jesus. The notion of Christ's bodily suffering was pivotal for the early development of a theology of compassion. Compassion was not an unproblematic affective response, however. Christian authors inherited Stoic philosophy's rejection of *misericordia*, and struggled to view bodily, affective compassion as a virtue. 'Compassion as an emotional response was rarely, if ever, taken for granted', Wessel writes.[18]

In the high Middle Ages, attention to Christ's bodily suffering was at the heart of the cult of affective piety. Whereas in the eleventh century Christ on the cross was still represented as a triumphant saviour, from the thirteenth century onward a different image of Christ, *Christus patiens*, became dominant: 'naked and disfigured, covered with blood, Christ ha[d] become a vulnerable human victim'.[19] The idea that Christ experienced bodily pain on the cross as a human being was central to late medieval devotion. His kinship with mankind enables both the meditator's compassion with Christ's suffering and Christ's compassion with man.[20] Late medieval piety was therefore characterised by a 'heightened experiential awareness of the humanity of Christ'.[21] Indeed, as Jan Frans van Dijkhuizen writes, 'because Christ's anguish is so physically graphic and outwardly visible, it lends itself so well to sustained meditation, and ... is open to human participation'.[22] The devotee's concentration on the physical and mental suffering of Christ was intended to kindle an intense experience of compassion.

We may wonder whether this co-suffering with the crucified Christ is the same emotion as Aristotle's *eleos*, since it occurs in such different contexts, involved different practices and shaped a different bodily experience. In meditations, prayers and reading, devotees were encouraged to concentrate on vivid images of Christ's suffering or the grief of his mother, Mary, in order to feel their pain as their own. Recall that Greek *eleos*, especially as we find it in Aristotle's writings, is characterised by an emotional distance between the pitier and the pitied. In affective devotion, in contrast, devotees are urged to enter into the suffering of Christ, to feel it as their own. For Aristotle, the sight of one's son being led to death is not pitiful, but terrible, since a son is so closely related that we would feel as if we were in danger ourselves.[23] Yet in late medieval affective devotion, it is precisely this familial situation that kindles compassion. Gendered feminine, it is predicated on the love of a mother for her son and of a female spouse for her beloved.[24] The drawing of the boundaries between 'us' and 'them' shifts across different historical contexts.

In analysing the social and political roles of compassion, we therefore insist on the significance of such historical differences. The cultural archive of compassion can help us to think beyond modern definitions of pity and compassion. Lauren Berlant's observation, for example, that 'in operation, compassion is a term denoting privilege: the sufferer is *over there*', applies more to Greek *eleos* than to late-medieval compassion. In the following section, we signal how conflicting historical traditions of thinking about and practising compassion come together and are reinterpreted at the time of a volatile mix of Neo-Stoicism and religious Reformation, and suggest how a richer engagement with the early modern period might bring us to a more complex understanding of compassion's operations today.

Early Modern Compassion

In the early modern period, the feeling and practice of compassion were recalibrated in a pressure cooker of social, religious and political changes. The rich philosophical heritage of classical ideas about the role of pity in virtuous citizenship and prudent statesmanship and the embodied practices of late-medieval affective meditation on compassion with the suffering of Christ jostled against new contexts of civil war, colonisation and capitalism. Cities such as London, Paris and Amsterdam expanded into metropoles, absorbing migrants from abroad as well as from the surrounding countryside. Notions of neighbourliness, charity and compassion became elastic as communities changed shape. With the opening of Exchanges in major European cities and an accompanying growth of credit culture, the beginnings of a capitalist economy shaped new economic relations among citizens that were experienced as conflicting with Christian ideals of compassion. Early empirical science gnawed at the foundations of humoral theory and its notion of bodily compassion when it confronted occult notions of sympathy between natural elements. Encounters with others, and exploitation of them, in travel, trade and imperial expansion invited a recalibration of the Christian circle of concern in the exercise of compassion; sometimes, disturbingly, they asked Europeans to imagine their violence against others as a form of compassion in itself.

Compassion's traditional practices and institutional affordances were revoked or reshaped in the context of the Reformation and Counter-Reformation, while authors all over Europe sought to reconcile Christian views of compassion with the revival of Stoic philosophy's problematisation of its social and political role. A seventeenth-century English sermon suggests how compassion ought to be experienced: 'hee must both haue compassion inwardly; and hee must shew it too outwardly: *Affectu*, and *Effectu*; pitying them in his heart, and helping them with his hand. It is not enough for him to see the Blinde, and the Lame, and the Poore; and to be sorry for them: but his compassion must be reall. Hee must lend his eyes to the blinde, to direct them; and he must lend his feet to the lame, to support them; and he must pitie the Poore as a father doth his children, so pitie them, that hee doe something for them.'[25] The sermon's distinction between inner emotion and exterior action is typical of debates in the wake of the Reformation that marked changing understandings of the path to salvation. If the discourse of a fervent inner emotion was in the first decades of the Reformation a peculiarly Protestant domain, Catholic responses to the Reformation later began to trouble that distinction. The growing Counter-Reformation interest in charitable practice, stemming from an understanding of the importance of the works of mercy to salvation, was also accompanied by a new emphasis on discourses of *caritas*. Both Protestants and Catholics argued the tension between abstract considerations of compassion and an exhortation to assistance, but the ways they conceptualised or drew distinctions between 'inner' and 'outer' were often different. Although both Catholics and Protestants drew on a rich textual tradition of compassion – reading the Stoics, Saint Augustine and sometimes even works of medieval piety – they often responded to it in different ways as their understanding of Christian charitable action shifted. Attention to the shifting scales of compassion, pity and fellow-feeling grants us a new look at the changes of the early modern period.

Our cover image, a detail from *Visiting the Sick*, part of the Master of Alkmaar's multipanel painting *The Seven Works of Mercy* (Rijksmuseum, 1504), suggests something of the changing practices of compassion in the context of the Reformation. The painting is assumed to have been commissioned by the regents of the Holy Spirit Almshouse in Alkmaar, who may be represented in the foreground (with Christ among them). An inscription on the frame encouraged charitable donations, promising that the reward for practising compassion with the sick 'will multiply eternally'. During the iconoclasms of the 1560s and 1570s in the Netherlands, the painting was severely damaged. Faces as well as the gifts carried by depicted figures were scraped away with knives, and the painting was later described as 'pitifully' damaged with black paint. With their removal of the proffered gifts, the iconoclasts seem to have targeted specific pre-Reformation practices of compassion, critiquing the outward performance of compassion in charitable donations.[26]

It was not only paintings that were changed. The Reformation brought about an anxious delineation of community, subject to constant redraftings. Where we tend to think of compassion as a warm or embracing emotion, the early modern emotion, drawing on Stoic tradition and anxious about the differences wrought by the Reformation, often stemmed from a series of restrictions. If compassion appeared as what John Staines terms for seventeenth-century England 'one model for public politics', then that understanding of the public was often hemmed in by enclosure or constraint.[27] Early modern compassion was also shaped by an extraordinary degree of confessionally marked violence across Europe. Katherine Ibbett has argued, for instance, that the restrictive form of compassion that marks seventeenth-century writing in France stems from the sectarian rhetoric of the 'pitiful spectacle' that marked the verbal storm accompanying the Wars of Religion, in which compassion was meted out within fiercely confessional structures of desert and worthiness, and those on the other side were deemed uncompassionable.[28] For others, as one disturbing example from France suggests, wartime atrocity brought about only a horrified sense that although onlookers might feel compassion, they could do little to intervene. The military man Henri de Campion, seeing the rape of local women by soldiers, writes that it made him feel 'a pity that I cannot express, but we couldn't do anything to stop it taking place'.[29] The large-scale devastation and suffering of conflict could make the compassionate gesture seem negligible. But, as many examples demonstrate in these chapters, compassion was also lived at the most intimate and neighbourly scale; sometimes it involved surprising reaches to those outside a narrowly defined community, sometimes it managed only to define that community more tightly still.

Early Modern Compassion and the History of Emotions

Our view of early modern compassion as entangled in a web of traditions, practices, sites and communities offers us a fresh way into a number of debates in emotion history. As Susan Matt has written, doing the history of emotions by tracing particular emotion words presents certain difficulties: 'We may have different words or no words for emotions and concepts that earlier cultures thought central, and vice versa. Even within a single society, at a given moment, the meaning of those words and the feelings they describe may be understood differently by different individuals.'[30] If we focus on the early modern English example of the word 'compassion', the complexity of the issue immediately becomes clear. The *Oxford English*

Dictionary stages an account of compassion that tells a particular seventeenth-century story. The word changes meaning in this period: its sense of 'suffering together with another, participation in suffering; fellow-feeling, sympathy' disappears from the dictionary around 1625.[31] In its newer and still current sense, 'compassion' refers not so much to a shared suffering, but to the feeling when a person is moved by the suffering of another, and by the desire to relieve it. Around the same time, the words 'sympathy' and 'fellow-feeling' begin to take flight as cognates of compassion. The noun 'sympathy' is first used to refer to shared suffering in the 1590s.[32] Also around the turn of the seventeenth century, the word 'fellow-feeling' is introduced into the English language to refer to the 'participation in the feelings of others, sympathy'.[33] Thomas Hobbes's writing testifies to the intermixing of these cognates in the period: he writes that 'griefe for the calamity of another is Pitty, and ariseth from the imagination that the like calamity may befall himselfe, and there fore is called compassion, and in the phrase of this present-time a fellow-feeling'.[34] As David Konstan also notes for antiquity, 'the notions conveyed by such terms as compassion, sympathy, pity, forgiveness, clemency, ... are not neatly bounded, and there are broad areas of overlap and combination'.[35]

Faced with this diversity in definitions and usages of compassion and its cognates, emotion historians have used various strategies to demarcate their source material. In his cross-historical study of sympathy Eric Schliesser took a conceptual approach to his object of study. He chose to define five underlying features 'incorporated in or presupposed by most usages of the term "sympathy"'.[36] Sarah McNamer, on the other hand, wonders if such a cross-cultural approach is possible, as she finds significant differences between ancient Greek *eleos* and late-medieval Christian compassion. 'Does "compassion" have an irreducible essence?' she asks, and therefore 'can these variations even be considered iterations of the same emotion?' Other historians base their selection of material on the use of a particular word. Seth Lobis, for example, focuses on the word 'sympathy' in seventeenth-century England, warning against 'semantic lumping – treating "pity", "compassion" and "sympathy", among other terms, as virtual fungibles – [since it] can yield a false sense of conceptual coherence'.[37] He signals that while sympathy and compassion are close cousins, their histories cannot be collapsed into one.

And yet, early modern authors were not too careful about the distinctions between compassion and its cognates. In early modern dictionaries, compassion, pity, fellow-feeling, commiseration, mercy, ruth/rue, yearning and other cognates are often defined as each other's synonyms. In his *World of Wordes*, John Florio translates the Italian *compassione* as 'pitie, compassion, or ruthe', *misericordia* as 'mercie, pittie, ruthe, compassion' and *pietà* as 'reuerent loue, naturall affection or zeale, reuerence, remorse, conscience, pitie, ruth, mercie, compassion, commiseration or compunction of anothers harme'.[38] Thomas Cooper's *Thesaurus Linguae Romanae et Britannicae* translates *misericors* as 'Merciful: pitifull: that hath pitie or compassion: that is sorie for an others ill: tender hearted: ful of compassion'.[39] At the beginning of the seventeenth century, Randle Cotgrave renders the French *pitié* as 'pitie, ruth, compassion, commiseration; charitie, kindnese, or tendernesse of disposition; also, grace, clemencie, mercifulnesse'; at its end, also in France, Antoine Furetière sees compassion as a 'Movement of the soul which brings us to have some pity'.[40] These often exhausting cross-references serve to remind us that, in contrast to the seamless definitions laid out by thinkers such as Arendt, early modern compassion (pity, mercy and so on) trips up constantly as it tries to set out semantic similarities and differences. Several contributors will return to the question of distinction and etymology in this volume's exploration of the diversity of compassion.

More broadly, early modern treatises on the passions can also sometimes be seen to question the desire to apply neat distinctions between quickly altering and ephemeral passions. Thomas Wright's *The Passions of the Mind in General* seems to mock the very idea of dividing the passions into categories. After introducing Aquinas' model of eleven passions (which include love, fear and sadness, but not compassion), he writes: 'If every diversity or change we finde in passions, were a sufficient reason to encrease their number, without doubt I could adde welnie eleven more; as, Mercy, Shamefastnesse, Excandescencie, Envy, Emulation, Anxitie, Confidence, Slouthfulnesse, Zelotypia, Exanimation, Iactation or Boasting, with many more.'[41] Wright's indeterminacy points to the precarious status of compassion: in many texts, compassion appears less like the early modern understanding of a passion that buffets the body, and something more like a virtue drawing on a set of classical exemplars; in still others, it looks more like a willed social practice. Where scholars often draw overly neatly on passion theorists to establish a norm for early modern emotional terms, this volume seeks to explore the confusion and diversity of compassion.

Early modern compassion was shaped by a broad range of different situated practices in early modern Europe. The present volume is neither a cross-historical exploration of one concept, nor a study of one emotion word in a specific historical setting and language. The chapters in this book negotiate different languages, different religious contexts and different practices of compassion. Our focus is on England, but we also reach to its European neighbours, and to its reflections on its imperial engagements; in placing a tradition usually considered in isolation in conversation with other places, we want to allow for a reflection on compassion's shared traditions, derived from a common if contested classical and Christian heritage, as well as its local practices and inflections. The authors in this volume take an equally broad approach to their sources. Rather than focusing on the use of the word 'compassion' and excluding its interrelations with sympathy, mercy, and other related concepts, they take an inclusive approach. Let us describe this as a compassionate methodology: overly strict definitions or concepts elide often productive entanglements and complexities. If compassion, in its ideal form, reaches across differences to form a new understanding, we hope that our clustering of diverse approaches to compassion's multiple forms can do the same.

Compassion in Practice

Our contributors bring the complex relations between different concepts of compassion into focus by tracing the kinds of words used in their source texts, in English, French, Spanish or Polish, and the contexts in which these words are used. Compassion's history is inseparable from the history of translation. Béatrice Delaurenti has shown, for example, that medieval medical texts in dialogue with Aristotle chose the term *compassio* instead of *sympathia* to figure the contagious bodily response of one being to the movements of another (ranging from the feeling of emotion for a sufferer to the need to urinate in seeing someone else do so). In Delaurenti's reading, scholastic inquiry thus bundled together the vocabulary of antiquity with later Christian overtones.[42] Compassion, which involves a reading and response of another's pain, also compels a careful reading and interpretation of the many forms of other traditions and texts that inhabit its vocabularies. Our authors therefore note not only the interrelations and overlaps between the various cognates for compassion, but also the ways in which compassion relates to other passions, and how other emotions can transition into or out of compassion. They also look beyond words, bringing into focus the rituals and practices, spaces and buildings, images and songs used in the evocation and experience of early modern compassion. For compassion hovers between a textual invocation and a lived practice, and the relation between the two was central to contentious debates. In some of the material covered in this volume, compassion is a set formula, borrowed from Aristotle or from the Bible, and recycled into a slew of different texts; in others, compassion appears as a spontaneous reaction to an event, as a gesture arising where least expected. This variance suggests something of the slipperiness of addressing such an ephemeral and yet erudite phenomenon as compassion. On the one hand, we tackle this project through textual traditions, and we take seriously the notion that these textual instances do something in the world. Yet we also try to glimpse, amidst the compassionate lexicon, something closer to a phenomenological experience of emotion: in gestures, in glances, in music, in audience response.

Much of today's critical impatience with compassion is predicated on its failure to follow through on its rhetoric, its incapacity to practice as it preaches. Yet early modern compassion was not merely an erudite textual tradition: it was also a set of practices that took on differing importance in different social and religious groups. These practices were impacted by and in turn shaped textual representations of compassion. The chapters in this volume analyse a broad range of sources to access the interplay between texts and practice in the early modern period. Some of our authors draw on prescriptive texts, such as Stoic philosophy, sermons or Counter-Reformation advice on self-compassion; others use literary texts as a source for discovering common emotional practices and to see how these texts shaped new emotional styles and vocabularies. Legal and administrative documents, too, can provide insight into practices of compassion: one of the chapters uses an archive of alms petitions to chart the ways compassion was exercised in early modern London. These petitions, like sermons, plays and literary texts, are not only useful to trace various discourses of compassion that circulated and conflicted in the period; they are also themselves what Monique Scheer has called emotional practices: 'habits, rituals and everyday pastimes that aid us in achieving a certain emotional state'.[43] As Bruce Smith notes in this volume, the pulpit and the theatre were probably two of the most important spaces for the kindling of compassion. Textual traces of sermons and plays provide insight into early modern emotions-as-practice. The affective impact of sermons, poems, petitions and plays thus blurs the dividing line between discourse and practice, between prescriptive and descriptive, since words have a performative effect: to extend Scheer's work to literary concerns, these are texts-as-practice.

In the field of the history of emotions, literary texts are sometimes regarded with a touch of distrust: cultural historians worry that poets and playwrights do not represent actual historical emotions, but only fictional feelings.[44] Literary texts are considered to be overly determined by genre characteristics and rhetorical traditions, and as such not trustworthy as sources for finding historical truth. Erin Sullivan and Marie Louise Herzfeld-Schild note that therefore 'in-depth studies of the arts ... have played a relatively muted role in the shaping of the history of emotions as a field'.[45] And yet, literary texts provide unique access to historical experiences of the emotions. Not only do these plays represent emotions at work, they also elicit an emotional response in their audiences. The complexity and performativity of literary texts make them especially fit sources for the exploration of the entanglements of compassion in the early modern period. Precisely because literature does not simply reflect existing vocabularies, theories and emotion scripts, but actively shapes them, it should be an integral part of the field of the history of emotions. In this volume, we take seriously the idea that literary topoi might, despite their familiarity, speak from and shape deeply felt emotion.

Structuring Compassion

Since compassion involves a confrontation across similarity and difference, we have organised our contributors into sectional pairs. Their paired descriptions of and responses to seven key aspects of early modern compassion sometimes bring out intellectual sympathies, and on other occasions suggest disagreement. They suggest the breadth of material encompassed by the exploration of compassion, as well as its capacity for a fine-grained response to the otherness of the past.

Theorising

Our first pairing addresses the theories of compassion which punctuated both secular and religious writing of the period. In 'The Ethics of Compassion in Early Modern England', Bruce Smith takes the conflict between Stoic and Christian views of compassion as his starting point for an exploration of the ethics of compassion in early modern culture. Taking up four aspects of ethics – character, culture, place and representation – he asks how they help in understanding the workings of compassion in the culture of early modern England. Smith's vision of compassion, which he relates to virtue theory rather than passion, allows for the emotion's generous relation to the other. In contrast, in 'The Compassionate Self of the Catholic Reformation' Katherine Ibbett worries over compassion's restrictions and its inwardness. Suggesting that the Stoic denial of the self was rewritten in some discourses of the Counter-Reformation, Ibbett explores how three writers of the Continental Catholic Reformation – François de Sales, Roberto Bellarmino and Pierre Le Moyne – understand compassion not only as a response to the suffering of the other, but also as an exercise of the will and a way to address the significance of the self. In these French and Italian writers, the engaged ethical compassion traced by Smith looks something more like a sociable civility.

Consoling

Our second pairing moves from theory to more practical questions, seen not at the scale of generalities sketched by the theorists but pitched to individuals responding to a particular suffering, be it emotional or physical. In '"Hee Left Them Not Comfortlesse by the Way": Grief and Compassion in Early Modern English Consolatory Culture', Paula Barros explores the changing role of compassion in the consolation of the bereaved in the early modern period. She shows how the sixteenth-century humanist tradition of consolation, which despite its Stoic rigor showed a real warmth of fellow-feeling, was perceived to be waning in the late sixteenth century. In this context, she reads Spenser's *Daphnaïda* as a defence of the humanist consolatory ethos. Barros demonstrates that the history of consolation cannot be understood as a linear progression towards a secularised understanding of sorrow and compassion, since early seventeenth-century sermons resist this linear movement and develop an ethics of shared vulnerability grounded in medieval traditions of spiritual mourning. Alongside Barros, Stephen Pender explores the role of compassion in doctor-patient relationships and conceptions of the ideal physician in 'Friendship, Counsel and Compassion in Early Modern Medical Thought'. Like Barros, Pender's chapter pushes against standard chronologies, here seeking to overturn the account of the physician's role seen in the standard history of medicine. Exploring the role of affective relations between patients and their doctors in philosophical, theological, medical and popular texts, he argues that compassion was central in physicians' roles of counsel and friendship in bedside practice in the sixteenth and seventeenth centuries. Taken together, these chapters suggest that the professionalisation of affect traced by sociologists like Arlie Hochschild has deep roots in a humanist assessment of emotion.[46]

Exhorting

Compassion is, of course, a response to another other person or being. But it can also be an exhortation to the other to respond to still another person. Our third pairing turns to the ways in which writers and orators sought to bring about compassion in other hearts, focusing on the theatrical draw of sermons. In '"Compassion and Mercie Draw Teares from the Godlyfull Often": The Rhetoric of Sympathy in the Early Modern Sermon', Richard Meek traces the transition in the meaning of the word 'sympathy' from a generalised sense of correspondence to a transferral of woe in late sixteenth-century sermons as well as in the theatre. Exploring the tensions between sympathy as a natural and automatic response, yet at the same time one that needs to be actively encouraged in sermons, he shows how the term is initially used by preachers to enforce a sense of a Christian body in which all members hurt if one part of the body experiences pain. Later sermons begin to use 'sympathy' as an imaginative, rather than a bodily, engagement with the other, paradoxically accompanied by a greater awareness of the separateness of individuals. Meek traces this treatment of the concept also in dramatic texts from the late sixteenth century, such as Shakespeare's *Romeo and Juliet* and his contribution to *Sir Thomas More*. Alongside Meek, in 'Mollified Hearts and Enlarged Bowels: Practising Compassion in Reformation England', Kristine Steenbergh views sermons from the perspective of practice theory, which takes as its starting point that emotions are engrained into body and mind through repeated practice. In early seventeenth-century sermons, the bowels of compassion are seen as the seat of fellow-feeling. These bowels need to be soft, tender and moist to enable them to enlarge and stretch towards the suffering other. Steenbergh argues that early seventeenth-century Protestant clergymen on the one hand laud the Reformation's eradication of late-medieval practices of compassion, but on the other hand can be seen to struggle to shape new practices for keeping the bowels of mercy soft and lithe. In both chapters, the Christian body, be it figurative or literal, is reworked through the exhortation of compassion.

Performing

The performance of the sermon model shifts sites in our fourth pairing, which turns its attention to the representation of compassion on stage. This section also takes us far from the Western European familiarities that dominate early modern scholarship. In 'Civic Liberties and Community

Compassion: The Jesuit Drama of Poland-Lithuania', Clarinda E. Calma and Jolanta Rzegocka analyse how compassion functions in the plays of Jesuit colleges in the multi-ethnic, multi-religious and multilingual context of the Polish-Lithuanian Commonwealth. Although the Jesuits were invited to Poland-Lithuania by the Catholic church authorities to strengthen the Counter-Reformation, their school plays do not map the limits of compassion onto religious fault lines. The objects of compassion in the school plays shift according to political allegiances as well as religious principles, responding to both Protestantism and Islam with a supple sense of political contingency. Calma and Rzegocka show how a familiarly Aristotelian understanding of compassion could be adapted for local circumstances. In 'Compassion, Contingency and Conversion in James Shirley's *The Sisters*', Alison Searle returns us to the English stage, analysing the formal procedures connected to compassion in James Shirley's *The Sisters* (1642), and focusing on its objects, performance, limits and role in policing community boundaries in the early modern Protestant state. Viewing compassion from the perspective of performance, she argues that compassion is figured in the play as inherently theatrical and politically contagious. It both responded to and shaped local political circumstances; indeed, she suggests, the compassion elicited by the theatre helped to pave the way for political revolution in the 1640s.

Responding

How did early moderns account for these performances which might push them to pity? Our fifth pairing examines the understanding of spectatorship and audience response elucidated not just in dramatic theory but also in canonical Shakespearean stagings of the response to suffering. In 'Mountainish Inhumanity in Illyria: Compassion in *Twelfth Night* as Social Luxury and Political Duty', Elisabetta Tarantino analyses the relations between compassion and community in Shakespeare's *Twelfth Night*. Starting from the question of whether Malvolio evokes audience compassion, she argues that even if the plot of the play focuses on the gulling of Malvolio, the play's semantic and compositional strategies undermine the idea of 'us' versus 'the other' as a discriminant for social and political action, thereby recommending compassion as a politically provident attitude. Eric Langley draws out the philosophical significance of this response to spectacles of suffering in 'Standing on a Beach: Shakespeare and the Sympathetic Imagination'. He explores how early modern writers revisit Lucretius' piteous spectacle of an observed shipwreck as the occasion for either sympathetic compassion or antipathetic dispassion. This topos provided occasion not only for the praise of sympathetic vulnerability, but also for a reassessment of the cost of emotional interaction. Langley's sensitive exploration of the oscillation between proximity and distance, contagion and isolation, tender sensibility and dispassionate rationality in early modern responses to Lucretius' commonplace, carefully traces not only Shakespeare's ethics but also his poetics of compassion.

Giving

Our sixth pairing takes up the practices of compassion, derived from medieval charitable traditions, and considers their relation to more abstract notions of fellow-feeling that emerge after the Reformation. In '"To Feel What Wretches Feel": Reformation and the Re-naming of English Compassion', Toria Johnson argues that the concept of compassion changed during the Reformation, moving away from the legacy of medieval charity towards concepts of interpersonal connection such as pity, fellowship and compassion. She reads the pre-Reformation morality play *Everyman* and Shakespeare's *King Lear* side by side to reveal this shift, and shows that changing discourses of compassion also change the way compassion is perceived by the characters in the plays. Alongside Johnson, Rebecca Tomlin takes up the question of the changes wrought by the Reformation in more practical questions of almsgiving. In 'Alms Petitions and Compassion in Sixteenth-Century London', Tomlin focuses on a specific practice of begging in sixteenth-century London, that of beggars equipped with alms petitions. Drawing on an archive of circa three hundred alms petitions at London's St Botolph's Church, she argues that these petitions moved parishioners to become donors not by emotive descriptions of their suffering, but by focusing on the economic consequences of disasters. In Tomlin's assessment, compassion for the other is also a form of insurance for the self.

Racialising

We investigate compassion's sharp assessments further in our final and most far-ranging pairing. How did compassion's gestures respond to, reach across or reify racial difference? In 'Pity and Empire in the *Brevísima relación de la destrucción de las Indias* (1552)', Matthew Goldmark describes the place of compassion in the work of the Dominican friar Bartolomé de las Casas, suggesting how affect's deployments helped organise the hierarchical differences necessary to imperial projects. Goldmark's chapter carves out a long genealogy for the imperial affect discussed by scholars of later periods. Likewise, in '"Our Black Hero": Compassion and Friendship for the Other in Aphra Behn's *Oroonoko*', John Staines considers compassion's restrictions and reach at a moment when a newly enlarged world put pressure on older models of fellow-feeling. Staines asks what room for difference, and especially racial difference, could be made within languages of humanity and friendship. Although Staines traces the failure of compassion in Behn's text, he shows too how by the eighteenth century it became a key text for abolitionists. Like Goldmark, Staines points to how the early modern period's understanding of affective relations to difference have come to shape our post-imperial shrinking world. We want to acknowledge that our field has been marked by a failure to attend to questions of racial identity in the early modern period and by a concomitant failure to build racial equality in the academy. In placing the work of Goldmark and Staines at the end of our volume's conversations, we suggest that a compassionate early modernism must take the history of race and of the violence wrought upon Black bodies seriously.

Early modern compassion, we have noted, marks a distinctive stand in the history of emotion's grappling with social division. It is not merely a preamble to the great Enlightenment projects of secular universalism that are usually associated with a later language of sympathy; we lose something when we draw on a genealogy that skips from the Stoics to Adam Smith. Goldmark's and Staines's gestures to later entanglements suggest how early modern compassion's distinctiveness provides us a painful purchase on our own times. They look not to the eighteenth century of philosophical abstractions, but to the global injustices of slavery and imperialism that underwrite our inequities today. Where Enlightenment thought pushed such questions aside to focus on the role of compassion in what Smith called the 'immense machine' of human society, early modern compassion draws attention to what makes that machine tick: in wrestling with the violence of religious and racial difference, it reveals the ghost in the affective machine of our own modernity.

In the final chapter, 'Contemporary Compassions: Interrelating in the Anthropocene,' Kristine Steenbergh explores how this volume's analyses of early modern forms of compassion might feed into the current pressing need to reshape more-than-human interrelations. The chapters in this volume trace the Reformation as a fault line in early modern concepts and practices of compassion. Our recent realisation of humanity's destructive impact on the planet similarly invites a radical rethinking of concepts and practices of witnessing and suffering-with. The final chapter connects the volume's exploration of early modern compassion to the work of Donna Haraway, Deborah Bird Rose and Thom van Dooren, and finds that the ecological crisis stimulates a search for new practices of compassion evoking similar questions of belonging and exclusion, identity and alterity, and inflecting them in new ways.

Notes

1 Lauren Berlant, 'Introduction: Compassion (and Withholding)' in Lauren Berlant (ed.), *Compassion: The Culture and Politics of an Emotion* (New York: Routledge, 2004), p. 1.
2 Didier Fassin, *Humanitarian Reason: A Moral History of the Present* (Berkeley: University of California Press, 2012); Miriam Ticktin, *Casualties of Care: Immigration and the Politics of Humanitarianism in France* (Berkeley: University of California Press, 2011).
3 Lauren Berlant, *The Female Complaint: The Unfinished Business of Sentimentality in American Culture* (Durham: Duke University Press, 2008), pp. xii; 6.
4 Hannah Arendt, *On Revolution* (Harmondsworth: Penguin, 2006), p. 76.
5 Nicolas Coeffeteau, 'Of Mercy and Indignation' in *A Table of Humane Passions: With Their Causes and Effects* (London, 1621), pp. 357 and 375.
6 On the unorthodox effects of compassion, see also Heather James, 'Dido's Ear: Tragedy and the Politics of Response', *Shakespeare Quarterly*, 52:3 (2001), 360–82.
7 David Konstan, *Pity Transformed* (London: Duckworth, 2001), pp. 125–26.
8 Aristotle, *Rhetoric*, 2.8.2, quoted in Konstan, *Pity Transformed*, p. 34.
9 Konstan, *Pity Transformed*, p. 60. But see Fred C. Alford, 'Greek Tragedy and Civilization: The Cultivation of Pity', *Political Research Quarterly*, 46:2 (1993), 259–80, for the argument that Aristotle misinterpreted the Greek tragedians' use of *eleos* and *oiktos*.
10 Martha Nussbaum, 'Tragedy and Self-Sufficiency: Plato and Aristotle on Fear and Pity' in Amélie Rorty (ed.), *Essays on Aristotle's Poetics* (Princeton University Press, 1992), p. 274.
11 See also Konstan, *Pity Transformed*, p. 18.
12 David Konstan, 'Senecan Emotions' in Shadi Bartsch and Alessandro Schiesaro (eds.), *The Cambridge Companion to Seneca* (Cambridge University Press, 2015), p. 180.
13 Susan Wessel, *Passion and Compassion in Early Christianity* (Cambridge University Press, 2016), p. 24.
14 Early Christians used *misericordia*, *compassio* and *caritas* in the Latin, and *splanchnon*, *eleos*, *sympatheia*, *oiktos* and *agapē* in the Greek (Wessel, *Passion*

and Compassion, p. 22). The Greek word *sumpatheia* is relatively rare in the vocabulary of the classical period, where it was used to refer to a sense of physical interrelatedness. In later Greek, particularly among Christian writers, the term comes to supplement pity (*eleos*). Konstan suggests that this may in part have happened because *eleos* 'had acquired something of the sense of "mercy" (it is often translated as such) and lost some of the quality of an emotion' in this period. Konstan, 'Pity, Compassion, and Forgiveness' in Michael Ure and Mervyn Frost (eds.), *The Politics of Compassion* (London: Routledge, 2014), p. 181.

15 Konstan notes that it has been suggested that *compassio* was coined as a replacement for the older Latin term *misericordia*, which had shifted in meaning from 'feeling with' to 'charity' or 'charitable works (*Pity Transformed*, p. 106).
16 Wessel, *Passion and Compassion*, p. 17.
17 Karl Morrison, 'Framing the Subject: Humanity and the Wounds of Love', in Karl F. Morrison and Rudolph M. Bell (eds.), *Studies on Medieval Empathies* (Turnhout: Brepols, 2013), p. 9.
18 Wessel, *Passion and Compassion*, p. 2.
19 Sarah McNamer, *Affective Meditation and the Invention of Medieval Compassion* (Philadelphia: University of Pennsylvania Press, 2010), p. 2.
20 See also Sarah Beckwith, *Christ's Body Identity, Culture, and Society in Late Medieval Writings* (London: Routledge, 1993), p. 50.
21 Steven E. Plank, 'Wrapped All in Woe: Passion Music in Late-Medieval England', in A. A. MacDonald, Bernhard Ridderbos and R. M. Schlusemann (eds.), *The Broken Body: Passion Devotion in Late-Medieval Culture* (Groningen: Egbert Forsten, 1998), p. 94.
22 Jan Frans van Dijkhuizen, *Pain and Compassion in Early Modern English Literature and Culture* (Woodbridge, Suffolk: D.S. Brewer, 2012), p. 63.
23 Aristotle, *Rhetoric*, 1386a.
24 McNamer, *Affective Meditation*, pp. 10 and 40. For a comparison between classical and medieval compassion, see also Ulrich Berton, *Eleos und Compassio: Mitleid im antiken und mittelalterlichen Theater* (Paderborn: Wilhelm Fink, 2016).
25 Robert Sanderson, *Ten Sermons Preached* (London, 1627), pp. 162–63.
26 Master of Alkmaar, *Panel of a Polyptych with the Seven Works of Charity: Visiting the Sick*, 1504 (Rijksmuseum Amsterdam, SK-A-2815-6). See J. P. Filedt Kok, 'Master of Alkmaar, Polyptych with the Seven Works of Charity, 1504', in J. P. Filedt Kok (ed.), *Early Netherlandish Paintings*, online coll. cat. Amsterdam 2008: hdl.handle.net/10934/RM0001.COLLECT.9048.
27 John Staines, 'Compassion in the Public Sphere of Milton and King Charles', in Gail Kern Paster, Katherine Rowe and Mary Floyd-Wilson (eds.), *Reading the Early Modern Passions: Essays in the Cultural History of Emotion* (Philadelphia: University of Pennsylvania Press, 2004), p. 92.
28 Katherine Ibbett, *Compassion's Edge: Fellow-Feeling and Its Limits in Early Modern France* (Philadelphia: University of Pennsylvania Press, 2018).

29 Henri de Campion, *Mémoires de Henri de Campion*, ed. Marc Fumaroli (Paris: Mercure de France, 1990), p. 87.
30 Susan J. Matt, 'Recovering the Invisible: Methods for the Historical Study of the Emotions' in Peter N. Stearns and Susan J. Matt (eds.), *Doing Emotions History* (Urbana: University of Illinois Press, 2014), pp. 43–44.
31 Interestingly, the majority of examples for this definition concern an attraction between two bodily parts, which was described as 'sympathy' from 1579 onwards. The *OED* signals that the entry has not yet been fully updated since its first publication in 1891.
32 The *OED*'s first example is from 1600. For the argument that this sense of sympathy was used earlier, see Chapter 5 by Richard Meek in this volume.
33 *OED*, 'fellow-feeling, *n.*', 1. The *OED* dates the first appearance of the word to 1604; a search in Early English Books Online (EEBO) renders earlier examples from 1578 onwards.
34 Thomas Hobbes, *Leviathan*, ed. Richard Tuck (Cambridge University Press, 1996), p. 43.
35 Konstan, 'Pity, Compassion, and Forgiveness', p. 179.
36 Eric Schliesser (ed.), *Sympathy: A History* (Oxford University Press, 2015), p. 7.
37 Seth Lobis, *The Virtue of Sympathy: Magic, Philosophy, and Literature in Seventeenth-Century England* (New Haven: Yale University Press, 2015), p. 5.
38 John Florio, *A Worlde of Wordes, or Most Copious, and Exact Dictionarie in Italian and English* (1598), pp. 78, 228 and 277.
39 Thomas Cooper, *Thesaurus Linguae Romanae et Britannicae* (1565), sig. GGgg3r.
40 Randle Cotgrave, *A Dictionary of the French and English Tongues* (1611), sig. Ppp6r; Antoine Furetière, *Dictionaire universel*. 2 vols. (La Haye et Rotterdam: Leers, 1690), s.v. 'compassion.'
41 Thomas Wright, *The Passions of the Mind in General* (1604), sig. C5v.
42 Béatrice Delaurenti, *La contagion des émotions. Compassio, une énigme médiévale* (Paris: Garnier, 2016), pp. 24–25.
43 Monique Scheer, 'Are Emotions a Kind of Practice (And Is That What Makes Them Have a History)? A Bourdieuian Approach to Understanding Emotion', *History and Theory*, 51:2 (2012), 209.
44 See also Sarah McNamer, 'Feeling' in Paul Strohm (ed.), *Middle English* (Oxford University Press, 2007), p. 245.
45 Erin Sullivan and Marie Louise Herzfeld-Schild, 'Introduction: Emotion, History and the Arts', *Cultural History* 7:2 (2018), 120.
46 Arlie Hochschild, *The Managed Heart: Commercialization of Human Feeling* (Berkeley: University of California Press, 1983).

PART I
Theorising

CHAPTER I

The Ethics of Compassion in Early Modern England

Bruce R. Smith

In today's terms at least, compassion would seem to be unequivocally A Good Thing. Does compassion *need* ethical investigation? Cicero, for one, answers in the affirmative. Here is what his chief spokesman M— says in John Dolman's 1561 translation of *Tusculan Disputations*:

> So as pity is a grief conceived of other men's adversity, so is envy a sorrow, for other men's prosperity. Whosoever therefore is subject to pity, he is also sometimes troubled with envy. But to envy is no point of a wise man: wherefore neither to pity.[1]

Any such *perturbation* – 'a motion contrary to reason, and against the nature of the mind' (sig. W5) – should be avoided by a wise man. Cicero's M— (is that Marcus Tullius Cicero himself? *Magister*, Master?) distances himself somewhat from such 'crooked conclusions' by dogmatic Stoic philosophers like Zeno, even as he commends the way these philosophers ground their arguments 'upon the stoutest and manliest opinion' (sigs. O2v–O3). Cicero's framing of the question is focused not on the object of pity, but on the person who feels pity, in the words of Katherine Ibbett in the chapter that succeeds this one, 'on the appropriateness of the self who metes out such an affective response'. What Cicero most definitely endorses in these passages from *Tusculan Disputations* is the need to *question* pity, envy and 'motions' in general. The full title of Cicero's dialogue in Erasmus's edition, printed and reprinted six times in London from 1574 to 1636, is *Quaestiones Tusculanae*, translated by Dolman as *Those five questions, which Mark Tully Cicero, disputed in his manor of Tusculanum*. Cicero's question-asking is an exercise in ethics.

For sixteenth- and seventeenth-century readers, Cicero's question-asking was even more urgent, given the way Stoic advice on pity runs absolutely counter to the examples of Christ's acts of compassion in the New Testament. The gospel of Mark, chapter six, records how Christ and his disciples were seeking rest by taking a ship to a deserted place when

Christ caught sight of the crowds waiting for him on shore. 'Then Jesus went out, and saw a great multitude, and had compassion on them, because they were like sheep which had no shepherd: and he began to teach them many things.'[2] Mark 6:34 provides a verbal template for how Christ's miracles are narrated in other New Testament passages – most of the recorded miracles begin with a feeling of compassion on Christ's part – as well as an implicit lesson for how Christ's followers should themselves feel in the face of other people's suffering and need. What would Zeno have made of *that*? The ethics of compassion in early modern England was rife with conflict. Recognising that fact should prevent us, looking back from the twenty-first century, from assuming on the one hand a sentimental universalism about compassion or on the other hand a monolithic cultural construction applicable to every early modern subject. When it comes to feelings as well as practices, ethics acknowledges conflicts. Ethical discourse is talk about choices. That fraught situation is evident in conflicts between Protestant and Counter-Reformation ethics, as well as conflicts within each of these confessions. This chapter will reveal some of the fault lines within Protestant ethics; Katherine Ibbett's chapter in this volume attends to differences of opinion within Counter-Reformation ethics.

By and large the history of feelings has been written in terms of nomenclature and cultural practices, and the reasons are not hard to seek. Names for particular feelings can be charted genealogically; evidence for particular ways of experiencing feelings and acting upon them can be catalogued and analysed objectively. The history of words like 'pity', 'compassion', 'sympathy' and 'empathy' can readily be traced in the *Oxford English Dictionary*. Each has a different linguistic source, each first comes into use, drifts in meaning, or falls out of use according to changing cultural circumstances. 'Pity', with its etymological associations with 'piety', is the oldest of the four terms.[3] *Compassioun* passed into English from French in the century of Chaucer, along with a great many other French words. Did 'compassion' refer to the same feeling as the indigenous Old English words it replaced? Was 'compassion' merely an updating of *besárgung* (literally, 'besorrowing') and *earmung* (taking pity) and their descendants in Middle English *sorwing* and *erending*?[4] The literal meaning of *besárgung* – sorrowing *about* or *near* – suggests something more physical and immediate than 'compassion'.[5] What's in a name? A great deal, when the subject at hand is the history of affects. As for cultural practices, we can find early modern indices of compassion in acts of *charity*, acts that are urged in books of conduct and piety, acts that can be observed in works of art, acts that can be quantified in wills and bequests.

Ethics takes into account these distinctions in language and deed, but it goes further. Aristotle in his *Poetics* gives us an entry point. *Ethos* (literally, 'character') is 'that kind of utterance which clearly reveals the bent of a man's moral choice (hence there is no character in that class of utterances in which there is nothing at all that the speaker is choosing or rejecting)'.[6] Ethos is also a set of social arrangements: 'the characteristic spirit of a people, community, culture, or era as manifested in its attitudes and aspirations', as the *OED* defines it ('ethos, *n.*', 39.b.3).

Ethos offers a way of understanding social institutions – in particular social institutions situated in particular geographical, architectural and acoustic spaces. It should come as no surprise that Roman Catholic ethics with respect to compassion should differ from Protestant ethics and that different Protestant confessions should manifest their own differences. As a qualifier to 'people, community, culture, or era', the *OED* adds 'the prevailing character of an institution or system'. Since institutions can often be located geographically – church, school, law court and theatre are examples – I would add 'place' to the meanings of ethos. Putting together character, culture and place, we arrive at a fourth definition of ethos: as an object that can be represented in words or visual media or music. Note the second phrase in the *OED*'s definition of 'ethos': 'character or characterization as revealed in action *or its representation*'. These four senses of ethos allow us to come at compassion from multiple directions. Ethics allows us to bring together four things: (1) character, (2) sets of protocols for behaving, (3) particular sites for that behaviour ('accustomed place' in the original Greek) and (4) ways of *representing* these entities of character, behaviour and action. Ethos marks the spot where character meets culture.

I have opted to refer to compassion as a 'feeling' because, in my view, it is a more capacious word than alternatives like 'affect' (in early modern English a synonym for 'intention' or 'disposition'), 'passion' (a physiological state) or 'emotion' (a synonym for 'commotion', 'disturbance' or 'agitation' that could be applied to political events as well as mental states). 'Feeling' does not eliminate the precise meanings of the other terms; it enfolds them. In English at least, 'feeling' can refer to (1) the *act* of sensing, (2) the *capacity* to sense, (3) the *state* of sensing and (4) the *consciousness* of sensing. An additional advantage of the term 'feeling' is that it comes to us already theorised in Raymond Williams's concept 'structures of feeling'. In *The Long Revolution* (1977), Williams demonstrated the phrase's utility in bringing together political ideology, subjective experience (individual and collective), genre and media. Williams is the inspiration for the attention I give to drama in the analysis that follows. No less important to my discussion is Williams's late idea of the 'pre-emergence' of new 'structures of feeling' in works of fiction, especially drama. That is to say, works of fiction may facilitate new ways of being and feeling and not just represent already-existing ways of being and feeling, as cultural materialist critics assume. Shakespeare attempts that 'pre-emergence', I believe, throughout his dramatic works (his contribution to the co-authored play *Sir Thomas More* will be examined below), but particularly in late works like *The Tempest*.

Character, custom, sites, representations: I shall take up these four aspects of ethos one by one and consider how each helps us understand the workings of compassion in the culture of early modern England. I will be limiting my frame of reference to the period I know best, 1560–1660. Politically, these dates extend from the first year of Elizabeth I's reign to the last year of the Commonwealth and the Restoration of monarchy with the accession of Charles I. Throughout this hundred-year period there was religious discord, ever more intense, which finally erupted in the establishment of a more radically Protestant church and then a return to the more liberal religious arrangements that had been overthrown. Amid these political changes, as we shall see, compassion toward religious dissenters became a huge issue. Philosophically, the period 1560–1660 witnessed a shift from an eclectic Humanistic philosophy that combined elements of Stoicism with Christian doctrine to the beginnings of Enlightenment rationalism, with important consequences for 'feeling' as a component of 'thought'.

Ethos as Character

Choice and utterance: those two external markers of ethos as character are explicitly addressed in philosophy books, advice books and religious writings. As I noted in the beginning of this chapter, early modern philosophy entertained two quite opposite ideas about compassion. Against the examples of Jesus Christ and the Good Samaritan had to be weighed condemnation of all the passions, even compassion, in Stoic philosophy. Bacon's encomium of compassion in his essay 'Of Goodness and Goodness of Nature' can stand as an expression of the Christian idea:

> The parts and signs of goodness are many. If a man be gracious, and courteous to strangers, it shows, he is a citizen of the world; and that his heart is no island, cut off from other lands; but a continent, that joins to them. If he be compassionate, towards the afflictions of others, it shows that his heart is like the noble tree, that is wounded itself, when it gives the

balm. If he easily pardons and remits offences, it shows, that his mind is planted above injuries; so that he cannot be shot. If he be thankful for small benefits, it shows, that he weighs men's minds, and not their trash. But above all, if he have St. Paul's perfection, that he would wish to be an anathema from Christ, for the salvation of his brethren, it shows much of a divine nature, and a kind of conformity with Christ himself.[7]

Diametrically opposite to such sentiments is the stark advice voiced by Cicero in *Tusculan Disputations*. Compassion is condemned as just another 'perturbation' of the mind that, according to the Stoics, a wise man will avoid. But the ideal, Cicero's spokesman M— ultimately concludes, is finding a middle way between conflicting passions: 'For virtue, is not contrary to any perturbation but a mean betwixt two of them' (sig. T3). It is worth observing that the Stoics' sense of passions, all passions, as 'perturbations', survives in our word 'emotion'. 'Every perturbation', M— observes, 'because of opinions troublously tossing to and fro, is always moving' (sig. T3). Movement, powerful movement, is common to both 'perturbations' and 'emotions'. As Michael Schoenfeldt has demonstrated in his book *Bodies and Selves in Early Modern England*, control of the passions was crucial to creating a sense of 'inwardness' – the very opposite of 'getting in touch with your feelings'.[8]

A middle way between Stoic control of the passions and Christian encouragement of compassion is spelled out in Thomas Wright's *The Passions of the Mind in General* (1604, rev. ed. 1630). It is ironic that someone generally so hostile to passions as Wright has become in our own time a major authority on early modern psychology. Steven Mullaney in *The Reformation of Emotions in the Age of Shakespeare* argues that most recent commentators on *The Passions of the Mind in General* have attended to only the first of Wright's concerns, the somatic workings of sensation, to the exclusion of his two other concerns: social formations (including rhetoric) and the rational soul, as the entity that is in ultimate control of 'mind' – or should be. The passions, as Mullaney quotes from Wright, are neither material like bodily humours nor immaterial like the soul. Rather, 'they "stand betwixt these two extremes," as Wright tells us, "and border upon them both", so that they "inhabit both the confines of sense and reason"'.[9]

Even in this more expansive scheme, however, Wright regards the passions as potentially dangerous. He makes an exception for compassion:

> if the passions of the mind be not moderated according to reason ... immediately the soul is molested with some malady. But if the humors be kept in a due proportion, they are the preservatives of health, and

perhaps health itself. By this discourse may be gathered that passions are not only not wholly to be extinguished (as the Stoics seemed to affirm) but sometimes to be moved and stirred up for the service of virtue, as learnedly Plutarch teacheth: for mercy and compassion will move us often to pity, as it did Job.... 'Compassion grew with me from my infancy, and it came with me out of my mother's womb'. Therefore he declareth what succor he gave to the poor (Job 31:18).[10]

If ethos as character is a moral choice, Wright offers here a way of combining Stoic restraint with an embrace of compassion's 'out-going-ness', if I can put it that way: compassion's emergence out of the compassionate person's very body.

Early modern writers recognised this bodily out-going-ness in the frequency with which they allied 'compassion' and 'bowels'. A proximity search of 'compassion*' and 'bowel*' in the database Early English Books Online Text Creation Partnership turns up no fewer than 3,264 instances within 40 characters of each other in books published in English between 1470 and 1699. The very first hit, a 1600 book of sermons on the Book of Jonah preached by George Abbot at St Mary's Church Oxford can serve as an example. Abbot told his listeners,

> the Savior of the world, according to those different inclinations, which his manhood brought unto him, did rouse himself the more, and did pierce the hearts of his hearers, with more pathetical speech, when he saw such troupes come about him, that he was forced to go to a mountain, or betake him to a ship, to teach so many of them. He who was moved in his bowels, with compassion, to see so many as sheep without a shepherd, may be more moved, in and with his tongue, to satisfy such a multitude.[11]

In such associations of compassion with bowels we should realise that we are not dealing here with a passion like other passions – anger, fear, lust, for example – which overwhelm the body from without. Rather, compassion is *visceral*, in the literal sense of that word. (For more on bowels, see Kristine Steenbergh's Chapter 6 in this volume.) Aristotle may locate character as ethos in moral choice and utterance, but compassion is first and foremost an internal matter, a bodily feeling. Unlike the other passions in Wright, which begin with sensations of sight and hearing, compassion begins in the guts.

Ethos as Cultural Values

John Donne in an undated early sermon hears Christ's words on the cross ('Father, forgive them, for they know not what they do' [Luke 23:24]) and addresses Christ directly, marvelling at Christ's forgiveness of his tormentors and executioners. It was one thing, Donne says, to show compassion to the thief who asked Christ directly for forgiveness of his sins; it was quite another thing for Christ to show compassion to his tormentors and executioners when they hadn't even asked for it: 'Was not thy passion enough, but thou must have compassion? And is thy mercy so violent, that thou wilt have a fellow-feeling of their imminent afflictions, before they have any feeling?'[12]

Christ may have displayed compassion to all mankind, but early modern men and women did not go so far. Proclamations and laws issued during the reigns of Elizabeth and James specify entire categories of people who are not deserving of compassion: 'masterless men', 'rogues, vagabonds and sturdy beggars', 'Negars and Blackamoors', the last group being further described as 'infidels, having no understanding of Christ or his gospel'.[13] Most of these people never got to speak up for themselves, but pamphlet literature in the sixteenth and early seventeenth centuries is full of 'complaints' from other categories of people, including common soldiers just back from religious wars on the Continent who never received the pay they were promised. It is remarkable how many of these categories of people not worthy of compassion – the homeless, people who refuse to work, military veterans – are precisely the same categories from whom compassion is widely withheld today. Foreigners – 'strangers' as they were called – constitute another ostracised group.

Concerning 'strangers', the manuscript of the group-authored never-produced play *Sir Thomas More* features a scene, usually ascribed to Shakespeare, in which More turns back a London mob intent on attacking immigrants from France and the Low Countries. More's appeal is to compassion, and again the parallels with the plight of migrants today is striking:

> You'll put down strangers,
> Kill them, cut their throats, possess their houses
> . . . . . .
>   Say now the King
> Should so much come too short of your great trespass
> As but to banish you: whither would you go?
> What country, by the nature of your error,
> Should give you harbour? Go you to France or Flanders,
> To any German province, Spain or Portugal,
> Nay, anywhere that not adheres to England:
> Why, you must needs be strangers. Would you be pleased

> To find a nation of such barbarous temper
> That, breaking out in hideous violence,
> Would not afford you an abode on earth,
> Whet their detested knives against your throats,
> Spurn you like dogs, and like as if that God
> Owed not nor made not you, nor that the elements
> Were not all appropriate to your comforts,
> But chartered unto them? What would you think
> To be thus used? This is the strangers' case,
> And this your mountainish inhumanity.
> (scene vi, ll. 133–35, 137–55)[14]

More's rhetorical ploy works. Through his speech More creates a new ethos in multiple senses of the word: he changes the character of his listeners by urging upon them a compassionate moral choice, he appeals to existing protocols by reminding them of their own status as subjects to the king, he turns the London street into a site for compassion, he represents compassion by word and example. (See Richard Meek's analysis of More's speech and the questions it raises about the relationship between self and other in Chapter 5.)

In the course of his survey of the passions, Wright takes up hatred and provides a list of precise reasons for hating 'a community, kingdom, province, or any society'. It is all right to hate people

- 'if they be our ancient enemies, if by nature bloody, crafty, proud, insolent in government, impatient of superiors or equals, if cozeners, extortioners, invaders unjustly of others' dominions, aiders or abetters of rebels or our adversaries
- 'if their religion be paganism, Judaism, heresy, or "Turcise" [i.e., Muslims]
- 'if in their temporal laws they have enacted any tending to tyranny and oppression, if to further vice and hinder virtue
- 'if they hold, pretend, or endeavour to bereave our state of any part of preeminence, dignity, signiory, province or country thereunto belonging, if they abused or injured our state, prince, or subjects any way ... ' (sig. S8–8v)

Needless to say, none of these people is worthy of compassion.

In general, compassion in early modern England seems to have been a commodity that was rationed carefully. There are only fourteen mentions of 'compassion' in Shakespeare's plays and poems, and the majority of them have to do with compassion graciously granted or stringently withheld by someone in power. Compassion is explicitly mentioned in a very unlikely assortment of plays, most of them early in Shakespeare's career: *Henry VI, Part One* (in which Gloucester and Winchester dole out compassion as royal favours), *Titus Andronicus* (in which Marcus cannot believe that heaven will not 'compassion' the suffering Titus) and most notably *Richard III* (in which Tyrrell reports that the 'fleshed villains' who murdered the young princes 'melted with tenderness and mild compassion' when they told him of their deed (IV.iii.6–7).

To be sure, certain categories of people in early modern England seem to have been deemed worthy of compassion: the physically ill, orphans, Protestant refugees and perhaps under certain circumstances beggars. Wright discusses beggars' tactics in the course of investigating the power of music to move 'mercy and compassion':

> for this purpose many beggars with songs demand their alms, and specially the Germans, where the man, the wife and their children make a full begging choir, according to the Italian proverb:
>
> *Cosi Vanno cattando*
> *Li Tudesci cantando,*
> *Li Francesi piangendo,*
> *Li Spagnioli biastemando.*
> Thus go a-begging
> The Germans singing,
> The Frenchmen weeping,
> The Spaniards cursing. That is, the poor needy
>   Spaniards will sometime curse if a man deny them alms.
>   (sig. M4)

In the contest for who was deserving of compassion, the biggest challenge was posed by religious differences. When the Puritan polemicist William Perkins declares that 'our hearts should be pitiful, full of compassion for the poor afflicted members of Christ: seeing they be our fellow members', one wonders if he was limiting 'the members of Christ' to John Calvin's 'chosen'.[15] Donne is more liberal. In a sermon preached on Candlemas Day 1623 on the scripture 'Therefore if thine enemy hunger feed him, if he thirst give him drink; for, in doing so thou shalt heap coals of fire upon his head' (Romans 12:20) stresses the *com-*, the 'with', in compassion:

> How much and how often St. Paul delights himself with that sociable syllable *syn, con, conregnare,* and *convisicare,* and *consedere,* of reigning together, and living, and quickening together. As much also doth God

delight in it, from us, when we express it in a conformity, and compunction, and compassion, and condolency, and (as it is but a little before the text) *in weeping with them that weep.*[16]

It is telling that Wright's list of 'communities' to be hated for religious differences does not include Catholics. He himself was a Jesuit priest. Increasingly in the first four decades of the seventeenth century people in England found it difficult to make community with fellow citizens whose religious convictions were different from theirs. Compassion for religious differences was in shorter and shorter supply.

John Milton, who was Latin secretary to Oliver Cromwell in the more deeply Protestant Commonwealth established in 1649, argued for tolerance of religious differences – but he drew the line at Catholics. In *Areopagitica* (1644), a plea for freedom of the press five years before the Commonwealth was established, Milton writes,

> if all cannot be of one mind, as who looks they should be? this doubtless is more wholesome, more prudent, and more Christian that many be tolerated, rather than all compelled, I mean not tolerated Popery, and open superstition, which as it extirpates all religions and civil supremacies, so itself should be extirpate, *provided first that all charitable and compassionate means be used to win and regain the weak and the misled* . . . .[17]

Note that qualifying phrase: 'all charitable and compassionate means' should be used to reason with people who hold different religious opinions. Ultimately Milton won his case for freedom of the press, if not toleration of especially aberrant sects like Quakers. Beginning in the early 1640s and continuing throughout the years of the Commonwealth (1649–1660) the number of religious and political books with the word 'compassion' and 'compassionate' in their titles increased exponentially. Take, for example, the following:

- *England's complaint, or the church her lamentation, pitifully bemoaning herself to her children, to move them to compassionate her, now in this troublesome time, and to bring them to a mutual agreement and reconciliation.* (1642)
- *The compassionate Samaritan unbinding the conscience, and pouring oil into the wounds which have been made upon the separation, recommending their future welfare to the serious thoughts and careful endeavours of all who love the peace and unity of Commonwealth's men, or desire the unanimous prosecution of the common enemy, or who follow our Saviour's rule, to do unto others what they would have others do unto them.* (1644)

- *Wholesome severity reconciled with Christian liberty. Or, the true resolution of a present controversy concerning liberty of conscience. Here you have the question stated, the middle way betwixt popish tyranny and schismatizing liberty approved, and also confirmed from Scripture, and the testimonies of divines, yea of whole churches: the chief arguments and exceptions used in* The Bloody Tenet, The Compassionate Samaritan, M.S. to A.S. &c. *examined. Eight distinctions added for qualifying and clearing the whole matter. And in conclusion a paraenetic to the five apologists for choosing accommodation rather than toleration.* (1645)
- *Bowels of compassion towards the fettered seed. Or a visitation to all, who hath been seeking the resting place, but hath not found it, the cause why showed, and the way to it manifested, wherein is something showed also, of the emptiness, and unsoundness of all profession, without the light of Christ, to be the guide. Also an information to all the honest-hearted who desires to know the truth in the simplicity of it concerning us, the people of the most high who is by the world called Quakers.* (1659)

The proliferation of books during the English republic turned on the 'common' in 'Commonwealth'. Religious reformists were partly responsible for the abolition of monarchy and the establishment of a republic in 1649. Once they had gained power, the question arose of how far religious liberty was to be extended to other dissident groups like Diggers, Muggletonians, Quakers, Ranters and of course Roman Catholics.[18] Each of these groups had in effect its own ethics. The question of how much compassion religious dissenters were due was ultimately a test of ethical boundaries. If the boundaries between worthy and unworthy objects of compassion seem severe in the English texts that I have cited, Katherine Ibbett's account of three Catholic writers in the following chapter reveals how central the questions of social differences were to the ethics of compassion that each of the three writers formulated.

Ethos as Place

The institutional 'character' of compassion, if I can be permitted that metaphor, invites us to consider the social geography of compassion: the sites in early modern England where compassion was fostered. Schools and universities would constitute one such site, since moral philosophy was part of the curriculum. We have seen already that the case for compassion in moral philosophy was anything but clear.

Law courts might be another site, especially in the levying of punishments. The evidence in Edward Coke's legal textbooks suggests an investment in the letter of the law, but digests of the court records for the counties around London during the reigns of Elizabeth and James reveal surprisingly low rates of conviction. Did local juries take into account more than the letter of the law? Were they more compassionate toward some defendants than others? Those possibilities have to be left as questions. We do, however, have the exhortation of no less an authority than Bacon, Queen's Counsel from 1594 and Attorney General from 1613, that offenders in some circumstances deserve compassion. In *The Wisdom of the Ancients* (published in Latin 1609, English translation 1619), Bacon has this observation to make about the story of Diomedes, who followed Pallas's order to wound Aphrodite if he encountered her during battles at Troy and was put to death for the crime by his host King Daunus:

> let there be never so nefarious an act done, yet there is some place left for commiseration and pity, that even those that hate offences, should yet in humanity commiserate offenders, and pity their distress, it being the extremity of evil when mercy is not suffered to have commerce with misery. Yea, even in the cause as well of religion as impiety, many men may be noted and observed to have been compassionate.[19]

How often Bacon's counsel was taken by his contemporaries is hard to determine from surviving legal records.

More certain as sites for compassion were 'hospitals' for housing and maintaining not only the ill, but also the elderly, the orphaned and the poor. Originally these were religious institutions – St Bartholomew's and St Thomas's hospitals in London are examples that still exist – but with the disestablishment of the Catholic Church and its monastic institutions during the Reformation, support shifted to private foundations. Under both regimes – the church and private charity – hospitals were devoted to long-term custodial care more than to cure. After the Reformation, stricter rules were established for the poor: they had to be 'the *deserving* poor', people who were unable to work and support themselves.

The two most important sites for fostering compassion in early modern England were, in my judgement, churches and – a shock, I'm sure, to Puritan detractors – theatres. We have seen already how sermons by Donne and Abbot explicitly exhorted compassion among the congregants.

The preacher's art and the actor's art were not so far apart as antitheatrical writers like Philip Stubbes might assume. Wright in *The Passions of the Mind in General* remarks on the way orators solicit compassion at the beginning of their speeches: 'A small trembling voice proceedeth from fear, and such an one commonly have great orators, or at least it were good they should have in the beginning of their orations, for thereby they win a certain compassion and loving affection of their auditors' (sig. K3). Donne was a master at stirring compassion in his listeners – and so, as we shall see in a moment, was Richard Burbage. The same people might flock to theatres as well as churches. The diary of John Manningham, a law student at the Middle Temple, contains notations not only about the sermons he eagerly attended but also about the first recorded performance of Shakespeare's *Twelfth Night* during Candlemas festivities in February 1602.[20]

In churches, it was not just sermons that encouraged compassion but liturgical music as well. Truth be told, compassion in this context most often came from Christ to the congregants and not from the congregants to other people. A stirring example is William Byrd's four-voice motet 'I will not leave you comfortless', based on two passages from the Gospel of John in which Jesus shortly before his arrest and crucifixion – that is to say, shortly before his Passion – promises his disciples, 'I will not leave you comfortless: but I will come to you' (14:18), 'And ye now therefore are in sorrow: but I will see you again, and your hearts shall rejoice, and your joy shall no man take from you' (16:22).[21] The effect of 'elevated' music on listeners is acknowledged by Wright: 'A sword serveth to defend right and is also an instrument to work wrongs: music in like manner elevateth the mind to devotion and piety, and abaseth the soul with effusion and levity' (sig. M2).

Testimony to the 'elevating' power of music on the mind is provided by the English world traveller Thomas Coryate, who describes the liturgical music he heard in Venice in 1608 on the feast day of San Rocco as being 'so good, so delectable, so rare, so super excellent that it did even ravish and stupefy all those strangers that never heard the like. But how others were affected with it I know not; for mine own part I can say this, that I was for the time even rapt up with St Paul into the third heaven.'[22] Coryate alludes here to 2 Corinthians 12:2–4, in which St Paul describes being in the presence of God. The site for Coryate's passionate experience may have been, given the occasion, the Scuola Grande di San Rocco. If so, the music he heard may have been composed and directed by Giovanni

Gabrieli, who was composer-organist at the Scuola as he was at St Mark's Basilica. The warmth of Coryate's response is remarkable, given that his father was a parish priest in the Church of England and that Coryate himself later in his travels risked reprisals for the vehemency with which he publicly lambasted the Catholic Church.[23]

No less remarkable in Coryate's account is the way he situates his intense feelings in the context of other people. He imagines that the performance did 'ravish and stupefy' anyone present who had not heard the like before – 'strangers' like himself – but he doesn't venture to speak for them. 'How others were affected with it I know not', Coryate says before describing his own ascent into St Paul's third heaven. In this juxtaposition of the public and the private Coryate points toward a dynamic at the heart of worship services. Each worshipper has his or her own experience at the same time that he or she is part of a 'congregation'. In spaces like St Paul's, Byrd's motet would have been taken to heart by worshippers as individuals even though the words that Byrd has set were originally spoken by Christ to the disciples as a group. So it would have been to all the congregants, not to individuals, that the choir would have sung. With respect to feelings, the situation would have left each listener in a double subject position. Mullaney notes in *The Reformation of Emotions* how many times during the sixteenth century the state-sanctioned religion changed, leaving individual worshippers in potentially conflicted positions vis-à-vis the worship services that the law compelled them to attend. The situation in London's churches, Mullaney argues, was replicated in London's public theatres. Both spaces functioned as arenas for playing out conflicts, not just in ideology but in feelings.

Ethos as Representations

The ethics of compassion in early modern England finds its most powerful exemplar, not in London's streets or even in its churches, but in London's theatres. Given the self-dramatisation of the title character's suffering, *Richard II* has some claim to being Shakespeare's most compassionate play. 'It boots thee not to be compassionate', Richard tells the just-banished Mowbray in I.ii. 'After our sentence, plaining comes too late' (1.2.168–69). This is typical of the power dynamics of compassion in *Henry VI, Part One*, and *Titus Andronicus*: a king grants or withholds compassion. By the end of the play, however, Richard himself is in need of compassion. When the defeated Richard, being escorted to the Tower under guard, encounters his wife on a street in London, he advises her there is nothing left but for her to tell the tale of his defeat by Bolingbroke:

> Tell thou the lamentable fall of me,
> And send the hearers weeping to their beds;
> For why the senseless brands will sympathize
> The heavy accent of thy moving tongue,
> And in compassion weep the fire out ...
> (V.i.44–48)

In the ensuing scenes, the imprisoned Richard, soon to be executed, puts the assembled *audience* in that position of compassion.

As Joseph Roach has demonstrated in *The Player's Passion*, a book that charts changing ideas of the actors' art, *com*-passion, 'feeling with', was the stock-in-trade of sixteenth- and seventeenth-century actors like Richard Burbage, who likely played the role of Richard II in 1595. In Roach's formulation,

> The rhetoric of the passions ... endowed the actor's art with three potencies of an enchanted kind. First, the actor possessed the power to act on his own body. Second, he possessed the power to act on the physical space around him. Finally, he was able to act on the bodies of the spectators who shared that space with him.... His passions, irradiating the bodies of spectators through their eyes and ears, could literally transfer the contents of his heart to theirs, altering their moral natures.[24]

The combination of Galenic psychology and classical rhetoric rendered the theatre a potent site of *com*-passion, even more potent, I would propose, than the church.

Prospero in *The Tempest* I.ii recognises compassion in Miranda's response to the shipwreck and at the same time elicits the audience's compassion as they hear the story of his overthrow and exile. Perhaps, as a storyteller, Prospero begins with the 'low' if not 'trembling' voice that, according to Wright, inspires 'a certain compassion and loving affection' on the part of auditors. Certainly before he begins his story Prospero puts aside the garment that gives him his power over other men. He is left with only his voice:

> 'Tis time
> I should inform thee farther. Lend thy hand,
> And pluck my magic garment from me.
>   *Miranda removes Prospero's cloak, [and he lays it on the ground]*
> Lie there, my art.

Miranda's tears he reads as an index of her compassion:

> – Wipe thou thine eyes; have comfort.
> The direful spectacle of the wreck, which touched
> The very virtue of compassion in thee,
> I have with such provision in mine art
> So safely ordered that there is no soul –
> No, not so much perdition as an hair
> Betid to any creature in the vessel
> Which thou heard'st cry, which thou saw'st sink. Sit down;
> For thou must now know farther.
>
> (I.ii.22–33)

And so begins the tale of the wrongs he has suffered.

At the end of the play Prospero himself shows compassion toward his malefactors, just as Bacon advises in *The Wisdom of the Ancients*. It is Ariel who gives Prospero his cue:

> Your charm so strongly works 'em
> That if you now beheld them your affections
> Would become tender.
> PROSPERO   Dost thou think so, spirit?
> ARIEL
> Mine would, sir, were I human.
> PROSPERO   And mine shall.
>
> (V.i.17–20)

The very sight of the shipwrecked nobles, Ariel says, would move compassion. We as spectators/listeners have, from the very beginning, been made *com*-passionate in witnessing and hearing the fictions of the play. That is how early modern theatre worked.

Virtue

When Prospero commends 'the very virtue of compassion' in his daughter, he is endowing the word 'virtue' with three meanings: a character trait or moral way of behaving (*OED*, 'virtue, *n.*', I.1.a), conformity to moral standards held by society (I.2.a) and 'power, efficacy, worth' (II.8), as in the power of a medicine. The third sense, in this particular context, extends to theatre as a site of compassion and to representation as a way of bringing compassion to life, both in actors and in their spectators/audiences. Prospero epitomises the entire play when he moves compassion in Miranda through the spectacle of shipwreck that he has staged with Ariel's help.

The 'ethics' of compassion is, in all the senses that we have explored here, a matter of virtue, and not just in the sense of feeling compassion or performing it. Cicero's sense of virtue as a middle way between two perturbations can be extended to virtue as a middle way among the multiple considerations embraced by ethics. 'Much virtue in if': Touchstone's quip in *As You Like It* about how to avoid a sword-fight (V.iv.101) extends to theatre itself. Theatrical performance is a particularly powerful – that is to say, particularly 'virtuous' – mode of representation. Theatre is fundamentally about hypothetical possibilities, about 'if', about virtuality as something 'that is such in essence, potentiality, or effect, although not in form or actuality' (*OED*, 'virtual, *adj.* and *n.*', II.4.a). With respect to compassion, let me take a cue from Touchstone and conclude thus: 'Much virtue in virtue'.

Notes

1 Marcus Tullius Cicero, *Quaestiones Tusculanae*, trans. John Dolman as *Those five questions, which Mark Tully Cicero, disputed in his manor of Tusculanum: written afterwards by him, in as many books, to his friend, and familiar Brutus* (London: Thomas Marsh, 1561), sig. O2v. In this and all other quotations from early modern English texts spelling has been modernised but original punctuation retained. Further references are cited in the text by signature number.
2 Mark 6:34 in *The Geneva Bible* [1560], facsimile rpt. ed. Lloyd E. Berry (Madison: University of Wisconsin Press, 1969), sig. EE4.
3 *Oxford English Dictionary*, 2nd ed., 'pity, *n.*', etymology, I.1, *OED Online*. December 2016. Oxford University Press. www.oed.com. Future citations from the *OED* will be given in the text.
4 Middle English Dictionary, http://quod.lib.umich.edu/, 'compassioun', 'sorwing', 'erending' and *OED*, 'be-, *prefix*'. I am grateful to my colleague David Rollo for helping me get beyond the usual translation of *besárgung* as 'compassion'.
5 For the etymology of 'sympathy' see Richard Meek's Chapter 5 in this book.
6 Aristotle, *Poetics*, trans. Gerald F. Else (Ann Arbor: University of Michigan Press, 1967), pp. 28–29.
7 Francis Bacon, 'Of Goodness and Goodness of Nature' in *The Essays and Councils, Civil and Moral*, ed. Michael Kiernan (Oxford: Clarendon Press, 2000), pp. 40–41.
8 Michael C. Schoenfeldt, *Bodies and Selves in Early Modern England: Physiology and Inwardness in Spenser, Shakespeare, Herbert, and Milton* (Cambridge University Press, 1999).
9 Steven Mullaney, *The Reformation of Emotions in the Age of Shakespeare* (University of Chicago Press, 2015), p. 55.

10 Thomas Wright, *The Passions of the Mind in General*, rev. ed. (London, 1630), sig. C1. Further quotations from Wright are cited in the text.
11 George Abbot, *An Exposition upon the Prophet Jonah Contained in Certain Sermons, Preached in St. Mary's Church in Oxford* (London, 1600), sig. BB3v.
12 John Donne, *LXXX Sermons* (London, 1640), sig. K2.
13 Statute of the Realm 14 Eliz. I, chap. 5 (Vagabonds Act, 1572); Statute of the Realm 39 Eliz. I, chap. 4 (1597–98); 'Licensing Casper van Senden to Deport Negroes [draft]' (1601), in *Tudor Royal Proclamations*, ed. Paul L. Hughes and James F. Larkin, 3 vols. (New Haven: Yale University Press, 1969), vol. III, pp. 221–22.
14 William Shakespeare, *The Complete Works*, 2nd ed., gen. eds. Stanley Wells and Gary Taylor (Oxford: Clarendon Press, 2005). Further quotations from Shakespeare and taken from this edition and are cited in the text by act, scene and line numbers.
15 William Perkins, *Lectures upon the First Chapters of The Revelation* (London, 1604), 66 (sig. K1v).
16 John Donne, *Fifty Sermons. The Second Volume* (London, 1649), sig. CC4v.
17 John Milton, *Areopagitica: A Speech of Mr. John Milton for the Liberty of Unlicensed Printing, to the Parliament of England* (London, 1644), sig. E4, emphasis added.
18 For a survey of the issues see Blair Worden, *God's Instruments: Political Conduct in the England of Oliver Cromwell* (Oxford University Press, 2012), pp. 313–54. Primary texts relevant to the controversies are collected in David Cressy and Lori Anne Ferrell, *Religion and Society in Early Modern England: A Sourcebook*, 2nd ed. (London: Routledge, 2005), pp. 201–44.
19 Francis Bacon, *The Wisdom of the Ancients, Written in Latin by the Right Honourable Sir Francis Bacon Knight, Baron of Verulam, and Lord Chancellor of England*, trans. Arthur Gorges (1619), rpt. in *The Essays, or Councils, Civil and Moral, of Sir Francis Bacon, Lord Verulam, Viscount St. Alban ... and a Discourse of The Wisdom of the Ancients* (London, 1969), sig. R5–R5v.
20 John Manningham, *The Diary of John Manningham of the Middle Temple 1602–1603*, ed. Robert Parker Sorlien (Hanover, NH: University of New England Press, 1976), excerpted in William Shakespeare, *Twelfth Night: Texts and Contexts*, 2nd ed., ed. Bruce R. Smith (Boston: Bedford St. Martin's, 2015), pp. 1–6.
21 *The Geneva Bible* (1560), introd. Lloyd E. Berry (Madison: University of Wisconsin Press, 1969). (Performances of Byrd's 'I will not leave you comfortless' can be found on YouTube; professional performances are available on iTunes and Amazon.)
22 Thomas Coryate, *Coryat's Crudities* (1611), excerpted in Carol MacClintock (ed.), *Readings in the History of Music in Performance* (Bloomington: Indiana University Press, 1979), p. 115.

23 Michael Strachan, 'Coryate, Thomas (1577?–1617)' in *Oxford Dictionary of National Biography* (Oxford University Press, 2004), online ed. Oct. 2006, www.oxforddnb.com.libproxy1.usc.edu/view/article/6364.
24 Joseph Roach, *The Player's Passion: Studies in the Science of Acting* (Newark: University of Delaware Press, 1985), p. 27.

CHAPTER 2

The Compassionate Self of the Catholic Reformation
Katherine Ibbett

If, as Bruce Smith's chapter suggests, we tend to consider compassion primarily as a response to the suffering of another, the discourse of early modern compassion also provides a surprising perspective on the self. Where early modern compassion announced itself as a generous gesture to the outside world, it also depended upon a sharp assessment of the self's capacity to be compassionate. Early modern writers considering how and to whom compassion was to be apportioned also reflected on the appropriate sort of person to make such a judgement; compassion's prism provided not only for a judgement on the suffering other, but also on the appropriateness of the self who metes out such an affective response, and the role of the will in assessing and deploying emotion. In looking at this figuration of this self within the wider ethical landscape of seventeenth-century Catholic writing in continental Europe, we can trace an evolving practice of Catholic compassion drafted for the sociable or secular life.

On the secular front, many early modern accounts of compassion circled around the structure posited in Aristotle's account of pity and terror in the *Rhetoric* and *Poetics*: upon seeing the suffering of another, we fear that such suffering might come to us, and our pity for the other is inseparable from our fear for our own self. Witness Hobbes, who in the *Leviathan* describes how 'griefe for the calamity of another is Pitty, and ariseth from the imagination that the like calamity may befall himselfe, and there fore is called compassion, and in the phrase of this present-time a fellow-feeling'.[1] For some writers influenced by the Stoics, like René Descartes, this tightly bound dynamic means that pity is only a narrow response to suffering that reveals our weakness. Descartes does acknowledge that a more generous (by which he means noble) individual can be capable of responding to another's pain without this soft concern for the self, but his tight-lipped concern that compassion's contagion indicates a weak self is common in the period, and in France that anxious parsing of the pairing of pity and fear shapes the work of the virtue theorists known as the 'moralists', giving rise to some of their sharp-tongued digs at the human tendency to self-love.[2]

Yet this anxiety over the place of the self in compassion's structures took a different and surprisingly more forgiving vein in religious writing. In this chapter, I address the place of the self in compassion as explored by three key writers of the European Catholic Reformation, and suggest that attention to the contours of the compassionate self provides an important perspective on the relation between the Christian and the world. I focus on three texts: the French devout humanist François de Sales's *Introduction à la vie dévote* / *Introduction to the devout life* (1609), the Italian Jesuit Roberto Bellarmino's *De gemitu columbae, sive de bono lacrymarum* /*The Mourning of the Dove, or the value of tears* (1617), and the French Jesuit Pierre Le Moyne's *La dévotion aisée* / *An easy devotion* (1652): all of these texts set out the role of compassion in response to suffering, but they also understand compassion as the proper measure of our will, and even the proper response to our own spiritual suffering. Instead of following the neo-Stoic rejection of the compassionate self, the writers of the Catholic Counter-Reformation looked to draft a new understanding of compassionate social interaction. But unlike the radical compassion for the poor that Bruce Smith describes in his account of Gospel compassion, this Counter-Reformation model pointed to a new and more worldly form of Christian civility, generated and underwritten by a sweet management of our own self.

François de Sales (1567–1622)

The Stoics, whose perspective shaped so much of early modern European discourse on the emotions, had shunned the sloppiness of compassion for the sufferings of another, and equally rebuffed the attachment to the self indicated by any form of self-compassion, and such resistance to self-regard shaped much religious writing on suffering: take as an example the missionary mystic Marie de l'Incarnation, who writes firmly that 'We must have great courage and be without pity with ourselves'.[3] Yet some theologians of the period worried about the difficulties of such ethical rigor for the broader Catholic population, and acknowledged instead our attachment to a softer way of living and believing. Foremost amongst such writers was François de Sales, whose 1609 *Introduction à la vie dévote* was one of the bestsellers of the century across Europe, bringing the Ignatian tradition of spiritual exercises to a new and feminised readership:

in his lifetime alone there were forty re-editions, and in English, translations mushroomed from 1613.[4]

François was the bishop of Geneva for twenty years, charged with converting the Calvinists, but he wrote for an audience outside of religious life, for people – chiefly women – exposed to, but also enjoying, the temptations of secular life, in towns, in households, or at court. This is not a guide for those who are already perfect, but for those who seek some help getting there gradually. In one of his many delightfully prosaic natural metaphors, François compares the ordinary Christian to a chicken, who can just about fly, if heavily, low, and rarely (18). It is only the rare swallow who can easily take to flight, and such a creature doesn't need guidance; instead, François's book is aimed at those of us who are more clumsy chicken than gliding swallow. François urges us to take the book's insights with us throughout the day, a little bouquet of devotion (35), as we might take flowers to ward off bad smells. The book is vigorously committed to self-improvement: through a gentle care for the self, François firmly believes, we can correct and moderate our imperfections (56).

François's book is chiefly addressed to gentlewomen, taking pains to nuance their marital status, since devotion might take on different forms for widows, virgins, and married women. The text is addressed to a 'Philothée', and François takes her through the spiritual exercises, meditations, and resolutions needed for a Christian life lived in the world, all to be performed in one's native language and 'with emotion' (67). Such exercises are a domesticated school of virtue: François advises his reader to avoid hankering after 'ecstasies, ravishments' as a spiritual model, but to focus instead on the virtues that can be attained through 'work and industry' (119). We should leave such marvels to elevated souls, he says; we don't deserve such a rank in the service of God, but 'we will be only too happy to serve him in his kitchen, in his bakehouse ...' (120). Salesian virtue is quotidian and content to be so.

Although his readership is feminised, François's text is not aimed at women alone, for he also suggests that this rescaling of notions of service or exemplarity might equally fit the new French nobility in the decades after the Wars of Religion, when occasions for great heroism had been displaced by new and more courtly concerns. François's rescaled sense of service responds to the obligatory activities of aristocrats in leisure time. For those who simply *must* dance (and even Elizabeth of Hungary did it when she had to, he acknowledges – 222), he notes that even such frivolity can in fact be an occasion for compassion:

> While you were dancing, several souls died in great anguish; thousands of men and women suffered great trials, in their beds, in hospitals and in the streets: gout, kidney stones, burning fever. Alas! They have had no rest! Will you not have compassion for them? (221)

This is one of the rare instances of compassion elicited on behalf of those different from the reader: that is, those beset by illness while the reader dances. Even the illnesses mentioned, gout and kidney stones, mark out the sufferers as genteel. François's very structured chivvying of his reader into compassion may suggest a small gesture across difference (you suffer, I dance), but it also reveals the homogeneous social world imagined through the text.

If compassion can be imagined as a perspective on difference, the central difference it underwrites here is the gulf between human weakness and divine strength. After the initial series of exercises, François asks the reader to imagine engraving the following text in her heart: 'I the undersigned ... having considered the immense mercy (*miséricorde*) of his divine goodness towards me ... having considered this incomprehensible sweetness (*douceur*) and clemency with which this good God has so benignly tolerated me in my iniquities ...' (56). God's compassion takes shape through a cluster of vocabulary: mercy, sweetness, clemency. At some moments this compassionate language is biblical: Christ's 'bowels (*entrailles*) of mercy' (315), the famous bowels of compassion of the Vulgate discussed by Kristine Steenbergh in this volume, are a point for reflection at the end of the text. Yet elsewhere François's language stems from a much more contemporary discourse of sociability: God, like a gallant courtier, is '*débonnaire* and full of pity'. In such formulations the language of *douceur* or sweetness tempers divine heterogeneity, and places it in the context of everyday civility.[5] The sweetness of God makes him an easy companion for those clumsy chickens starting out in their own exercise of compassion; this is not a God whose corrections sit well with Stoic admonishment, but a gentle friend who shows us how to do compassion in the context of social life.

How will our hesitant Christian begin to exercise similar sweetness in her own life? In the third section of the book, François addresses the virtues in a series of paired chapters. Chapter 8, 'Of kindness (*De la douceur*) towards one's neighbour', sets out a compassionate ethic also tempered by the language of sweetness so central to Salesian discourse: we are urged to practise humility, *douceur*, *débonnaireté*: this civil practice of emotion is far distant from the fierce Aristotelian reflections that animate Descartes. Instead, it takes inspiration from recycled fragments of Pliny to imagine the place of the human within a larger compassionate ecology, in which animal compassion figures human potential:

> We must resist the ills and reprove the vices of those who are in our charge, constantly and valiantly, but *doucement* and peacefully. Nothing so calms the angry elephant as the sight of a lamb, and nothing breaks the force of cannon balls as well as wool. (143)

François's compassion is pedagogical and corrective: it calls us to intervene not to alleviate suffering but to correct imperfections that might block the route to salvation. But it corrects sweetly and kindly; compassion's corrective impulse must not lead us into temper, lest the heart 'being thus troubled can no longer be master of itself' (144). Compassion's reach to the other can sometimes endanger the peaceful security of the self.

But this chapter is followed by its surprising complement, 'Of *douceur* towards ourselves', urging compassion not just for others but for our own selves:

> One of the good practices we can make of *douceur*, is that where the subject is in ourselves, never raging (*dépitant*) against ourselves nor against our imperfections; since even though reason desires that when we make faults we should be unhappy, we must also stop ourselves from having a bitter and chagrined, pitiless (*dépiteuse*) and angry *déplaisance*. (146)

Far from being a gesture to assist another, in this new spiritual practice compassion is mobilised as a continual effort to reshape the self. This gently compassionate correction is contrasted with one that is 'dépiteuse', without pity, and François makes a further temporal distinction between these two forms of self-correction: the compassionate correction will be 'a displeasure with our faults [that is] peaceful, well-tempered and unfaltering' whose steady 'peaceful and constant repentances' are contrasted with 'bitter, hurried and angry repentances'. Compassion for the self allows for a constant and measured practice, rather than an immediate or punctual intervention.

This new temporality of self-compassion marks a departure from the standard discourses of early modern compassion, which tends to proclaim its response to an emergency event, responding heroically to a scene of suffering, as in the story of the Good Samaritan. Throughout the *Introduction* François shuns such heroics, suggesting at one point that although his readers may never be martyrs they can understand suffering through a more quotidian domestic unhappiness: a headache, a toothache, a broken glass or a lost glove (223). Here the continual small-scale compassionate corrective dampens down any notion of compassion as drama, and instead figures compassion as quotidian labour, a household practice turned towards the interior:

> Believe me, Philothée: just as the remonstrances of a father made *doucement* and cordially have much more power over a child to correct him than does anger and wrath, so when our heart has made some fault, if we correct it with *douce* and tranquil remonstrances, having more compassion with him than passion against him, encouraging him to amendment, the repentance that he will imagine will work better and penetrate more than a repentance that is without pity (*dépiteuse*), angry and tempestuous. (147)

François asks us to imagine addressing our own heart, in a sort of interior dialogue, 'reasonably and using the compassionate way'. In his reading, compassion is not a passion, not an emotion that is opposed to reason or that overcomes the passive individual; instead, emotion is a practice deliberately directed by an individual with agency, a practice that couches reason comfortably and allows it to find an easy place.[6] François's sweet corrections make him the Mary Poppins of early modern spiritual life: the spoonful of sugar of compassion makes the correction easier to take. The sites of compassion, to use Bruce Smith's terminology in the previous chapter, have shifted from scenes of suffering in the world to scenes of genteel inwardness.

François's turning of compassion to the self changes the norms of compassionate scenarios. Yet there is a social landscape to be glimpsed even in the interior worlds of gentlewomen, and even François's revised compassion provides some angle on understandings of inequality. In a grouping of chapters on the humility that can be practised in wealth and the richness of spirit that can be practised in material poverty (3.15–16), François addresses our emotional relation to social positioning. François asks wealthy women worried about their own salvation to detach emotionally from their ease and embrace what he calls moments of real poverty, reflecting on moments when the wine is spoiled or they don't have enough in the house to treat a guest the way they feel is right (167): these moments are enough, he suggests, to let such fortunates *feel* the position of poverty. François's movements around the question of wealth and poverty reveal to what extent this text addresses only an enclosed world of peers. For his audience, material suffering is rarely made visible, and these women are not yet encouraged either to look to the suffering around them or to attend to the potential miseries of distant others, as they will be some twenty years later in movements urging social action.[7]

François's compassion regulates conversation about difference, rather than social action. For the women he addresses, compassion is brought about more by gossip-induced suffering than by hunger: in a set of detailed instructions, he counsels the reader to avoid labelling others according to their vices, but notes that we can speak of such things 'as long as it is in a spirit of charity and compassion, and not arrogance or presumption' (213). Likewise, he urges us to feel compassion for those who are quietly like us rather than those who might be theatrically distant from our estate: everyone has compassion for the sufferings of a ragged freezing hermit, he says, but we mock 'a poor artisan, an impoverished gentleman or lady' (134). His called-for compassion would soften the scorn of social interaction, and encourages us to form a social compact with those who most resemble us.

Far from reaching out to the other, François's compassion urges a closer binding to those to whom we are most proximate. For François, the difference which counts the most is the spiritual divide: those souls who find themselves in spiritual drought are 'worthy of compassion' (282). (Blaise Pascal, who scorned the softness of François, was nonetheless in agreement with him on this front.) In a landscape of differing scales of spirituality, those fortunate enough to be nourished by Salesian bouquets of devotion can allow themselves to be 'moved by pity' for the loss of faith of their peers (289).

François's self-compassion suggests that in Salesian spirituality the key difference is not that between social types, but rather the difference between our own interior states. Calling for the importance of retreating to our 'little inner oratory' (85), François makes of emotion a continual system for self-surveillance, something akin to what Michel Foucault called a technology of the self, practices 'which permit individuals to effect by their own means or with the help of others a certain number of operations on their own bodies and souls, thoughts, conduct, and way of being, so as to transform themselves in order to attain a certain state of happiness, purity, wisdom, perfection, or immortality'.[8] Foucault describes how the injunction to know oneself is replaced by that to *take care* of oneself.[9] For François, this work is ongoing and sweetly undramatic, but it is always directed by a self with a clear sense of purpose and potential. There can be no social project without such attention to the self.

Roberto Bellarmino (1542–1621)

François's sweetness shapes a feminised self who is mostly concerned with private life, with domestic troubles, and the dances that punctuate them. Yet the proper disposition of the compassionate self was equally central to writers looking to a male readership and concerned largely with activities in a wider public sphere. The Italian Jesuit Robert Bellarmine (as he is known in English) is best known as the disputatious senior churchman and chief dogmatist of the Catholic Reformation, in which role he was the interrogator of Giordano Bruno. Yet towards the end of his life, during annual spiritual retreats, he also wrote a series of seemingly less contentious spiritual reflections. The penitential guide *De gemitu columbae* was written in 1617 during one such retreat, and as befitted the work of such a significant figure of the Church, appeared across Europe in swift translation; it found an eager Catholic audience, was greatly praised by François de Sales, and was reported to be the favoured devotional reading of James I.[10] Bellarmine's text, like that of François, articulates concerns about the place of the self in relation to wider suffering, but also explores concerns about the distinction between proximate and distant suffering, indicating what will become a pressing professional concern for the Jesuit missionary order. If François addressed dancing gentlewomen, Bellarmine writes as and for a weary statesman, and his self is imagined in relation to institutional need. How should the statesmanlike Catholic imagine his compassion in response to the world?

For all the baroque sentimentality of its title, Bellarmine's text also presents a difficult vision of compassion that wrestles with the question of social difference. How, asks the anti-Protestant polemicist, is it possible to maintain one's faith in the face of social inequities? Bellarmine lays out a long account of the categories and causes of tears in scriptural tradition, from those provoked by misery through to those 'holy tears' brought about through divine agency. In this first part of his account the tear functions as a motif that allows for spiritual and scriptural reflection, much as the 'tear poetry' of contemporary baroque poets like the French poet Jean de La Ceppède drew on the notion of the tear in order to reflect upon the mysteries of incarnation and salvation. But Bellarmine moves on to a discussion of the tear as a reflection on social ills in a chapter on human suffering. In this chapter, the tear trickles away from a strictly Christian context, and instead marks a shared humanity; tears, writes Bellarmine in a telling formulation, are 'common both to children of the Church and to all the peoples of the world'; the conjunction 'and' bears much weight here, but refrains from elucidating the relation between children of the Church and the wider world (150). Tears are shed for three principal reasons, Bellarmine notes, namely sickness, poverty, servitude, but they can also be shed because of an excess of wealth or health, as François had also affirmed. This language of legitimacy is central to the Counter-Reformation consideration of compassion; so too is the hesitation over who precisely is our neighbour.

For Bellarmine, compassion is not just the effect of private reflection; it is also a public emotion elicited by the sight of suffering in the world: 'Hospitals, public squares and sometimes even the high roads are so full of the suffering that they surpass by many the number of those who are sick in their own houses' (153). In early modern Europe, those 'sick in their own houses' would tend to be the affluent ill, whose domestics could provide assistance. But public disorders – wars, sieges, food shortages – brought the rest of the population into public disarray. Bellarmine, who had been in Paris on a papal mission when that city suffered under the siege of Henri de Navarre, posits compassion as the natural response to such disaster: 'What water can all these sick people everywhere ask of us, if it is not that which charity and compassion must make run from our eyes, at the sight of such sufferings?' For an instant, this plaintive formulation seems to bear within it a hint of the limitations of compassion, to be merely a conservative compassion: are tears then the only water that the sick can ask of us, and must they be content with that? Bellarmine rushes to clarify: 'Let us not imagine that I want to say that charity demands only tears of us, when we can add in visits, exhortations, donations. I speak only of those who, far from us, can hope for no other assistance than that of our prayers' (153–54). Tears are not enough when we see the suffering at hand; they must be supplemented by the works of mercy. But Bellarmine imagines a sort of universal charity, for those far distant from us who can nonetheless be imagined to draw upon our emotions and prayers.

Bellarmine's account of compassion is not merely an account of our own emotional reaction to what we see; it also furnishes some degree of analysis as to why we see so much suffering in the world. The analysis of poverty, for example, takes in what we today would term both a progressive and a conservative view of the question. There are so many poor because of the avarice and prodigality of the rich, Bellarmine argues, and if one man has too much, that means he is taking from others who deserve better (154). At this point, Bellarmine's radical compassion seems to anticipate the social justice tradition for which much later generations of Jesuits would become known. But in the next section it is the negligence and vanity of the poor, who fail to trust in providence, which is to be blamed for their suffering. The same rich who might be blamed for their avarice are also to be pitied, for wealth pushes them to pointless desires and thus 'The rich are unhappy, and worthy of compassion' (166). This chiasmus of the abstract and the material, the poor and the rich, recalls

François's gesture to those who suffer spiritually rather than materially; it also draws on the long tradition of distinguishing between the worthy and unworthy poor, a commonplace in early modern writing since Juan Luis Vives's influential *De subventione pauperum* (1526). This teeter-totter between those that have too little and those who have too much, between pity and blame, suggests that a fine judgement might be needed to gauge the appropriate amount of compassion required in any given case: compassion is not the impulsive response of the weak, as Descartes suggests, but rather the work of a discerning and informed agent.

Bellarmine's compassion is also motivated by a particular theological variant on the interests of the self. The great quantity of suffering in the world allows for greater potential for religious works, and allows the 'we' of the readership to ensure their own salvation: 'However given that these sufferings excite in us real feelings of compassion for our brothers, and that they serve to reanimate our zeal for their salvation, we will have cause to console ourselves, and it will come back to us with great advantages' (264). Bellarmine's text hesitates between a desire to see the end of suffering and the salvation of others, and a more self-interested sense of the salvatory possibilities such suffering offers to his order. If compassion doesn't quite save the other, at least we can save ourselves.

From a secular vantage point, this position seems ethically treacherous, but of course it is squarely within an orthodox Catholic perspective on suffering and salvation. But Bellarmine also proposes another reflection on charity and compassion that stands out sharply from that tradition and points to a more worryingly self-implicated model of understanding compassion in the world. Towards the end of the text, Bellarmine describes a number of acts of charity that might be understood as a self-description. Thus one important way to demonstrate neighbourly charity is to write corrective books, as indeed Bellarmine's vast bibliography indicates he had done throughout his career (248). Bellarmine had worked at the highest levels of state diplomacy and negotiation, and in the closing pages of his book he indicates how such work might be considered as a kind of charity: 'As for giving advice to those who need it, true charity demands that one does not flatter great men, that one does not only say sweet and agreeable things to them, and that one never disguises the truth' (271). Again, charity in this formulation demands a fine ability to judge and to consider the proper course of action. It is not merely an instinctive reaction, but in these most sophisticated manifestations entails a high degree of skill. So much skill, indeed, that the greatest pity must be reserved for those whose job entails the cautious assessments required when dealing with great figures:

> Who then, if he is wise, would want to claim such high positions, or could stop themselves feeling compassion for those who have them? And yet it is a necessity that there are in the Church and State people who are exposed to all these dangers: we must groan for them, be compassionate with their sufferings, help them in our prayers to he who alone can protect them from danger. (274)

In speaking of these difficult tasks in church and state, Bellarmine appropriates a distinctly biblical language of suffering (his verbs recalling the trials of Job) to describe his own role in the Catholic Reformation. Where François had urged kindness towards the self, suggesting that we correct ourselves kindly, Bellarmine goes further: we should not just show compassion to our own selves but instead – if we are high-ranking church- or statesmen – urge the wider world to feel compassion for our lot. If writing on compassion typically involves a manipulative choreography of 'us' and 'them', here Bellarmine pulls off the even greater coup of asking 'us' to pray for a 'them' behind whom it is not hard to decipher his own self. Those who are most worthy of compassion, in short, are those whose positions most resemble that of Bellarmine himself.

Pierre Le Moyne (1602–1671)

The Jesuit Pierre Le Moyne wrote a number of works central to French Counter-Reformation culture: the *Galerie des femmes fortes* (1647) and a vast work on the passions, *Les peintures morales* (1640–1643). His discussions of compassion come in *La dévotion aisée* of 1652, in which Le Moyne, heavily influenced by François de Sales, shows how devotion can be sweetly accessible to those who wish to remain anchored in the pleasures of the world. But, like Bellarmine, Le Moyne also suggests what it is to think about a self within the institution of an order: his is a distinctly Jesuit self, active in the world but thinking also about his own order's concerns, and in his work the direction of the self so central to François's pedagogy is dissolved into a broader and less willed understanding of human behaviour that builds a new figuration of human sociality as natural.

Le Moyne defines this natural neighbourliness in a rather socially particular way:

> The love of one's neighbour depends on and follows from, flows from, and reflects the love of God, and is as natural and as easy. And it would be very

strange, if it needed constraint and violence to go down a slope that the senses had prepared; if it needed springs and machines, to make it go where resemblance was drawing it. Whatever kind of man we have, he resembles another man; and resemblance is the stuff of inclinations and sympathies, the knot of hearts and minds, the bond between couples and gatherings. Through resemblance a savage is the familiar of all savages, a lion is at home with (*privé pour*) other lions, a tiger is the natural friend of all tigers.[11]

Le Moyne's exuberant insistence that we love one another is kept in check by a strong sense of where the limits of the 'we' might lie, and he insists on our similarities as humans by insisting on our differences from animals. A man resembles a man, a savage a savage, and a tiger a tiger, and it is similarity that binds us; we cannot imagine other forms of neighbourliness. The connection between 'man' and 'savage' is not articulated, and seemingly not imagined; the savage is what separates man from the lions and tigers, and he is as different from them as are those beasts, whose habits are presumably gleaned from travellers' tales, including those by Le Moyne's fellow Jesuits. The lion is '*privé*' for all other lions, in the sense that he is tame or domesticated for lions, but presumably still savage to other beasts; there is to be no crossing of party lines in Le Moyne's structure of fellow-feeling. The natural both binds together and rigorously separates. Le Moyne stumbles over the delineation of difference that nonetheless relies on an analogical understanding: man's friend is to man as tiger's friend is to tiger. Ontologically humans and tigers might not be similar, but our bonds are of the same order. We love each other because we are made that way, but our maker made us in very particular and separate ways.

In his delineation of such creatures, Le Moyne holds firmly to a Creator-centric understanding of the natural. But elsewhere his language lets us glimpse a new Jesuit science at work. His Christian reading of emotion's sociality draws on a scholastic vocabulary in sharp conflict with more recent discoveries. *La dévotion aisée* appeared four years after a bitter debate between Pascal and the Jesuits on the nature of the vacuum. For the Jesuits, drawing on scholastic tradition, the notion of the horror of the vacuum figured a world naturally gathered together in unity, an inexorable human movement.[12] Jesuit scientific assertions underwrote Jesuit beliefs in the natural sociability of humans, a notion also fiercely opposed by Pascal: for the Jesuits, just as the natural bodies of physics were drawn together, so too were humans.[13] Le Moyne's reading of compassion stems from this Jesuit natural philosophy. In accordance with this tradition, Le Moyne describes the love of one's neighbour as 'natural', but he defines this natural neighbourliness in a rather socially particular way:

> The commerce of good deeds, which is the proper commerce of noble souls, is made of the plenitude which is on one side, and the vacuum that is on the other; it is made of the compassion that the poor and afflicted inspire, and the relief that the rich and happy give to them. For on one side the vacuum naturally draws us to it, and misery naturally gives rise to pity; on the other hand it is also natural for plenitude to spread, and the most natural happiness of the happy is the good deed. (256–57)

The Jesuit science of sociability brings physics to bear upon human bonds. Where Le Moyne's earlier passages insisted on God as maker and regulator of difference and similitude, here compassion obeys the impersonal laws of physics, moving goods and emotions in seamless and natural exchange, an exchange that builds a moral economy: the noble soul participates not in the usual bourgeois exchange of goods (*biens*) but rather of good deeds (*bienfaits*). This scientific figuration of emotion displaces the individual judgement that was so important in the texts of François and Bellarmine, who praised the delicate judgement needed to properly identify and respond to suffering. In contrast, Le Moyne's naturalising compassion mechanism systematises affect and suggests that it happens even without our agency, flattening out our particularised reactions to a human other into a normalising landscape of redistribution in which our will has no place, and that is a good thing:

> Rivers which are full and constrained break their levees; fountains which brim and are held back, burst their canals; in ourselves repletion brings about illness, and generally all abundance which has no outlet is ruinous, and felicity which is not communicated is an imperfect and awkward happiness. (25)

Le Moyne says that we do not need springs and machines to keep compassion flowing where resemblance draws it, but his commerce of compassion is in its own way a mechanism that regulates our assessment of similarity and difference. Where François and Bellarmine both attended to a self that is able to exercise will and discretion, Le Moyne disintegrates such a self and attends instead to a larger emotional ecology in which the human struggles to determine the levers.

In recent work on early modern English emotion, scholars have emphasised the importance of individual will in considering the early modern emotions: although often the early modern emotions were imagined as forces (be they humours or passions) to which an individual was subjected, some writers also insisted on a form of emotional agency, a choice to respond affectively in a particular fashion or to school one's emotions to do so.[14] This question takes on still greater urgency in the context of the Catholic Reformation. The question of the will was central to Catholic reformist thought; the Council of Trent had stressed the importance of freedom of the human will to questions of salvation, something that John D. Lyons has suggested is central to François's interest in spiritual exercises, which stem from the encounter of this Tridentine focus with Stoic tradition.[15] For François, as for Bellarmine, the will is central not only to self-compassion but also to the self's direction of compassion: the proper selection of a worthy object, the considered response, the understanding of its significance within a wider salvatory schema, what Bruce Smith calls its ethical 'investigation', directed by human consciousness. For Le Moyne, in contrast, the will is emptied out, and although we are urged to humanist civility in the tradition of François, we are also opened up to a vista of non-human forces that spur the ebb and flow of emotion: this time not passions, nor humours, but the laws of physics. Le Moyne, writing thirty years after François, still sees himself within the sweet, easy Salesian framework, but his easy devotion is buffeted by new understandings that have come to erode the self he seeks to direct.

Our conversations about emotion and affect today often return to similar territory: from Rei Terada's emotion after the subject to Brian Massumi's virtual dissolution of intention, from William Reddy's first-person emotives to Eve Sedgwick's working-over of what we thought we knew about the emotional self, across our different critical idioms, in positivist accounts or post-structuralist, we still worry about the place of the self in a larger emotional ecology, about the capacity of the will or of language to direct or account for what we experience.[16] Even popular compassionate rhetoric today also depends on a willed direction that skirts close to self-help's emotional entrepreneurialism: witness the marketing of the Dalai Lama's book *How to Be Compassionate* alongside cheery guides to business in airport bookstalls and other pitiless places of modern life. In therapeutic circles, self-compassion is in vogue, emphasising the technique of the self that enables what two psychologists call 'portable therapy': in this model, mental health becomes an entrepreneurial exercise, just as wider public provisions for it fail. This language echoes the compassionate conservatism of the 1980s, when influential US Republicans insisted on compassion as a privatised form of action. Central to the rhetoric of conservatives from the 1980s on, compassionate conservatism turns its head away from structural inequity; it does not ask (as the Stoics recommended) how the sufferer came to be, but rather showcases its gesture of self-regard. We tend to imagine this entrepreneurial emoter as the legacy of a nineteenth-century Protestantism, defiantly modern; but the Counter-Reformation shaping of the compassionate self reminds us that these intellectual concerns stem from a longer and very partisan theological past.

Notes

1 Thomas Hobbes, *Leviathan*, ed. Richard Tuck (Cambridge University Press, 1996), p. 43.
2 On these French early modern discourses of compassion, see Ibbett, *Compassion's Edge* (Philadelphia: University of Pennsylvania Press, 2018), chap. 2.
3 Marie de l'Incarnation, *Lettres* CLXIII, 18 October 1654, p. 549.
4 For a good introduction to the text, see Richard Parish, '"Une Vie douce, heureuse et amiable": A Christian *joie de vivre* in Saint François de Sales' in Susan Harrow and Timothy Unwin (eds.), *Joie de vivre in French Literature and Culture* (Amsterdam: Rodopi, 2009), pp. 129–40; on François and the language of civility, see Ruth Murphy, *Saint François de Sales et la civilité chrétienne* (Paris: Nizet, 1964); on what he calls worldly sociability in both François and Le Moyne, see Richard Strier, *The Unrepentant Renaissance* (Chicago, 2011), pp. 189–98. References to the text from Saint François de Sales, *Introduction à la vie dévote* (Paris: Seuil, 1962): all translations throughout this chapter are my own.
5 On the language of *douceur* see Eric Méchoulan, 'La douceur comme politique' in Marie-Hélène Prat and Pierre Servet (eds.), *Le doux aux XVIe et XVIIe siècles: écriture, esthétique, politique, spiritualité* (Lyon: Université Jean Moulin-Lyon 3, 2004), pp. 222–37.
6 John D. Lyons insists on the importance of Tridentine understanding of the will for François's understanding of the individual imagination: 'Triumph of the Will: Imagination and Self-Cultivation in François de Sales', *Seventeenth-Century French Studies*, 25:1 (2003), 21–35, arguing that imagination, too, is 'a practice, something that one deliberately does' (25).
7 See Susan E. Dinan, *Women and Poor Relief in Seventeenth-Century France: The Early History of the Daughters of Charity* (Aldershot: Ashgate, 2006); Barbara Diefendorf, *From Penitence to Charity: Pious Women and the Catholic Reformation in Paris* (New York: Oxford University Press, 2004).
8 Michel Foucault, 'Technologies of the Self' in Luther H. Martin, Huck Gutman, and Patrick H. Hutton (eds.), *Technologies of the Self: A Seminar with Michel Foucault* (Amherst: University of Massachusetts Press, 1988), p. 18.
9 Foucault addresses François at two moments in his work: in the lectures of 1973–74 he discusses him as a spiritual director, and in his lecture on *Modes of Life* he discusses François's famously chaste elephant.

10 In French it appeared as *Trois livres du gémissement de la colombe ou du bien des larmes* in 1617 and then again in 1686. I am quoting from a later edition (Avignon: Séguin aîné, 1835). On Bellarmin and de Sales, see Robert Bellarmine, *Spiritual Writings*, ed. John Patrick Donnelly and Roland J Teske (Paulist Press, 1988), p. 23. In English, Thomas Everard ('A.B.') translated another work of Bellarmine for the English College at Douai in 1638 (*Of the eternall felicity of the saints, five books*) – with an appendix on the torments of hell taken out of *Mourning*. On the text's success, see Giorgio de Santillana, *The Crime of Galileo* (Chicago, 1955), p. 102.

11 Pierre Le Moyne, *La dévotion aisée* (Paris: A. de Sommaville, 1652), pp. 251–52. My discussion of this passage briefly revisits a more developed argument I made in *Compassion's Edge*, pp. 102–107.

12 See Matthew L. Jones, 'Three Errors about Indifference: Pascal on the Vacuum, Sociability, and Moral Freedom', *Romance Quarterly*, 50:2 (2003), 99–119.

13 Jones, 'Three Errors', 107.

14 See, for example, the recent volume edited by Richard Meek and Erin Sullivan, *The Renaissance of Emotion* (Manchester University Press, 2015), especially the introduction, the essay by Meek, and the afterword by Peter Holbrook.

15 John D. Lyons, 'In Love with an Idea' in Jennifer R. Perlmutter (ed. and foreword), *Relations and Relationships in Seventeenth-Century French Literature* (Tübingen: Gunter Narr, 2006), pp. 17–32.

16 Rei Terada, *Feeling in Theory: Emotion after the 'Death of the Subject'* (Cambridge, MA: Harvard University Press, 2003); Brian Massumi, *Parables for the Virtual: Movement, Affect, Sensation* (Durham: Duke University Press, 2001); William M. Reddy, *The Navigation of Feeling: A Framework for the History of Emotions* (Cambridge University Press, 2001); Eve Kosofsky Sedgwick, *Touching Feeling: Affect, Pedagogy, Performativity* (Durham: Duke University Press, 2002).

PART II

Consoling

CHAPTER 3

'Hee Left Them Not Comfortlesse By the Way'
Grief and Compassion in Early Modern English Consolatory Culture

Paula Barros

After performing ritual gestures of mourning, Job's friends sat with him in silence for seven days and seven nights. They 'thoght that he wolde not have hearkened to their counsel', the annotators of the Geneva Bible explained.[1] Early modern English culture acknowledged bereavement as a harrowing experience and recognised the challenges consolers faced when trying to offer solace. Overwhelmed by the loss of a loved one, grief-stricken mourners might, like Job, be reluctant to accept the remedies of religion and philosophy. To be sure, those who indulged in excessive sorrow were castigated, but so were consolers when their insistence on faith and reason was felt to betray a lack of sympathy for the bereaved. The fictitious author of an answer letter included in Angel Day's *The English Secretorie*, a letter-writing manual published in 1586, pointed out the inefficiency of the consolatory epistle sent to him by his 'brother', whose severity, he implied, was ill advised: 'Follie were it for mee to thinke or you to beleeue, that the pensiue imagination of a thing so neere ... coulde with the vehemencie of a fewe specches (more of zeale then equitie deliuered) be sodenly remooued'.[2] The multiplication of formal templates for such replies shows that in England as well as on the Continent, consolation came to be perceived as a dialogic exchange.[3] Epistolary practice and friendly 'conversation' opened up a conceptual space for debating the ethical and rhetorical limits of consolation.[4]

Three decades ago, in a groundbreaking study, George Pigman drew attention to the emergence of early modern discourses resisting the perceived 'rigorism' of humanist consolation; he showed that towards the end of the sixteenth century, the development of the English elegy signalled a shift to 'a more sympathetic, less anxious attitude towards mourning'.[5] More recently, Fred B. Tromly demonstrated that Shakespeare questioned the consolatory ethos by staging manipulative or downright dishonest consolers; according to Tromly, Cordelia in *King Lear* shows that sorrow is best alleviated 'not by assuming the detached, impersonal stance of the traditional consoler, but by a complete denial of moral privilege' and, crucially, by the 'mutuality' of 'a shared grief'.[6] In the early 1630s, Sir Kenelm Digby rejected consolation in the letters he wrote after the death of his wife, begging his correspondents to 'compassionate the sad condition I am in'.[7] These examples all point towards a tension between compassion (particularly in its early modern acceptation of '[s]uffering together, when two or three feele the same greefe'[8]) and consolation (defined as an exhortative discourse based on reason and rhetoric).

Though there have been numerous studies of grief and mourning in early modern England, the precise relationship between compassion and consolation has yet to be examined. This chapter aims to clarify the role of compassionate companionship in situations of bereavement in early modern English consolatory culture. It begins with a discussion of the humanist tradition of consolation that flourished in England from the mid-sixteenth century onwards. I argue that the Erasmian conception of compassion as a potentially disruptive force must be understood in the light of the neo-Stoic critique of pity, which articulated an ethics of consolation grounded in a deep commitment to the well-being of others. For all its 'rigorism', humanist consolation – which intersected with the culture of counsel discussed by Stephen Pender in the next chapter – was not incompatible with fellow-feeling. The following section examines Edmund Spenser's *Daphnaïda*, which I propose to read as a comment on the perceived erosion of the humanist consolatory ethos in late sixteenth-century England. Spenser published his funeral elegy in 1591, at a time when resistance to consolation was, as Pigman and others have shown, gaining momentum. I contend that *Daphnaïda* warns against the social and ethical consequences of compassionate mourning and should be read as powerful defence of the humanist tradition of consolation. The final section explores early seventeenth-century justifications of compassionate mourning in Protestant sermons and commentaries on John 11:35 ('Jesus wept'). I demonstrate that these texts developed an ethics of shared vulnerability that is best understood in the broader context of the revival of the medieval tradition of spiritual mourning. As such, they resisted the humanist movement towards the secularisation of sorrow, the groundwork for which had been laid by Petrarch who, in George McClure's formulation, 'shifted *miseria* from its status as an ascetic remedy to that of a worldly malady, offering as its long-awaited cure the anthropocentric consolation of human dignity'.[9] The Protestant divines and theologians I consider rejected the humanist ideal of self-sufficiency while closely articulating human and spiritual sorrow. Their interpretations of John

11:35 suggest that the history of consolation cannot be understood as a linear progression to a secularised understanding of sorrow and compassion. Using Christ's exemplary tears to justify compassionate weeping, these authors encouraged the expression of shared grief as a token of Christian fellowship.

The Humanist Ethos of Consolation: Compassion as Strategy

Rooted in classical literature, the humanist tradition of consolation framed an approach to grief based on the belief in the therapeutic efficiency of reason and rhetoric. Consolatory manuals and epistles by Petrarch, Cardano, Erasmus and others provided formal models and lists of *topoi* for the composition of speeches and letters aiming at offering solace to the bereaved.[10] Geared towards the moderation, if not the outright eradication of grief, humanist consolation acknowledged the use of pathos as one of the three modes of persuasion. In Renaissance consolatory literature, therefore, the expression of compassion was an important rhetorical strategy. Functioning as a *captatio benevolentiae*, it was essentially confined to the *exordium* of consolatory letters and speeches where, according to ancient rhetorical theory, assertions of sympathy helped establish the consoler's ethos and enhance the mourner's receptivity to arguments against grief.[11] The Greek rhetorician Aelius Theon, for example, underlined the expediency of voicing compassion in consolatory discourses:

> Expressing pity has great power for consolation, especially when someone is composing a speech for bereavement; for those in distress are naturally resentful of those who think they have experienced nothing dreadful, ... but they naturally accept consolations in a better spirit from those who join in their lamentations, as from relatives.[12]

In his augmented edition of *The Arte of Rhetorique* (1560), Thomas Wilson explained that there were two different methods for composing consolatory speeches, a straightforward one, consisting in the unadorned rehearsal of the arguments against grief, and an indirect one, best suited when consolers needed to capture the goodwill of 'excedyng sorowfull' persons:

> the other [method] is when we graunte, that thei have juste cause to be sadde, and therefore we are sadde also in their behalfe, and would remedie the matter, if it could be, and thus entering into felowshippe of sorowe, we seke by a little and little, to mitigate their greefe. For all extreme heavinesse, and vehement sorrowes can not abide coumfort, but rather seke a mourner, that would take parte with them.[13]

In early modern England, as in classical antiquity, discourses of consolation routinely expressed such 'felowshippe' with the bereaved in the *exordium*, as a prelude to the philosophical and religious arguments against grief. After the opening lines, expressions of compassion all but disappeared.[14]

Wilson's *Arte of Rhetorique* drew heavily on Erasmus's *De conscribendis epistolis*, a letter-writing manual published in 1522 that not only set out a method for writing consolatory epistles, but also included several models, among which Erasmus's influential consolation to his friend Antoine Sucquet.[15] In the section discussing the letter of consolation, Erasmus followed standard rhetorical theory when he recommended an 'indirect' method (*per insinuationem*) to comfort 'persons plunged into grief' while insisting on the need to *simulate* compassion, a stance which seemed to rule out any real identification with the bereaved:

> we shall give comfort in such a way as to transfer to ourselves the feelings of the person we wish to console, *so adapting our language that we seem [videamur] to wish rather to give in to our own grief than to assuage his sorrow* . . . . For persons plunged into grief [*quos dolor adhuc totos possidet*] must be treated in exactly the same way as those whose deranged state of mind leads them to believe that they have horns, or too long a nose, or are dead, or are made of clay. *They dislike those who disagree with them, and like those who humour their fancy by dissembling [per dissimulationem]. Hence those who are eager to cure them sometimes pretend [simulant] that they themselves are victims of the same evil.* Then once they have gained their good will, they easily convince them of the cure, and by this gradual approach remove the false imaginings in the end. This is how one must deal with those whose state of mind does not yet permit the hand of the healer.[16]

This passage reveals a tension between compassion and consolation that must be understood in relation to Erasmus's conception of grief. In the Latin text, the 'persons plunged into grief' who must be tricked into accepting consolation are described as 'entirely possessed' by sorrow, to the extent that they descend into madness. Erasmus here endorses the Stoic doctrine of grief as an error of judgement and a disease of the mind, a passion, in other words, it would be dangerous for the consoler to identify with. In ancient and early modern thought, nurturing grief, through imitation or otherwise, was believed to have potentially debilitating consequences. As Stephen Pender has pointed out, early modern conceptions of grief were influenced by Plato's warnings against 'affective mimesis' in book 10 of the *Republic*. Threnody, for example, was a perilous practice, because of 'the susceptibility of grief (and perhaps of all passions) to imitation: if one indulges grief, one indulges the sensitive part of the soul and thus potentially occludes reason and deliberation'.[17] Such worries about the effects of grief may explain why Erasmus, through his emphasis on simulated compassion, seems to set a limit to the consoler's emotional involvement and depart from Quintilian's precept that (as Pender reminds us in his contribution to the present volume) efficient oratory 'entails being moved oneself'.[18]

The Stoic and neo-Stoic critique of pity provides another illuminating context for Erasmus's prescription of simulated compassion. As editor of Seneca's works, Erasmus would have been familiar with the distinction the Roman philosopher had made between mercy (*clementia*) and pity (*misericordia*), which Justus Lipsius and Pierre Charron later contributed to disseminate in early modern Europe.[19] In the eyes of the Stoics, pity was a sentimental and despicable response to the suffering of others, a sign of effeminacy and moral depravity.[20] As such, it was incompatible with the ideals of rationality, wisdom and constancy that underpinned the humanist approach to consolation. Since therapeutic efficiency depended on the orator's capacity of marshalling rational arguments, one understands why Erasmus seems to have believed that consolers should protect themselves from the emotional contagion of grief. The prospect of the consoler's emotional miscarriage was likely to raise concerns about the possible failure of consolation.

By contrast, however, there were important points of convergence between the Stoic sage's commitment to mercy and Erasmus's ethos of consolation. Seneca insisted that the sage

> will assist his neighbour that weepeth, without weeping himself . . .; hee will lodge him that is famished, feede him that is poore . . .; But he will doe all this with a peaceable minde, and without change of countenance. He will not therefore be mooved, but will helpe, will profit, as being borne for the common good and the service of the Common-weale, whereof he will give every one his apart.[21]

The same preference for a rational, virtuous and action-orientated response to suffering characterised the humanist approach to consolation, which envisaged the task of alleviating grief as part of a broader mission, involving the advancement of civic virtue and the quest for human dignity and self-sufficiency.

Two additional remarks are necessary to clarify Erasmus's view of compassion. Though the pragmatic, therapeutic and psychagogic orientation of the consolatory ethos justified deception and emotional manipulation, such methods were acceptable only as long as the consoler's ends remained within the ethical boundaries of classical oratory, linking the honourable (*honestum*) to the expedient (*utile*).[22] The consoler, in other words, had to be a *vir bonus dicendi peritus* ('a good man skilled in speaking'),[23] which implied conforming to the model of the *vir civilis*, a core ideal of the educational programme promoted by Tudor humanists and rhetoricians.[24] Second, as Stoic and neo-Stoic defences of mercy make clear, Erasmus's rejection of compassion implied neither indifference nor insensitivity to the suffering of others. The Renaissance ethos of consolation was rooted in the culture of friendship, which meant that offering solace ranked among the duties of amity, as did the obligation of giving sound advice.[25] Erasmus thus reminded his readers that 'Timely and friendly consolation is no ordinary act of kindness; for in times of distress, when it is not possible to remedy the anguish of those whom we love through deeds, it at least enables us to ease their suffering by words.'[26] In his *Poetices Libri Septem* (1561), the Italian humanist Julius Caesar Scaliger agreed: 'Consolation is a discourse that restores tranquillity to the soul of the afflicted. It can only come from a friend.'[27] If the expression of compassion was a rhetorical strategy, the practice of consolation – through epistolary exchange or friendly conversation – involved feelings of amity, good will and kindness, as well as concern for the common good. Exchanges between the consoler and the bereaved required the same balance between 'admonition' and 'affability' as the physician-patient relationships discussed by Stephen Pender in the next chapter. This link between 'friendship, counsel and compassion' has not been sufficiently recognised so far, and it is important to underline its significance for the humanist consolatory ethos. But it is equally important to stress that for Erasmus, caring for the welfare of one's friends seems to have stopped short of feeling sorry for them: far from participating in the suffering of others, the Erasmian consoler was expected to demonstrate an active, rational and virtuous commitment to the alleviation of misery.

Compassionate Mourning and the Failure of Consolation in Edmund Spenser's *Daphnaïda*

The humanist ethos of consolation, particularly when it is examined through the lens of Erasmus's emphasis on the potentially disruptive effects compassion, sheds light on what William A. Oram has described as one of Edmund Spenser's 'least loved works'.[28] *Daphnaïda* is a funeral elegy originally published in 1591 to commemorate the death of Douglas Howard, the wife of Arthur Gorges, a courtier and poet whose relationship with Spenser remains obscure.[29] The poem, which takes the form of a pastoral eclogue, stages an encounter between a bereaved shepherd named Alcyon and a melancholy narrator. The two characters are literary representations of Gorges and Spenser. They meet at dusk, in a gloomy autumnal landscape of 'open fields, whose flowering pride opprest / With early frosts, had lost their beautie faire' (27–28). In this perverted pastoral setting, their exchange takes an ill-fated turn. The grief-stricken shepherd laments the death of his love, Daphne, in a protracted complaint. Impervious to the narrator's attempts to comfort him, he remains utterly disconsolate. The final stanza sees him hasten to desolation and ruin:

> But without taking leave, he foorth did goe
> With staggring pace and dismall lookes dismay,
> As if that Death he in the face had seene,
> Or hellish hags had met upon the way:
> But what of him became I cannot weene.
> (563–67)

Ending on a tragic note, *Daphnaïda* is, as Ellen Zetzel Lambert explains, 'a pastoral elegy which seeks but does not find pastoral consolation'.[30] Other critics have pointed out the poem's didactic engagement with the consequences of excessive grief, underlining not only Alcyon's 'self-centredness and self-absorption' but also his impaired poetic faculties.[31] A. Leigh Deneef, for instance, convincingly argues that Alcyon is 'a bad reader and writer of pastorals', who 'makes the ... mistake of assuming that the poetic conventions [he relies on] are literal records of his own emotional condition and his own experiential situation'.[32] Because of their focus on Alcyon, however, critics have tended to neglect the part played by the narrator. Those who, like Paola Baseotto, rightly consider him to play a pivotal role, suggest that his compassion for Alcyon redeems him from his narcissistic melancholy.[33] For Oram, thus, the narrator 'manages to control and transcend his own melancholy. His active sympathy as he attempts to help Alcyon ... demonstrate[s] a Christian charity that rises above personal misfortune'.[34] Focusing on the interaction between the narrator and Alcyon, I will offer an alternative reading, arguing that the narrator's compassionate attitude is a key element in the breakdown of the consolatory ethos dramatised in the poem.[35] Because the narrator is a thinly disguised persona of Spenser, *Daphnaïda* can be read as a comment on the ethical and social role of the elegiac poet in the face of bereavement.

The poem suggests that the narrator's compassion, because it undermines the power of the consolatory logos, is ultimately counterproductive.

Alcyon's very appearance as he enters the stage – his 'carelesse locks', his 'bearde all over growne', his downcast eyes and his heartrending sighs (43–49) – aligns him with stereotypical representations of melancholy mourners.[36] He fails to submit to God's providential plan, disregards the words of comfort spoken by Daphne on her deathbed, and indulges in self-destructive behaviour. The poem, moreover, casts him as a figure of effeminate grief, not only because his name is a masculine form of Alcyone, the disconsolate queen in Chaucer's *The Book of the Duchess*, which Spenser revisits in *Daphnaïda*,[37] but also because he replicates gestures of ritual weeping that were habitually marked as feminine: 'Did rend his haire, and beat his blubbred face' (551). His moral and spiritual distraction is such that he can easily be recognised as one of those 'excedyng sorowfull' persons whom the rhetorical and epistolary tradition of consolation advised to approach with compassion and condolence before administering the remedies against grief.

Cast as a narrative dialogue, the poem leads readers to expect a standard consolatory exchange. It soon becomes clear, however, that Spenser plays with the generic conventions not only of pastoral but also of *consolatio*. After recognising the once 'jollie' shepherd behind the 'disguize' of mourning (50–58), the narrator addresses Alcyon with words of sympathy that read like a conventional *captatio benevolentiae*:

> [Alcyon] Who is it that dooth name me, wofull thrall,
> The wretchedst man that treades this day on ground?
> [Narrator] One, whome like wofulnesse impressed deepe,
> Hath made fit mate thy wretched case to heare,
> And given like cause with thee to waile and weepe:
> Griefe findes some ease by him that like does beare.
> Then stay, *Alcyon*, gentle shepheard, stay,
> (Quoth I), till thou have to my trustie eare
> Committed, what thee dooth so ill apay.
>
> (62–70)

Invoking a shared experience of grief, the narrator takes up the stance of the confidant, to whose 'trustie eare' Alcyon should confess his woes. Yet, as the opening stanza has indicated, the poem's avowed purpose is not to assuage grief but to give the 'mournfull' reader '[f]it matter for his cares increase' (1–4). Overwhelmed by his melancholy, the narrator is ill suited to the role of the consoler. By his own confession, he is obsessed by 'a troublous thought' that 'empassion[s]' his soul and encourages daily meditations '[o]f this worlds vainnesse and lifes wretchednesse' (29–35). His claim that he is Alcyon's co-sufferer is not a strategic move, but must indeed be taken literally.

The narrator's sympathetic attitude, though it ignores Erasmus's advice to simulate compassion, is nonetheless in keeping with early modern beliefs (shaped by Galenic medical knowledge) about the negative effects of suppressed grief.[38] Furthermore, consolatory theory underlined that comfort had to be given at the 'right moment', a view that encouraged consolers to allow the outpouring of extreme grief to intervene only when the worst pain had calmed down.[39] Erasmus himself insisted that consolation had to be 'timely', cautioning that 'we must perform this duty skilfully, lest like unskilled doctors we aggravate rather than alleviate a wound that is still raw and fresh'.[40] In *Daphnaïda*, however, the exchange between the narrator and Alcyon does not unfold according to this familiar script.

Indeed, the narrator's attempts at comforting the bereaved shepherd all end in failure. First, in response to Alcyon's enigmatic but woeful tale about the death of a lioness, the narrator gives in to the contagion of grief and sheds tears of pity: 'Therewith he gan afresh to waile and weepe, / That I for pittie of his heavie plight / Could not abstaine mine eyes with teares to steepe' (169–71). Next, after trying to revivify Alcyon, who has swooned when spelling out the harsh truth of Daphne's death, he tries to 'comfort [him] all my best', and 'with milde counsaile str[ives] to mitigate / The stormie passion of his troubled brest' (190–92). But all he achieves is to rekindle Alcyon's grief, prompting the mournful shepherd to vent his sorrow in a long complaint. The violence of this lament is such that Alcyon loses consciousness again, which incites the narrator to redouble his efforts: 'I [...] / Amooved him out of his stonie swound / And gan to comfort him as I might' (544–46). This attempt, however, only intensifies Alcyon's passion, the extremity of which once more elicits the narrator's compassion: 'Did rend his haire, and beat his blubbred face, / As one disposed wilfullie to die, / That I sore griev'd to see his wretched case' (551–53). In these pivotal passages, phrases such as 'all my best', 'strove to mitigate' and 'as I might', because they are not backed up by any conventional consolatory speeches, suggest that the narrator's efforts are weakhearted at best. The two characters seem caught in a vicious circle of excessive grief and compassion. Though well intentioned, the narrator is clearly not a skilled consoler. His urge to reach out seems dictated by passion rather than reason, and his identification with Alcyon prevents him from exercising the self-control that is necessary for coolheaded and efficient consolation.

He makes a final (and fatal) mistake when he fails to understand that, with the abatement of Alcyon's passion, the time may be ripe at last for offering consolation:

> Tho when the pang was somewhat overpast,
> And the outragious passion nigh appeased,
> I him desirde, sith daie was overcast
> And darke night fast approched, to be pleased
> To turne aside unto my Cabinet,
> And staie with me, till he were better eased
> Of that strong stownd, which him so sore beset.
>
> (554–60)

Moved by compassionate kindness, the narrator opens up the doors of his 'cabinet', a gesture that is as generous as it is ill advised, as he fails to take advantage of what a competent consoler might have identified as the 'right moment'. The grieving shepherd turns down the proposal and wanders off to meet his tragic fate.

The poem's opening indicates that the narrator's incompetence is linked to his melancholy, which encourages his compassionate identification with Alcyon. Described as a death-bearing mother giving birth to a 'long borne Infant, fruit of heavinesse' (32), his disease has an emasculating effect that contributes to align his response to Alcyon's grief with the effeminate compassion decried by neo-Stoic thinkers. Even though the narrator is less self-centred than Alcyon, his blindness to the demands of reason and wisdom makes it difficult to redeem him. In the poem, the only character capable of exercising 'manly virtue' is the dying Daphne, who puts forward the Christian vision of death in the poem's only consolatory discourse. Alcyon reports the speech in his complaint, but neither he nor the narrator pays any heed to it.[41]

Spenser suggests that when responding to the suffering of others, it is dangerous to substitute compassion for consolation, emotion for discourse. In the 1590s, the need to issue a warning against the danger of emotional contagion would have been all the more pressing as England was affected by what was perceived as an 'epidemic' of melancholy.[42] At the same time, the rise of the English funeral elegy contributed to shaping an emotional landscape where sorrow seemed to outweigh consolation as an adequate response to bereavement. In his *Arte of English Poesie*, George Puttenham (1589) recommended poetic lamentation as a valid therapeutic response to the grief caused by the loss of a loved one.[43] Against this backdrop, the poem's dramatisation of the failure of consolation betrays a profound concern about the disintegration of the values of civic humanism. In the final line, the narrator professes ignorance about Alcyon's fate, even as evocations of 'Death' and 'hellish hags' leave little doubt about the endpoint of the shepherd's journey. The reader is left to contemplate the disquieting consequences of this disengagement, which signals the demise of the consolatory logos.

'Jesus Wept': Compassionate Mourning, Shared Vulnerability, and Emotional Communion

Far from disappearing, the therapeutic and logocentric approach to consolation was perpetuated in England, most notably by Robert Burton, whose *Anatomy of Melancholy* comprised a consolatory method predicated on humanist principles.[44] Even so, sorrow was increasingly valued in late sixteenth- and early seventeenth-century England. This was particularly the case of spiritual sorrow, which Paul had commended in the second epistle to the Corinthians: 'For godly sorrow worketh repentance to salvation not to be repented of: but the sorrow of the world worketh death' (2 Cor. 7:10).[45] Calvin had been careful to point out that repentance and salvation were 'inseparable graces', thus making it clear that Paul's praise of godly sorrow was not to be construed as a validation of justification by works: 'he dooth not enquire of the cause of salvation: but onely commending repentance of the fruite which it bringeth forth, sayth, that it is lyke unto a waye, by which we come to salvation'.[46] On the basis of Paul's and Calvin's authority, Protestant preachers and divines, from the turn of the century onwards, published sermons and treatises on the virtues of godly sorrow that renewed the tradition of spiritual mourning, a tradition rooted in medieval piety, but now brought into line with Calvinist orthodoxy.[47]

At the same time, Protestant writers produced unambiguous defences of human sorrow, thus complicating the Pauline dichotomy between the carnal and the spiritual. Richard Sibbes, for instance, remarked that though 'a little of spirituall sorrow is better than a great deal of naturall', yet '[n]aturall griefe is allowable, which if a man have not, he is in a reprobate sense: for the Apostle reckons this up as a great sinne; that in the latter dayes men should bee without affection'.[48] The norm of moderate sorrow for the dead had always been standard Christian doctrine, but early seventeenth-century English Protestants (partly, it seems, in response to the rise of neo-Stoicism) went to great lengths to prove that moderate grief was not only acceptable, but indeed expected in the practice of Christianity.[49] As a corollary, special emphasis was placed on the role of compassionate weeping when trying to help others cope with bereavement, while the humanist ethos of consolation was questioned, or at least put into perspective.

A biblical text used to defend compassionate mourning was John 11:35, where Jesus weeps over the death of Lazarus. In a treatise 'bewailing the want of weeping' published in 1631, John Lesley explained that through his tears, Christ had meant

> to excite in us mutuall compassion, teaching us by his owne example to weepe with them that weepe in a moderate manner; that neither ... [a]fter the manner of mad-men wee should be swallowed up with overmuch sorrow, nor forget Christian humanity and compassion towards the dead, and distressed.[50]

Almost two decades earlier, in a funeral sermon on John 11:35 entitled *Sinneless Sorrow for the Dead*, Thomas Jackson had described compassionate weeping as a natural response to the suffering of others: 'Nature hath so provided, that teares beget teares, and the sight of those that weepe in passion, provoketh others to weepe in compassion.'[51] Taking his audience through the biblical narrative, Jackson emphasised the emotional intensity of Jesus' encounter with Mary and Martha:

> *Lazarus* is dead, and Christ is absent, his sisters *weepe*; the Jewes come to comfort them, and they *weepe*; when they understand that Jesus is comming, *Martha* she runneth to meete him, & saluteth him with words of bitter complaint, *Lord, if thou hadst beene heere, my brother had not beene dead*: No sooner had hee with words of consolation, shut the sluces and flood-gates of her teares, but *Mary* shee commeth and breaketh out into the same words of dolefull complaint, *Lord, if thou hadst beene heere, my brother had not beene dead*: the Jewes, they *weepe*. and Christ he *wept*; the sluces are broken up again, as if all should be drowned with a *deluge of teares*.[52]

Here, Jackson was echoing the common belief that compassion was communicated through the senses, that it originated, in other words, in the 'mournful' sight of other persons' misfortunes or the sound of their 'complaints, sighes, teares, and lamentation'.[53] But he did more than just refrain from censuring this visceral response to the suffering of others: he also considerably amplified the original biblical narrative, which merely states that Jesus 'groaned and was troubled' when he saw Mary and the Jews weep, and that he wept himself when he went to see Lazarus' grave. Jackson's additions, particularly the 'sluces' that were 'broken up again' and the ensuing 'deluge of teares', validated an intense, if temporary, communion in grief as an adequate response to bereavement.

It is true that Jackson's reading of John 11:35 was uncommon in the exegetical tradition. In his commentary on John 11, Calvin argued that Jesus wept out of respect for the Jews' and the two sisters' grief: 'unless Christ had sorrowed togeather with them, he woulde have stood rather with a fierce countenance'; even so, Calvin was convinced that Christ 'had respect unto some higher matter: namely, unto the common miserie of man'.[54] The annotators of the Geneva Bible saw Jesus' groans as a sign of his general 'compassion' for 'our miseries' but did not extend this interpretation to his tears; their gloss on John 11:35 merely emphasised the 'measure' of Christ's 'affections'.[55] In a biblical commentary published in 1646, John Trapp explained that Jesus

> wept with those that weep. And the same tendernesse he retains still toward his afflicted. As Aaron, though he might not lament his two sonnes slain by Gods hand in the sanctuary, yet he had still the bowels of a father within him: he hath lost nothing by heaven.[56]

In his 1623 sermon on John 11:35, John Donne merged these different interpretive strands with many others culled from the exegetical tradition. He took up the idea of civility foregrounded by Calvin, arguing that Jesus had shed tears 'in a Condolency of a humane and naturall calamity fallen upon one family'. He also believed that Christ wanted to comfort the bereaved even though he knew that he would bring Lazarus back to life:

> He wept, *Et si suscitandus*; Though he knew that *Lazarus* were to be restored, and raised to life again: for as he meant to declare a great good will to him at last, so he would utter some by the way; he would do a great miracle for him, as he was a mighty God; but he would weep for him too, as he was a good natured man. . . . Jesus would not give this family, whom hee pretended to love, occasion of jealousie, of suspition, that he neglected them; and therefore though he came not presently to that great worke, which hee intended at last, yet hee left them not comfortlesse by the way; *Jesus wept.*[57]

Though none of these interpretations displayed the emotional intensity of Jackson's paraphrase, taken together, they all stressed the role of compassion in comforting the bereaved. First, they construed the expression of condolence as an act of civility and kindness while choosing to ignore its strategic usefulness. But more importantly, Jackson, Donne and Trapp emphasised the need to consider the humanity of the bereaved. In different ways, all three writers referred to essential precepts of Christian consolation. Jackson and Donne suggested that one should not sorrow because of the prospect of the resurrection – Donne by mentioning the 'greate worke' that Christ 'intended at last' and Jackson by reminding his readers of the 'words of consolation' uttered by Jesus in the biblical narrative.[58] Trapp, through his evocation of Aaron, pointed out the need to submit to God's will. None of them questioned the supreme validity of the eschatological perspective, but all three stressed that tears of unfeigned compassion were necessary to minister to the emotional needs of the bereaved, who, like Aaron, felt their loss in their 'bowels' and, therefore, ought not to be left 'comfortlesse by the way'.

Ultimately, these commentaries on John 11:35 suggested that consolatory speeches rehearsing arguments based on faith and reason were inadequate to provide a comprehensive response to the experience of bereavement. They delineated an alternative approach to comfort that acknowledged human vulnerability rather than promoting fortitude and self-sufficiency. They valued sincerely felt compassion as the bond that united the Christian community, a point Jackson made when he asked:

> Is there that *Simpathie* and fellow-feeling in the members of the natural body, that if *one member be honoured, all the rest rejoyce with it: if it be hurt, all doe suffer with it*; that if the elbowe receive a rappe even the fingers ends will tingle? and is there not much more such fellow-feeling in the misticall members of Christ?[59]

Calvin had commended compassion in very similar terms in his commentary on the Eucharist. In order to benefit from the sacrament, he wrote, the faithful had to remember

> that what care we have of our owne body, such also we ought to have of our brethren which are members of our body: as no part or our body is touched with any feeling of greefe, which is not spreade abroad into all the other partes, so we must not suffer our brother to bee greeved with any evill whereof wee should not also be touched with compassion.[60]

Through their participation in Christ's mystical body, the members of the Church militant and of the Church triumphant were linked by indissoluble bonds of solidarity, manifested by their ability to participate in each other's suffering.

Conclusion

I have argued that the rise of humanist consolation encouraged a rhetorical approach to compassion that was questioned in the late sixteenth and early seventeenth centuries, when the vogue of melancholy and the theological defence of human and spiritual sorrow fostered a more positive appreciation of heartfelt sympathy and condolence. As early seventeenth-century conceptions of grief and consolation make clear, the neo-Stoic view of compassion was rejected by Protestant preachers and divines, who articulated a vision of community grounded in a Christian ethics of shared vulnerability. Though criticised by John Milton, as Jan Frans van Dijkhuizen has shown, the 'common bond of frailty' signified by compassion nonetheless remained meaningful for these writers, not least because of their opposition to the humanist ideal of the autonomy of the sage.[61] Furthermore, though they foregrounded an 'anthropocentric' point of view, Donne and Jackson did not envisage the task of comforting the bereaved in secular terms. Whereas, according to George McClure, Petrarch and his successors had reaffirmed the 'legitimacy of worldly consolation' through a secularisation of sorrow, Donne and Jackson located compassion within an all-encompassing affective experience, in which the human was closely enmeshed with the spiritual.[62] As Donne pointed out, tears of bereavement, tears of compassion, and tears of repentance were interconnected.[63] Human tears, though less prestigious than spiritual tears, were nonetheless essential because they signalled an emotional predisposition that could be used as a stepping stone to the more trying but infinitely more rewarding experience of spiritual sorrow.

Notes

1 Annotation to Job 2:13 in *The Bible and Holy Scriptures Conteyned in the Olde and Newe Testament* (Geneva, 1562).
2 Angel Day, *The English Secretorie* (London, 1586), p. 222.
3 See Paula Barros, '"Piety to a dead man": les limites de la consolation dans la pratique épistolaire de Sir Kenelm Digby (Angleterre, 1633)', *Exercices de rhétorique*, 9 (2017), https://doi.org/10.4000/rhetorique.527.
4 On the importance of conversation for successful counsel, see Stephen Pender's Chapter 4, 'Friendship, Counsel and Compassion in Early Modern Medical Thought', in this volume.
5 George W. Pigman, *Grief and English Renaissance Elegy* (Cambridge University Press, 1985), here at p. 52. For a more recent study of elegy, see Andrea Brady, *English Funerary Elegy in the Seventeenth Century: Laws in Mourning* (Basingstoke: Palgrave Macmillan, 2006).
6 Fred B. Tromly, 'Grief, Authority and the Resistance to Consolation in Shakespeare' in M. Swiss and D. A. Kent (eds.), *Speaking Grief in English Literary Culture: Shakespeare to Milton* (Pittsburgh: Duquesne University Press, 2002), p. 40.
7 Vittorio Gabrieli, 'A New Digby Letter-Book: "In Praise of Venetia"', *The National Library of Wales Journal*, 9:4 (1956), 138; Barros, '"Piety to a dead man"'.

8 This is the first meaning of 'compassion' given by Thomas Wilson in his *Christian Dictionarie* (London, 1612), p. 60.
9 George McClure, *Sorrow and Consolation in Italian Humanism* (Princeton University Press, 1991), p. 58.
10 On the humanist tradition of consolation, see McClure, *Sorrow*. On the classical tradition, see Han Baltussen (ed.), *Greek and Roman Consolations: Eight Studies of a Tradition and Its Afterlife* (Swansea: The Classical Press of Wales, 2013).
11 See *Rhetorica ad Herennium*, vol. VI, trans. Harry Caplan (Cambridge, MA: Harvard University Press, 1954); Thomas Wilson, *The Arte of Rhetorique* (London, 1560), f. 51r–v.
12 *Progymnasmata: Greek Textbooks of Prose Composition and Rhetoric*, ed. and trans. George A. Kennedy (Atlanta: Society of Biblical Literature, 2003), p. 49.
13 Wilson, *Arte*, ff. 33v–34r.
14 See for instance: Day, *The English Secretorie*, pp. 211–17; John Evelyn's letter to his brother on the death of his son in *The Diary and Correspondence of John Evelyn*, ed. William Bray (London: Henry G. Bohn, 1863), vol. 3, pp. 79–81. The letters of Coluccio Salutati are an important counter-example (see McClure, *Sorrow*, pp. 73–92).
15 About the significance of Erasmus's contribution to the consolatory tradition in northern Europe, see McClure, *Sorrow*, n.32, p. 279.
16 Erasmus, *On the Writing of Letters*, trans. Charles Fantazzi, in *Collected Works of Erasmus*, vol. 25, ed. J. K. Sowards (University of Toronto Press, 1985), pp. 148–49 (my italics); between square brackets are words from the Latin text taken from *De Conscribendis Epistolis*, ed. Jean-Claude Margolin, in *Opera Omnia Desiderii Erasmi Roterdami*, vol. 1/2 (Amsterdam: North Holland Publishing Company, 1971), p. 433.
17 'Rhetoric, Grief, and the Imagination in Early Modern England', *Philosophy and Rhetoric*, 43:1 (2010), 54–85 (quotation on 62). I wish to thank Prof. Pender for graciously sending me his article.
18 By comparison, Scaliger does not emphasise the need to *simulate* compassion, while Vossius closely follows Erasmus. See Julius Caesar Scaliger, '*Poetices libri septem* (1561), III, 122. La consolation' and G. J. Vossius, 'Rhetorices contractae (1621), II, 24. De la consolation', *Exercices de rhétorique*, 9 (2017), https://doi.org/10.4000/rhetorique.515. About Quintilian, see Chapter 4, 'Friendship, Counsel and Compassion', this volume.
19 On the nuances of Erasmus's appreciation of Stoicism, see Barbara Pitkin, 'Erasmus, Calvin, and the Faces of Stoicism in Renaissance and Reformation Thought' in John Sellars (ed.), *The Routledge Handbook of the Stoic Tradition* (London: Routledge, 2016), pp. 145–59. On the humanist critique of Stoicism, see Richard Strier, *The Unrepentant Renaissance: From Petrarch to Shakespeare to Milton* (University of Chicago Press, 2001), pp. 29–36.
20 See Seneca, *A Discourse of Clemencie* in *The Workes of Lucius Annæus Seneca*, trans. Thomas Lodge (London, 1614), pp. 607–8; Justus Lipsius, *Two Bookes*

of Constancie, trans. John Stradling (London, 1595), pp. 28–30; Pierre Charron, *Of Wisdome*, trans. Samson Lennard (London, 1608?), pp. 98–99.
21 Seneca, *A Discourse*, p. 608.
22 Quintilian, *The Orator's Education*, III.8.1, vol. I, ed. and trans. Donald A. Russell (Cambridge, MA: Harvard University Press, 2002).
23 Quintilian, *The Orator's Education*, XII.1.1, vol. V.
24 Quentin Skinner, *Reason and Rhetoric in the Philosophy of Hobbes* (Cambridge University Press, 1996), pp. 66–110.
25 On friendship, see Paul Trolander, *Literary Sociability in Early Modern England: The Epistolary Record* (Newark: University of Delaware Press, 2014), pp. 77–84. See also Stephen Pender's Chapter 4 in this volume.
26 Erasmus, *On the Writing of Letters*, p. 148.
27 '*Consolatio est oratio reducens maerentis animum ad tranquillitatem. Nequit autem proficisci nisi ab amico.*' English translation mine (Scaliger, '*Poetices libri septem*').
28 *Daphnaïda*, in William A. Oram et al. (eds.), *The Yale Edition of the Shorter Poems of Edmund Spenser* (New Haven, CT: Yale University Press, 1989), pp. 487–515, here at p. 487. All quotations from *Daphnaïda* are taken from this edition.
29 William A. Oram, '*Daphnaïda*', in A. C. Hamilton et al. (eds.), *The Spenser Encyclopedia* (University of Toronto Press, 1990), p. 546.
30 Ellen Zetzel Lambert, 'elegy, pastoral', in *The Spenser Encyclopedia*, p. 318.
31 Oram, '*Daphnaïda*'; Paola Baseotto, '*Disdeining life, desiring leaue to die*'. *Spenser and the Psychology of Despair* (Stuttgart: Ibidem, 2008), pp. 109–35; A. Leigh Deneef, *Spenser and the Motives of Metaphor* (Durham, NC: Duke University Press, 1982), pp. 41–50. The quotation is taken from Baseotto, p. 117. See also Pigman, *Grief*, pp. 75–6.
32 Deneef, *Spenser*, p. 49.
33 Baseotto, '*Disdeining life*', pp. 114, 118–20.
34 Oram, '*Daphnaïda*', p. 548.
35 This preoccupation with the consolatory ethos posits Spenser, along with Robert Burton, as one of Erasmus's chief heirs in early modern England. See Angus Gowland, *The Worlds of Renaissance Melancholy. Robert Burton in Context* (Cambridge University Press, 2006), pp. 124–28.
36 On the 'visual vocabulary of melancholy', see Roy Strong, 'The Elizabethan Malady. Melancholy in Elizabethan and Jacobean Portraiture' in *The English Icon: Elizabethan and Jacobean Portraiture* (London: Routledge and Kegan Paul, 1969), pp. 352–54.
37 Oram, Introduction to *Daphnaïda*, p. 489.
38 See for instance Timothy Bright, *A Treatise of Melancholie* (London, 1586), p. 161.
39 For a classical example, see Plutarch, *Letter of Condolence to Apollonius*, I, in *Moralia*, vol. II, trans. Frank Cole Babbitt (Cambridge, MA: Harvard University Press, 1928); on the theory of the 'right moment', see Horst-Theodor Johann, *Trauer und Trost. Eine quellen- und strukturanalytische*

Untersuchung der philosophischen Trostschriften über den Tod (Munich: Wilhelm Fink, 1968), pp. 37–38.
40 Erasmus, *On the Writing of Letters*, p. 148.
41 *Daphnaïda* thus celebrates manly virtue as the keystone of consolation. The *Fairie Queene*, on the contrary, 'casts compassion as a specifically female virtue': see Jan Frans van Dijkhuizen, *Pain and Compassion in Early Modern Literature and Culture* (Cambridge: D.S. Brewer, 2012), p. 198.
42 See Angus Gowland, 'The Problem of Early Modern Melancholy', *Past & Present*, 191 (2006), 77–120.
43 Pender, 'Rhetoric, Grief, and the Imagination', pp. 71–72.
44 See in particular subsections 2.2.6.1 and 2.2.6.2 discussed by Stephen Pender in Chapter 4.
45 Bible quotations follow the 1611 King James Version.
46 John Calvin, *A Commentarie upon S. Paules Epistles to the Corinthians*, trans. Thomas Tymme (London, 1577), f. 261v.
47 See for instance Thomas Playfere, *The Meane in Mourning* (London, 1596); James Buck, 'Beati Lugentes' in *A Treatise of the Beatitudes, or Christs Happy Men* (London, 1637), pp. 49–87; Richard Sibbes, 'The Art of Mourning' in *The Saints Cordialls* (London, 1637), pp. 39–58. On the medieval tradition, see Piroska Nagy, *Le Don des larmes au Moyen Âge. Un instrument spirituel en quête d'institution, V*^{e}*–XIII*^{e} *siècle* (Paris: Albin Michel, 2000); on spiritual mourning in early modern Protestantism, see Alec Ryrie, *Being Protestant in Reformation Britain* (Oxford University Press, 2013), pp. 48–62, 187–95.
48 Richard Sibbes, *The Art of Mourning*, p. 53. The biblical reference is Rom. 1:31.
49 See Ralph Houlbrooke, *Death, Religion and the Family in England, 1480–1750* (Oxford: Clarendon Press, 1998), pp. 220–54.
50 John Lesly, *An Epithrene: or Voice of Weeping; Bewailing the Want of Weeping* (London, 1631), p. 32.
51 Thomas Jackson, *Sinnelesse Sorrow for the Dead* (London, 1614), p. 20.
52 Jackson, *Sinnelesse Sorrow*, p. 10.
53 Nicolas Coeffeteau, *A Table of Humane Passions*, trans. Edward Grimeston (London, 1621).
54 John Calvin, *A Harmonie upon the Three Evangelists ... Whereunto is Also Added a Commentary upon the Evangelist S. John*, trans. Eusebius Pagit (London, 1584), pp. 269–70 (separately paginated).
55 See annotations to John 11:33 and 11:35.
56 John Trapp, *A Brief Commentary or Exposition upon the Gospel according to St John* (London, 1646), p. 65.
57 John Donne, 'Jesus Wept' in *The Sermons of John Donne*, vol. 4, ed. George R. Potter and Evelyn M. Simpson (Berkley: University of California Press, 1959), pp. 325, 335.
58 'I am the resurrection, and the life: he that believeth in me, though he were dead, yet shall live' (John 11:25).
59 Jackson, *Sinnelesse Sorrow*, p. 20.

60 John Calvin, *The Institution of Christian Religion*, trans. Thomas Norton (London, 1587), ff. 472r–73v.
61 Van Dijkhuizen, *Pain and Compassion*, pp. 173–215.
62 McClure, *Sorrow*, p. 29.
63 Donne, 'Jesus Wept', p. 326.

CHAPTER 4

Friendship, Counsel and Compassion in Early Modern Medical Thought

Stephen Pender

In the less-studied second part of *Religio Medici* (1643), a meditation on charity and compassion, Sir Thomas Browne supplements his anatomy of self: he has no 'Idio-syncrasie, in dyet, humour, air, any thing', he claims, yet his 'generall and indifferent temper' is inclined to charity.[1] Browne's 'Philosophy of Charity' impugns not only 'self-love' but what he terms 'moral charity', a 'sinister and politick kind of charity' directed as much at oneself as at others, arising from overmuch passion, unevenly distributed to recipients deemed deserving of mercy (pp. 71–72, 74–77). True 'Eleemosynaries' are compassionate, for 'by compassion we make anothers misery our own, & so by relieving them, we relieve ourselves also' (pp. 71–72); they 'cast an eye upon the soule' (p. 79), on 'that insensible part that our armes cannot embrace' (p. 92). Similarly, at the sickbed, only 'barbarous' physicians add 'unto an afflicted parties misery, or endeavour to multiply in any man, a passion, whose single nature is already above his patience' (p. 77). These passages are typically civil, ecumenical. Browne then offers a brief treatment of friendship, in which he declares that charity has the power to 'translate a passion out of one breast into another, and to divide a sorrow almost out of it selfe' (p. 78). The constituents of friendship – trust and counsel, charity and compassion – animate his 'finely sensitive'[2] medical practice: he desires 'rather to cure [his patient's] infirmities than my owne necessities' (p. 85). In his otherwise insipid response to *Religio Medici*, Sir Kenhelm Digby endorses this self-portrait: Browne possesses a 'compassionative nature', 'æquanimity' and 'magnanimity', a 'strong and generous heart'.[3]

Amity and relief, charity and counsel, the 'compassionative' character of a physician: this chapter explores the intersections of medical care and friendship at the sometimes crowded early modern bedside. This semi-private, deliberative scene was a setting for equable advice, conversation, physical and spiritual inventory. 'Emotional trauma' was among a practitioner's concerns: cures for sorrow enjoin sufferers to seek 'holsome counsayles' in scripture and read 'bokes of morall doctrine', and abjure 'Romance'.[4] Most physicians were certain that remedying physical suffering meant 'care must be taken, to sweeten and abate the troubles of the mind with pleasing words . . . . *A good speech is a Physitian for a sick mind*'.[5] Evidence for attending to 'the accidents of the mind' is sparse in early modern *historiae* and *consilia, observationes* and records of cure, but advice for physicians, critiques and encomia of the profession, tracts by sufferers, letters and devotional and doctrinal treatises often retail relationships between counsel and advice, psychic remedy and recovery.[6] Yet few scholars have investigated the rich store of medical advice in these texts, in which the sick court reciprocal duty – self-care, conformity to counsel – and physicians are urged to embody and exhibit the constituents of friendship.[7] This chapter explores the confected relationship between counsel, compassion and friendship – in doctor-patient relationships, in conceptions of ideal physicians as virtuous friends – in medical thought between c. 1500 and 1780.

Histories of this 'moral state in action' suggest compassion appears in early modernity, in which the term has a skein of meanings.[8] As Paula Barros argued in the preceding chapter, compassion and consolation are distinct, the latter influenced by humanist conceptions of grief, by humanism's debts to neo-Stoicism and Calvinism.[9] Proper spiritual sorrow receives wide endorsement, while sympathisers and consolers were urged to immure themselves from superabundant feeling. In Barros' terms, there was a reflexive 'resistance to consolation'. In her examination of early modern conceptions of Christ's tears at John 11:35, for example, Barros reveals a dedication to moderate grief, 'an all-encompassing affective experience' opening men and women to licit spiritual sorrow.[10]

Spiritual, dispositional concord also characterises friendship. As we shall see, fellow-feeling, suffering together, is transacted via timely frankness, flexible and fortuitous counsel. As it establishes trust, compassion seeks egress: its means are developed and refined from ancient and early modern treatises on friendship, and its register is moral. Thus the 'medical thought' of my title is a broad church, and includes philosophers, theologians and populariseres concerned with regimen and therapy. I argue that conversations between physicians and patients were characterised by trust and compassion, and offer several instances in which friendship is advanced as a framework, a structure of feeling, for exploring vulnerability, suffering, physical and psychic distemper. In particular, troubles and accidents of mind were assuaged by embracing and exhibiting qualities associated with a well-meaning, virtuous friend. Compassion knows few sharper outlines, or deeper, variegated tones, than in clinical encounters at the early modern bedside.[11]

This chapter is also meant to correct two forms of misprision. Marjorie O'Rourke Boyle notes Erasmus' claim that 'the art of admonishing friends, like the art of medicine, requires not merely devotion but tact as well, in case we undermine friendship itself even while we clumsily try to cure our friend's faults'. The article is spurring and, as we shall see, Erasmus' analogy is ubiquitous. But, in a passing remark, Boyle asserts that 'therapeutic oratory' was 'a medical technique recommended by ancient philosophers, although not decisively practised by physicians'.[12] On the contrary, such counsel was essential to theories and practices to which most healers and sufferers subscribed.[13] Second, recent work on trust, compassion and the 'moral imagination' in contemporary medicine continues to treat the beside as an ethical domain.[14] A similar medical-moral philosophy, with its attendant habits of thought and styles of conversation, flourished in the sixteenth and seventeenth centuries,[15] belying claims that 'the physician as a professional' and medicine as a profession 'in the intellectual and moral senses of the term' did not exist before the eighteenth century.[16]

Trust and Compassion

In *De tradendis disciplinis* (1531), the Spanish humanist Juan Luis Vives advises novice physicians to inquire about their patients' illnesses, manners and habits 'in an urbane and affable fashion', listening patiently. Should a patient be disinclined to conversation, physicians should use 'few and especially sober words'. If a patient can 'endure talk', the physician 'will narrate some anecdote, wittily, pleasantly, suited to the mood of his patient, and to enliven those present without lapsing into buffoonery'.[17] Vives recommends the Hippocratic *On Decorum* (pp. 224; 344), a text which urges physicians to exhibit propriety in speech and conduct. They must be quick-witted and affable, 'ready to reply', and know 'what conduces to friendship'.[18] In bedside conversation, practitioners should embrace equity, *aequitatem animi*, and endeavour to express paternal feeling, *patrio ... affectu*, towards sufferers. 'Is there anything which inclines us more to good-will and good action', Vives concludes, 'than the fact that we are trusted?' (pp. 226; 346).

Trust, compassion and affability underwrite the French physician Laurent Joubert's views of patient-physician conversation. He urges physicians to be gentle, present and prudent (pp. 71–72, 73–75, 78). For 'the good opinion patients have of their physician gives them a certain confidence that helps them to recover better, and more steadily, under his treatment than under another's', and this success depends on trust, the imagination:

> This is why we commonly say in our schools: 'He in whom many trust heals more patients' . . . . one sees great changes in the patient just with the arrival of the devoted awaited physician. For desire and hope being satisfied, the soul awakens and withstands the disease; very often nature will make a courageous sally, impetuously driving out the sickening substance in what is called a crisis . . . . On the other hand, if the patient does not like the physician and does not see himself treated as he would wish, the physician will not get very far. In this instance, the patient, saddened and discouraged, will become weaker than he otherwise would. For his dashed spirits have no vigour because of the fear and mistrust that have seized his heart. (p. 76)

Desire, hope and trust enliven; sadness weakens. The patient 'will do for a physician he trusts what he will refuse to do for one he does not' (p. 77). Joubert's contemporary, the Salisbury physician John Securis, agrees: so that the patient may be 'delited', a doctor must possess a good disposition, a fine reputation, and persuade his patients gently, with 'dexteritie' and 'modest talke', while he comforts them with 'a lively & merry countenance'.[19] The French physician and poet Auger Ferrier 'enjoyed the reputation of being very successful, mostly because, according to one of his early biographers, Scévole de Sainte-Marthe, he was of a cheerful disposition in his demeanour, speech and actions'. Ferrier himself recommends that carers 'keep [a patient] in good spirits and prevent him from becoming depressed or angry and from shouting'.[20] Some sufferers, Joubert concludes, 'say that the presence of the physician consoles, rejoices, and gives them courage, making them feel the illness give way and their strength grow' (p. 78).

Patients agreed. John Burges, a minister with a Leiden medical degree, treated Lucy, Countess of Bedford, in 1613. John Chamberlain writes: 'Doctor Burgess, who is turned physician, was much about her in her sickness, and did her more good with his spiritual counsel than with natural physic', for which he was recommended to the king.[21] John Finch, writing to his sister Anne, discloses similar sentiments: in Padua, suffering the 'bitterest fitt of sicknesse', Finch consulted a number of prominent physicians, who pronounced him 'a dead man'. Their remedies – glisters, purges, cupping glasses – were impotent. Fortunately, his lifelong friend, Sir Thomas Baines, a physician, '3 whole nights satt up with me, and indeed was the onely Comfort I had in my disease by his care and vigilancy'.[22] Similarly, Princess Elisabeth of Bohemia is called to her ill brother's bedside, 'either to make him, through the fondness he has for me, abide by the rules set by the doctors, or to show him my fondness by diverting him'.[23] Of course, there is some scepticism about talking cures and fellow-feeling, epitomised in Petrarch's invectives.[24] An instance is John Hales – member of Parliament and translator of Plutarch's *Preceptes of Helth* (1543) – writing to Sir William Cecil in 1559: when they cannot secure 'the best physicians', the 'extremely sick' are 'contented with every one that seameth to have any skyle in phisik, and if no such can be founde, yet to they thynk themselves moche eased, when they may have to whom they may utter ther griefs, albeit he can do them no good'. Still, most practitioners, counsellors and divines agreed with Joubert: 'It is therefore no small thing to have indebted and endeared to oneself some learned and wise physician who will always have more concern for friendship than grandeur' (p. 74). 'Concern for friendship' is concern for care and counsel, virtue and vulnerability, and rarely is it tested more sharply than in the clinic.[25]

Physicians and Friends

If Erasmus' adage, *amicorum communia omnia*, opens up an 'ocean of philosophy', as he claims, and folds many into one via consensus, commonplaces and proverbial knowledge, the 'ocean' itself is formed in conversations between friends.[26] Friendship is philosophy's *praxis*, activating its therapeutic commitments, presenting living *exempla* of virtue: philosophy should cure, conversation should refresh, counsel should ballast. What has been called the public, explicitly political 'rhetoric of counsel'[27] was tested in the relatively private space of the bedside, in which physicians often occupied the roles, and adopted the armaments, of friends.

The ancient distinction between true, whole friendships and those founded on advantage, utility or pleasure is sustained throughout the Middle Ages and early modernity, though there was a flourishing of literature concerned with another category – Christian, spiritual friendship – in later periods. Central to these conceptions is Cicero's *De amicitia*: its ideas are reflected or refracted in most treatments of what he calls, next to wisdom, the greatest good (6.20.131; see also 5.17.127). As Cicero argues, friendship is devoted to practical, active virtue (6.21–22.131, 11.38.149–50). He criticises several philosophical sects for indulging in mere theory, for undervaluing practical wisdom, for faux austerity. His purview is wide, and includes his views about choosing 'frank, sociable, and sympathetic' friends (18.65.175), the boundaries of love and affection, the phenomenology of acquaintance (for the latter, see 9.32.144–45, 20.76.185), flattery and disengagement (25.91.199ff., 21.76.185ff.). Friendship's 'innumerable' benefits include adding 'radiance' to prosperity, dividing grief (6.22.133), the famous *alter idem* (21.80.189), the proper attainment of virtue, which cannot be done 'unattended' (22.83.191). A related question recurs in these treatises, first posed by Cicero: does friendship emerge as a response to human weakness or for some other 'more beautiful' cause (8.26.139)? For Cicero, 'friendship springs rather from nature than from need' (8.27.139). Although 'things human' are frail, fleeting (27.102.209), friendship marks virtue, not vulnerability (8.29–30.141; 13.48.159; 14.51.163).

Paradoxically, those who find friendship secure autonomy, and they do so largely through counsel. Its offices – frankness, compassion and patience, amongst others – are prophylaxes against hypocrisy, flattery and, as Plutarch has argued, underwritten by medical models and metaphors. Genuine friends play physicians, offer remedies, restore health: a friend is 'like a physician, who, if it be for the good of the patient', sometimes prescribes gentle remedies and baths, sometimes harsh cures, 'endeavouring through either course to bring his patient to one state – that which is for his good'. Similarly, a friend either 'gladdens' us or 'assails with stinging words and all the frankness of a guardian' (55a–c, 295–97). Plutarch insists that frankness, *parrhesia*, is therapy, but it must be applied in season: 'like any other medicine, if [frankness] is not applied at the proper time, does but cause useless suffering and disturbance' (66b, 351). Especially for the sick, timely, amicable counsel is a fine art, 'the greatest and most potent medicine in friendship' (68d–69c, 363–67; 74d, 393). Sufferers' circumstances leave little room for frankness, so they require 'gentle usage and help' (69c, 367). A 'troubled spirit' balks at 'plain reproof' (72c, 383), so 'ill-advised counsel' must be avoided; instead, a question, a story or an example may serve as opening for frankness (69e, 369; 70c, 371). Frances Meres summarises Plutarch in 1636: 'As a Physitian doth his endeavour to maintaine and encrease health: so also doth a friend . . . . A Medicine applyed to a wrong place, doth afflict without fruit: so doth admonition being used out of due time'.[28]

The medical metaphors point to the fact that, from antiquity on, the sickbed was a testing ground for friendship, consolation, counsel. As we have seen, Hippocrates recommends that doctors be affable and know the 'use of what conduces to friendship'. He advises frequent visits, close observation: arriving at the sickbed, physicians were to 'bear in mind your manner of sitting, reserve, arrangement of dress, decisive utterance ... bedside manners, care, replies to objections, calm self-control' (3.12.295). Celsus agreed. For patients suffering from fever, a physician does not 'seize the patient's forearm, as soon as he comes', but 'first sits down and with a cheerful countenance asks how the patient finds himself; and if the patient has any fear, he calms him with entertaining talk, and only after that moves his hand to touch the patient' (3.6.6). As Cicero claims, sternness is always tempered with urbanity, 'affability of speech and manner' (17.66.177)

Perhaps the *locus classicus* is Seneca, who argues frequently that 'peace of mind' is as efficacious as medicine. 'My friends, too', he writes, 'helped me greatly toward good health; I used to be comforted by their cheering words, by the hours they spent at my bedside, and by their conversation' (*Ep.*, 78.3–5). At another time, he was comforted by a physician, whom he came to call 'friend': this physician was attentive, applied his own remedies, 'sat at my bedside among my anxious friends', performed every difficult service, 'not indifferent to my moans'. Such a doctor 'has placed me under obligation, not as a physician, but as a friend. (*De benficiis*, 6.16.4–5). Not only attention and care, but discourse itself is curative, and an eloquent physician is a better physician: 'if it so happens that the physician who can cure him likewise discourses elegantly about treatment which is to be followed, the patient will take it in good part' (*Ep.*, 75.5–7; see also 76.2, 84.14ff.).

The alacrity is characteristic, moderated by a concern for overburdening one's friends, as well as the risk of offering callow, inopportune advice. Deliberation and counsel, virtue and vulnerability – figures on the ground of conversation and amity – animate early modern thought. Early modernity inherited 'a broad river of ideas and practices' of friendship, in all of which virtue, goodness and 'dispositional agreement' held sway as dominant forms of conceiving association. Still, most pictures of friendship, even those defined by 'mutual self-interest',[29] allow plenty of space for *parrhesia*. Frankness is central to scores of early modern treatises, here represented by a few examples. The sections on 'the right godly example of friendship' in Sir Thomas Elyot's *Boke Named the Governour* (1531), which draw on Aristotle, Cicero, Plutarch and Seneca, advance typical views: friendship is rare, reserved for those 'inclined to beneficence, liberalitie, and constance'. For Eylot, frankness sieves flatterers.[30] A number of years later, claiming that friendship can only arise between 'faithfull and trued hearted Christians', Lambert Daneau describes the 'mutuall knitting together of myndes, and a like inclination and conformitie of willes'.[31]

Counsel is singled out for attention.[32] Daneau claims that 'admonitions and frendly directions' must be given frankly, and point up 'faultes worthie of reprehension' (sig. C1r).

There were more mixed views. In his pithy, impacted style, Bacon summarises much of this material in 1612. Classical examples accrue in order to testify to friendship's threefold benefit: it provides outlets for 'swellings of the heart', clarifies ratiocination and enlarges capacity. With respect to the latter, friendship distributes and widens the performance of 'all offices of life'. Subtly revising Cicero, Bacon notes that, of course, there are things we cannot accomplish alone, but we may 'rest almost secure' with the aid of friends, 'bearing a part in all actions and occasions'.[33] So, too, with passion. Friends are *participes curarum*, partners in care, to whom we impart grief and joy, suspicion and counsel, easing oppression in what is a traditional hydraulic conception of passional egress. Bacon's model is medical: 'diseases of stoppings and suffocations are the most dangerous to the body; and it is not much otherwise in the mind': various remedies heal bodies, 'but no receipt openeth the heart, but a true friend; to whom you may impart ... whatsoever lieth upon the heart to oppress it, in a kind of civil shrift or confession'. The friendless are 'cannibals of their own hearts' (60–61).

Friendship's signal effect is intellectual, for 'it maketh day light in the understanding', resolving and clarifying confused, disorderly thought in conversation, a term Bacon uses liberally to mean not only discourse but all forms of familiar exchange. Faithful counsel from a friend illumines, freeing us from 'affections and customs' (63). We tend to flatter ourselves, Bacon continues, the remedy for which is 'the liberty of a friend'. Of two sorts of counsel, public and private, advice about active living 'setteth business straight' (64). Private counsel, the counsel of a friend, ensures or restores the health of the mind: 'calling of a man's self to strict account is a medicine, sometime, too piercing and corrosive. Reading books of morality is a little flat and dead. Observing our faults in others is sometimes improper for our case. But the best receipt ... is the admonition of a friend.' The theatre and the bedside shape Bacon's description: if we cannot engage as we would, we seek assistance, so if one does not have a friend on which to call, 'he may quit the stage'. Various capacities are buoyed by the 'manifold use' of true friendship, as long as it is subtle, timely, holistic. Poor counsel is bad physic (64).

Unalloyed, benign counsel's rarity presses into service diagnostic acumen: deep, abiding acquaintance is most, if not all. As Nicolas Coeffeteau argues, 'What content to have a friend whose discourse sweetens our cares?

whose counsells disperse our feares? whose conversation charmes our griefs?'[34] For Pierre de la Primaudaye, friends conform in manners, desires, passions, studies, speech, inclinations, and achieve together 'tranquillitie of minde'. Since the correct trial of friendship is adversity, La Primaudaye suggests conversation and counsel, goods and comfort are its defining elements.[35] Thomas Newton, Daneau's translator, calls to mind 'the varietie of mans inclynacion': 'some are enclined and have delight to refresh wearinesse, in reading & conferring with notable writers, other some have great pleasure in comfortable Music, and others in the conversation of faithfull and loving freends'.[36] A variety of suffering enjoins an eclecticism of response.

Eclecticism is medical counsel's virtue: the qualities associated with friendship conditioned the ways in which early moderns saw clinical encounters. 'There is nothing more miserable *then to want the Counsell of a friend, an admonisher in time of neede*'. Friends are signs of a virtuous disposition.[37] Joseph Hall expresses the orthodox view: 'Visitation of the sicke is a dutie required both by the law of humanitie, and of Religion; Bodily infirmitie is sad; and comfortlesse; and therefore needs the presence, and counsell of friends to relieve it.'[38] 'Presence' and counsel organise physician-patient interaction, in which trust and confidence were desirable – as Vives insisted – and appear at the intersection of friendship and cure. Still, overmuch amicability could rile: in one case, a surgeon contrived to 'satisfie the Relations and By-standers' of a patient, even allowing another patient's 'Relations and Friends' to choose surgical instruments.[39] The chymist Robert Crouch lamented the 'perswasion of Friends' at the bedside: 'when any one is taken sick, one Friend adviseth him to such a thing, another perswades another, and a third another; telling him if it does him no good it will do him no hurt'.[40]

Physicians as Friends

For the French courtier Eustache de Refuge, compassion arises when we are 'afraid to see in our selves the miseries and afflictions which we see befals [sic] others', but not just any 'other', only those who are not 'too farre distant from our consideration' nor those with whom we are very intimate, 'so neere as their afflictions and ours seeme to sympathise and make but one'.[41] Compassion depends on intimacy, proximity. Patients have the precise 'moral distance' for compassion, and physicians express compassion as they court trust and confidence.

What inspires confidence in a physician? What inspires 'good opinion'? Petrus Pomarius puts it simply: 'A Physition must be learned, judiciall, sober, of honest conversation, not full of words, but secret, chast, truely Religious, not covetous, or given to wine, and finally, me must be a Phylosopher, according to the saying, *Ubi desinit Philosophus, incipit Medicus*'.[42] Similarly, recommending that his colleagues read Browne's *Religio Medici*, Christopher Merret, physician and fellow of the Royal Society, describes a doctor's character thus: 'His Morality is sober, grave, continent, pitiful to, and careful of his Patients; Writing his Receipts solely for their good, and not for the gain of others their Subordinates. He is continent, wise, and prudent, mild and modest, hath veracity and clearness in all his Sayings .... He is decent in Habit, courteous in Behaviour, neither morose nor talkative, able and ready to satisfie any of his Patients in hearing the Sick man's Complaint, and rationally to satisfie him in his Scruples.' He smiles at 'flattering Language, commending all, enslaving his Judgement to the hearer's Opinion' in his frequent bedside visits.[43] Angry physicians cannot cure.[44] These guidelines specify behavioural and discursive decorum, instantiating relationships between rhetorical and moral categories and criteria. Unorthodox practitioners frequently endorsed medical compassion, too. J. B. van Helmont insists that physicians should adopt a 'humility of spirit', and express 'compassion towards the Sick', for medicine 'alone of Arts', is founded on compassion.[45] So that they possess this disposition, God endows physicians 'with a Heart communicative', as George Starkey writes in 1656.[46]

In one sense, Merret's and others' ideal physician has taken to heart a central tenet of rhetorical inquiry: feel the passion, the mood, one wishes to convey. The classical expression of this notion is Cicero's *De oratore*, in which his interlocutors suggest 'kindling feelings' in an audience by means of 'rhetorical fireworks' (2.48.199, 2.51.205) is accomplished by a threefold method: the use of a particular style, intense in diction, sentiment, delivery; forms of application, in which listeners are spurred to apply a speech to their own situations; and the gradual intensification of an oration from logical to 'spirited and emotional' (2.44.188–92; 2.52.213–14; 2.52.211). And it entails being moved oneself: 'for the very quality of the diction, employed to stir the feelings of others, stirs the speaker himself even more deeply than any of his hearers' (2.45.191–92; see 189–90). The same notion appears as paradox in Quintilian: we end up feeling the passion we 'feign' (6.2.26–27; 11.3.61–62). This is summed up nicely, and with scepticism, by Montaigne, who mentions that Quintilian was 'still weeping' (637) long after his own speeches: 'even though they go through borrowed emotions ... they are often entirely carried away and inwardly affected with a genuine melancholy' (636). The orthodox Ciceronian Thomas Wilson, Montaigne's contemporary, argues much the same, without the magistrate's scorn. We cannot move an audience, Wilson writes, 'except we bring the same affections in our own heart ... no man's nature is so apt straight to be heated except the orator himself be on fire and bring his heat with him'.[47] That speakers become, or should be, 'inwardly affected' is a durable notion. While there is some risk here – as Digby writes, one should not intermingle oneself 'in the others *Woe*'[48] – in these early modern texts, we are not far from Hippocratic strictures: physicians should be serious, eloquent, graceful, solicitous, know the 'use' of friendship, always poised to converse. If the bedside is a deliberative scene, then deliberation is in part dependent on what might be called 'fellow-feeling'.

If 'true humanity' is 'fellow feeling', asks Richard Brathwaite in 1635, how might we engage another's misery? With care, with delicacy: 'much discretion is required, that the sufferer may become more eased, by having his griefes in some proportion shared: for it is not so hard to give comfortable counsell to the sorrowfull, as to find a fit season to give it.' A 'discreet conceit' is required for such work.[49] Counsel's yield depends on its season, on the affability of the advisor, on conceit. Brathwaite's advice is orthodox. 'As for the Griefs of others', Henry Jenkes writes, 'their ailes and maladies make them your own, be always sensible of their Calamities, pity them and relieve them to the uttermost of your power, share with them in their Sufferings, alleviate their Sorrows as much as you can, and leave the rest to the God of all Consolations.' Sufferers are to be treated with gentleness, their afflictions met with commiseration, their distempers comforted and relieved.[50] Reciprocity is camaraderie: 'wee shall finde a friend to cheere *us*, when the sharpest gusts of seeming discontent assaile us'.[51] As the physician Theodore Turquet de Mayerne has it, 'I participate in the evils which happen to my Friends, and suffer by consent, or sympathy with them, chiefly if they be such to whose advice I have devoted myself.'[52] Earlier, Lodowick Bryskett comments that 'it is not sufficient for recovery of the sicke patient, that the Physition be well disposed to cure him ... but that other things must likewise concurre for the recovery of his health, as the care and sollicitude of such as watch and tend him, with other exteriour things'.[53] The care of family and friends tends to cure: patients are to be offered 'good Counsel for their Souls' and 'chearful converse'.[54]

I offer a few final examples of the ways in which 'cheerful', compassionate conversation between patients and physicians enlivens, for as Timothy Nourse argues, when 'a Man hath a good Opinion of his Physician, and of what he gives him, his Heart seems to dilate it self with a kind of Joy', which helps the humours circulate, and revives the spirits, 'Vehicles of Life'.[55] A physician's greatest sagacity and industry should be devoted to assuaging a sufferer's spirits via 'fair Words', agreeable medicines, 'pretending' that the remedies to hand are the most effective.[56] As an English physician insists, when 'a Sick Person comes to stand in need of the *Physitians* help, those surely of all others are most likely to do him good, who may be presumed to sympathize with him the most feelingly in his Afflictions'.[57]

In a work he revised and expanded until his death, as if to question its own remedial efficacy, Robert Burton claims the 'chiefest cure' for melancholy is rectifying the passions, and his therapy takes several forms, resolved in a surprising crescendo, should patients be unresponsive to 'art and insinuation' (2.2.6.2: 474; all references to 6.1 and 6.2). These subsections *The Anatomy of Melancholy* (1621–1651) are complex, but they are conditioned by, as much as they question, a distinctly humanist faith in forms of mollification: individual rectitude, inuring oneself against affective turbulence; redescription, in which 'evil is persuaded for good' (469); diversion, which might occlude or assuage immoderate, unhealthy feeling; mastering one passion with another; and counsel. As Burton urges, 'persuade him, advise him', for 'the body cannot be cured till the mind be satisfied' (475; cf. 467). 'Many are instantly cured, when their minds are satisfied' (473). Satisfaction takes several forms. While 'from the Patient himself … the first and chiefest remedy must be had', by, for example, 'moderat[ing] ourselves in those six non-natural things' (468–69; cf. 470), responses other than rectitude are available to the intermittently wise. If we cannot 'seek our own good, or moderate ourselves', the 'best way for ease is to impart our misery' to 'some discreet, trusty, loving friend' (471). A 'simple narration' can ease us, he continues, 'so divers have been relieved, by exonerating themselves to a faithful friend' (471–72). But 'how shall it be effected, by whom, what art, what means?' (468).

His answer is curious, and little noticed: 'by any art or means possible' friends are to discover distemper's causes. In a passage that echoes Seneca, Burton argues that it behoves a friend 'by counsel, comfort, or persuasion, by fair or foul means, to alienate his mind, by some artificial invention, or some contrary persuasion, to remove all objects, causes, companies, occasions, as may anyways molest him, to humour him, please him, divert him ... to give him security and satisfaction' (473; cf. 475). Quoting Galen, Burton contends that many 'have been cured by good counsel and persuasion alone. ... a gentle speech is the true cure of a wounded soul' (475; the same point is made at 468). What follows is a long list of citations substantiating the therapeutic value of discourse, including sending healing words by post. When such remedies fail, when 'satisfaction may not be had', this friend is to 'threaten and chide ... terrify sometimes', and the patient is to be 'lashed and whipped' (476–77). Lashed and whipped? The 'powerful ... charm of a discreet and dear friend' finds its end in witty devices, in deception, in modulated roughness.

Or in laughter.[58] In a text that treats public attitudes towards medicine, novice physicians' dress and address, and his own views from the sickbed, the French physician Samuel Sorbière offers similar advice: physicians 'should bring feelings into play, even the violent ones as well those that are milder'.[59] They should be neither chatterers nor 'the taciturn one who has no elegance of discourse whatever' (289), and 'it might be that a smiling face, a fine appearance, a pleasing voice, and neatness in a physician would contribute to the well being of a patient, by drawing the vital spirits to the surface through the joy he inspires' (279). Imagining himself in a sickbed, Sorbière wishes his doctor to have 'sweet breath', to speak to him 'amiably', to tell him 'diverting stories', even to 'unfold with good grace some pleasant story to make me laugh' (279–80).

Such advice finds fictional expression in Bernard de Mandeville's 1711 book-length *historia*, in the form of a dialogue between a patient and physician, Misomedon and Philipirio. Frustrated with his care, ill for most of his life, the patient initially claims that he would have tripled his first physician's fees 'if he would only have kept his Temper, and invented new Reasons, to sooth my fancy, tho' he had done nothing to my disease'.[60] But he is continually riled, buoyed only at the prospect of a good conversation: 'You can't imagine', Misomedon says, 'how a pertinent lively discourse, or anything that is sprightly revives my Spirits' (41). His physician, whose name means 'lover of experience', prescribes erudition. As he explains at the end of the text, distempers in which 'Fancy has so great a share' are treated by mooring medical practice to his patients' inclinations, matching his discourse with theirs: 'I am not only careful of the *Idiosyncrasis*, but likewise strive to fall in with the very Humours and Inclinations of my Patients ... as soon as I heard you [Misomedon] was [sic] a Man of Learning and lov'ed Quotations from Classick Authors, I answer'ed you in your own Dialect, and often strain'd my self to imitate, what in you is natural' (277). In the course of a life punctuated with inadequate care, conversation revives the spirits, pressing into service the constituents of friendship – shared aims, concerns, 'natures' – for the purposes of cure. Even for Mandeville, though, compassion has limits: 'A Surgeon may be as compassionate as he pleases, so it does not make him omit or forbear to perform what he ought to do.'[61]

The Scottish physician John Gregory insists on 'that sensibility of heart which makes us feel for the distresses of our fellow-creatures, and which of consequence incites us in the most powerful manner to relieve them'. We should have sympathy for patients, he continues in *Lectures on the Duties and Qualifications of a Physician* (1772), a feeling that 'naturally engages the affection and confidence of a patient, which in many cases is of the utmost consequence to his recovery'.[62] Affection and confidence point Gregory towards friendship, as he muses on doctors' character, manners and dress: in a 'depression of spirits', visits may distress, so physicians present 'easy, cheeful, soothing behaviour'. A patient will then 'forget the physician in the friend' (53–54). The physician 'lost' in the friend: Gregory's conception of physician-patient interaction conjures Hippocrates' sense that physicians should know what conduces to amity. In cases where medical remedies are impotent, a physician's 'presence and assistance as a friend may be agreeable and useful, both to the patient and his nearest relations' (35–36). Still, they must be frank, though not from pique or obduracy (32–35). A physician's conversation must be 'cheerful and entertaining' (101), for belief in the efficacy of a remedy depends more on the imagination than rational conviction, and the former is rarely 'warmed' by the fustian (62). Should the physician fail to charm, a clergyman's 'conversation' could compose a sufferer's mind (36). Gregory recognises an expansive province for bedside rhetorical work: mollifying the imagination frequently comforts, often heals, for sufferers 'readily take the alarm, when they discover any diffidence in their physician' (18–19).[63]

Friendship and its offices, especially timely, frank counsel, then, are potent. In physicians' and *adstantes*' clinical advice, counsel aspires to realise the effects it claims to develop: in the very ways in which it is conceptualised, physicians and philosophers demonstrate, even as some question, its salutary qualities. From antiquity on, ideal physicians and true friends shared virtue, care, timeliness, moderate candour; portraits of friends borrowed medical metaphors, while physicians mobilised the qualities of friendship to aid, and to describe, their care. As Browne claims, physicians are 'the most successful' counsellors. The entanglement of comfort and frank talk, consolation and counsel, is brought into relief at the early modern bedside by the physician-as-friend. In these clinical conversations, and in its treatment of passions, the imagination, psychic distemper, for physicians rhetoric becomes a 'life science': the 'moral no less than the rational faculties' are susceptible to rhetorical interventions,[64] and this is perhaps another way that 'medicine is politics on a small scale'.[65]

Notes

1 *The Works of Sir Thomas Browne*, ed. Geoffrey Keynes, 4 vols. (London: Faber and Faber, 1964), vol. I, pp. 69–72, 80–81, 91.
2 Reid Barbour, *Sir Thomas Browne: A Life* (Oxford University Press, 2013), p. 267; *passim*, esp. pp. 69ff., 262–72.
3 *Observations upon Religio Medici* (London, 1643), pp. 12, 29, 75.
4 Sir Thomas Elyot, *The Castel of Helth* (1541 [c. 1533]), sig. 64v.; Richard Baxter, *A Treatise of Self-Denial* (London, 1675), p. 157. Reading could sicken, too; see Roy Porter, 'Reading: A Health Warning' in Robin Myers and Michael Harris (eds.), *Medicine, Mortality, and the Book Trade* (Folkstone: St Paul's Bibliographies, 1998), pp. 131–52.
5 Levinus Lemnius, *The Secret Miracles of Nature*, no trans. (London, 1658), p. 65. There are dozens of similar instances; see, for example, William Vaughan, *Approved Directions for Health*..., 4th ed. (London, 1612), p. 90; Johannes Jonstonus, *The Idea of Practical Physick*, trans. Nicholas Culpeper (London, 1657), 8.4.21; and Thomas Beverly, *The Great Soul of Man* (London, 1675), p. 214.
6 See Jole Agrimi and Chiara Crisciani, *Les 'Consilia' Médicaux*, trans. Caroline Viola (Turnhout: Brepols, 1994).
7 Harold J. Cook, 'Good Advice and Little Medicine: The Professional Authority of Early Modern English Physicians', *Journal of British Studies*, 33 (1994), 1–31; 24, 13; and see Nancy Siraisi, 'Oratory and Rhetoric in Renaissance Medicine', *Journal of the History of Ideas*, 65 (2004), 191–211.
8 Natan Sznaider sees the emergence of compassion in seventeenth-century latitudinarian thought, and calls sympathy its 'weak form' while noting that the imagination is 'key to compassion'. See 'The Sociology of Compassion: A Study in the Sociology of Morals', *Cultural Values*, 2 (1998), 117–39; 124–26.
9 Chapter 3, this volume.
10 Chapter 3, this volume.
11 The term 'clinic' is not out of place in the period; as Daniel Le Clerc writes, it is 'from a Greek word signifying a ... Bed, to shew that he was the first that *visited the sick in their beds*' (*The History of Physick*, trans. Dr. Blake and Dr. Baden [London, 1699], p. 46).
12 'Erasmus' Prescription for Henry VIII: Logotherapy', *Renaissance Quarterly*, 31 (1978), 161–72; 163, 167, 164.
13 For the ways in which patients and practitioners spoke a 'common language', see Michael Stolberg, *Experiencing Illness and the Sick Body in Early Modern*

Friendship, Counsel & Compassion in Medical Thought 97

Europe, trans. Leonhard Unglaub and Logan Kennedy (Basingstoke: Palgrave Macmillan, 2011 [2003]), p. 79, *passim*.
14 See, for example, the special issue about authority and trust, *Journal of Medicine and Philosophy*, 24 (1999) and Kjetil Rommetveit et al., 'The Role of Moral Imagination in Patients' Decision-Making', *Journal of Medicine and Philosophy*, 38 (2013), 160–72.
15 Nancy Struever, 'Petrarch's *Invective Contra Medicum*: An Early Confrontation of Rhetoric and Medicine', *Modern Language Notes*, 108 (1993), 659–79; 677.
16 Laurence B. McCullough, *John Gregory and the Invention of Professional Medical Ethics and the Profession of Medicine* (Dordrecht: Kluwer, 1998), p. 4, *passim*.
17 Juan Luis Vives, *Vives on Education: A Translation of the* De tradendis disciplinis *of Juan Luis Vives*, trans. Foster Watson (Cambridge University Press, 1913), p. 226; Johannes Lodovic Vivis, *De disciplinis. Hi de corruptis artibus ... illi de tradendis disciplinis* (London, 1612), pp. 345–46.
18 *Hippocrates*, trans. W. H. S. Jones, 8 vols. (Cambridge, MA: Harvard University Press, 1923), vol. II, 3.3.281–83, 12.295, 16.298–99, 12.287. Indeed, the physician should be 'a gentleman in character' and dress, act, smell and speak in ways 'pleasing to patients' (*The Physician*, vol. II, 3.311).
19 *A Detection and Querimonie of the Daily Enormities and Abuses Com[m]ited in Physick* (London, 1566), sigs. Aiiiv–Avr.
20 Quoted in Ingrid de Smet, 'Of Doctors, Dreamers, and Soothsayers: The Interlinking Worlds of Julius Caesar Scaliger and Auger Ferrier', *Bibliothèque d'Humanisme et Renaissance*, 70:2 (2008), 351–75; 354–55.
21 *The Chamberlain Letters: A Selection ...*, ed. Elizabeth McClure Thomson (London: John Murray, 1965), p. 129.
22 Finch to Conway, 30 November / 10 December 1653, in Marjorie Hope Nicolson (ed.) *Conway Letters: The Correspondence of Anne, Viscountess Conway, Henry Moore, and their Friends, 1642–1684* (London: Oxford University Press, 1930), p. 90.
23 *The Correspondence between Princess Elisabeth of Bohemia and René Descartes*, ed. and trans. Lisa Shapiro (University of Chicago Press, 2007), p. 101.
24 See Nancy S. Struever, 'Petrarch's *Invective contra medicum*: An Early Confrontation of Rhetoric and Medicine', *Modern Language Notes*, 108 (1999), 659–79.
25 It is not my purpose here to rehearse the history of friendship, already well documented; the most comprehensive survey, including a rich bibliography, is Barbara Caine (ed.), *Friendship: A History* (London: Equinox, 2009), but see also Albrecht Classen and Marily Sandidge (eds.), *Friendship in the Middle Ages and Early Modern Age* (Berlin: de Gruyter, 2010); Daniel T. Lochman et al. (eds.), *Discourses and Representations of Friendship in Early Modern Europe, 1500–1700* (Farnham: Ashgate, 2011).
26 Kathy Eden, '"Between Friends All Is Common": The Erasmian Adage and Tradition', *Journal of the History of Ideas*, 59 (1998), 405–19.

27 John Guy, 'The Rhetoric of Counsel in Early Modern England' in Dale Hoak (ed.), *Tudor Political Culture* (Cambridge University Press, 1995), pp. 292–310.
28 *Witts Academy: a Treasurie of Goulden Sentences, Similies, and Examples* (London, 1636), pp. 276–77.
29 Carolyn James and Bill Kent, 'Renaissance Friendships: Traditional Truths, New and Dissenting Voices' in Barbara Caine (ed.), *Friendship: A History* (London and Oakville: Equinox, 2009), pp. 122, 150–51, 132. Keith Thomas, *The Ends of Life: Roads to Fulfilment in Early Modern England* (Oxford University Press, 2009), pp. 189, 191.
30 Thomas Elyot, *Boke Named the Governour* (1531), ed. Henry H. S. Croft, 2 vols. (New York: Burt Franklin, 1967 [1883]), 2.119–185, quotation at 2.133, and see pp. 127, 162–66, 220.
31 *True and Christian Friendshippe*, trans. Thomas Newton (London, 1586), sig. A3r–v.
32 See, for example, Richard Brathwaite, *The English Gentleman* (London, 1630), pp. 238–89, 244, 275, pp. 293–97.
33 'Of Friendship', in *The Essays*, ed. Brian Vickers (Oxford University Press, 1999), pp. 64–65. All in-text references refer to pages from this work.
34 *A Table of Humane Passions*, trans. Edward Grimeston (London, 1621), p. 81.
35 *The French Academie*, no trans. (London, 1618), pp. 57, 58–59.
36 Dedicatory letter, prefaced to Pedro Mexia, *A Pleasaunt Dialogue, Concerning Phisicke and Phisitions*, trans. Thomas Newton (London, 1580), sig. Aiiiv.
37 Henry Peacham, *The Compleat Gentleman* (London, 1625), p. 197.
38 Joseph Hall, *Contemplations upon the Principall Passages of the Holy Storie* (London, 1628), book twenty, p. 22.
39 Richard Wiseman, *Severall Chirugicall Treatises* (London, 1676), pp. 28, 36, 397.
40 Robert Crouch, with additions by Christopher Pack, *Praxis Catholica: or, the Countrymans Universal Remedy* (London, 1680), sigs. b1r–b2v.
41 *A Treatise of the Court, or Instructions for Courtiers*, trans. John Reynolds (London, 1622 [1616]), pp. 83–84.
42 *Enchirdion medicum*, no trans. (London, 1612), p. 1.
43 *The Character of a Compleat Physician, or Naturalist* (London, 1680), pp. 6–7; see also his *The Accomplisht Physician* ... (London, 1670).
44 Leonard de Marande, *The Judgment of Humane Passions*, trans. John Reynolds (London, 1629), p. 185.
45 *Van Helmont's Works*, trans. J[ohn] C[handler] (London, 1664), p. 4, sig. Nnnnn3r; see also pp. 3, 7ff., 1074ff., 1080–82. Van Helmont claims his own medical studies arose from compassion for ignorant practitioners, their suffering patients (p. 1016).
46 *Nature's Explication or Helmont's Vindication* (London, 1656), p. 7.
47 Wilson, *Arte of Rhetorique (1560)*, ed. Peter E. Medine (Philadelphia: Penn State University Press, 1993), p. 163.
48 *Observations*, pp. 96–97.

49 *Essaies upon the Five Senses*, 2nd ed. (London, 1635), pp. 125–26.
50 *The Christian Tutor* (London, 1683), pp. 52–53.
51 Brathwaite, *Essaies*, 135.
52 *Medicinal Counsels or Advices*, trans. Thomas Sherley (London, 1677), p. 94.
53 *A Discourse of Civill Life: Containing the Ethike Part of Moral Philosophy* (London, 1606), pp. 134–35.
54 Richard Baxter, *Compassionate Counsel to All Young-Men* (London, 1681), pp. 162–63.
55 *A Discourse upon the Nature and Faculties of Man* (London, 1686), pp. 99–100.
56 Giorgio Baglivi, *The Practice of Physick*, no trans., 2nd ed. (London, 1723), pp. 171, 162.
57 Richard Griffith, *A la Mode Phlebotomy No Good Fashion* ... (London, 1681), p. 184.
58 On the therapeutic effects of laughter, see Stephen Pender, 'The Moral Physiology of Laughter' in David Beck (ed.), *Knowing Nature in Early Modern Europe* (London: Pickering and Chatto / Routledge, 2015), pp. 29–48.
59 Frank L. Pleadwell, 'Samuel Sorbière and his *Advice to a Young Physician* [1672]', Bulletin of the History of Medicine, 24 (1950), 255–87; 277.
60 *A Treatise of the Hypochondriack and Hysterick Passions* (London, 1711), p. 19.
61 *The Fable of the Bees: or, Private Vices, Publick Benefits* [1732], ed. F. B. Kaye, 2 vols. (Indianapolis: Liberty Fund, 1988 [1924]), 1.260.
62 *Lectures on the Duties and Qualifications of a Physician*, new ed. (London, 1772), pp. 19–20, 69–70.
63 As Guenter B. Risse notes, for Gregory 'the patient and physician need to become friends' (*Hospital Life in Enlightenment Scotland: Care and Teaching at the Royal Infirmary of Edinburgh* [Cambridge University Press, 1986], p. 185).
64 L. J. Rather, *Mind and Body in Eighteenth-Century Medicine: A Study Based on Jerome Gaub's* De regimine mentis (Berkeley: University of California Press, 1965), pp. 40, 53, 70, 71.
65 Pedro Laín Entralgo, *The Therapy of the Word in Classical Antiquity* (New Haven: Yale University Press, 1970), p. 177.

PART III
Exhorting

CHAPTER 5

'Compassion and Mercie Draw Teares from the Godlyfull Often'
The Rhetoric of Sympathy in the Early Modern Sermon

Richard Meek

John Prime's *An Exposition, and Observations upon Saint Paul to the Galathians* (1587) contains a powerful description of Christ's Passion and its effect upon the surrounding environment:

> When our Saviour suffered, we read that the sun was darkened, the earth moved, the powers of heaven and earth were shaken, the rock did rive asunder, the vaile was rent, and the graves were open, & al things felt a sympathy & a compassion at the passion of Christ.[1]

In Prime's account, both heaven and earth are shaken by Christ's suffering: the earth is literally 'moved' by the experience. This idea derives from Matthew 27, which describes how 'the vaile of the Temple was rent in twayne, from the top to the bottome, and the earth did quake, and the stones were cloven. And the graves did open them selves.'[2] Yet Prime's creative reworking of these biblical verses ascribes a certain degree of feeling to the landscape, describing how 'al things felt a sympathy & a compassion'. The term *sympathy* is especially suggestive here; in the sixteenth century the word could refer not only to occult affinities between objects in the cosmos but also to emotional affinities between individuals.[3] In this passage, the term hovers between these two overlapping senses, suggesting both unseen forces at work and a compassionate response to Christ's death. Prime's *An Exposition* is based upon sermons that he had been preaching at Abingdon in Oxfordshire 'every other weeke', which makes his emphasis upon sympathetic transference even more suggestive.[4] Of course, it is difficult to say how closely the text reproduces the sermon on which it is based; nevertheless, this description of Christ's Passion is immediately followed by an exhortation to Prime's audience: 'and shal not man have a feeling of these sufferings, for whom onely hee suffered them? Shal he not, should hee not mourne for these sins, that caused the son of God to take upon him the shape of man, and the shame of the crosse?' (pp. 308–9). These rhetorical questions encourage Prime's listeners to emulate the sympathetic landscape he has just described, and to 'have a feeling' of Christ's Passion. This is an emotional and rhetorical performance, designed to stir up sympathy and compassion in Prime's listeners – and indeed readers.

This example reveals how early modern religious writings played an important part in the process whereby the meaning of *sympathy* narrowed from a generalised sense of correspondence to a transferral of woe. In what follows I explore the ways in which sermons in the late sixteenth century are fascinated with ideas of sympathy and compassion, and often draw upon natural philosophical ideas to make analogies between the human body and the body of the church. These sermons also contain an intriguing performative and self-reflexive element whereby they invoke the concept of physiological agreement as a way of uniting a socially diverse audience into a single compassionate body. At the same time, however, I want to question the assumption that early modern individuals were passive creatures who were easily affected by either sympathetic forces or powerful orators.[5] Rather, the materials I explore suggest a considerable degree of emotional agency and imagination, increasingly so as we move into the 1590s. My approach corresponds with that of Arnold Hunt, who has argued that 'sermons were addressed to the emotions as well as to the intellect, and were designed not merely to impart doctrinal information but to elicit an affective response from the audience, with the help of voice, gesture and all the other rhetorical skills at the preacher's command'.[6] Hunt's emphasis on affect and rhetoric is certainly welcome; but I want to make a more specific observation about the particular words and concepts that preachers used. I argue that late-Elizabethan sermons both reflect and help to facilitate a shift in the understanding of sympathy from the physical and physiological to the emotional and imaginative – and that this process existed alongside similar developments taking place in dramatic culture.

By tracing the development of the term *sympathy*, the chapter highlights the important cultural work performed by sermons in making a more complex conception of compassion – as an active and imaginative engagement with the other – available to early modern subjects. This investigation also seeks to raise wider questions about the individual and communal aspects of worship, as well as the individual and communal aspects of compassion. As we shall see, there are some revealing tensions apparent in several of these texts, in the sense that sympathy is presented as a natural and automatic process, but simultaneously one that needs to be activated and encouraged. This chimes with Kristine Steenbergh's interest in compassion as an 'emotion-as-practice', which has to be 'cultivated and habitually trained'.[7] While Steenbergh is interested in changes in compassionate and charitable practices during the Reformation, the present chapter focuses on shifting conceptions of sympathy and selfhood during the period. It argues that religious writings about compassion reflect certain cultural anxieties about early modern English society, and about what happens when a social group recognises itself as a gathering of individual selves rather than a unified or homogenous body.[8]

Sermons and the Social Body

We might begin by considering the history of the terms *sympathy* and *compassion*, both of which appear in the passage from Prime quoted above. *Compassion* was current in English from the fourteenth century onwards, and appears 73 times in the 1560 Geneva Bible, the primary bible of English Protestantism.[9] *Sympathy*, conversely, was a more recent addition to the language and first appears in printed English texts in the late 1560s. Deriving from the Greek *sympathia* and the French *sympathie*, the word was originally a much more general term, and not necessarily concerned with affect. According to the *OED*, the primary meaning in the period was 'A (real or supposed) affinity between certain things, by virtue of which they are similarly or correspondingly affected by the same influence' (*OED*, 1; first cited usage 1579). It could also refer to 'A relation between two bodily organs or parts (or between two persons) such that disorder, or any condition, of the one induces a corresponding condition in the other' (*OED*, 2). The more familiar sense of 'The quality or state of being thus affected by the suffering or sorrow of another; a feeling of compassion or commiseration' (*OED*, 3c) appears to have grown out of these physiological and pathological understandings of the term. The *OED*'s first cited usage of this affective sense is 1600, although I would suggest that this meaning was available considerably earlier.

Certainly the word *sympathy* was current in medical discourse by the 1580s. For example, in an English translation of Galen's works from 1586 we find a discussion of the ways in which parts of the body affect each other, explicitly drawing upon the Greek concept of *sympathia*: 'at this time the causes of these intemperatives are to be considered, whether these be common to all the whole bodie, or else proper of some partes, which should infest the ulcerate member by societie, the Greekes call it *Simpathia*'.[10] In the same year, early modern readers could have encountered the concept of sympathy in Timothy Bright's *Treatise of Melancholy*, which describes how the brain communicates with the heart, and how both parts then affect the rest of the body: 'these being troubled carie with them all the rest of the partes into a simpathy, they of all the rest being in respect of affection of most importance. The humours then to worke these effectes, which approch nigh to naturall perturbations grounded upon just occasion, of necessity, alter either brayne or hart.' The heart is then 'moved to a disorderly passion'.[11] Thus *sympathy* was used by medical writers to describe a form of compassionate contagion between bodily parts, and was understood in humoral terms.

At the same time, however, these correspondences within the human body were seen as part of a larger system of sympathies and antipathies, which included the cosmic order of the earth and the heavens, as well as the natural order of society. In William Lightfoot's *The complaint of England* (1587), a polemic against papists, he offers this rapturous celebration of unity: 'And therefore Nature in all her actions intending *unitie*, buildeth her whole frame upon the groundworke of sweete harmonie, and musicall concent: tempering the qualities in each severall body with such indifferent proportion, that albeit some one overrule the rest, yet it is not permitted to overthrow them: but they all by a secret *sympathie* & mutual agreement, indevour to support the one the others burden.'[12] Similarly, William Averell's *A mervailous combat of contrarieties* (1588), a political dialogue between parts of the body, uses *sympathy* to describe a kind of agreement between fellowships of men: 'In this order we knowe there is a continuall *Sympathie*, no shew of contrarietie, for if there were, it could be no order but a disorder, no *Sympathie* but an *Antipathie*, so ye whole course of natural things should either be dissolved or unnaturally be mervailously confounded.'[13] Averell's text was one of the sources for Menenius' fable of the belly in Shakespeare's *Coriolanus* (c.1608), reminding us that metaphors involving the body had particular currency in the late sixteenth and early seventeenth centuries. As Averell suggests, we are all part of God's creation, and our bodies are not only part of a larger creation but also resemble it: man is a 'lesser world, in respect of the greater, participating both of the heavenly and terrestriall matter, and bearing also a simililtude of the heavens and elements ..., a natural agreement there should be among the fellowships of men, to the making up of a politique bodie, knit together in the unitie of mindes' (sig. D1r).

This desire for a 'unitie of mindes' clearly has a political dimension in Averell's text, which was printed in the year of the Armada crisis, and concludes with a plea for loyalty for Queen Elizabeth.[14] Yet this rhetorical strategy also relates to several late sixteenth-century sermons, which are also preoccupied with concepts of social and emotional unity. And it is here that we can see the word *sympathy* being used to describe a mutual suffering between individuals. One sermon from the 1580s preached by Edwin Sandys, Archbishop of York, and recorded in his *Sermons* (1585), takes as its text Philippians 2:2: '*Be like minded, having the same love, being of one accord and of one judgement.*'[15] One of the central concerns of this sermon is 'unitie and concord', and Sandys cites an analogy made by St Paul between three forms of unity: the mystical body of Christ, the company of men professing the Christian faith, and the parts and members of a natural body.[16] As Sandys writes, 'the bodie by nature is a thing whole and perfect, consisting of all his members; if any part be wanting or cut off, it is maimed' (pp. 83–84). It is the same with the mystical body of Christ:

> All the members and every one of them labour not for themselves onely, but for the use and preservation of the whole bodie. So are we borne not for our selves alone, but for others also, for whom we should travell as for our selves .... The members rejoice and suffer together: Even so should wee bee kindely affected eche to other, mourning with them that mourne, and being glad with them that doe rejoice. That member which hath not this sympathie, this mutuall suffering, this feeling of other mens hurts is dead and rotten. (p. 84)

In Sandys's reworking of Paul's analogy he begins with the idea of the members of the 'whole bodie', and how they do not labour 'for themselves onely'. Similarly, he suggests, human beings do not exist in isolation but rather experience the same emotions as the other members of the church. In this way, the natural philosophical concept of bodily parts sympathising with others develops into a discussion of emotional correspondence. More specifically, Sandys claims that any 'member' who does not experience this 'sympathie' with others – glossed as a 'mutuall suffering' – is dead and rotten. His comments may reflect the wider anxieties in Reformation culture about a lack of compassion discussed by Steenbergh in the next chapter. Indeed Sandys's declaration that an individual without sympathy is 'dead and rotten' anticipates Robert Bolton's assertion in the 1620s that such a person is 'rotten at the heart-roote'.[17] For Sandys, this notion is part of his larger argument that an essential aspect of being a living human is being part of a larger whole, and thus responsive to and affected by the suffering of others.

The penultimate sentence in this passage recalls Romans 12:15, an oft-cited verse describing compassion: 'Rejoyce with them that rejoyce, & wepe with them that wepe.' Sandys also explicitly cites Hebrews 13, which encourages his audience and readers to imagine themselves in the bodies of those who are suffering: '*Remember them* saith the Apostle, *that are in bonds, as though yee your selves were bound with them, and them that are in affliction as if yee your selves were afflicted in their bodies*' (p. 84). This is a fairly accurate quotation of Hebrews 13:3, which asks people to imagine the bodily suffering and incarceration of others.[18] However, Sandys goes on to make a further analogy with the body politic: 'Even so in this resembled bodie, and civil societie there must be diversitie as of members so of functions. The prince is as the head, without whose discreete and wise governement the Lawes would cease, and the people being not ruled by order of Lawes, ruine and confusion would soone followe, eche contending and striving against other the end would be the utter subversion of all' (p. 84). The political import of this section is underscored by the fact that this sermon was preached before Queen Elizabeth herself. In this way, the knitting together of individual selves has political as well as ethical implications, and encourages the listeners to see themselves as part of a natural hierarchy: 'Men of lower degrees are set as inferior parts in the bodie, painefully to travel for the necessarie sustentation both of themselves and others. All these members are so necessarie that none can want without the ruine of the whole. For everie one hath need of other & by the help of the other is maintained' (p. 85). Here the rhetorical and political aspects of Sandys's argument are most explicit: individuals can – and indeed should – experience a mutual suffering of others' hurts, but should also remain in their appropriate place in the social hierarchy. The further implication is that they are part of a receptive and compliant audience: obeying the preacher, the monarch, and, above that, God.

William James and the Limits of Sympathy

Sandys's sermon thus serves as a fascinating example of a natural philosophical concept being imported into a religious context, and used as a way of describing social emotions and relationships. At a time when analogical thinking was widespread, the concept of sympathy appears to have been eminently translatable across a wide range of medical, political and religious discourses. While not strictly speaking an 'emotional practice', to borrow Monique Scheer's useful phrase, the use of *sympathy* as an emotion word can nevertheless be regarded as a new form for nurturing (as well as expressing) the capacity for compassion.[19] We can see this process at work in a sermon preached by William James at Paul's Cross on 9 November 1589. This is the second of James's published sermons, and is a strong defence of episcopacy – the idea that bishops should retain their position at the top of the body of the church. The sermon takes as its text three verses from 1 Corinthians 12: '*25 Least there should be any division in the body, but that the members should have the same care one for another. 26 Therefore if one member suffer, all suffer with it: if one member be had in honour, all the members rejoyce with it. 27 Now yee are the body of Christ, and members for your part.*'[20] Mary Morrissey has discussed this sermon in relation to puritan controversies, suggesting that treatments of these verses 'are dominated by dissuasions from contentions within the Church'.[21] However the sermon offers a wide-ranging discussion of the ethics of compassion that goes beyond these topical considerations.

Like some of the writers whom we have already examined, James discusses various natural forms of discord and harmony. In the first part of the sermon, James suggests that Nature has 'tempered and mingled all things, that there is not onely not any division and discord, but (if we beleeve some Philosophers) such and so sweete a harmony, that, as he saith of vertue, if it might be seene with bodily eies, it would stirre up incredible love thereof' (sig. B3r). In other words, while there is 'division and discord' in the world, there is nevertheless a sweet harmony that joins everything together. The same idea applies to human bodies: 'In this litle world, this tabernacle of our bodies, this *microcosmos*, albeit it consist altogether of contrarie elements, and of those whereof every one seeketh to destroy another, and that by most contrarie qualities, as the extremities of heate, colde, moisture, and drought: and albeit there be never any peace or rest, untill (as Aristotle teacheth) there be *elementum praedominans,* a predominant element that ruleth all the rest' (sig. B3r–v). Here we move from nature, where there is variety and division, to the microcosm of the human body, which contains various contrary elements but a predominant element that 'ruleth' the rest. Thus, while this part of the sermon is ostensibly concerned with natural philosophical ideas, there is once again a political aspect to James's arguments.

These arguments are presented in a highly rhetorical form that seeks to bind the audience together in agreement. For example, in the following passage James uses various forms of repetition and alliteration, and concludes with a powerful rhetorical question:

> Seeing we all inhabite here one and the same vale of miserie, the valley of teares, having all one and the same sworne enemie, the olde malicious and canckred serpent: Seeing there is but one God, one faith, one baptisme: Seeing we are all branches of the same vine, drawing all juice & moisture alike from the same roote, all servants of the same master, children of the

same father, and (as the Apostle saith) all members of the same body: why do we either contemne or contend one with another? (sig. B4v)

James's emphasis upon hierarchy and authority feeds into the rhetorical movement of the passage, unifying the listeners into a sympathetic and compliant body. Once again, the orator seeks to unify his audience in acceptance of an intellectual argument about unity. Division across various sections of society is presented as undesirable: 'Dissension, division, is a most miserable thing, whether you respect the church, Commonwealth, or private families' (sig. C1v). All individuals take their place within this respective hierarchy, and simply by listening to the speaker the audience's assent is implicit.

But as well as these political elements, the sermon also focuses closely on ideas of compassion and care. The second part of the sermon considers verse 25, '*Let the members have the same care for another.*' Once again, James makes a powerful analogy between the members of the body, and the members of the church. His description of the body recalls Galen's interest in sympathy and infection: 'if one [member in the body] perish or putrifie, it infecteth first the next, and so in time anoieth all: or if any one in a common calamitie deny helpe to another, all thereby are brought into danger'. Just as the body cannot function with one part that is ill, there must also be a mutual care between members of the Church: 'Let the members care. Let no man thinke his brothers matters not to appertaine unto him. Let the members not only have a care, but the same care, let the members have the same care, let there be no distraction or separation of mindes' (sig. F1r–v). Here James uses a similar formulation to William Averell, describing the unity of minds between members of the church, and implicitly between members of the audience listening at Paul's Cross. This example further highlights how preachers sought to knit together the minds of their congregations in order to convince them of the importance of compassionate behaviour. Indeed, it is an effective rhetorical strategy to join listeners together in a unity of minds – especially when a preacher's primary aim is to persuade his audience of the need for societal and emotional harmony.

James spends a considerable amount of the sermon reflecting on mutual love, before realising that he has not quite addressed the last verse of his main text, and what he calls 'the third part of mutuall compassion, and the application' (sig. G4r). In the suggestive final pages of the sermon James uses the term *sympathy* to describe the relationship between the different parts of the body and the members of the church:

> *Yee are the bodie of Christ, and members for your part*, to your Christian consideration. Onely this I wish you all consider, that as in the griefe of the bodie, the very heart sigheth, the eies shead teares, the head aketh, the stomacke refuseth foode, the whole bodie is made feeble, though it be but the griefe of a finger, or of a toe: so in the church there ought to be a sympathie, and fellowe feeling, to weepe with them that weepe, to rejoyce with them that rejoyce. (sig. G4r)

This is a striking example of the word *sympathy* in transition; it looks back to the earlier, physiological concept but it also points forward to the more modern emotional usages. James suggests that his audience should respond to the suffering of others in the same way that parts of the body respond to each other. But it is worth noting that James says that there 'ought' to be a sympathy with others, suggesting that it is not necessarily automatic. He combines the word with the more familiar phrase 'fellowe feeling' and a biblical verse on the same theme: Romans 12:15. We might also note that this important verse itself employs repetition and rhetorical mirroring to reflect the sharing of emotions – weeping and rejoicing – that it describes. In this way, the rhetorical strategies employed by the sermon might contradict, or at least complicate, its central proposition. James's argument that sympathy is a natural process is belied by the very form of the sermon itself and its reliance upon rhetoric and biblical authority to persuade its listeners to feel compassion for one another.

James goes on to discuss Chrysostom's *Commentary on Matthew*, Homily 35: 'Doeth thy brother suffer trouble or losse? if thou be sorie for him, thou art placed as a member in the bodie of the Church: if thou sorow not, if thou suffer not, thou art cut off, and peradventure thou therefore sorowest not, because thou art cut off' (sig. G4v). As James suggests, feeling sorrow for one's brother effectively makes one a member in the body of the church. If a member is cut off, he will have no sorrow precisely because he is no longer part of this metaphorical body. This discussion leads on to a second usage of the word *sympathy*:

> This your Sympathie and commiseration should shewe it selfe in releeving your needie brethren, in helping and succouring the poore maimed souldiers, in aiding and assisting your afflicted brethren in Fraunce and Flaunders for the Gospels sake. (sig. G4v)

Here the argument moves from a general consideration of sympathy and commiseration to a specific political situation: the French wars of religion. Clearly there is a desire for sympathy and commiseration to be an active process, and for the listeners to relieve the sufferings of others. Sympathy should 'shewe it selfe'; in other words, it is not just an inward experience but needs to reveal itself through one's deeds. As Steenbergh puts it in the following chapter, 'The experience of compassion is engendered through practice – not only in the sense of doing compassion, but practice also in the sense of exercising and training it.'[22] Of course, it is impossible to know whether James's original audience – or readers of the printed text – put these ideas into practice; but certainly this discussion was of considerable interest to at least one early modern reader, as we can see from the Huntington Library copy of James's sermon.[23] This reader seems to have been particularly interested in the Latin and biblical phrases used, which are highlighted and joined up by lines traced in the margin. However, the two usages of *sympathy* are also highlighted, suggesting that they were regarded as a notable part of the argument and attracted this reader's attention.

This case study thus reveals how the word *sympathy* was now being used in the public sphere as a way of describing commiseration – and for putting such feelings into practice. But it is also noteworthy that the unity James describes is bound up with the contemporary political situation; there is no sympathy for people from Continental Europe, who 'seeke to displace your dread Soveraigne ... to conquere & subdue this nation to a forraine yoke, to spoile man, woman, and childe, and to make us all slaves to their Romish and Spanish crueltie' (sig. G4v). Certainly James's sermon makes the term *sympathy* available to listeners and prompts them to reflect upon their Christian duty to be compassionate. And yet sympathy is not an automatic response to human suffering but mediated by religious and political considerations. Rather than bringing about a deeper understanding of the 'other', James's conception of sympathy and compassion only extends to brethren who closely resemble his Protestant audience.

'[A]s if wee were in their case': Imagining the Other in Sermons and Plays

While James's sermon tends to figure the sympathetic 'other' as someone rather similar to the self, other preachers were exploring the ways in which sympathy and compassion could involve putting oneself in another individual's situation. The bodily concepts and practices of early modern compassion – in which members of the church are encouraged to see themselves as parts of a single body – become increasingly inadequate.[24] Indeed by the mid-1590s there appears to be a notable shift, whereby *sympathy* is used by preachers to describe an imaginative engagement with the other. According to the *OED*, this more complex understanding of *sympathy*, 'The quality or state of being affected by the condition of another with a feeling similar or corresponding to that of the other; the fact or capacity of entering into or sharing the feelings of another or others' (*OED*, 3b), does not appear until the later seventeenth century. However, several preachers in the 1590s clearly use the term in this sense, drawing upon biblical narratives and exemplars as a way of exploring this form of imaginative fellow-feeling.

One notable example of this creative (and emotive) use of biblical stories is to be found in the sermons of Henry Holland, a writer on witchcraft who was also a priest. Holland was made vicar of Orwell in Cambridgeshire in 1580, and moved to St Bride's, London, in 1594.[25] In *The Christian Exercise of Fasting* (1596), which was based on his sermons and written after his move to London, Holland discusses the causes of private fasting, the third of which is the cure and comfort of the sick: 'so also when their brethren were in like dangers, they prepared themselves to cry unto God for them, in a religious abstinence'.[26] Holland suggests that God commands us 'to cherish this Christian sympathie in our hearts', and – like several other writers during this period – cites Romans 12:15–16: '*Weepe with them that weep, be of like affection one towards another.* And the sicke wee bee commanded to have in speciall regard, and to consider of them as if wee were in their case, for the time present' (p. 22). In this description of 'Christian sympathie', Holland implies a degree of separateness between individuals. He describes how it is possible to reflect upon the sick and imagine oneself (temporarily) in their situation. The idea of imagining the other as if we were 'in their case' clearly draws upon and extends biblical ideas; yet it also anticipates eighteenth-century conceptions of sympathy. In *The Theory of Moral Sentiments* (1759), Adam Smith writes that 'Though our brother is upon the rack, as long as we ourselves are at our ease, our senses will never inform us of what he suffers ... it is by the imagination only that we can form any conception of what are his sensations. Neither can that faculty help us to this any other way, than by representing to us what would be our own, if we were in his case.'[27] Smith's text is usually regarded as one of the foundational philosophical treatments of sympathy, with its emphasis upon imaginative perspective-taking. Yet Holland's sermon questions the idea that this form of sympathy only emerged in the Enlightenment, and suggests that it can be traced fruitfully back to the sixteenth century at least.

Holland continues his emphasis upon the imagination in his discussion of the love of Job's friends, who came to lament with Job, and to comfort him: 'when they came to that place, whether because of smell, or infection, or both, it is uncertaine, standing a farre off, they lift up their voyces and wept' (p. 23). At first glance, this formulation might suggest a form of emotional contagion, and confirm the sense that conceptions of sympathy in the period were primarily physiological or Galenic. Yet this idea is soon replaced by a focus on the men's ability to imagine themselves in Job's situation. Job's friends are said to exemplify the kind of Christian sympathy Holland has already referred to:

> I finde also in these men a christian sympathie, this appeares in their weeping, and rending of their clothes: they felt in the beginning such passions in themselves, as if their soules had been in his soules stead: as Job after wisheth, chap. 16.4. that is, they mourned as if they had been in the same case: such men onely can minister comfort and pray effectually for the sicke. (p. 24)

Holland suggests that Job's friends felt his passions, as if their souls 'had been in his soules stead'. This is a paraphrase of Job 16:4, in which Job says, 'I colde also speak as ye do: (but wolde God your soule were in my soules stead) I colde keep you companie in speaking, and colde shake mine head at you.' Holland's reworking of this verse extends its emphasis upon emotional exchange, and suggests that Job's friends mourned as if they had been in his situation: 'in the same case'. This is a sophisticated conception of sympathy, which does not imply contagion or embodied compassion but rather involves role-playing and imaginative substitution.[28] Holland implies that godliness is dependent upon 'christian sympathie', which is presented as an imaginative inhabiting of another's sorrowful situation. The wider implication is that, if Job's friends can imagine themselves in Job's situation, then the audience listening to the sermon can imagine themselves in the situation of Job's friends. This citation and amplification of scripture provides further evidence that the recollection of biblical narratives and figures played a key role in shaping the understanding of compassion in the period – arguably a more important one than humoral or medical models.

Holland's fascination with perspective-taking and the imagination resonates with other treatments of sympathy that we find in dramatic texts from the same decade. In Shakespeare's *Romeo and Juliet* (c.1595; first printed 1597), for example, the distressed Romeo suggests to his friend Friar Laurence that it is impossible for someone to experience his feelings unless he is in the same predicament.[29] Friar Laurence offers to 'dispute with thee of thy estate' (III.iii.63), but Romeo declines this offer:

> Thou canst not speak of that thou dost not feel.
> Wert thou as young as I, Juliet thy love,
> An hour but married, Tybalt murderèd,
> Doting like me, and like me banishèd,
> Then mightst thou speak, then mightst thou tear thy hair,
> And fall upon the ground as I do now,
> Taking the measure of an unmade grave.
> (III.iii.64–70)

Romeo claims that sympathy – the experience of feeling another person's sorrow – is impossible. Nevertheless this speech offers a moving evocation of Romeo's emotions, and provides a summary of his plight and a description of his sorrowful actions. Indeed, the emotional power of the play surely depends upon the audience's ability to put themselves in the lovers' position.[30]

In the same scene, we also find an important Shakespearean use of the word *sympathy*. Juliet's Nurse arrives, and identifies Romeo as being in the same state as Juliet:

> O, he is even in my mistress' case,
> Just in her case! O woeful sympathy,
> Piteous predicament! Even so lies she,
> Blubb'ring and weeping, weeping and blubb'ring. –
> Stand up, stand up, stand an you be a man;
> For Juliet's sake, for her sake, rise and stand.
> Why should you fall into so deep an O?
> (III.iii.84–90)

As with several other Shakespearean works from the 1590s, the word *sympathy* is associated with woe and pity – and is used here in the context of two individuals being in the same 'case'. According to the Nurse, Romeo is 'Just in [Juliet's] case!'; that is, in precisely the same situation. In her Oxford edition of the play, Jill Levenson glosses *sympathy* as 'likeness in misery'.[31] And indeed, like the sermon by William James we examined earlier, the Nurse's speech is replete with repetition and doubling; her description of Juliet's weeping and blubbering is a striking example of the figure of *antimetabole*, in which the verbal repetition itself repeats and mirrors the emotional agreement of the two lovers.[32] The emotional effect of this passage is, however, complicated by the Nurse's unintentional double entendres, which arguably detract from the 'woeful sympathy' that the audience might experience for Romeo.[33] Nevertheless, this scene not only debates the complex relationship between the self and the other but also further associates *sympathy* with grief and fellow-feeling.

While *Romeo and Juliet* presents sympathy as likeness in grief, or simple correspondence, other dramatic texts go further in emphasising the imaginative aspects of compassion. In *Sir Thomas More* (c.1601–4), a passage that appears to be in Shakespeare's hand has More addressing an anti-immigration riot in the streets of London. He urges the rioters to imagine themselves banished to a land where the inhabitants

> Whet their detested knives against your throats,
> Spurn you like dogs, and like as if that God
> Owed not nor made not you, nor that the elements
> Were not all appropriate to your comforts
> But chartered unto them, what would you think
> To be thus used? This is the strangers' case,
> And this your mountainish inhumanity.[34]

This remarkable passage differs from William James's sermon on sympathy inasmuch as it invites the audience to extend their selves into 'the strangers' case'; that is, feeling compassion as a result of imagining oneself in the situation of someone from a different ethnic group.[35] The passage also raises complex questions about the relationship between the self and the other – and about the individual and the group. Does compassion stem from identification or from difference? Does being part of a collective make one more or less compassionate? Such questions are pertinent to both the pulpit and the playhouse during this period – not least because both involve social performances that employ rhetoric and storytelling to move audiences. Henry Holland's hostile description of London's '*divellish theaters*', which he paints as '*the nurceries of whoredome and uncleannesse*', may confirm our sense that preachers did not learn about sympathetic perspective-taking from Shakespeare.[36] Yet it is certainly plausible that Shakespeare and other playwrights drew upon the vocabulary and ideas contained in sermons, and that there was a degree of cross-fertilisation between these two cultural forms.[37] Either way, there appears to have been a parallel exploration of ideas of correspondence and harmony, and the social body, which gave rise to the term *sympathy* being redeployed from the natural philosophical realm to the dramatic, the imaginative and the ethical.

Conclusion

As we have seen throughout the present chapter, sermons in the late sixteenth century were especially concerned to explore the mechanics of compassion – in terms of both their form and content. The intellectual arguments made by preachers about religious unity and social cohesion often appealed to the emotions of their listeners, reminding us that moving an audience to compassion was an important aspect of rhetorical persuasion. This idea certainly informs Thomas Wright's *The passions of the minde in generall* (1604), which contains an extraordinary account of an Italian preacher who had a particular ability to manipulate the passions of his listeners:

> I remember a Preacher in *Italy*, who had such power over his Auditors affections, that when it pleased him he could cause them shedd abundance of teares, yea and with teares dropping downe their cheekes, presently turne their sorrow into laughter: and the reason was, because hee himselfe being extremely passionate, knowing moreover the Art of moving the affections of those auditors, and besides that, the most part were women that heard him (whose passions are most vehement and mutable) therefore he might have perswaded them what hee listed.[38]

Wright describes this ability as a 'commoditie' that can be employed and exploited by other orators as well is preachers. As Wright puts it, if orators can 'stirre a Passion or Affection in their Hearers, then they have almost halfe perswaded them, for that the forces of strong Passions marvellously allure and draw the wit & will to judge and consent unto that they are moved' (p. 4). Various sixteenth-century preachers attempted to tap into this cultural commodity, and sought to move the 'wit & will' of auditors, bringing about 'consent'. At the same time, however, their sermons raise larger questions about human agency, and whether sympathy and compassion are natural phenomena, or qualities to be stirred up or cultivated. Indeed, it seems ironic that the shift in the usage of the word *sympathy*, whereby a concept from natural philosophy is used to refer to human relationships, goes hand in hand with an increasing sense of the separateness of individuals. Both of the early modern cultural forms that I have been exploring – sermons and plays – seem to have been fascinated by social relationships and emotional affinities. And, as we have seen, both preachers and playwrights required a new word to express the notion of imaginatively transporting oneself into the other's case.

This complex understanding of sympathy implicitly complicates the Renaissance commonplace that passions could be automatically transferred from orator to audience, provided the orator is sufficiently moved himself. As Wright puts it, 'It cannot bee that hee which heareth should sorrow, hate, envie, or feare any thing, that he should be induced to compassion or weeping, except all those motions the orator would stir up in the judge, be first imprinted & marked in the Orator himselfe, & therefore *Horace* well observed, that he which will make me weep must first weepe himselfe' (p. 172). And yet, the texts I have been discussing suggest that the reality was somewhat more complex, and that articulations and representations of sympathy presupposed an active – and participatory – audience. These materials allow us to question some of the rhetorical commonplaces of the period, as well as the broader critical assumption that sympathy in the Renaissance was a primarily physiological or pathological process. Moreover, ideas of sympathy and compassion in the late sixteenth century were bound up not only with wider political and religious debates, but also with shifting concepts of the social body and the self. We might even suggest that the very idea of a homogenous social group was beginning to seem outmoded, and that this is one reason why preachers and playwrights began to address audiences as a compassionate network of individual selves, and not simply – as William Averell might have it – as a 'unitie of mindes'.

Notes

1 John Prime, *An Exposition, and Observations upon Saint Paul to the Galathians* (London, 1587), p. 308.
2 Matthew 27: 51–52. Unless otherwise stated, quotations from the Bible are taken from *The Geneva Bible: A Facsimile of the 1560 Edition*, with an introduction by Lloyd E. Berry (Madison: University of Wisconsin Press, 1969).
3 See Ann E. Moyer, 'Sympathy in the Renaissance', in Eric Schliesser (ed.) *Sympathy: A History* (Oxford University Press, 2015), pp. 70–101.
4 See Prime's Dedication to John Piers, Bishop of Salisbury (sig. ¶2r). Prime became a fellow of New College, Oxford in 1571, and gained a university preaching licence in 1581. See Julian Lock, 'Prime, John (1549/50–1596)', *ODNB*.
5 Mary Floyd-Wilson has argued that sympathies and antipathies 'produced involuntary emotional relationships' in the early modern period (*Occult Knowledge, Science, and Gender on the Shakespearean Stage* [Cambridge University Press, 2013], p. 2).

6 Arnold Hunt, *The Art of Hearing: English Preachers and Their Audiences, 1590–1640* (Cambridge University Press, 2010), p. 11.
7 See Kristine Steenbergh's Chapter 6 in the present volume.
8 Steven Mullaney has recently argued that there was a 'reformation of emotions in the early modern period' and that it took place 'in the domain of what we might call the social emotions, in the social and hence the lived world of feeling, as opposed to the theoretical or polemical discourses of medical treatises' (*The Reformation of Emotions in the Age of Shakespeare* [University of Chicago Press, 2015], p. 22). Mullaney is interested in the concept of 'cultural performances' and mentions the importance of the pulpit for delivering stories that shaped social practices (p. 23), although his primary focus is early modern drama.
9 For further discussion of the term *compassion* see the Introduction to this volume.
10 *Certaine workes of Galens, called Methodus medendi ... all translated into English, by Thomas Gale Maister in Chirurgerie* (London, 1586), p. 84.
11 Timothy Bright, *A treatise of melancholie, Containing the causes thereof, & reasons of the strange effects it worketh in our minds and bodies* (London, 1586), p. 93.
12 William Lightfoot, *The complaint of England* (London, 1587), sig. A2r–v.
13 William Averell, *A mervailous combat of contrarieties* (London, 1588), sig. D1r.
14 See William E. Burns, 'Averell, William (*bap.* 1556, *d.* 1605)', *ODNB*.
15 *Sermons made by the most reverende Father in God, Edwin, Archbishop of Yorke* (London, 1585), p. 78.
16 Cf. 1 Corinthians 12:12: 'For as the bodie is one, and hathe many membres, and all the membres of the bodie, which is one, thogh they be many, *yet are but* one bodie: even so is Christ.'
17 See Steenbergh's discussion of Bolton's *Some generall directions for a comfortable walking with God* (London, 1626) in Chapter 6.
18 'Remember them that are in bondes, as thogh ye were bonde with them: and them that are in affliction, as if ye were also *afflicted* in the bodie' (Hebrews 13:3).
19 Monique Scheer, 'Are Emotions a Kind of Practice (And Is That What Makes Them Have a History)? A Bourdieuian Approach to Understanding Emotion', *History and Theory*, 51:2 (2012), 193–220.
20 William James, *A sermon preached at Paules Crosse the IX. of November, 1589* (London, 1590), sig. B1r.
21 Mary Morrissey, *Politics and the Paul's Cross Sermons, 1558–1642* (Oxford University Press, 2011), p. 214.
22 See Steenbergh, Chapter 6.
23 Huntington Library shelf mark 20681. Some earlier pages are also highlighted, but the sermon's final pages contain the most concentrated and sustained markings.
24 By contrast, Steenbergh emphasises the continuing importance of the 'bowels of compassion' in the period, and the centrality of this bodily concept to early modern practices of fellow-feeling and charity. Chapter 6, this volume.

25 See Clive Holmes, 'Holland, Henry (1555/6–1603)', *ODNB*.
26 Henry Holland, *The Christian Exercise of Fasting* (London, 1596), p. 22.
27 Adam Smith, *The Theory of Moral Sentiments*, ed. Knud Haakonssen (Cambridge University Press, 2002), p. 11.
28 William Perkins, writing in 1608, describes a compassion of the heart as 'one man ... put[ting] on the person of another' (*A godly and learned exposition of Christs Sermon in the Mount* [Cambridge, 1608], quoted in Steenbergh's Chapter 6, this volume). Yet Perkins's emphasis is upon a bodily transferral of misery, whereas Holland implies an exchange of souls.
29 Quotations are taken from *Romeo and Juliet*, ed. Jill L. Levenson (Oxford University Press, 2000).
30 For further discussion of sympathy in the play, see my chapter on 'Sympathy' in Katharine A. Craik (ed.), *Shakespeare and Emotion* (Cambridge University Press, 2020).
31 See Levenson's note to III.iii.85.
32 See Eric Langley, *Narcissism and Suicide in Shakespeare and His Contemporaries* (Oxford University Press, 2009), p. 128.
33 See Levenson's note to III.iii.88–90.
34 Addition II.D, 149–55, quoted from Gary Taylor and Stanley Wells (gen. eds.), *The Oxford Shakespeare: The Complete Works* (Oxford University Press, 1988).
35 Cf. Bruce Smith's discussion of this passage in Chapter 1 in the present volume.
36 Holland, *Spirituall preservatiues against the pestilence: Or A treatise containing sundrie questions* (London, 1593), The Epistle Dedicatory, sigs. A5v–A6r.
37 Hunt cites the example of the Wiltshire preacher John Andrewes, who includes an extract from Portia's speech about mercy from *The Merchant of Venice* in his *Christ his crosse or The most comfortable doctrine of Christ crucified* (Oxford, 1614). See *The Art of Hearing*, pp. 171–72.
38 Thomas Wright, *The passions of the minde in generall. In Six Bookes. Corrected, enlarged, and with sundry new Discourses augmented* (1604; rpt. London, 1630), p. 3.

CHAPTER 6

Mollified Hearts and Enlarged Bowels
Practising Compassion in Reformation England

Kristine Steenbergh

> *Labour for a tender heart [...] then shall your compassion extend itself more viscerally towards your afflicted brethren.*[1]

How to practise compassion? This question was pressing for English Christians during the long process of the Reformation. Protestant preachers worried about a lack of charitable practices in Reformation culture. The Church of England clergyman Henry Smith, for example, draws a striking contrast between the generosity of his pre-Reformation forefathers and the hard-heartedness of his own generation.

> Where is the large liberallity be come, that in time past was rooted in our forefathers, they were content to be liberall, though they applied it to evil purposes, the successours of those which in time past gave liberallie to maintain Abots, Friers, Monks, Nunnes, Masses, Durges, Trentals, and all idolatrie: seeing the abuses thereof, may now bestow it to a better use: namely, to foster and feed the pore members of Christ. [...] Oh howe liberall were people in times past to mainetaine superstition: and nowe howe harde hearted are they growen to keepe the poore from famine[.][2]

Even as he frowns upon late medieval practices of charity, Smith looks back nostalgically to an era in which people were 'content to be liberall'. He disapproves of pre-Reformation practices that involved giving charitably to religious orders, or singing dirges to express compassionate ties with the dead: these only served to sustain idolatry and superstition. His church therefore does not function as an intermediary between the charitable giver and the poor; his congregation could give directly to 'the pore members of Christ' rather than to religious orders. And yet, he wonders what has become of his forefathers' liberality. He is acutely aware that for them, traditional devotional habits ensured that charity was firmly 'rooted' in their daily lives. A similar sentiment can be found in the work of Thomas Becon (1512/3–1567) theologian, Church of England clergyman and spokesman for Protestant reform. He complains that the charitable habits of the previous generation have been forgotten: 'with what a Godly pitie & charitable affectioun dyd our ancestors burne toward the poore members of Christ, which as I may speake nothynge of Abbeyes, Colleges, Chauntries, frechapels &c bilt with theyr greate cost hospitals & suche other houses, enduing [endowing] the same with yerely revenewes for the relife [sic] of the poore? Men crie fathers, fathers, but the maners of these fathers are clene forgotten'.[3] Like Smith, Becon disapproves of the abbeys, colleges, chantries and chapels that the church built with money donated by his forefathers. Yet he also looks back with approval and nostalgia at the 'Godly pitie & charitable affectioun' with which his parents regarded the poor. He regrets that the compassionate habits of the previous generation are 'clene forgotten' and that his contemporaries have become more covetous than compassionate. The 'love towarde the poore compared with the love of our Auncestoures, is very cold, yea it is almost nothing'.[4]

Sermons like Smith's and Becon's show that the Reformation's uprooting of traditional habits and rhythms of charitable practice was experienced as having an impact on people's capacity to feel compassion. Since Protestant Reformers distrusted ritual, ceremony and structured pious practice, a wide range of devotional practices ceased to exist or lost their moorings in the common liturgy.[5] Traditional modes of arousing and expressing compassion were discontinued. Compassion with dead family members, for example, was no longer expressed in dirges after the abolition of Purgatory. Fellow-feeling with the suffering of the poor was no longer practised in donations to monasteries, and the practice of compassion with the suffering of Christ in Passion meditations was problematised.[6] Worried that the disappearance of former habits resulted in a waning of compassion, Smith warns that if a generation grows up to harden their hearts against the poor, 'doubtlesse gray heares will come upon our heads before we can find the right waie to pittie and compassion'.[7] As Steven Mullaney suggests, the generation that was born Elizabethan was not only uncertain what to believe, they also 'did not know what or how to feel'.[8]

In this chapter, I argue that while late sixteenth- and early seventeenth-century sermons reveal a concern over the disappearance of traditional habits of charitable giving and compassionate meditation, they also explore new forms of nurturing a capacity for sharing in the suffering of others. Like Smith and Becon, other authors also realise that a mollified heart susceptible to the suffering of others requires constant practice. With the loss of traditional habits of charity, they fear their congregations' hearts are in danger of hardening against the sight of suffering. These concerns are expressed in a recurrent image: clergymen worry that the members of their congregation suffer from hardened, closed and dry bowels.

In the preceding chapter in this section on 'exhorting' compassion, Richard Meek traces early modern understandings of sympathy in sermons and Shakespeare's plays from the physical and physiological to the emotional and imaginative. He makes the crucial point that although sympathy is often seen as an automatic process of emotional contagion, the early moderns also began to conceive of fellow-feeling as an active process requiring the audience's participation and use of their imagination. Sermons were an important instrument in this active process of compassion: they exhorted their congregations to put themselves in the other's case by relying on rhetoric and biblical authority. Indeed, Meek argues that 'the recollection of biblical narratives and figures played a key role in shaping the understanding of compassion in the period – arguably a more important one than humoral or medical models'.[9] In this chapter, I will argue that this active cultivation of compassion was seen as a long-term process of softening the bowels of compassion – a concept that brings together religious terminology with humoral and bodily notions of the workings of compassion. As I will show, the concept of the 'bowels of compassion' is central to early modern practices of charity and fellow-feeling: these organs need to be soft and moist to open and stretch towards those in need, to share in their suffering. Early modern texts view compassion as bowels that need to be enlarged and stretched to cultivate a lasting compassionate response to the suffering of others. As Protestant clergymen criticise the devotional practices of the traditional faith as idolatrous, they explore new practices to cultivate their congregations' compassion. In so doing, they walk a tightrope between inspiring an inward experience of compassion and inciting the outward performance of charitable deeds that do not spring from the bowels of compassion (and therefore evoke the same censure as pre-Reformation practices of charity). Paradoxically, one of the most productive modes of training dry and closed bowels to open themselves to the suffering of others is precisely the performance of charitable deeds.

Compassion as Practice

During the Reformation, late medieval devotional practices of cultivating compassion became unsettled.[10] A key devotional practice in the late Middle Ages – in England as elsewhere – was affective meditation on the

Passion. It was shared among a wide range of believers: lay devotees as well as the clergy, men and women, the lower as well as the upper classes. Meditators were encouraged to imagine Christ's suffering in such a way as to be able to partake in it, even to imagine it as their own. This focused concentration on the pains of Christ on the cross was meant to kindle an intense experience of compassion. As one of the influential devotional texts puts it: through meditation 'we sholde be stirede to inwarde compassion, & wondere'.[11] With chapter headings such as 'How a man shal have cristeis passion in mynde', devotional texts read like self-help books, instructing lay readers in the step-by-step cultivation of a practice of affective meditation, guiding them towards the goal of experiencing compassion with the suffering of Christ.[12] The meditations use various strategies to cultivate the desired affective response:

> Many are scripted as first-person, present-tense utterances, designed to be enacted by the reader. Others work through interpellation, hailing the reader as 'you' and directing affective response, even proscribing the gestures that will generate compassion ('behold him', 'embrace him'). Still others stage detailed, vividly imagined scenes from the Passion and cast the reader as feeling eyewitness and participant. The participatory, performative character of these texts is often enhanced through the use of apostrophes and exclamations, deictic rhetoric ('here', 'there'), and the regular use of the dramatic present.[13]

Compassion in late medieval devotional practice, then, is not conceived of as a contagious phenomenon, or as the spontaneous sharing of Christ's grief. Rather, it requires mental, and in some cases also bodily, effort: it is an emotion-as-practice that needs to be cultivated and habitually trained. The scripts told their readers 'through iterative affective performance, how to feel'.[14] The repeated kindling of compassion was thought to nurture a sustained capacity for sharing in the pain of others. Practices of meditation were considered to have long-term consequences: the regular arousal of compassion with the suffering of Christ on the cross was thought to make devotees more susceptible to the suffering of others' also in daily life. As Ellen Ross notes, in fourteenth- and fifteenth-century spirituality the affective, bodily engagement with the Passion and an understanding of Christ's suffering were thought to instil an ethical response to suffering in devotees.[15]

The idea that compassion is not a spontaneous reaction to the sight of suffering, but needs to be cultivated in regular practice, resonates with the insights of practice theory. Focusing on the ways emotions are 'done' in specific social, cultural and religious contexts, practice theory offers a model for understanding historical changes in the arousal, experience and expression of emotions. In brief, it posits that emotions are ingrained into people's bodies through a process of habituated, regular practice. Practices are not simply vehicles for emotions; rather, emotions are themselves practices: they come into being in the doing.[16] Monique Scheer has shaped a model for thinking about emotions and historical change that is anchored in Bourdieu's concept of the habitus. For Bourdieu, the body is a knowing, mindful body, which stores past experiences in habituated processes. His concept of 'habitus' is a set of dispositions that incline a person to act, think or feel in specific ways. These dispositions are not learned conceptually; they are formed by the repeated performance of practices that thereby become lodged in the body. As Margaret Wetherell describes, 'past practice and social location are embodied in an over-developed muscle, in the callous on a writing finger, in a cringe and timorous stoop, or in a confident stride and a braying voice in a London street'.[17] Similar to the way this 'over-developed muscle' of the habitus unconsciously determines the bodily comportment of individual persons, habitus determines what is 'feelable' in a specific setting.[18] Scheer writes that 'the habits of the mindful body are executed outside of consciousness and rely on social scripts from historically situated fields. That is to say, a distinction between incorporated society and the parts of the body generating emotion is hard to make'.[19] Emotions are interwoven with emotional practices, the bodily habits that arouse the experience of the emotion. Therefore, emotions are bodily, but the particular ways to arouse, experience and express an emotion are acquired through cultural and social context. Through repeated practice these ways become ingrained in the body of the individual. When the practice ceases to exist, the emotion-as-practice also gradually wanes: Scheer refers to the historically specific feeling of honour engendered by the eighteenth- and nineteenth-century European practice of the duel, which was lost when duels were no longer fought.[20]

During the Reformation, the removal of practices of affective devotion and charitable donation from official religion spurred a search for new modes of cultivating compassion. The need to find new practices was especially pressing because the experience of sharing in another's suffering was so central to Protestant faith as to be considered a prerequisite for Christian charity. As a Church of England clergyman puts it: 'we can doe but little good to any body, except we haue a feeling pitie and compassion of them'.[21] Indeed, sermons stress that it is precisely the experience of compassion that distinguishes the Protestant faith from traditional religion. Thomas Becon, for example, writes that Christians are not merely bound to help another, but should share an embodied experience of grief: 'when I haue a neighbour that is nedie or sycke, I ought not only to be redie to helpe, but I must be sorie for his miserie, and that at my very heart, as though it were min owne euil'.[22] Compassion here is a 'being sorie', a feeling of grief or sorrow 'at my very heart', as if the grief suffered by the other is also one's own. In his *Christian armorie*, the Church of England clergyman Thomas Draxe draws on Pope Gregory's writing to stress that any act of charity should be preceded by compassion:

> Q. What duties are we to perform to persons afflicted and persecuted?
>
> A. First, wee must haue a fellowlike feeling of their misery, and sympathize with them; otherwise we cannot effectually comfort them: for as iron cannot be ioyned, and fastened to iron, unlesse both of them bee made red hote, and beaten together: so one Christian can yeeld no comfort to another, unlesse both suffer together, (if not in action) yet in fellow feeling.[23]

The image of two pieces of iron that both need to be heated for them to be beaten together reinforces the idea that the sufferer and the charitable person first need to 'suffer together', to forge their bodies into the same vulnerable affective condition, before any help can be given. On the one hand, then, compassion was considered a key element of charity, while on the other hand, clergymen worried about finding new ways to arouse and practise compassion.

Bowels of Compassion

At the root of Protestant religious experience lies a concern over hardened hearts. 'The bane of the earnest Protestant's spiritual life', Alec Ryrie writes, 'was a condition variously described as dullness, hardness, heaviness, dryness, coldness, drowsiness, or deadness. This insidious malaise could creep into your heart unnoticed; its symptom was numbness, not pain.'[24] It is clear from the sermons that hard-heartedness was not only diagnosed in terms of spiritual insensitivity, but also conceived of as a lack of compassion for the suffering of others. In the case of compassion, however, it is not only the heart that suffers from a hardened state: the bowels also contract and harden. The notion of the bowels as the seat of compassion derives from several passages in the New Testament, where the Greek reads 'σπλάγχνα' and the Vulgate '*viscera*' to refer to the seat of compassion.[25] As Susan Wessel explains,

The Greek word the Gospels often use in this context, '*splanchnizomai*', is derived from the noun '*splanchna*', meaning 'guts' or 'entrails'. While most of the internal organs were designated, together and separately, by the word '*splanchna*', its meaning was extended metaphorically to indicate the seat of the feelings, emotions, and affection. The guts were thought to be the place where the feelings were felt.[26]

From the late fourteenth century onwards, the bowels in English came to stand for 'the seat of the tender and sympathetic emotions, hence: pity, compassion, feeling, "heart"'. Early modern English texts speak of the 'bowels of compassion' and the 'bowels of mercy'. Where were these bowels located in the body? In Greek, the word could refer to most of the internal organs, like *viscera* in Latin. In early modern English, the word *bowels* could, as now, refer to 'the intestines or entrails; the portions of the intestinal canal contained within the abdomen', but also more generally to 'the interior or inside of the body'.[27] William Jones, for example, interprets the bowels as 'our internall and vitall parts: the longues, the liver, especially the heart the seat of love and affection'.[28] The bowels of compassion were occasionally associated with the digestive tract: in a sermon, an onlooker sees hungry children scour the fields for something to eat and comments that 'the emptines of their bowels did justly fill our bowels with compassion. Famine is a sore plague.'[29] The effect of the image rests on a contrast between the empty (digestive) bowels of the children and the onlookers' bowels filled with compassion. This connection, however, is far less frequent in early modern texts than the association of the bowels of compassion with the organ of the heart.

Some critical disagreement exists over the question whether the bowels of compassion are a Catholic or a Protestant phenomenon. John Staines has described embowelled compassion as a typically Catholic 'visceral notion of compassion' which he argues was met with growing distrust in the Protestant context of the rejection of mass and the real presence.[30] John Yamamoto-Wilson, on the other hand, has shown that the phrase becomes more common in seventeenth-century Protestant texts. He shows that these texts refer to the bowels in the visceral sense that Staines viewed as typically Catholic. Yamamoto-Wilson ascribes this rising popularity of the bowels of compassion in the seventeenth century to a Protestant sense of inwardness: 'just as Protestant doctrines of repentance focused on an internalized sense of guilt, rather than on outward acts of penance, so, perhaps, the visceral nature of compassion hinges on the extent to which one makes the attempt to enter into the feelings of another, rather than on the performance of outward acts of mercy'.[31] His observation here is crucial also in the context of the search for new practices of compassion during the long Reformation: as we will see, Protestant faith distrusted the outward works of compassion that were such an integral part of late-medieval devotion and therefore sought to base charity in an inward, embowelled, experience of co-suffering – an experience that is unexpectedly visceral.

The concept of the bowels of compassion can be visualised as a movement within and between bodies. This movement begins inside the body, causing an inward sensation, and then moves outward, to finally return inward again. First, another person's suffering is felt inwardly, in the bowels. As Bruce Smith succinctly puts it in this volume, 'compassion begins in the guts'. The initial movement of compassion is often described as an inner experience: it 'wil worke in vs a fellow-feeling, and moue euen the bowels of compassion in vs'.[32] The experience is described as painful: the bowels 'yearn' within. Indeed, the bowels are described as the most tender part of the body, a place where pain is intensely experienced. Lancelot Andrewes thinks that 'of all parts, the bowells melt, relent, yeeld, yerne soonest. Consequently, the mercies from them, of all other, the most tender, and (as I may say) the mercie most mercifull.'[33] The bowels do not operate in isolation: in what is often described as a rolling movement, the heart and the liver stir with the bowels. Sometimes the heart is seen as the initiator of this movement, as, for example, in 'my heart is turned within me, and my bowels of compassion are rolled together'; in other texts the movement begins in the bowels.[34]

The early modern compassionate body is not self-contained. After the initial movement within, there follows a movement outward. The bowels of the person who experiences compassion are described in early modern texts as expanding, dilating, opening and pouring out towards the person they feel compassion with. The compassionate self is porous, extending beyond the boundaries of the physical body, stretching towards the other. This movement outwards is underlined by the use of the preposition 'towards' in many phrases for compassion. If in modern English compassion is felt *with* someone, in early modern sermons, people stretch forth their bowels of compassion *towards* the afflicted, or enlarge their bowels *towards* mankind. A sermon could urge the congregation 'to stretch forth the bowels of compassion towards the afflicted', for example.[35] The sight of suffering triggers a bodily response of opening towards the other, of pouring out compassion towards them. The workings of compassion are conceived of in terms of capaciousness, of enlarging and opening, of a movement outward.[36] A sermon exhorts its audience if they have any bowels of mercy to 'receive this counsell of Christ thy saviour, persuading thee to express thy bowels of mercie towardes the poore'.[37] These images of bowels opening and pouring forth compassion may cause merriment in modern readers, but they find a basis in humoral notions of the relation between the passions and the opening and closing of organs. Pierre de la Primaudaye – if you will allow me a brief excursion into a French source – explains the opening movement as a result of the effect of love on the organs: 'For before wee can finde this in vs, wee must first haue love in our hearts, which causeth us to open our bowels, and mooveth us to compassion towards our like.' He clarifies that the heart 'is either opened or closed up, as the affections are disposed that moove it: [...] Therefore as love or hatred is great or small, hote or cold, so doth the heart open or close it selfe.'[38] The bowels, then, seem to mimic this movement of the opening of the heart. Conversely, closed and dry bowels were inimical to the experience of compassion. Like the Protestant heart, bowels could be dull, withered, dried up, hardened and congealed, straightened, or even laid aside and absent.[39] Such a condition would render a person uncompassionate: 'the bowels of compassion are in some men so maruellously dried and closed vp, that they turne away their faces from all men that desire any thing at their hands'.[40] Closed bowels caused a close-fistedness in charity: 'it doth [...] harden the heart, and shut vp the hands, and close the bowels of compassion'.[41]

Besides opening, the bowels also stretch and extend beyond the limits of the body, dissolving the boundaries between within and without. The epigraph to this chapter sees it as a visceral mode of extending, as if the organs themselves stretch towards the object of pity. The greater one's compassion is, the greater the extent of opening and stretching forth. Thomas Wilcox, for example, urges Christians to 'excite and stir up [...] al christian pitie & bowels of compassion, to inlarge themselves to their uttermost, yea beyond it, if they coulde tell howe, towards such afflicted soules'.[42] The intensity of compassion could take bowels to the point of rupture, as appears from the words of a pitying father: 'What heart would not dissolve to see you misse? / What tender bowels would not burst at this?'[43] The acme of expansive compassion is God's: 'There was never a city of refuge so open to transgressors, never holes in the rockes so open for doves; never lappe of the mother so open to her babes, as the bowels of God's compassion are open to beleevers.'[44] Note that these images of extreme openness also express an inward movement, welcoming believers into the bowels, like a dove flies into a hole in the rock, or a child jumps onto her mother's lap.[45] The opening of the bowels enables receptiveness of the suffering of the other.

This receptiveness is also expressed in bodily metaphors. Like the dove who flies into a cave, the physical suffering of the other is absorbed in the body of the compassionate onlooker. For William Perkins, this compassionate movement within and between bodies takes the form of a transplantation of bowels:

> I call it a compassion of heart, because it makes one man to put on the person of an other, and to be grieved for the miseries of an other, as if they were his owne: and therfore it is called the bowells of compassion, because when a mans heart is touched therewith his very liver and entralls doe stirre in his bodie, and are rouled within him, as the Prophet speaketh: and he is affected, as though the bowells of him that is in miserie were in his bodie.[46]

Perkins explains the phrase 'bowels of compassion' as a movement of the liver and the entrails together with the movement of the heart, stirring and rolling within him, which occurs 'when a man's heart is touched' with compassion. Although this passage does not stress the outward movement of the bowels, it does make clear that compassion brings the bodily of experience of the suffering person into the onlooker: he 'puts on the person of an other' and feels his suffering 'as though the bowells of him that is in miserie were in his body'. If modern empathy is often described as placing oneself in the other's situation, the bowels of compassion move outward into the suffering body of the other and back in again.[47] Richard Meek in the preceding chapter discusses how Holland encourages his congregation to imagine themselves into the situation of Job, 'as if their soules had been in his soules stead'. He interprets this as a sophisticated conception of sympathy, involving role-playing and imaginative substitution. Perkins's image of the adoption of the bowels of a suffering person into the onlooker's body offers listeners a more embodied visualisation of the outward and inward movement of their feeling of another's pain.

Cultivating Bowels of Compassion

If the experience of fellow-feeling with other human beings was central to Reformed faith, and if the capacity to share in another person's suffering was determined by the softness and openness of one's bowels, which practices did Reformed ministers recommend to soften and open the bowels? Alec Ryrie has shown that in the case of a hardened heart, the diagnosis was easier than the cure. 'Some ministers made specific suggestions, such as seeking spiritual counsel, adopting new regimes of reading and fasting, or simply turning up to more sermons,' he notes. The prime remedy, however, was sheer effort. If devotees vigorously engaged in acts of prayer and religious exercises, their hearts would soften spontaneously. This performative cure, however, was 'theologically dubious and, sometimes, ineffective'.[48] In the case of dried and closed bowels of compassion, we find similar remedies – eliciting similar theological objections – in seventeenth-century sermons. Practical recommendations are characterised by a tension between words and deeds, between inward and outward compassion.

Church of England clergyman Henry Bedel (1536/7–1576), for example, thinks it shameful that the poor are scorned by Protestants, since his congregation's faith should be grounded in love: 'surely it is a shame to see and knowe the contempt of the poore, especially nowe in the time of the Gospel, when faith shuld so spread her selfe in our heartes: faith I say that is exercised in love, that bragging much of faith in wordes, do not correspondantly aunswer the same in deede'. He asks his congregation: 'is this the life of Christians? Is this the fruite of our Gospell? Is this the mercye that we learn by the word?'[49] Bedel's concerns, like Smith's, focus on 'words' as opposed to 'deeds', on the proper way to 'exercise' love and compassion. His final exasperated question seems unwittingly to reveal a despair that the church's focus on the Word no longer offers an infrastructure for the practice, the doing, of compassion.

Other ministers also think of practices as a way to kindle compassion: they urge their congregation to engage in good works. The sheer doing would have a mollifying effect on the bowels, rekindling their capacity for compassion. As Edward Topsell told his church audience and the later readers of his sermon:

> put on compassionate hearts towards your poore bretheren in this time of dearth, and thinke not sufficient to distribute once, but stretch out your hands againe and againe, to help the necessities of the poore sainets which dayly cry vnto you, give, give: that your love may increase, your compassion augment, and your fellow-feeling of the same hunger, may worke a fellow feeding on the same reliefe.[50]

Topsell proposes the recurrent act of stretching out one's hand to give charitably as a mode of training to increase love and augment compassion. Bodily practices are seen to alter the state of mind: just as the closing of the bowels caused tightfistedness, the stretching of the hand to give to the poor increases the capacity for compassion. Once compassion has been sufficiently kindled, the giver will be able to attain a 'fellow-feeling of the same hunger', which will in turn 'worke a fellow-feeding' – a charitable sharing of food with the poor. Like Scheer, early modern ministers thought that the practice of charity generated the experience of compassion. With Thomas Becon, they thought that the practice of charity incrementally increases one's capacity for fellow-feeling: 'let us go forwarde dayly somwhat in modestie, lenitie, softnes, gentlenes, mercie, compassion, & in suche other workes of godlines. For if thou haste but ones begunne, there is a good hope: halfe the matter is done, when it is ones well begunne. And although thou procedest but slowly, yet geve not over.'[51] The experience of compassion is engendered through practice – not only in the sense of doing compassion, but practice also in the sense of exercising and training it: the repeated rehearsal of works of compassion strengthens the capacity for fellow-feeling.

This performative mode of kindling compassion was not recommended across the Protestant spectrum, however. The Puritan minister Robert Bolton, for example, frowns upon such a practical remedy for frozen bowels:

> If the world hath locked up thine heart, and congealed the bowels of thy compassions towards the poore; let the blaze of thine outward profession shine never so faire, manage the heartlesse representations of externall holinesse never so demurely; keepe the times and taskes of daily duties with never so great austeritie; nay, though thou bee able to amuse weaker Christians with some affected straines, and artificiall fervency in Prayer (for by the meere power, or rather poyson of hypocrisie and vaineglory, a man may pray sometimes to the admiration of others, especially lesse judicious, having cunningly collected the most mooving passages for that purpose, from the best-gifted in that kinde, and then giving an enforced action and life unto them in the deliverie, as some in other cases act other mens inventions to the life.) I say, for all this, if the holy heate of brotherly love doth not warme thine heart, and upon occasion worke affectionately and effectually, I dare say, thou art rotten at the heart-roote, there is no true love of God in thee, no grace, no hope of salvation.[52]

For Bolton the case is clear: if a devotee's frozen bowels cannot be thawed by the heat of brotherly love, he cannot be saved. He may go through the motions of daily piety, hoping that the exercise of his Christian duty will eventually warm his heart, and he may even convince some that he does indeed experience compassion, but there is no hope of grace from God.

Bolton's suspicion of 'enforced action' is in part caused by theological anxieties about the relation between the inward experience of compassion and the outward performance of good works. Because the experience of inward compassion with a fellow Christian's suffering was the litmus test to distinguish virtuous Protestant charity from pre-Reformation traditions of good works, ministers hesitate to recommend the mere performance of good works as a remedy for closed bowels. Only if charitable deeds were accompanied by an inward feeling, were they safe from the appearance of outward deeds of hypocrisy. Robert Aylett walks this tightrope between inward and outward, Christian and hypocritical compassion in a poem on Mercy:

> Grant I may rightly sing and practise Mercy here.
> [...]
> And since 'tis not in outward workes alone,
> But inward Bowels that God doth delight,
> (Though by the one the other is best knowne)
> [...]
> Lord grant that as I of sweet Mercy sing,
> Her in my heart, deed, word, I practise may,
> Not for vaine praise or any outward thing,
> But for thy Mercy sake, my good and gracious King.[53]

The poem testifies to the fraught interdependence of outward works of mercy and the inner feeling of compassion. The speaker asks his Lord to enable him to practice Mercy 'rightly', which requires a subtle balance between good works and 'inward Bowels', so that it is clear his compassion is 'in [his] heart' and not performed for outward gains. His parenthetical remark neatly sums up the double bind between the experience of compassion and the practice of good works that this chapter focused on. Mercy in Protestant faith is grounded in a fellow-feeling between Christians that is experienced inwardly, in the bowels of compassion. It can only manifest itself, however, in the movement outward, towards the suffering other. Hardened bowels could be softened through the practice of charitable deeds; inward experience and bodily practice are intertwined: 'by the one [outward workes] the other [inward Bowels] is best knowne'.

Conclusion

Monique Scheer's view of emotions as historical practices, rooted in repeated actions in which body and mind are inextricably intertwined, provides a window onto anxieties over the 'doing' of compassion in Reformation England. Scheer's argument that certain historical inflections of emotions will slowly disappear when the practices in which they are exercised are no longer in use, throws light on the worries of

Reformed preachers over the loss of 'charitable affection' among their congregation. Although these preachers condemn traditional practices of compassion as outward and hypocritical, they remember them fondly for their capacity to cultivate fellow-feeling. Since interpersonal, social compassion was central to Protestant faith, the bowels of mercy were a vital organ: charitable deeds could only be virtuous if they sprang from the movement of these bowels. Entangled with conflicts between words and deeds, inward and outward faith, the search for religious exercises to soften and moisten the bowels of mercy reshaped the emotion of compassion in Reformation England.

Beyond the context of the Reformation, this view of compassion as a cultivated, embodied emotion can renew our thinking on the political potential of compassion. If compassion has by some been hailed as a radical spur to action and social change, the concern of critics like Lauren Berlant, Elizabeth Spelman and Sara Ahmed is that a mere transient feeling like compassion does not inspire (or even come to takes the place of) the sustained commitment required for real political transformation.[54] The early modern paradigm of compassion as an embodied experience offers a fresh perspective on this problem. If cultural theorists worry that fleeting experiences of compassion do not stimulate enquiry into the causes of suffering, Reformed clergymen and their congregations in contrast did not understand compassion as an ephemeral experience. Rather, they conceived of compassion as a capacity for sharing and responding to the suffering of others ingrained in the body through training. The bowels of compassion needed to be kept soft, moist and supple through constant practice, to root a vulnerable, open and responsive mode of being deeply inside believers' bodies.[55] As the clergyman Charles Fitz-Geffry emphasises in the epigraph to this chapter, compassion for these early modern Protestant preachers is a response embodied through practice: 'Labour for a tender heart [...] then shall your compassion extend itself more viscerally towards your afflicted brethren.'[56]

Notes

1 Charles Fitz-Geffrey, *Compassion Towards Captives* (Oxford: Leonard Lichfield, 1637), sig. E3v.
2 Henry Smith, *The Poore Mans Teares Opened in a Sermon* (London, 1592), sigs. B6v–B7r. On concerns over a lack of charity and the disappearance of charitable institutions, see also Toria Johnson's Chapter 11 in this volume.

3 Thomas Becon, *The Fortresse of the Faythfull Agaynst [ye] Cruel Assautes of Pouertie and Honger Newlye Made for the Comforte of Poore Nedye Christians* (London, 1550), sig. A8r.
4 Becon, sig. B1r.
5 Alec Ryrie, *Being Protestant in Reformation Britain* (Oxford University Press, 2013), p. 2.
6 On the redefinition of devotees' relation to Christ's suffering during the Reformation, see Jan Frans van Dijkhuizen, *Pain and Compassion in Early Modern Culture* (Oxford: Boydell and Brewer, 2012).
7 Smith, sig. A6v.
8 Steven Mullaney, *The Reformation of Emotions in the Age of Shakespeare* (University of Chicago Press, 2015), p. 16.
9 See Meek, Chapter 5, in this volume.
10 See also Richard Viladesau, *The Triumph of the Cross: The Passion of Christ in Theology and the Arts* (Oxford University Press, 2008), who writes that 'conspicuously missing' from Reformation meditations on the Passion 'are two important points that late medieval preachers insist on: exciting the heart to compassion with Christ in his suffering, and turning to [. . .] good works as a result of conversion' (p. 138). On women and the practice of affective meditation, see Femke Molenkamp, *Women and the Bible in Early Modern England: Religious Reading and Writing* (Oxford University Press, 2013), pp. 185–217.
11 Nicholas Love, *Mirror of the Blessed Life of Jesus Christ*, ed. Michael G. Sargent (New York and London: Garland Publishing, 1992), p. 163, ll. 20–21.
12 Eleanor McCullough, '"Þenke We Sadli on His Deeþ": The Hours of the Cross as a Short Passion Meditation' in S. Kelly and R. Kelly (eds.), *Devotional Culture in Late Medieval England and Europe: Diverse Imaginations of Christ's Life* (Turnhout: Brepols, 2014), p. 325.
13 Sarah McNamer, *Affective Meditation and the Invention of Medieval Compassion* (Philadelphia: University of Pennsylvania Press, 2010), p. 12.
14 McNamer, *Affective Meditation*, pp. 13 and 2.
15 Ellen Ross, *The Grief of God: Images of the Suffering Jesus in Late Medieval England* (Oxford University Press, 1997), p. 133.
16 Monique Scheer, 'Are Emotions a Kind of Practice (And Is That What Makes Them Have a History)? A Bourdieuian Approach to Understanding Emotion', *History and Theory*, 51:2 (2012), 209.
17 Margaret Wetherell, *Affect and Emotion: A New Social Science Understanding* (Los Angeles and London: Sage, 2012), p. 106; see also Herman Roodenburg, *The Eloquence of the Body: Perspectives on Gesture in the Dutch Republic* (Zwolle: Waanders, 2004).
18 Scheer, 'Are Emotions a Kind of Practice?', 205.
19 Scheer, 207.
20 Scheer, 219.
21 Richard Greenham, *The workes of the reuerend and faithfull seruant af Iesus Christ M. Richard Greenham* (London, 1612), STC 12318, sig. B6v.

22 Thomas Becon, *A New Postil* (London, 1566), sig. Qq7v.
23 Thomas Draxe, *The Christian armorie wherein is contained all manner of spirituall munition* (London, 1611), sig. X7r.
24 Ryrie, *Being Protestant*, p. 20.
25 For an overview of the connotations of the bowels in the Bible, see John Durham Peters, 'Bowels of Mercy', *BYU Studies*, 38:4 (1999), 27–41.
26 Susan Wessel, *Passion and Compassion in Early Christianity* (Cambridge University Press, 2016), p. 17.
27 *OED*, 'bowel, n, pl. collectively' sv II.3, 1 and 2, respectively.
28 William Jones, *A Commentary Upon the Epistles of Saint Paul to Philemon, and to the Hebrewes Together With a Compendious Explication of the Second and Third Epistles of Saint Iohn* (London, 1635), p. 28.
29 Thomas Adams, *The Barren Tree: A Sermon Preached at Pauls Crosse, October 26. 1623* (London, 1623), sig. H3r, in: *Five Sermons Preached upon sundry especiall Occasions* (London, 1626).
30 John Staines, 'Compassion in the Public Sphere of Milton and King Charles' in Gail Kern Paster, Katherine Rowe and Mary Floyd-Wilson (eds.), *Reading the Early Modern Passions: Essays in the Cultural History of Emotion* (Philadelphia: University of Pennsylvania Press, 2004), p. 101.
31 John R. Yamamoto-Wilson, *Discourses of Pain, Pleasure and Perversity in Early Modern England* (Abingdon: Routledge, 2016), pp. 135–36.
32 William Gouge, *The Whole Armor of God* (London, 1619), p. 376.
33 Lancelot Andrewes, *XCVI Sermons* (London, 1629), sigs. Mmmm3r–v.
34 Francis Mason, *The avthoritie of the Church in making canons and constitutions* (London, 1607), p. 15.
35 Richard Humfrey, *The Conflict of Job* (London, 1607), sig. B2r.
36 In Chapter 10, Eric Langley thoughtfully reads this movement in terms of stretching of attention to achieve a 'receptive ability to receive their pain'.
37 Anon., *Three Sermons Moving Towards Compassion* (London, 1596), sig. H3r.
38 Pierre de la Primaudaye, *The second part of the French academie*, trans. Thomas Bowes (London, 1605), sig. Q7r.
39 I base this brief overview of the various conditions of the bowels on searches in EEBO using the 'EEBO-TCP Keywords in Context' search at Early Modern Print (http://earlyprint.wustl.edu/).
40 Edwin Sandys, *Sermons made by the most reuerende Father in God* (London, 1585), sig. N5r.
41 George Downame, *Lectures on the XV. Psalme read in the cathedrall church of S. Paule, in London* (London, 1604) sig. R7r.
42 Thomas Wilcox, *Large Letters Three in Number* (London, 1589), sig. F8r–v.
43 Edward Calver, *Passion and Discretion in Youth and Age* (London, 1641), sig. I3r.
44 John King, *Lectures upon Jonas* (London, 1599), p. 311. Compare 'If God requireth such mercie of man whose bowels in ye widest are not of a *span*

breadth, what shall hee doe, whose compassions are rouled together into bowels broader than the Sea, yea, wider than the heauens?' in Zacharie Boyd, *The Last Battell of the Soule* (London, 1629), p. 344.
45 Although the opening of the lap could also refer to birth: associations between the womb, motherhood and the bowels of compassion in early modern culture would be a fruitful subject for further research.
46 William Perkins, *A godly and learned exposition of Christs Sermon in the Mount* (Cambridge, 1608), STC 19722, sig. B4r. For a slightly different version, see also his *Garden of Spiritual Flowers*.
47 On indwelling or co-inherence as a form of medieval selfhood, see Barbara Newman, 'Indwelling: A Meditation on Empathy, Pregnancy, and the Virgin Mary' in Karl F. Morrison and Rudolph M. Bell (eds.), *Studies on Medieval Empathies* (Brill: Turnhout, 2013), pp. 190–91.
48 Ryrie, *Being Protestant*, p. 24.
49 Henry Bedel, *A sermon exhorting to pitie the poore Preached the. xv. of Nouember. Anno. 1571. at Christes Churche in London* (London, 1573), sigs. D1r and B4r.
50 Edward Topsell, *The Reward of Religion* (London, 1596), sig. O5v.
51 Thomas Becon, *A new postil conteinyng most godly and learned sermons vpon all the Sonday Gospelles* (London, 1566), sig. Kk5r.
52 Robert Bolton, *Some generall directions for a comfortable walking with God* (London, 1626), sigs. S2v–S3r.
53 Robert Aylett, *The Song of Songs, which was Salomons metaphrased in English heroiks by way of dialogue* (London, 1621), pp. 159, 174 and 176.
54 On compassion's reinforcement of the status quo, see Lauren Berlant, *Compassion: The Culture and Politics of an Emotion* (New York: Routledge, 2004); Elizabeth V. Spelman, *Fruits of Sorrow: Framing Our Attention to Suffering* (Boston: Beacon Press, 1998); Sara Ahmed, *The Cultural Politics of Emotion* (London: Routledge, 2004); on compassion's capacity to inspire social and political transformation, see John D. Staines, 'Radical Pity: Responding to Spectacles of Violence in *King Lear*' in James R. Allard and Matthew R. Martin (eds.), *Staging Pain, 1580–1800: Violence and Trauma in British Theater* (Farnham: Ashgate, 2009), p. 76; Paul Hogget, 'Pity, Compassion, Solidarity' in Simon Clarke, Paul Hoggett and Simon Thompson (eds.), *Emotions, Politics, Society* (Houndmills, Basingstoke: Palgrave, 2006), pp. 145–61.
55 See also Carolyn Pedwell, who argues that 'imagination, affect and habit can be vital collaborators in the workings of social transformation. [...] [Affect] can help establish new embodied capacities and material assemblages, including those premised on empathic imagination and attunement between bodies', in 'Transforming Habit: Revolution, Routine and Social Change', *Cultural Studies*, 31 (2017), 22–23. Science is increasingly interested in the nature of compassion and the possibility of cultivating this social emotion

through exercise. The Center for Compassion and Altruism Research and Education at Stanford, for example, focuses on this subject. See: Hooria Jazaieri et al., 'A Randomized Controlled Trial of Compassion Cultivation Training', *Motivation and Emotion*, 38 (2014), 24.

56 Charles Fitz-Geffrey, *Compassion Towards Captives* (Oxford: Leonard Lichfield, 1637), sig. E3v.

PART IV

Performing

CHAPTER 7

Civic Liberties and Community Compassion
The Jesuit Drama of Poland-Lithuania

Clarinda E. Calma and Jolanta Rzegocka

Discussions of the Protestant Reformation in the Polish-Lithuanian Commonwealth tend to centre on the questions of success and failure of the religious reform in the country.[1] This chapter focuses on the ways the multi-religious public sphere of the Polish-Lithuanian Commonwealth was negotiated in theatre, and on 'the feelings of compassion which the affective technologies of the theatre could elicit'.[2] In her insightful study of compassion in James Shirley's *The Sisters* in Chapter 8, Alison Searle writes from an early modern English perspective about the ways plays exposed the limits of existing groups and made a direct appeal to spectators' compassion. A very similar process, we argue, was taking place in the Jesuit school theatre of Poland-Lithuania where compassion and pity featured prominently within the poetic theory and stage practice. The difference, however, lies in the nature of the state and political system that informed and often overshadowed the 'performance of compassion' (Alison Searle) in early modern Poland and England. 'The complexities of policing the performance of compassion within the early modern protestant state' which Alison Searle tackles in her analysis are altogether different from the realities of a republican state with an elective king (*respublica mixta*), where religious toleration became law and common good was the governing principle in public life. When King Sigismundus Augustus (1520–1572) famously said in the parliament, 'I am not the king of your consciences', refusing to take either Catholic or Protestant side, he expressed the general feeling among the nobility that religious dissent is not a matter of state politics and should rather be embraced for the sake of peaceful co-existence. Bearing these structural differences in mind, we consider the possible venues of contact where religious boundaries were negotiated and mapped onto a politics of tolerance and compassion.[3] In this chapter, we specifically look at the Jesuit school theatre as one of the venues where the multi-denominational, multi-ethnic and multi-linguistic public sphere of the Polish-Lithuanian Commonwealth was debated.

As in other European countries of the period, attempts were made in the Commonwealth of Poland-Lithuania to unify the state with the Catholic Church. However, the political class of Poland-Lithuania, with at least three major religions represented, officially secured toleration as the law of the country. One of the key legal regulations was the Warsaw Confederation of 1573, a legal guaranty of religious tolerance and civic mobilisation in the time of the *interregnum*.[4] This law, passed during a time of political instability, is in stark contrast to the situation in England in 1642, when the court of Charles I withdrew to York, described in the prologue of Shirley's *Sisters* as: 'the whole Town is not well'. A political vacuum, as Searle notes, was in England 'rapidly filled by politic opportunists', and the theatre expressed these tensions very well days before it was closed. In Poland, the political vacuum generated a situation in which huge common effort was directed at strengthening the bonds between multi-religious nobility to ensure all groups had their proper representation. To some, it was political freedom and civic mobilisation, to others a sign of discord and anarchy. So pressing was the issue that Jesuit Piotr Skarga (1536–1612), later a preacher to King Sigismundus III Vasa (1587–1632), criticised the 1573 law in several tracts.[5]

The Polish-Lithuanian nobility held on to the articles of the Warsaw Confederation to secure their political rights and peaceful coexistence when the *cuius regio, eius religio* principle was adopted in most of Europe. The Polish-Lithuanian Commonwealth provided a safe haven for religious refugees from other parts of Europe – Protestants as well as Catholics, and also people of Orthodox, Judaic and Muslim faiths.[6] Although throughout the sixteenth and seventeenth centuries the degree of political and religious tolerance varied and was contested by political parties, an ideal of common good, faith, good will and conscience prevailed in this multi-religious country.

Members of the political class of the nobility acknowledged a brotherly bond between them, a bond that made them all, irrespective of their economic status, members of the same family (estate). It is fellow-feeling and political wisdom that permeate the preamble to the Warsaw Confederation in which the nobles agree 'to maintain and observe among ourselves peace, justice, order and the defense of the Commonwealth'.[7] Common good was the cementing force that allowed the nobility to overcome their religious and political differences.[8] Compassion subsumed under the early modern Polish word *miłosierdzie* (mercy) was part of *vita activa civilis* and had a huge political impact in early modern Poland-Lithuania. It strengthened the brotherly bonds within the nobility, cemented political bonds across the country and transformed the idea of common good into real political principle.[9]

One of the key decisions in the Catholic Church authorities' response to the Reformation was to bring the Jesuits to Poland-Lithuania in 1564. They were invited to the town of Braunsberg (Braniewo) in Royal Prussia in northeast Poland by Cardinal Stanislaus Hosius, who generously supported their house and college. An academy run by the Jesuits was soon opened in Wilno (Vilnius) in 1579, one of the two capitals of the Commonwealth. The Wilno college was granted the status of an academy by the royal charter of the King of Poland Stefan Batory and the bull of Pope Gregory XIII. The Jesuits were undoubtedly in the avant-garde of secondary and higher education in the country; when the Society of Jesus was dissolved in 1773, there were 66 colleges in Poland-Lithuania (35 in Poland and 31 in Lithuania) with circa 20,000 students.[10] With 126 secondary schools in total in the country, the Jesuit schools comprised half of the number of schools. The Jesuit system of education was thereby one of the key institutions in the Catholic Reformation movement; their preaching and their educational efforts, supported by the king and some members of the nobility, were one of the reasons for massive reconversions in the country. Within the span of two generations of Polish-Lithuanian nobility, the Catholic Church in Poland-Lithuania was able to radically reform itself, and offer a modernised model of education and a new style of preaching that appealed to the nobility.

Piotr Skarga's Economy of Mercy

Piotr Skarga, the royal preacher and the rector of the Jesuit Academy in Wilno, extensively preached on mercy in relation to the political and moral life of the country.[11] He gave his fullest examination of the concept of mercy in *Sermons on Mercy* (*Kazania o miłosierdziu*, 1610), where he presented mercy as coming from God and as a foundation of all other virtues.[12] In his *Sermons for Sundays and Feast-days* (*Kazania na niedziele i święta*, 1597), Skarga gave love priority over mercy, and claimed that mercy and all acts of charity follow from love.[13] Through his extensive pastoral and charitable work, Skarga developed a deep understanding of the act of mercy as a mutually enriching reciprocal act. In his famous *Second Sejm Sermon* (*Kazanie wtóre*) in the series of *Sejm Sermons* (*Kazania Sejmowe*, 1597), written for the Polish-Lithuanian parliamentarians, Skarga subtly graded the stages of love and mercy:

> The wider the brotherly love, the better. It is good to love a neighbour, it is better to love all the people living in town, and the best is to love all the citizens of the kingdom and do good to them or suffer for their sake. It is worthwhile keeping peace and concord among the simple folk, it is even more worthwhile to keep peace among the lords who rule or who establish laws, and it is the most worthwhile to keep peace among the kings who bring peace to the world with their concord. It is to this wide and profound love that you must inspire yourself, virtuous Lords, who have come here to consider and debate the ways to protect your people, and to show your deep and sincere love for the Republic.[14]

In his preaching, Skarga proposed a certain economy of mercy: it is bestowed first of all on confessors and converts. Skarga's first and foremost practical recommendation to his fellow Catholics was to offer mercy in a proper order, first of all to the kin, then to the strangers, first to a Catholic, then to a heretic, Jew or Turk.[15] Mercy entails a judgement, since it should be bestowed on the good rather than on the evil. Skarga repeated this recommendation even when he cited the fathers of the Church who spoke in favour of the indiscriminate use of mercy. In his study of Skarga's concept of mercy, Jacek Kwosek sees a close link between mercy and the virtue of prudence. The theological virtue of love must accompany the cardinal virtue of prudence. Therefore, according to Skarga, love or emotion which prompts us to help others, to sympathise with them, has to be guided by reason and prudence.[16] It is rather a far cry from the indiscriminate compassion of the Parable of the Good Samaritan. Skarga's approach to compassion did not entail toleration: his highly influential writings also feature a language of anti-Protestant debate. He preached against the 'false teachers and heretical poison' and he also spoke about the ways the Church of his time fought 'fierce heretics and poisonous wolves'.[17] Some echoes of this approach are also to be found in the Jesuit school plays, discussed next.

Compassion and Virtue in Dramatic Theory and Performance

The political culture of Poland-Lithuania was largely shaped by the Aristotelian tradition that prevailed in the public life of the country. The state was seen as a natural society and a fulfilment of the drive for humans to associate with one another, to be part of the community.[18] Rhetoric and the art of persuasion were at the heart of public debate and they also became the strategic tools of the early agents of the Counter-Reformation. One of those tools was the Jesuit school theatre – a well-honed instrument of persuasion.[19] Jesuit books on poetics, theatre documentation and school theatre playbills from the Jesuit Province of Poland-Lithuania between 1614 and 1773 testify to the fact that theatre was an important channel for the transfer of ideas, attitudes and moral codes into the public sphere of Poland-Lithuania. Because the theatres had a huge community-building potential, much stress was put on the presentation and teaching of civic virtues to the students of the college and members of the audience.[20] While some plays were class exercises and were staged by the pupils for the pupils, most of the plays were produced for larger audiences, as they were meant to tighten links with the school patrons and city or church authorities. The audience of these plays was, like the country itself, very mixed in terms of language and religion. While the Catholic college patrons were invited and celebrated on these occasions, the plays also attracted distinguished guests of other denominations, as these were social and public events not to be missed.[21] Many Protestant parents from the lesser nobility also came to see Jesuit plays since their children were pupils at the Jesuit schools.

In addition to the school regulations, or *Ratio studiorum*, first implemented in all Jesuit colleges in 1599, Jesuit pedagogy was also largely informed by the virtues cherished by the members of the nobility who were among both the chief advocates and adversaries of the Jesuits in the country.[22] Given the Society's strong opposition to the spirit of toleration expressed in the Warsaw Confederation of 1573 on the one hand, and their firm commitment to the teaching of civic virtues on the other hand, this situation created a tension in the Jesuit portrayal of compassion. Thus, the question that must be asked is: were the Jesuit pupils and audiences encouraged to experience compassion across religious lines, or did compassion in the plays function mainly to strengthen a Catholic emotional community?

The school theatre in the Jesuit province of Poland-Lithuania may be accessed through its rich performance records collection in the form of theatre playbills[23] as well as through a treatise on practical poetics, *De perfecta poesi sive Vergilius et Homerus* (written between 1619 and 1626) by Matthias Casimirus Sarbievius (1595–1640), a Jesuit poet laureate also known as the Christian Horace. Sarbiewski was a professor of theology, rhetoric and poetics who taught at several colleges in the Jesuit Lithuanian province (Polotsk, Wilno, and Kroże).[24] Playbills or play synopses (*periochae*) were introduced by the Jesuits of Poland-Lithuania around 1614 as a means to promote the school in a given town and region. Typically consisting of four pages, the playbills were presented to students' family members, patrons of the school and distinguished guests. They served as invitations, practical summaries of the argument and elucidation of the allegorical meaning, and also as a souvenir or token of respect and gratitude. A playbill summarised the plot, choruses as well as the prologue and epilogue of the play, usually containing an allegorical message. Some playbills also contain lengthy dedications to the patrons as well as the cast list (elenchus).[25] While school theatre playbills give an overview of themes and topics that were taken up by the Jesuit professors of poetics responsible for theatre production in the colleges, the treatises on poetics provide insight into the theoretical outlook on poetry, drama and theatre in the Jesuit Polish-Lithuanian province. Thus, the sources – playbills and handbooks – may be analysed alongside each other in order to determine the degree to which compassion was present in Jesuit dramatic theory and practice.

The Polish early modern concept of compassion is expressed in the word *miłosierdzie* (mercy). It was a remarkably broad term and it carried both the meaning of compassion and sympathy (Latin, *misericordia, animus misericors, miseratio*) as well as the meaning of love (Latin, *amor, caritas*).[26] It was, first, a quality intrinsic to the nature of God, a concept crucial to an understanding of God's dealings with humankind, hence the meaning of forgiveness inherent in the concept. Mercy is a quality of God and one that God requires of his people, and sixteenth-century Polish dictionaries also note the meaning of *mercy* as pity, compassion, forgiveness and brotherly love (Latin *misericordia, miseratio, commiseratio, clementia*.)[27] *Commiseratio* and *misericordia* are also rhetorical concepts used in drama theory and performance practice, and in the Jesuit plays the emblematic figures of Amor and Caritas often appear on stage.

The Polish-Lithuanian Jesuits largely depended on Aristotelian poetics in the ways they thought about imitative arts including drama, the ways of interesting the audience (*delectare*), the ways of moving the audience (*movere*) and managing the pathos of the plot of the narrative (*pathos fabulae*). In terms of his contribution to the seventeenth-century European poetics, Sarbiewski has to be read alongside Jacobus Pontanus SJ (member of the Society of Jesus) (c. 1542–1626) and Joseph Justus Scaliger (1540–1609). Sarbiewski relies on Aristotelian poetics in most of his work, with occasional references to Scaliger's *Poetices libri septem*.[28] He is at times critical of the work of Pontanus, a highly influential Jesuit playwright and author of several works on poetics, active in Dillingen and Augsburg.[29] It is first of all Sarbiewski's Book VIII[30] and Book IX[31] of *De perfecta poesi* that focus on the affective side of poetry and dramatic theory, and are therefore particularly relevant to the theme of compassion on stage.

Book VIII discusses the means to move the reader and has a chapter on pathos, or suffering.[32] Sarbiewski claims that a definition of poetry should be broader than the Aristotelian imitation of human actions, but at the same time as a true Aristotelian and admirer of classical poetry, he criticises some of the Jesuit dramatic practices of the day, for example, the Jesuit custom of making the entire life of a saint a subject of tragedy.[33] In his criticism of the contemporary Jesuit dramatists, Sarbiewski is very much like Pontanus, who regrets that his fellow dramatists completely ignore the Aristotelian unities.[34]

Sarbiewski's theory features compassion in Book VIII of *De perfecta poesi*, where he writes on the means necessary to move the reader and focuses on pathos, which contains an element of both terror and pity.[35] There are no major differences between Aristotelian theory and Sarbiewski's treatment of it. There are some actions, he repeats after Aristotle, that incite interest rather than passion ('because of the various probable but miraculous events they contain'), and there are actions that move rather than interest ('because they contain more elements of terror and pity'). In both of these, terror and pity (*terribilium miserabiliumque*)[36] are crucial and, as they eventually also serve to stir interest, they therefore must be part of the action. Sarbiewski then discusses questions of logical and causal connections in action and the question of probability, which have to be observed in order for the reader to be moved. Thus, variety, a proper degree of terror and pity, causal connections and concern for probability are the rules of the game. They are to be followed if a reader/spectator is to be truly moved and entertained.

In Sarbiewski's theory, commiseration and pity (*commiseratio* and *misericordia*) are the words that come closest to the sense of compassion, and they are to be taken as theoretical Latin concepts that circulated in the Polish-Lithuanian province as well as beyond it thanks to the outstanding popularity of Sarbiewski's lectures in Latin Europe.[37] Dramatic practice in the Polish-Lithuanian province of his times significantly differed from the theory Sarbiewski aimed to codify. In Book IX, Sarbiewski describes some aspects of theatre production that he thinks are important for the overall effect, for moving the audience and creating the context for the expression of terror and pity in drama. He discusses in separate chapters theatre lighting,[38] the layout of the stage,[39] the stage set[40] and ways of designing the backdrop.[41] Almost every chapter of Book IX concludes with a brief reference to the way 'they do it in Rome'.[42] Sarbiewski spent his early years in the Society in Rome (1622–1625), and he may be referring to the Jesuit theatre practice in the Collegium Romanum. In any case, the Roman theatre of the period is taken as exemplary and the diagrams of the stage mechanics that one of the manuscript copies contains are drawings based on Roman prototypes. Sarbiewski emphasises that stage sets and mechanics are crucial in evoking the emotional response to tragedy and in building the necessary pity and terror. In his handbook, we see a mechanical theory of stage compassion.

The Playbills: Compassion in and across Religious Communities?

Mercy, compassion and commiseration were frequently evoked in the surviving play synopses (playbills) that document individual performances in Poland-Lithuania, though it is the term *mercy* rather than *compassion* that is contained in the playbills.[43] In the playbills that have been found so far, the theme of compassion is never signalled in the title. There are, however, three groups of plays that were staged in Wilno, the centre of the Jesuit Lithuanian Province, that take on the theme of compassion in the broad sense: 1) a large group of plays on the persecution of Christians in different countries (English Catholics,[44] Jesuit missionaries to Japan and China,[45] Orthodox Christians in pagan Lithuania); 2) plays about tyrants whose heart is softened by mercy and compassion; and 3) plays that feature Poles and Lithuanians taken as captives by the Tartars and Turks in the seventeenth century. Above all, these performances express sympathy for human beings opposed to those in power. All the plays documented in the playbills pose a variety of questions: what are the obligations of those in power, how does one behave in the face of a tyrant, what are the limits of mercy and brotherly compassion? The playbills also raise questions about the sources and limits of compassion. While there are plays in which the limits of mercy and compassion are mapped onto religious boundaries, there are also plays that arouse compassion for other Christian denominations. For example, a 1727 play from Minsk, *Sacrum foedus*, features Constantinus Ostrogski (c. 1460–1530), a commander of Lithuanian military forces who was Orthodox and remained in steady loyalty to the Catholic Sigismund I, the King of Poland and a Grand Duke of Lithuania.[46] It is symptomatic that there are almost no fiercely anti-Protestant plays, one possible reason being a largely tolerant and open political culture that excluded straightforward attacks on religion.[47] The principle of religious denomination is used in the school plays in various, often contrasting, contexts: pagan rulers are represented as merciful and compassionate, even if the same rulers may in another play persecute Orthodox Christians whom the audience is invited to sympathise with and pray for. For example, a 1732 Vilnius play, *Sacra fames*, produced at Shrovetide, tells the story of martyrdom of three Orthodox monks: Johannes, Antonius and Eustachius. Duke Olgierd (c. 1296–1377), the pagan duke of Lithuania, ordered the monk, and members of his court, to be executed in c. 1347 as they insisted on observing a holy fast. The play is a warning against gluttony and debauchery and teaches a moral lesson of moderation, a fitting message before Lent. Interestingly, Duke Olgierd was the father of Duke Jogaila (c. 1352/1362–1434) who converted to Western Christianity in 1386 and became the Christian King of Poland and Lithuania, and a founder of the powerful Jagiellonian dynasty whose four generations of kings ruled in Central Europe for two centuries. However, rather than celebrate the forefather of the Polish-Lithuanian kings (as, for example, did the 1687 Vilnius play *Olgerdus magnus*), this Jesuit play represents him as a tyrant persecuting Christians.[48] The play makes use of a very well-known chapter of Lithuanian history, and it focuses on the theme of Christian martyrs opposing a tyrant rather than on the specific politico-historical issues. The first Christian martyrs in Lithuania were Orthodox and by making them the main protagonists of the play, the Jesuits transcended religious divisions and commemorated the three martyrs who stood up to a tyrant, thus inviting community compassion and celebration of religious orthodoxy in the Polish-Lithuanian context.[49]

Plays like *Sacra fames* show that compassion in Jesuit school theatre occasionally cut across religious differences. It is more difficult to establish how exactly the limits of compassion were set in relation to the Protestants, as there is only one surviving clearly anti-Protestant play and no depictions of Protestants in the Polish-Lithuanian playbills except for the allegorical characters of Heresy, Infidelity and Impiety (*Heresia, Infidelitas, Impietas*).[50] Yet while the Jesuit university and its theatre waged war against Protestantism, it was usually careful enough not to point to individual Protestants as their enemies, considering the strong political bonds among religiously mixed Polish-Lithuanian nobility. This tension marks performance practice well until the dissolution of the Order in 1773. Still, some plays mapped the limits of compassion seamlessly along religious fault lines. A 1731 end-of-the-school-year play from Wilno *Signaculum Supra*, set in the late sixteenth century, represents the Protestant community opposing the founding of the Jesuit academy.[51] The play's main protagonist, the Transylvanian noble Gáspar Békés (1520–1579), argues that the new academy will limit the rights and liberties of the nobility. In the play Békés, an Arian, is stricken by apoplexy and dies. Békés did indeed take part in the triumphal royal entry in Vilnius in 1579, but died soon afterwards having caught a cold. He was refused a burial in all the cemeteries of religious denominations in Vilnius and was eventually buried at royal command on one of the hills of Vilnius, which is still today called the Békés hill (Polish, *Góra Bekieszowa*, Lithuanian, *Bekešo kalnas*). While the play uses some historical facts, it offers an uncompassionate view of the country's Protestant community and brands them as enemies of true learning. This view of the country's Protestants is clearly in conflict with the political practice of the day, where the principle of tolerance was adopted on a wide scale, and it thus testifies to a Jesuit educational agenda that limited compassion to certain communities.

Compassion with the Captives

One of the most numerous groups of playbills depicting compassion on stage features Poles and Lithuanians taken as captives by the Tartars and Turks in the seventeenth century. The playbills engage with the political realities of the period, as well as with fears shared by many members of the audience. The Polish-Lithuanian Commonwealth bordered in the south-east on the Ottoman Empire, and raids of the Crimean Tartars and Turks were not infrequent. Inhabitants of the south-eastern territories who were taken captive would become slaves of the Ottoman Empire for many decades, sometimes for life. An organised border defense, military actions and the need for constant vigilance became part of the Polish-Lithuanian identity and this is where the idea of Poland as the outpost of Western civilization, *antemurale* or the bulwark of Christianity, came from.[52] It was specifically the task of the Order of the Most Holy Trinity for the Redemption of the Captives to ransom Christians held captive by non-Christians. Invited from France to Poland-Lithuania in 1685 by King John III Sobieski, the Trinitarians established their churches and monasteries along the eastern borders of the Commonwealth, enabling them to organise missions to ransom people from the Tartar captivity.[53] The Trinitarians introduced to Poland-Lithuania the cult of Jesus the Captive. Plays that aroused compassion for Polish captives of the Ottoman Empire therefore served to shape a Christian, specifically Catholic, emotional community. Considerable iconographic and historical evidence suggests that captivity was the reality of many Polish-Lithuanian border households, as families preserved stories over generations about people gone missing or miraculously recognised in captivity and ransomed. In their plays featuring 'Captivi Poloni', the Jesuits therefore struck a familiar note. Since many Jesuits were sons of the local nobility, they knew the motif would sound familiar to their students and their families who came to see the theatre performances. In accordance with Aristotelian dramatic theory, their familiarity with the threat of being captured may have made these audiences more susceptible to the experience of compassion.

In view of these politico-religious tensions at the border, it is perhaps not surprising that plays on this subject reserved their appeal to compassion for Catholic protagonists. A good example is a 1684 playbill from Vilnius, *Victoria Mariae seu Vienna Austriae*.[54] The source of the play is a letter King John III Sobieski sent to his royal consort, Queen Maria, after the victorious battle at Vienna against the Turks on 13 September 1683. The audience follows the story of a Polish captive in the Ottoman court. The Pole brings the news of the approaching battle; he is then interrogated and eventually dies unwavering in his faith. Compassion for the Polish captive assumes an important place in the play as the audience moves from compassion with the inhabitants of the besieged city of Vienna, to fellow-feeling with the 'Captivus Polonus' who dies in the Turkish camp. In this play, the audience is asked to pity the soul and sympathise with the Polish captive before the final victorious battle ensues. Compassion with one's fellow Catholic, a martyr whose fate was dangerously familiar to that of the inhabitants of the southern provinces of the Commonwealth, in this play serves to shore up the celebration of the victory of Christianity over the Ottoman Empire.

Whereas the boundary between Catholic and Protestant religious communities could sometimes be broached in Jesuit school theatre by not making direct reference to the Protestants or by resorting to allegorical rather than to historical characters, the limits of compassion prove far less porous in the case of the Islamic faith. The play that comes closest to arousing compassion for Turkish victims of the war is able to do so only after these Turkish captives have converted to Catholicism. *Zodiacus Poloniarum* (Vilnius, 1718) features 12 'Poloni Captivi' balanced by 12 'Ephebi Turcici' and 12 'Hospites Sarmatici'.[55] We see twelve young Polish prisoners in Turkish captivity who are unsure of their fate. They are admitted to the Ottoman court to replace 12 young Turks who are dismissed from their service. The Turkish emperor is willing to keep the Polish boys at his court provided they renounce the Catholic faith. The captives refuse to do so and therefore die as martyrs. The audience's compassion for these Catholic martyrs would have been further stimulated by the choice of actors. What is more, a few of the Turkish courtiers express admiration and sympathy for the Polish captives. They are executed together with the captives, and die expressing their wish to become Christians. The compassion expressed by the Turkish courtiers may have been intended as a dramatic device to channel the audience's compassion with the captives, an onstage example of the reaction expected from the playgoers. Moreover, compassion functions in the play as a litmus test for conversion to the Catholic faith: since the Turkish courtiers are able to experience compassion for the Polish captives, they are eligible to join the Christian community. The play thereby seems to reinforce rather than trouble the boundaries of religious emotional communities.

Conclusion

In the multi-ethnic, multi-religious and multi-linguistic reality of early modern Poland-Lithuania, the limits of compassion were shifting and did not depend only on religious principles; they also depended on political ones, as can be seen from the examples discussed in this chapter. The normative poetics of the day suggested that pity and commiseration were crucial elements of tragedy, and the playbills testify that although the poetic rules were often bent (when, for example, allegorical characters appeared on stage), the plays incited both terror and pity in their audiences. Some plays seem to extend compassion across confessional lines, if the dramatic argument requires it; others refuse such emotional flexibility. The Jesuits arriving in Poland-Lithuania found themselves in a complex multi-ethnic and multi-religious reality where a clear anti-Protestant message could not be easily followed, and thus their theatre, homiletics and poetic theory became spaces where mercy, compassion and tolerance were continually questioned, debated and negotiated in the shifting context of the Polish-Lithuanian political tradition.

Notes

1 For a well-balanced perspective see Maciej Ptaszyński, 'The Polish-Lithuanian Commonwealth' in Howard Louthan and Graeme Murdoch (eds.), *A Companion to the Reformation in Central Europe* (Leiden: Brill, 2015), p. 40.
2 Alison Searle, Chapter 8, this volume.
3 This chapter presents preliminary results of the research project 'Civic Education in Jesuit School Theatres of the Polish-Lithuanian Commonwealth: Playbills in the Jesuit archives of Vilnius, Rome and selected Polish libraries', funded by the National Science Centre of Poland UMO-2014/13/B/HS2/00524.

4 Full text in English translation: www.reformation.org/confederation-of-warsaw.html.
5 Skarga opposed the idea of inter-confessional confederation in a number of polemical tracts: *Proces konfederaciej* (Kraków, 1595), rev. ed., *Proces na konfoederacją z poprawą i odprawą przeciwnika* (n.p., 1596), *Discurs na Confoederacją* (Krakow, 1607). Paradoxically, while being uncompassionate towards the reformers and critical of the tightening of inter-confessional relations in the public sphere, Skarga contributed enormously to philanthropy and charitable works in the country. He almost single-handedly started that 'sanctified Contagion' of Mercy (Senault) and compassion towards fellow-citizens in Poland-Lithuania by establishing the Archconfraternity of Mercy in Krakow in 1584 which is still in operation. The motto of the Archconfraternity is 'Semino metam' (I sow so that I reap). Skarga also opened in Krakow a *mons pietatis* – a pawnbroker office run as a charity offering financial loans without interest to those in need.
6 For a recent examination of the exchange of ideas and book circulation between Elizabethan England and the Polish-Lithuanian Commonwealth, see Teresa Bela, Clarinda Calma and Jolanta Rzegocka (eds.), *Publishing Subversive Texts in Elizabethan England and the Polish-Lithuanian Commonwealth* (Leiden: Brill, 2016).
7 'We have all sedulously attempted at the Warsaw meeting, as an example to our descendants to maintain and observe among ourselves peace, justice, order and the defense of the Commonwealth. Therefore, we swear and commit ourselves, according to our faith, our good will, and our conscience'. Warsaw Confederation (1573): www.reformation.org/confederation-of-warsaw.html.
8 Two recent studies on the Polish-Lithuanian Commonwealth focus extensively on the idea of common good in the political life of the country: Robert Frost, *The Oxford History of Poland Lithuania*, vol. 1: *The Making of the Polish-Lithuanian Union, 1385–1569* (Oxford University Press, 2015); Benedict Wagner-Rundell, *Common Wealth, Common Good: The Politics of Virtue in Early Modern Poland Lithuania* (Oxford University Press, 2015).
9 Consensus was the primary rule of operation of the Polish-Lithuanian parliament (the Diet); see Michał Kulecki, 'A Parliamentary Procedure' in Wojciech Gilewski (ed.), *Poland: The Heritage of Parliamentarism until 1791* (Brussels, n.p., 2009), pp. 124–26. Consensus and the so-called concordant election (Pl zgodny obiór) were also applied in the dietines (local parliaments).
10 Kazmierz Puchowski, *Edukacja historyczna w jezuickich kolegiach Rzeczypospolitej 1565–1773* (Gdańsk: Wydawnictwo Uniwersytetu Gdańskiego, 1999), p. 20.
11 For a study of the concept of mercy in the preaching of Piotr Skarga, see Jacek Kwosek, *Kategoria miłosierdzia w kazaniach księdza Piotra Skargi* (Katowice: Wydawnictwo Uniwersytetu Śląskiego, 2013).
12 Piotr Skarga, 'Kazania o miłosierdziu' in *Kazania przygodne z inemi drobniejszemi pracami o różnych rzeczach wszelakim stanom należących* (Kraków, 1610).

13 Kwosek, *Kategoria miłosierdzia*, p. 241.
14 Piotr Skarga, *The Second Sejm Sermon* (Kazanie sejmowe wtóre), http://literat.ug.edu.pl/skarga/0002.htm (translation Jolanta Rzegocka).
15 Kwosek, *Kategoria miłosierdzia*, p. 242.
16 Kwosek, p. 242.
17 Skarga. *The Second Sejm Sermon.*
18 Cf. the recent studies on the political ideas and values of the Polish-Lithuanian Commonwealth: Anna Grześkowiak-Krwawicz, *Regina libertas. Wolność w polskiej myśli politycznej XVIII wieku* (Gdańsk: Słowo/Obraz Terytoria, 2006) and Dorota Pietrzyk-Reeves, *Ład rzeczypospolitej. Polska myśl polityczna XVI wieku a klasyczna tradycja republikańska* (Krakow: Księgarnia Akademicka, 2012). See also Dorota Pietrzyk-Reeves, 'O pojęciu *Rzeczypospolita (res publica)* w polskiej myśli politycznej XVI wieku', *Czasopismo Prawno-historyczne*, 1 (2010), 38–64; Norman Davies, *God's Playground A History of Poland*, vol. 1: *The Origins to 1795*, rev. ed. (Oxford University Press, 2005).
19 The mutual impact of the pedagogy of the Polish-Lithuanian Jesuits and the public and political life in the country has been the subject of research of Kazimierz Puchowski, *Edukacja historyczna w jezuickich kolegiach Rzeczypospolitej 1565–1773* (Gdańsk: Wydawnictwo Uniwersytetu Gdańskiego, 1999), *Jezuickie kolegia szlacheckie w Rzeczypospolitej Obojga Narodów* (Gdańsk: Wydawnictwo Uniwersytetu Gdańskiego, 2007).
20 Major studies on Polish-Lithuanian school theatre: Irena Kadulska (ed.), *Europejskie związki dawnego teatru szkolnego i europejska wspólnota dawnych kalendarzy* (Gdańsk: Wydawnictwo Uniwersytetu Gdańskiego, 2003); Jerzy Axer, 'Polski teatr jezuicki jako teatr polityczny' in *Jezuici a kultura polska*, ed. Ludwik Grzebień (Kraków: WAM, 1993), pp. 11–21; Jan Okoń, *Dramat i teatr szkolny. Sceny jezuickie XVII wieku* (Wrocław: Zakład Narodowy im. Ossolińskich, 1970); Jan Poplatek, *Studia z dziejów jezuickiego teatru szkolnego w Polsce* (Wrocław: Ossolineum, 1957).
21 For example, the Grand Chancellor of Lithuania, as well as the Palatine of Vilnius, Mikołaj Krzysztof Radziwiłł (1549–1616), then a Calvinist, saw the play *Tragoedia Absalonis Rebellis* that the Jesuits produced at the start of the winter term in Wilno in 1585. The Palatine came with his wife and a young son to see a play on the necessity of the proper upbringing of children.
22 Janusz Tazbir, *Literatura antyjezuicka w Polsce, 1578–1625* (Warszawa: Ludowa Spółdzielnia Wydawnicza, 1963).
23 So far, we have been able to retrieve c. 400 theatre playbills from the Vilnius University Library alone. These pertain to the Jesuit theatre in Vilnius, Warsaw, Braniewo (Braunsberg) and a number of other colleges in the Polish-Lithuanian Jesuit province. The main bibliography of all Jesuit playbills in Poland-Lithuania as well as in the former German Province (e.g. Wrocław, Świdnica) lists 770 playbills: Władysław Korotaj (ed.), *Dramat staropolski od początków do powstania Sceny Narodowej. Bibliografia*, vol. II:

Programy drukiem wydane do r. 1765, part 1: Programy teatru jezuickiego (Wrocław: Ossolineum, 1965).

24 Matthias Casimirus Sarbievius, *De perfecta poesi, sive Vergilius et Homerus* (in ms before 1626). Book IX of the treatise entitled "De Tragoedia et comoedia, sive Seneca et Terentius" discusses dramatic poetry. Two student manuscript copies of lecture notes of *De perfecta poesi* are kept in the Princes Czartoryski Library, Krakow, Poland: Czartoryski Library Ms 1446 and Czartoryski Library Ms 1858 (this copy includes original stage set drawings). It was first published by V. I. Rezanov, *K istorii russkoj dramy. Poetika M. K. Sarbiewskogo* (Nieżin: Tipo-litografija W.K. Melenskogo, 1911). A modern critical edition of the mss, including drawings from Ms 1858, can be found in Matthias Casimirus Sarbievius, *De perfecta poesi, sive Vergilius et Homerus. O poezji doskonałej czyli Wergiliusz i Homer*, Biblioteka Pisarzów Polskich. Seria B, nr. 4, ed. Stanisław Skimina, trans. Marian Plezia (Wrocław: Ossolineum, 1954). All subsequent refences will be to the critical edition.

25 Arguably, the Jesuits invented the playbill in the early modern era. As opposed to the early modern English playbills that would be attached to posts all around a city on the day of a performance, the Jesuit playbills were handed out or sent to the members of the audience beforehand or even after the play as a souvenir. Since they are not as ephemeral as the English playbills, they are still found all across Europe, as well as in Polish and Lithuanian libraries, although they were often miscatalogued or misplaced in library holdings as the understanding of the function of the Jesuit theatre and its records waned in the late eighteenth century. A seminal study of Polish-Lithuanian Jesuit playbills is Jan Okoń, *Dramat i teatr szkolny* (1970).

26 '*Miłosierdzie*' (English 'mercy') in *Słownik staropolski*, vol. IV, ed. Władysław Kuraszkiewicz et al. (Wrocław, 1965).

27 '*Miłosierdzie*' (English 'mercy') in *Słownik polszczyzny XVI wieku*, vol. 14, ed. Maria R. Mayenowa (Wrocław, 1982).

28 Sarbievius relies on a translation by Alessandro Pazzi (Paccius): *Aristotelis poetica, per Alexandrum Paccium Patritium Florentinum in latinum conversa* (Venice: Aldus, 1536). See Skimina, 'Introduction', p. LII–LIII.

29 Sarbievius, *De perfecta poesi*, Liber IX, p. 228. Rezanov argues that Sarbiewski's theory also shows the influence of the unpublished work of Italian Jesuit Alessandro Donati, *De arte poetica libri tres* (Köln, 1633), Rezanov, *Kisstorii russkoj dramy*, p. 14.

30 Sarbiewski, *De perfecta poesi*, Liber VIII, 'De iis rebus, quae necessariae sunt ad movendum, seu pathis fabulae', pp. 219–27.

31 Sarbiewski, *De perfecta poesi*, Liber IX, 'De tragoedia et comoedia sive Seneca et Terentius', pp. 228–511, illustrated with the drawings of stage sets from Ms Czartoryski Library 1858.

32 Sarbiewski, *De perfecta poesi*, Liber VI, 'De perturbatione', pp. 224–27.

33 Sarbiewski, p. 231: 'As we have earlier mentioned in the part on stage and machines, we shall deal with those issues here, as there are many who commit mistakes in this respect, such as in writing the story of the tragedy or comedy

or when they portray the whole life of a certain character' (translated by Clarinda Calma).
34 Fidel Rädle, 'Jesuit Theatre in Germany, Austria and Switzerland' in Jan Bloemendal and Howard B. Norland (eds.), *Drama and Theatre in Early Modern Europe* (Leiden: Brill, 2013), vol. III, p. 268.
35 'Haec ut dixit Aristoteles, est actio letifera continens terrificum quid et commiserabile', 'This is, says Aristotle, a lethal action which has something terrible and pity-inspiring' (translated by Jolanta Rzegocka), Sarbiewski, *De perfecta poesi*, Liber VIII, caput VI. 'De perturbatione', p. 224. Redaction B of the manuscript (Ms Czartoryski Library 1446) has *'miserabile'*.
36 Sarbiewski, *De perfecta poesi*, p. 219.
37 Sarbiewski's poetic theory was hugely popular all across Europe throughout the seventeenth century and well into the eighteenth century when many manuscript copies were still in circulation in Europe. A regular canon priest from Köln, Jan Michael van der Ketten was known to have planned an edition of Sarbiewki's work on poetics around 1721; unfortunately, the plan was never carried out. Cf. Skimina, Introduction, pp. XXXIV–XXXV.
38 Sarbiewski, *De perfecta poesi*, p. 231.
39 Sarbiewski, p. 231.
40 Sarbiewski, p. 232.
41 Sarbiewski, p. 232.
42 Sarbiewski, pp. 231, 232, 233.
43 Polish theatre historical studies of playbills: Wanda Roszkowska, 'Uwagi o programowości teatru barokowego w Polsce', pp. 47–79; Władysław Korotaj, 'Z problematyki staropolskich programów teatralnych', pp. 81–109; Tadeusz Bieńkowski, 'Na marginesie lektury staropolskich programów teatralnych' in Wanda Roszkowska (ed.), *Wrocławskie spotkania teatralne* (Wrocław: Ossolineum, 1967), pp. 111–19. The 'grammar' of playbills has been discussed by Jan Okoń in his study of Jesuit school theatre, *Dramat i teatr szkolny* (1970), pp. 12–79.
44 Thomas Pounde (Thomas Pondus) playbills and plays in Jesuit school theatre in the former Polish-Lithuanian Jesuit Province: [Brzozowski Marcin?]: *Lusus in feria desinens* (Vilnius, 1733), Warsaw National Library (Warszawa BN), XVIII.3.5027; [J. Katenbring] *Próżność nad różnościami albo Tomasz Poundus, tragedia Teofili i Katarzynie Radziwiłłownom przypisana od młodzi w szkołach nieświeskich Societatis Jesu ćwiczącej się, na Sali książęcej wyprawiona roku 1755 dnia 27 lipca* (Nieśwież, 1755). One play on Thomas Pounde is documented in a playbill from Świdnica (D Schweidnitz, L Suidnicium), the German Jesuit Province (present-day Poland): Siegl, Johannes: *Heroica de instabilitate gloriae vindicto seu Thomas Pondo caducam anlae [!] pompam cum Jesu societate mutans* (Świdnica, 1722), Korotaj, *Dramat staropolski*, n. 385 (all subsequent references will be to this bibliography).
45 Playbills on Japan: *Arbor Vita seu Crux meliorem* (Vilnius, 1691), Korotaj, *Dramat staropolski*, n. 523; *Trophaeum innocentiae* (Braniewo, 1717), Vilnius University Library (VUB) IV 32427; *Conviva dolus, ad laetas Bacchi*

(Braniewo, 1723), *VUB IV* 31647; *Arbor Vitae crux Christi* (Braniewo, 1723), *VUB IV* 30545; *Terminus interminabilis amoris crucis* (Grodno, 1712), *VUB IV* 16832; *Solitudo popularis et solitaria caelestis* (Warsaw, 1713), *VUB IV* 30911; *Wet za wet chrześcijańskie* (Vilnius, 1704), The Wroblewskis Library of the Lithuanian Academy of Sciences, Vilnius F-266-203; *Solium regnantis a lingo Dei* (Vilnius, 1714), Korotaj n. 581; [Berzański, Michał], *Flaminia inversae Romae amoris* (Vilnius, 1723), *VUB IV* 31331; [Wazgird, Kazimierz?] *Scena post triste Deo et Angelis* (Vilnius, 1737), SD XVIII.3.8475, http://polona.pl/item/16427470/0/; *Foecunda tyrannis* (Vinius, 1743), Korotaj n. 639; *Felicitas constantiae comes seu Titus* (Vilnius, 1749), Korotaj n. 643. Playbills on China: *Candidatus eloquentiae* (Braniewo, 1729), *VUB IV* 31589.
46 *Sacrum foedus*, Minsk, 1727, *VUB IV* 23578.
47 This is a hypothesis that needs further research, as on the one hand the political writing of Poland-Lithuania provides ample evidence of calls for religious differences to be curbed by the principle of the common good and peaceful co-existence. See Pietrzyk-Reeves, *Ład rzeczypospolitej* (The Order of Respublica) (Kraków: Księgarnia akademicka, 2012). On the other, Lithuanian cities of Wilno, Mińsk, Nowogródek saw a series of anti-Protestant tumults at the end of the seventeenth century, with the case of the infamous Wilno tumult of 1682 being discussed by the Parliament. See Tomasz Kempa, *Konflikty wyznaniowe w Wilnie od początku reformacji do końca XVII wieku* (Toruń: Wydawnictwo Naukowe Uniwersytetu Mikołaja Kopernika, 2016).
48 *Olgerdus magnus Lithuaniae dux*, Vilnius, 1687, VUB III 19755 adl.
49 [Obrąpalski P.], *Sacra fames inter profans dapes*, Vilnius, 1732, VUB IV 32040. The playbill has been edited and analysed by Darius Baronas, *Trys Vilniaus kankiniai. Gyvenimas ir istorija* (Vilnius: Aidai, 2000). The play's argument mentions 'the Holy martyrs Joannes, Antonius and Eustachius, courtiers of Olgierd, the grand duke of Lithuania, of noble decent... executed in Vilna in 1328, buried in the Greek-Orthodox Basilica of the Holy Trinity in Vilna'. The play is based on the historical work of Albert Wijuk-Kojałowicz (SJ) (1609–1677), *Miscellanea rerum ad statum eccleciasticum in Magno Lithuaniae Ducatu pertinentia* (Vilnius: Typis Academicis, 1650), fol. 8–9.
50 For example, in a playbill *Constantinus Magnus*, Vilnius, 1688, Korotaj n. 529; Heresy attempts to shorten the life of Pope Gregory XIII in a playbill *Solennitas secunda*, Vilnius ca. 1691, Korotaj n. 533. The play also celebrates Pope Alexander VIII (1689–1691) as a champion of heresy and Bishop Walerian Protaszewicz as the founder of the Jesuit Academy.
51 [Wazgird Kazimierz], *Signaculum supra cor Lituaniae* (Vilnius, 1731), Korotaj n. 627.
52 Norman Davies, *God's Playground: A History of Poland*, vol. 1: *The Origins to 1795*, rev. ed. (Oxford University Press, 2005), ch. 6, 'Antemurale: The Bulwark of Christendom', pp. 126–55.

53 In Polish and Ruthenian, there exists a term, *jasyr*, for Turkish or Mongolian captivity; it comes from the Turkish *jesir* or Arabic *asir*, meaning 'caught, tied'.
54 [Puciłowski Krzysztof], *Victoria Mariae seu Vienna Austriae* (Vilnius, 1684), Czartoryski Library, Kraków 11169.
55 *Zodiacus Poloniarum Poli pro duodecim signis, duodecim insignibus, pro fide Christi et Agelica extinctis puritate luminaribus distinctus, theatrales inter umbras ab Oratoriae facultatis propositus anno 1718 die 9 Aprilis* (Vilnius, 1718), Vilnius University Library IV 17009, IV 31333.

CHAPTER 8

Compassion, Contingency and Conversion in James Shirley's The Sisters

Alison Searle

This chapter examines the formal procedures connected to compassion in James Shirley's *The Sisters* (licensed 26 April 1642). I focus on the problems posed by outsiders: the compassion of bandits dwelling as an anti-society in the woodlands, the recurring trope of the vagrant/beggar/gypsy/actor used to interrogate histrionic techniques deployed to evoke compassion, and the complexities of policing the performance of compassion within the early modern Protestant state. Consideration is given to the role played by the audience in Shirley's drama, particularly the rhetorical function of the prologue and epilogue, which directly appeal to the spectators' compassion. Shirley's play elucidates the ways in which compassion could create new, dangerous communities, as well as exposing the limits of existing groups. By postulating the ruler as a potential object of compassion, the play proleptically examines some of the most pressing political questions of the English Civil War: Can the monarch be an object of compassion? How are the limits of fellow-feeling inflected by one's ideological affiliation, class, gender and age? With whom should the audience sympathise? Even though the theatre presents a fictional drama, the emotions that its affective technologies evoke in the audience are real.[1] The play's invitation to feel pity for the plight of the king creates a political space for subversive action. If one can empathise with the king, is he a potential peer?

These aspects of compassion – its objects, performance, limits and role in policing community boundaries – will be contextualised by Charles Taylor's philosophical reading of the parable of the Good Samaritan. Taylor's assessment of how the state 'ordered by [a] system of rules, disciplines and organizations can only see contingency as an obstacle', which must be mastered, provides a way of thinking about the legal and social mechanisms established in early modern England to control beggars, actors and vagrants. Taylor's analysis is complemented and exemplified by Nicholas Terpstra's historical analysis arguing that charity was a key link between belief and action, or mind and body. Terpstra demonstrates that the exercise of compassion both succoured the needy and actively policed community boundaries, particularly in refugee contexts throughout Europe following the Reformation, where needs and tensions were often high and resources (material, civic and social) were limited.[2]

Following the Reformation no part of English culture was excluded from the logic of conversional transformation. Conversion operated both as a sublime instrument of state power and a potential site for resistance. As Jean-François Senault noted: 'Mercy is a sanctified Contagion, which makes us sensible of our Neighbours sufferings; we ayd him to comfort ourselves: and we help him at his need, to free our selves from the Grief we feel.' John Staines elucidates this: 'The grief of compassion is good and holy because, as it touches each person – in the root sense of *contagion*, contact – it spreads virtuous behaviour. This contact spreads what is, in effect, a physiological disease, but it is a 'sanctified' infection.'[3] Jesus' parable advocates indiscriminate compassion without limits and this disrupts the state's desire to control contingency through rules. *The Sisters* similarly creates an imaginative space enabling the audience 'to escape from the monomaniacal perspective in which contingency can only be an adversary requiring control'.[4] Compassion is thus figured as inherently theatrical and politically contagious.

The Sisters was Shirley's final play to be performed before the closure of the London theatres due to the civil war. He interrogates the relationships between theatricality, politics and the limits of compassion in both the personal and public spheres. The complex interconnections between professional acting and cynical imposture are foregrounded alongside the tension created by harsh English laws against vagrancy and customary expectations about aristocratic hospitality and charity. Shirley probes the theatricality inherent in constructing one's identity as a worthy recipient of compassion and the gender and class politics that limit a person's ability to experience or demonstrate compassion. These issues relate directly to the political instability of the play's initial performance context, created by Charles I's abrogation of authority as he himself became a vagrant of sorts, and intensified the playwright's attempt to elicit compassion from the audience at Blackfriars. This was in part an economic concern as the absence of the king and court entailed a real loss of patronage opportunities for Shirley.[5]

The plot of Shirley's play is, in many ways, a typical exemplar of Caroline comedy. It tells the story of two sisters – the proud, rich Paulina and the humble Angellina destined for a nunnery. Impostures and mistaken identities form the crux of the action as Frapolo, a bandit pretending to be a prince, seduces Paulina (who turns out to be the natural daughter of peasants). The true leader, Farnese, only asserts his political authority as Prince of Parma (where the drama is set) with great difficulty at the end of the play. The fairy-tale aspect of the narrative invites an unambiguous moral response from the audience. Paulina's pride is grotesquely crushed: she is an object of contempt, not compassion. Angellina marries the true prince, and the natural order of authority associated with aristocratic birth, wealth and good character is re-established. However, this is complicated by the subplot, which focuses on Frapolo's bandits, who masquerade as astrologers, and a lengthy scene where a separate group of wandering vagrants pretend to be disabled as a result of war and natural disasters, attempting to gain money from the credulously compassionate Angellina.

Many critics have observed that English penal legislation established a relationship between actors and vagrants in the early modern period. For Barry Taylor, vagrants and actors 'embody a double principle of evasion': 'a physical wandering from the places … where identity and relationship are constituted and fixed; and an uncoupling of the "natural" relationship between … the appearance and the reality of social position'. The 'vagrant's delinquent acts of impersonation and forgery' offer a 'radical challenge … to the conceptual order of the sign'.[6] William Carroll suggests that 'the histrionics of poverty found a natural home on the stage' due to a twofold relationship established between beggar and stage. The theatre was denounced as a site of sedition where masterless men might gather and rebel, and descriptions of 'false beggars' often 'employed theatrical language' to expose their 'fraudulence'.[7] Charles Whitney concludes: 'Beggars and vagabonds are seen as performers, and professional performers are lumped with them … . Anxieties associated with the development of the commercial theater helped spark this antitheatrical consolidation.'[8]

Representing gypsies, beggars and vagrants in semi-utopian terms was a well-established tradition in English theatre. Ben Jonson's *The Gypsies Metamorphosed* (1621) and Richard Brome's *A Jovial Crew* (1641–1642) are just two examples. Shirley's drama is often dismissed as derivative and to some extent it is, but he also deploys well-worn generic tropes to astute political and theatrical effect. In *The Sisters*, the prologue notes that 'the whole Town is not well', '*London* is gone to *York*' and 'a Play / Though ne'r so new, will starve the second day'.[9] The epilogue, delivered by the chief bandit, Frapolo, undercuts the authoritative summary given by the nondescript Prince of Parma moments before in terms that would have resonated with the subjects of Charles I: 'his graces word is but mortall, and not security enough for me; for all this Sun-shine he may hang me ... and therefore I have chosen, rather to trust to my legs, than a reconcil'd State-Enemy' (E6r). Frapolo then makes a direct appeal to the audience's compassion: 'Two'not be worth your glory to betray / A man distrest, whom your own mercy may / Preserve to better service; rather then / Go back I'l stand your justice Gentlemen. / I've plaid the thief, but you, as the case stands, / May save or kill, my lif's now in your hands' (E6r). As Julie Sanders observes: 'with Parliament inactive, London theatres constituted alternative spaces and talking-shops for ideas. Nowhere is this more evident than in plays performed on the threshold of war in the early 1640s.'[10]

The metatheatrical frame provided by the prologue and epilogue is one way in which Shirley deploys the actor/vagrant association to make a contemporary political point: 'It is not far-fetched to suppose that in the parallel that Shirley suggests between Charles and Frapolo he is hinting that Charles's failure validly to maintain his regality has already reduced his credibility to little more than that of a mock king.'[11] The play itself includes numerous variations on this theme. There are the bandits, led by Frapolo, who live in the forest and enact by turns a group of fortune-telling mathematicians and the prince and his retinue. There are the tradesmen who come seeking to exploit the commercial opportunities opened by Antonio's announcement that Angellina is his heir. These are closely followed by a group of able-bodied beggars who appeal to Angellina's compassion, but in another twist are exposed as charlatans by her uncle, Antonio, who has pretended to be one of them. Finally, the actual prince, Farnese, comes to Paulina's castle as an ordinary citizen and is almost outfaced by the brazen Frapolo in a final stand-off. Piperollo, one of Paulina's retainers and an erstwhile thief, suggests a trial by lion to determine which of them is the true prince. This can be read as the final uncoupling of the 'natural' relationship 'between signifier and signified' or 'the appearance and reality of social position and status' in the play.[12]

Shirley interrogates the limits of compassion in this politically fraught and overtly self-conscious theatrical context. Even the subplot, dismissed as extraneous and 'dull' in a 1924 edition of the play, foregrounds this question.[13] This scene offers an intriguing angle on the complex interrelationships that Shirley sets up between gender, patronage, theatricality and compassion. Angellina's uncle, Antonio, is horrified by his niece Paulina's arrogance in presuming to be sole regent of her own territory.[14]

His somewhat counterintuitive response is to make her sister Angellina his heir, and he attempts to transform her anodyne humility into a pride that undercuts Paulina's pretensions to nobility. Angellina's newfound wealth and status attract a series of hangers-on and solicitors that enable Shirley to satirise the commercial and self-interested exploitation of patronage and fashion in Caroline London and also to expose the credulous nature of his heroine's compassion. She is first accosted by two gentlewomen, who attempt to offer her various beauty-enhancing services and then by a witty student who seeks to flatter her through poetry (D2v–3r). Hard on their heels come a tailor, a perfumer, a jeweller and a spurrier. Each tries to sell Angellina something she does not want, or need, as a way of gaining 'the Credit of [her] name' and the 'privilege to swell above [their] neighbors' (D4r). They are brusquely dismissed, and Angellina requests her maid, who is aiding Antonio in his attempt to convert his niece to aristocratic pride and conspicuous consumption, to repel further suitors. Francescina needs no encouragement to refuse access to the next group of visitors. Ironically, though, they receive a ready welcome from Angellina.

FRANCESCINA   You are rude and sawcy fellows to intrude
              So far without my Ladies licence.
ANGELLINA   What makes thee so impatient? will they not
              Be gone?
FRANCESCINA   Gone? here's a new regiment is pressing forward.
ANGELLINA   What are they?
FRANCESCINA   Beggars.
ANGELLINA   How?
FRANCESCINA   And tell me I abuse your Charity,
              To keep off their petitions; we must have
              A Court-du-guard, I think, and Centries plac'd
              At every dore.
ANGELLINA   I prethee let 'em enter.

Enter three Petitioners.

FRANCESCINA   The room will not be sweet again this three days;
              But if it be your pleasure — know your distance.
ANGELLINA   The blind, and lame, what's your condition Sir?
                                                    (D4r–v)

As Angellina's rapid inference reveals two of the three beggars are visually performing their need — they are blind and lame — and the third claims to have suffered shipwreck and gives her 'a Paper' where she may 'Peruse [his] tragick story'. The blind beggar asserts that a fire not only spoilt his eyes and ruined his estate but 'ravish'd' him of all that 'was precious to 'em, / A wife and pretty Children' (D4v). The lame beggar claims to be a soldier who lost his limbs in the service of his country: 'I've had more lead in bullets taken from me / Than would repair some Steeple' (D4v). Francescina adds in an aside: 'Ring the bells, / That was a loud one!' (D4v–D5r). Angellina, who had no difficulty seeing through the commercial stratagems of the scheming gentlewomen and tradesmen, is entirely convinced by the performance of these beggars. She concludes: 'Poor souls! I pitty'em, here honest men, / Divide this bag, and pray for my good Uncle' (D5r). However, a fight over how to divide up the money between them exposes the beggars' charade and reveals the ringleader to be none other than Angellina's uncle, Antonio, who threatens to 'send for some Officers' (D5r). He concludes:

> They have found their eyes and legs again.
> Neece I observe your Charity, but you see not
> The inside of these things, and I did mean
> And hope these sums might serve your self;
> Some Ladies would have considered
> A new gown and trinkets; Francescina,
> I see little amendment, she'l undo me
> In pious uses.
>
> (D5r)

The performance of the able-bodied beggars has been co-opted by Antonio as a mechanism to determine whether his attempts to convert his niece from a would-be nun to an affluent gentlewoman have been successful. In the process, Shirley deconstructs both the false narratives and artistic props deployed by the beggars to obtain charitable funds and the formation of noble ladies through flattery and the conspicuous consumption of luxury goods. Of particular interest here, however, is the fact that Angellina is able acutely and satirically to undercut the spurious performances of the commercial and courtly solicitors but is incapable of discerning the subterfuge employed by the beggars and actively resists her maid's attempts to protect the room from smells and falsehood. Her humility and charity inure her to some forms of exploitation and deceit but also render her vulnerable to the predatory performance of the beggars.[15] Antonio critiques Angellina for her refusal to purchase the accoutrements of the role that was naturally hers and suggests that an inordinate humility limits her ability to discern the subterfuge of the beggars. Angellina's compassion can be seen as a conversional affect, entwined with her ambition to become a nun, which frustrates Antonio's attempts to use conversion as a strategic tool to effect her social and economic transformation.

The relationship between compassion and performance is a contested issue throughout the play. The exercise of compassion as it operates within the natural social order, aristocratic distribution of patronage or largesse to those in need, is thwarted by the myopic pride of those like Paulina who instead spend large sums on flattering parasites. Yet failure to perform and fulfil one's role within the traditional hierarchy, such as the Prince of Parma's decision to go incognito or Angellina's desire to become a nun rather than take her place as her uncle's heir, also created opportunities for subversive action. Charismatic charlatans are swift to capitalise on these whether they result from selfishness on the part some nobles or inappropriate withdrawal from the public sphere by others. These include individuals like those who solicit Angellina in the subplot, but, more significantly, Frapolo and his group of bandits in the main plot. Shirley here references the king's abdication of his authority as he withdrew from the capital in 1642, creating a vacuum that would be rapidly filled by politic opportunists.[16] This opportunism is balanced by the regenerative potential that Frapolo's band of performers also offered in their green woodland retreat. The forest was home to 'a network of every day relationships' configured partly by the crown's desire to regulate its resources and 'in part by a desire of local residents to benefit from these resources'.[17] The forest signified a mixture of lawlessness and utopian promise in the dramatic imagination of the period, though Sanders notes that liberty was not an automatic attribute of groups who dwelt there; rather, it was 'the special practice of it by particular communities that achieves this condition'.[18] In Chapter 7 of this volume, Clarinda E. Calma and Jolanta Rzegocka examine the ambivalence expressed by Jesuit playbills when interrogating a similarly dangerous, liminal space on the Polish-Lithuanian border with the Ottoman Empire; the duty to exercise compassion and its limits was shaped by a complex combination of religious and political imperatives. Such borderlands were permeable: the threat of captivity also offered the possibility of conversion.

The first guise adopted by Frapolo and his bandits to gain access to Paulina's castle and steal her wealth was that of mathematicians (also described as Chaldeans, fortune-tellers, Ethiopians, canting rogues and black-faced Egyptians). Pandering to Paulina's overwhelming ambition by telling her precisely what she wants to hear – that it is her fortune to marry the Prince of Parma – they gain easy access to the house. It is only Antonio's scepticism and resourcefulness in rousing the tenants to arms that prevent them from carrying out their purpose. His reflection on

Paulina's ready distribution of largesse to such, in contrast to other 'Poor men', is telling.

ANTONIO Her house is open for these Mountebanks,
Cheaters and Tumblers, that can foist and flatter
My Lady Gugaw; Every office open,
When Poor men that have worth and want an Alms,
May perish ere they pass the Porters lodge;
What are you Sir?
STROZZO One of the Mathematicians noble Signior.
ANTONIO Mathematicians? Mungrell,
How durst thou take that learned name upon thee?
You are one of those knaves that Stroul the Country,
And live by picking worms out of fools fingers.
(C4r)

Antonio is shown to be just such a 'fool' as Strozzo picks his pocket while he laments. However, he expresses a complaint common in publications from the period. Early modern English legislation was driven by an obsessive fear of vagrancy and the protean capacity of beggars to form themselves into diverse shapes. Arguably, though, what Paulina is doing here is precisely what Antonio critiques Angellina for not doing in the subplot. In contrasting the sisters in this way, Shirley exposes the limits of a natural ideology of compassion based on an idealised social hierarchy that was no longer viable, if it ever had been. He does not resolve this conflict, although at the level of the plot he reaches a compromise by resorting to a fairy-tale ending. The proud, ungenerous sister turns out to be the natural daughter of peasants and is trapped in an unhappy union with the leader of the bandits, while the virtuous, beautiful sister becomes sole heir to the family's wealth and marries the prince.

Frapolo and his troupe deploy an even more daring theatrical ruse in their second attempt to rob Paulina's house, by impersonating the Prince of Parma and his court, and persuading Paulina to marriage as part of the pretence. This is also the most radical aspect of the play in political terms. Absent monarchs feature frequently in early modern English drama, so it is important not to overemphasise the contemporary political resonance of this part of the plot. But there are two reasons this can be seen as a deliberate choice on Shirley's part. The prologue expresses clear disappointment in the king's removal to York and sets out the negative implications for London, particularly its playwrights and their audiences. Second, the play pits the two leaders – Frapolo and Farnese – directly against each other at the end of the action. Frapolo's charismatic performance of Farnese deceives Paulina and her household and almost convinces her sceptical uncle. His enactment of royalty is so effective that the prince himself is momentarily unsettled: 'I am at a loss to hear him; sure I am / Farnese, if I be not lost by the way' (E4v). Piperollo is unable to make up his mind and with typical resourcefulness states: 'Stand off Gentlemen, – let me see – which? / Hum! this – no, th'other. Hum! Send for a Lion / And turn him loose, he wo'not hurt the true Prince' (E4v). Though Frapolo ultimately succumbs by admitting he is a prince of rogues, he maintains his flamboyance till the end by thanking his loving uncle for wishing 'joy to thy invisible Grace' and promising to beget multiple children with his bride. He also solicits audience sympathy in the epilogue by refusing to entrust himself to 'a reconcil'd State-Enemy' and metatheatrically resigns his life into their hands (E6r).

The play exposes the theatricality that is at the heart of all forms of identity: whether one is a prince, a gentlewoman and heir to the family fortune, a vagrant dependent on charity or a lawless rogue. At a point when Charles I's performance of kingship was visibly unravelling before the eyes of his often bewildered subjects, Shirley's depiction of the theatricality and fragility that characterised any performance of identity in the public sphere had significant political clout. The theatre, as a public institution, is thus operating quite differently at this moment in English history to Calma and Rzegocka's depiction of the Jesuit school theatre as 'a well-honed instrument of persuasion' deployed in the services of Counter-Reformation agents, though there is a shared emphasis on the important contribution that theatrical performances, with their emphasis on rhetoric and the art of persuasion, could make to public debates.[19]

There is one final element in the play that foregrounds tensions between natural bonds, self-preservation, thievery and compassion. Piperollo, Paulina's brother (though this is unknown until the end), finds himself under threat from the bandits and saves his skin by offering to give them access to the life savings of his parents.

PIPEROLLO ... you need not fear
           The Court-du-Guard; if you please let me go
           An honest theeves part, and furnish me
           With a Devills complexion, to hide my own
           I will conduct you.
FRAPOLO   A very honest fellow!
PIPEROLLO I do not love to be ingratefull where
           I'm kindly us'd, my heart is honest.
FRAPOLO   Is he thy own Father?

PIPEROLLO   My own Father and Mother, Sir, the cause
            Would not be so natural else, and meritorious.
FRAPOLO   A precious rogue, fit him instantly
            With a disguise, and let him have that face
            The Devill wore in the last anti-masque.
PIPEROLLO   It cannot be too ugly Sir to fright'em.
                                                  (B3r)

However, when confronted with the bound bodies of Piperollo's parents, the two bandits Longino and Strozzo experience a change of heart. His father, Fabio, pleads: 'Have some compassion, tis our whole estate.' His mother, Morulla, cries: 'O pity Gentlemen' (B5v–B6r). Piperollo is indifferent. Not so the bandits, who succumb to feelings of compassion.

STROZZO   I begin to find a kind of compunction,
            Let us be charitable thieves for once –
LONGINO   And return half,
            What say you?
PIPEROLLO   Not a gazet, y'are not such foolish theeves;
            Part with present money? part with my life first.
STROZZO   Not to your Parents?
PIPEROLLO   ... not a penny –
            If you will be so charitable, defalk
            From your own shares, mine is a just theeves part;
            I look for thanks, distribute your own alms;
            These things must be employ'd to better uses.
            Is a Father and Mother considerable
            To ready mony ...
                                                  (B6r)

Piperollo is left bound by the bandits and is unmasked by his mother, Morulla, who draws a knife and kicks him out of doors. There is a clear comic dimension to this scene, but Shirley is also interrogating the connections between natural bonds, the performance of roles, feelings of compunction or compassion and the exercise of charity. Piperollo requests a devil's mask and a direct allusion is drawn to the tradition of anti-masques at the Stuart court. The unravelling of the plot as the three collaborators fight about how to divvy up the money bags is echoed later in the scene where Antonio unmasks the beggars. This exposes the inextricable entanglement of feelings of compassion and acts of charity with mercenary considerations. However, there is also a moment where the thieves suddenly realise that they are implicated in 'networks of living concern'. Faced with the bound bodies of an elderly couple pleading with them to have pity, and Piperollo's crass lack of feeling towards his parents, a sense of 'compunction' leads to 'charity', which Piperollo describes as a 'foolish' distribution of 'alms'. The compassion exhibited by these bandits forms a stark contrast to the theatrical utility of its deployment by the vagabonds who seek to manipulate Angellina in order to gain some of her uncle's wealth. Shirley actively interrogates the parameters of compassion as a social quality or virtue by probing the ways this human emotion can be instrumentalised.

The authorities in early modern England attempted to control poverty and vagrancy through the creation of sharp distinctions (worthy/unworthy or vagrant/settled poor) and the legislation of which types of performance were acceptable and which were not. Charles Taylor has noted that a 'world ordered by this system of rules, disciplines and organizations can only see contingency as an obstacle, even as an enemy and a threat. The ideal is to master it, to extend the web of control so that contingency is reduced to a minimum.' The improvisational performances and rough, not always self-serving, justice of Frapolo's bandits are governed by contingency (opportunistic or otherwise) rather than a desire for control. Contingency is also 'an essential feature of the story of the Good Samaritan as an answer to the question that prompted it. Who is my neighbour? The one you happen across, stumble across, who is wounded there on the road. Sheer accident also has a hand in shaping the proportionate, the appropriate response. It is telling us something, answering our deepest questions: this is your neighbour. But in order to hear this, we have to escape from the monomaniacal perspective in which contingency can only be an adversary requiring control.'[20] In his dramatic representation of the bandits in their woodland home and, to a lesser extent, in the prospect of freedom from the inheritance of wealth and conventional marriage that a nunnery offered Angellina, Shirley is exploring the consequences of escape from a monomaniacal perspective. This was something that the political and economic conditions required of him, rather than a freely exercised choice. *The Sisters* presents a series of contingencies and accidents that asks actors and audiences alike to consider what constitutes an appropriate or proportionate response: compassion, poetic justice or charismatic theatrical opportunism?

In conclusion, I will consider the hermeneutic, epistemological and affective affordances that Taylor's account of the genealogy of early modern Christianity offers for rethinking the lived experience or dramatic enactment of compassion. Conversion is inherently contingent and affective. As with Shirley's play, it required individuals and their communities in early modern England to consider the degree of freedom available to the subject within a constrained set of circumstances, the imperatives of personal conscience and the potential for strategic theatrical opportunism (defined in theological terms as hypocrisy at best, apostasy or heresy at worst). The affective weight and theatrical dynamic of conversion results from its dual nature as both a change of heart and a shift in communal religious identity during this period.[21] Taylor takes the doctrine of the incarnation, 'the enfleshment of God', which was central to cross-confessional thinking about the role of compassion, and explores how it effects personal conversions through the formation of relationships producing a 'network' or 'skein of relations which link particular, unique, enfleshed people to each other' leading to new communal identities.[22] Taylor draws on Ivan Illich's reading of the Good Samaritan, which exposes the radical logic inherent in conversion as an affective, personal transformation that inevitably subverts aspects of the dominant culture. Illich notes that 'the relationship between the Samaritan and the beaten-up Jew is a voluntary and bodily tie .... The Samaritan, Jesus says, is "moved with compassion." He undergoes a conversion, an inward turning around which begins in his guts .... .'[23] The Samaritan's decision to step outside what his culture has declared sacred enables the creation of a 'new relationship and, potentially, a new community'.[24]

These intersections between compassion, personal conscience and the development of a nascent public sphere in seventeenth-century England have important implications for how we think about theatre or, indeed, the heuristic role of biblical parables and their interpretation. Theatre's capacity to present fakeries that elicit real emotions on the part of its audience make it an instrument of conversion. The types of conversion taking place and the ways in which these relate to religious morphologies of conversion are beyond the scope of this chapter, but the opening scene of *The Sisters* demonstrates Shirley's conscious determination to use theatre's capacity to put conversion, and the complex implications of compassion as a contagious, unpredictable emotion, into serious play. A conversation between Frapolo and the company of bandits makes the social, political and ideological stakes very clear.

RANGONE   I'l be of no Religion.
FRAPOLO   Who was so bold
          To say he would have no Religion?
          What man is he, hopes to be drunk, to whore,
          To scape the wheels, the Gallies, and the gallowes
          And be of no Religion?
LONGINO   He says right.

FRAPOLO	Yee shall be of what Religion I please.
PACHECO	Tis fit we should, *Frapolo* is our Monarch.
FRAPOLO	And yet I must consider of some fit one That shall become our trade And constitutions; hum! Silence.
STROZZO	Nay, nay Prince, take time to think on't, Ther's no hast.
FRAPOLO	I have thought, And you shall be no *Pagans*, *Jews*, nor *Christians*.
LONGINO	What then?
FRAPOLO	But every man shall be of all Religions.
RANGONE	I like that well.
FRAPOLO	Why should I clog your Conscience, or confine it? Do but obey your Prince, and I pronounce You shall live Grandees, till the State Phangs catch you, And when you come unto the Wheel, or Gibbet, Bid figo for the World, and go out Martyrs.
OMNES	A Prince, a Prince!
FRAPOLO	Provided, that no theef Makes a Confession at his Death, or 'peach His Tribe, or make a shew of penitence, To make the Butter-women melt, and draw Compassion from the toothless musty rabble; This will exclude the benefit of that Canon Declares you Martyrs for the Cause.

(B2r)

The bandits are both an anti-society and a utopian community living precariously in the woodland fringes of the play. Shirley uses this space to interrogate issues of freedom of conscience, conversion and a contagious compassion that might persuade the masses to sympathise with a compelling performance of penitence at the scaffold by a martyr/thief. Though the dramatic context is comic, its satirical presentation of a commonwealth of outlaws makes serious comment on the religious and political issues confronting the English nation in April 1642. Staines has argued that appeals by preachers to the masses to choose between competing churches led to the 'gradual creation of private consciences that frequently stand at odds against the official public sphere' constituted by the sovereign and his or her government. The humanist public sphere of the Reformation was formed by individual 'consciences making practical judgments about the rhetorical performances presented before them'. Arguably, plays like Shirley's *The Sisters* were engaged in an analogous project – the theatrical production of compassion and conscience through rhetorical performances staged before public audiences. The English political system almost completely conflated church and state and this resulted in a breakdown in distinctions between religious, cultural and political criticism. Staines concludes: the 'institutions that made up this sphere of religious criticism ... reached all strata of society ... who all had consciences that needed to make a choice for belief. This criticism paved the way for revolution.'[25] Frapolo models a commonwealth that allows freedom of conscience to all its members, provided they remain loyal to their prince. This is precisely the situation that Calma and Rzegocka, in Chapter 7, argue existed in the Polish-Lithuanian Commonwealth, where the multi-denominational nature of the political class necessitated a pragmatic toleration such as that enshrined in the Warsaw Confederation of 1573. But in Shirley's play this delicate balance between freedom and loyalty is shadowed by the judicial apparatus of the state authorities whose fangs threaten an ever-present martyrdom or death for the bandit/outlaw defying their laws. To confess publicly on the gibbet, to impeach his companions, or to make a show of penitence deliberately designed to elicit compassion from the crowd gathered to watch their execution will, Frapolo warns, prevent members of the fraternity from being revered as martyrs for the cause.

If, as Todd Butler argues, imagination is 'the instrument by which human beings know their world and then communicate their knowledge and desires through speech to others, providing for both the formation of a commonwealth and its potential subversion',[26] Shirley is offering a powerful alternative model that exposes the oppression of individual conscience in the public sphere at the heart of the Elizabethan church settlement inherited and strengthened by the Stuarts. Nonetheless, the limitations of a semi-utopian anti-society existing precariously on the fringes of the state are also revealed. Compassion is figured as a contagious, indiscriminate emotion elicited by a 'shew of penitence' that is sufficient to melt butter-women and deceive the 'toothless musty rabble'. It is a 'contagion' that 'remains problematic for the very reason that the spectacle touches the viewer in such an immediate and powerful way'.[27] The spectators are categorised contemptuously by Frapolo in terms of class and gender. However, the fact that an effective theatricalisation of penitence can move members of the public observing a judicial execution with compassion is shown to be both viable and reprehensible. Such compassion has the power to deconstruct the bonds of loyalty that unite the bandits and that are essential to the preservation and security of their anti-society. To this extent, the state fangs are effective. The imminency of death ensures a compliant performance of penitence on the part of the captured thief that affectively reinscribes the authority of the state by evoking a compassionate response from the indiscriminate rabble gathered to observe the spectacle.

But compassion also has a radical, destabilising edge. At the denouement of the play, when Farnese is determined to execute justice on Paulina and Frapolo as traitors, Angellina requests a pardon for their lives so that no part of her story will be remembered as a tragedy. Farnese acquiesces but confines Frapolo and Paulina, if she chooses, to the castle because completely to waive the requirements of justice would encourage treason. Angellina responds to this by noting: 'Because I call'd her Sister, / I will contribute something to their fortune.' Farnese leaves this to the direction of 'her goodness' (E5v). Though Antonio's attempt to convert Angellina from a novitiate to his heir has had some success – she agrees to marry the prince – there is no indication that she has lost her shrewd ability to assess, critique and reject the commercial stratagems of courtly society and its parasites nor her commitment to indiscriminate compassion for those in need, neglected by the institutions of the state, or oppressed by fortune. Compassion for her sister, and other more self-conscious charlatans, might bleed the coffers of the state dry if Farnese sets no restraints on Angellina's charitable spending. Shirley does not advocate an undiscerning generosity to all in need within this play. However, throughout his oeuvre he repeatedly scripted verbally dexterous and outspoken female characters that challenged the social and ideological mores of Caroline society in various ways. Angellina is comparatively compliant, but any attempt to construe a political critique within Shirley's output needs to pay careful attention to his dramatisation of gender. Angellina remains an unknown quantity at the conclusion of the play. Her marriage to the prince places her in a powerful political position, but she has not been effectively converted to performing her role according to conventional scripts for female generosity, compassion or conspicuous consumption. Her uncle, Antonio, acknowledges that his pedagogical project to convert her to patriarchal norms has partially failed. Alongside Frapolo's determination to trust to his legs rather than a reconciled but ambivalent state-enemy this means that the political status quo at the end of the action is fraught.

Compassion as figured within the play can both reinforce the authority of the state, through ensuring a coercive performance of compliance on the part of captured thieves, and deconstruct it by the indiscriminate exercise of charity to all, including charlatans who effectively performed disabilities resulting from war and natural disasters. Perhaps most unsettlingly, the king himself became an object of compassion. The feelings of compassion that the affective technologies of the theatre could elicit, and exposure to the associated emotional contagion, created a dangerous synergy between fiction and fact – as the paratextual material of the play makes clear – helping to pave the way for political revolution.

Notes

1 Steven Mullaney, *The Reformation of Emotions in the Age of Shakespeare* (University of Chicago Press, 2015), especially the introduction and chapter 1.
2 Nicholas Terpstra, *Religious Refugees in the Early Modern World: An Alternative History of the Reformation* (New York: Cambridge University Press, 2015), pp. 218–40.
3 Cited by John Staines, 'Compassion in the Public Sphere of Milton and King Charles' in Gail Kern Paster, Katherine Rowe and Mary Floyd-Wilson (eds.), *Reading the Early Modern Passions: Essays in the Cultural History of Emotions* (Philadelphia: University of Pennsylvania Press, 2004), p. 100.
4 Charles Taylor, preface to *The Rivers North of the Future: The Testament of Ivan Illich as told to David Cayley* (Toronto: Anansi, 2005), p. xiii.
5 This chapter is deeply indebted to discussion with and feedback from participants of the seminar on Conversion and Theatre in Early Modern Europe led by Professors Steven Mullaney and Paul Yachnin from 3–27 May 2016 at the University of Michigan. In particular, I am grateful to Dr Tiffany Hoffman for her comments.
6 Barry Taylor, *Vagrant Writing: Social and Semiotic Disorders in the English Renaissance* (New York: Harvester, 1991), pp. 9, 11.
7 William Carroll, *Fat King, Lean Beggar* (1996), pp. 2–3, cited by Paola Pugliatti, *Beggary and Theatre in Early Modern England* (Aldershot: Ashgate, 2003), p. 1.
8 Charles Whitney, 'Beggary and Theatre in Early Modern England', *Clio*, 34:3 (2005), 361.
9 James Shirley, *The Sisters* (London, 1652), A3r. All subsequent citations are taken from this octavo edition and are provided in text.
10 Julie Sanders, 'Beggars' Commonwealths and the Pre-Civil War Stage: Suckling's *The Goblins*, Brome's *A Jovial Crew*, and Shirley's *The Sisters*', *The Modern Language Review*, 97:1 (2002), 4.
11 Martin Butler, *Theatre and Crisis, 1632–42* (Cambridge University Press, 1984), pp. 264–25.
12 Taylor, *Vagrant Writing*, pp. 9, 11.
13 C. M. Edmondston (ed.), introduction to James Shirley, *The Sisters* (London: Wells Gardner, Darnton & Co., 1924), p. xxxvii.
14 This theme is picked up as a central motif in the comic opera based on Shirley's play *The Fancy'd Queen. An Opera* (London: Charles Corbett, at Addison's Head without Temple-Bar, 1733).

15 Sarah McNamer observes that compassion and gender are not necessarily inextricably connected in other traditions as they have been in Western Christendom and highlights the importance of exploring the historical roots of associations that assume a normative status in *Affective Meditation and the Invention of Medieval Compassion* (Philadelphia: University of Pennsylvania Press, 2010), pp. 11–14.
16 As Todd Wayne Butler notes: '... those who succeeded Charles found themselves drawing upon similar patterns of expressing authority ... . Legitimacy thus became a matter of performance, and even with a radical transformation in the institution of government, the means by which authority was instantiated remained the same.' *Imagination and Politics in Seventeenth-Century England* (Aldershot: Ashgate, 2008), p. 14.
17 Adam Zucker, cited by Julie Sanders, *The Cultural Geography of Early Modern Drama 1620–1650* (Cambridge University Press, 2011), p. 69, n. 10.
18 Sanders, *Cultural Geography*, p. 68.
19 Calma and Rzegocka, Chapter 7.
20 Charles Taylor, preface to *The Rivers North of the Future: The Testament of Ivan Illich as told to David Cayley* (Toronto: Anansi, 2005), p. xiii.
21 Molly Murray, *The Poetics of Conversion in Early Modern English Literature* (Cambridge University Press, 2009), p. 7.
22 Taylor, preface, pp. xi–xii.
23 Ivan Illich, *The Rivers North of the Future: The Testament of Ivan Illich as told to David Cayley* (Toronto: Anansi, 2005), p. 31.
24 Illich, *Rivers*, p. 31.
25 Staines, 'Compassion in the Public Sphere', pp. 96–97.
26 Butler, *Theatre and Crisis*, p. 16.
27 Staines, 'Compassion in the Public Sphere', p. 100.

PART V

Responding

CHAPTER 9

Mountainish Inhumanity in Illyria
Compassion in Twelfth Night *as Social Luxury and Political Duty*

Elisabetta Tarantino

There is no compassion in *Twelfth Night*; or rather, the term 'compassion' does not occur in the play. And yet pathos is the dominant mood in this story of shipwrecked twins – effectively refugees who believe each other dead – where the female twin's male disguise potentially gives rise to more heartbreak for those, of either sex, who love her thinking that she is a man, and for herself, in love with a master who feels mysteriously and disturbingly drawn to this young manservant. Even the final recognition and resolution cannot be completely happy, because in the meantime the Steward Malvolio, in one of the two noble households in the story, has been the subject of a cruel joke, which was meant to teach him to tolerate other people's propensity for 'cakes and ale' but in fact only gave him a masterclass in intolerance. The Steward storms off at the end of the play, vowing revenge: characters go after him. We must take it on trust that he will be found and pacified. Never named, our compassion is continually evoked as the play challenges the bases on which it is withheld.

Certainly compassion's synonym makes its presence felt. The word 'pity', apart from an idiomatic phrase, appears in act I scene v and in act III scene i.[1] In both these situations, 'pity' is a synonym for 'love' in the conventional Petrarchan tradition. As so many other aspects of this play, the two occurrences of the word 'pity' mirror each other: in the first instance (the famous 'willow cabin' speech, I.v.237–45) Viola, disguised as Cesario, envisages receiving 'pity' from Olivia, whom she is frustratingly expected to court on behalf of her master Orsino; in the second it is Olivia who tries to construe Cesario's proffered 'pity' as love in response to her own, of whose hopelessness she is entirely unaware. In reply to this, Cesario debunks the Petrarchan situation by pointing out as 'vulgar proof' that 'very oft we pity enemies' (III.i.117).

Given that the play sets in motion a riotous gang's revenge against Malvolio, Viola's confidence in the natural human propensity to feel compassion even towards one's enemy seems rather misplaced. In fact, this conviction allies her with the ruling élite within the play: at the lower social levels compassion is suppressed by a sense of one's own social and economic vulnerability, and, as I argue in the final section of this chapter, it is a luxury that only the higher classes can afford.

The question of the treatment of the Steward Malvolio is one of the crucial interpretive issues in *Twelfth Night*, and the placement of our compassion is central to the history of that debate. Few readers and spectators of any age would go as far as Charles Lamb, who found actual 'tragic interest' in this character in the late nineteenth century. Not uncommonly, we come across a historicising and contextualising response, which points out that 'in practice, observing the scene on stage, we are not in a position to sympathise with Malvolio' because 'Shakespeare makes us look at [the Steward] through the eyes of Sir Toby and Maria, and, from that perspective, the smiling yellow-stockinged Malvolio is ridiculous and we laugh'.[2] However this kind of response only refers to the trickery to which Malvolio is subjected. The full story of his punishment is a tale of deceit, false imprisonment and serious psychological harassment, and few spectators laugh at that.

Recent readings focusing on the social function of laughter have again reached diverging conclusions. After surveying a variety of responses to Malvolio in critical literature and in performance, Bridget Escolme opts for a reading of this character as the legitimate victim of a 'community of laughers'.[3] At the same time, other critics point out the failure of laughter as an instrument of social correction and cohesion in the play.[4] These positions show a tendency to equate the issue of a 'compassionate' response to Malvolio, or lack thereof, in the community within the play and among the play's viewers. By contrast, in this chapter I argue that the play's audience is expected to achieve a higher understanding of the motives why compassion may be granted or withheld by different groups of characters within the play.

In terms of the latter, nearly sixty years ago, Leo Salingar had already identified the root of the problem as Malvolio's inability 'to live spontaneously as one of a community'. However, in doing so Salingar briefly pointed to an alternative, reality-based, community where Malvolio would fit in: 'He belongs ... to the world of law and business, outside the festive circle of the play.'[5] An assessment of 'the problem of Malvolio' must then consider what the play tells us about its 'community'.

As for the audience's response, I discuss new intertextual evidence that suggests that *Twelfth Night* addresses issues of community and compassion in a direct historical and political sense, with reference to the contemporary relationship between England and Europe, and that an ambivalent representation of Malvolio is a central part of the play's semantic strategy. While at the level of plot the play depicts Olivia's household as a community that gangs up against 'Monsieur Malvolio', its textual and compositional strategies – the high number of mirrorings and surprising instances of identification between opposites – undermine the very idea of 'us' versus 'the other' as a discriminant for social and political action.

In the next chapter, Eric Langley insightfully discusses the storm and shipwreck of human life in the face of which different gradations of compassion (or lack thereof) are possible, with a special focus on the late plays and with a wealth of cultural references from Lucretius to Montaigne. In the reading I offer below, this 'storm' takes the form of the struggle to survive in specific material and economic conditions, where the degree of compassion that characters can afford is directly linked to their social status.[6]

Malvolio and Bonifacio

We have long known that the ultimate source for the main plot in *Twelfth Night* is a play by the Accademia degli Intronati in Siena, called *Gli Ingannati*, i.e. *The Deceived* (1532).[7] Recently, however, another Italian play has been adduced as the main source for the gulling of Malvolio, allowing us to make comparisons between the analogous situations in the source and target texts. Such comparisons bring to the fore the idea of 'desert', which is closely linked to that of compassion. 'Desert' creates a chiastic relationship between 'punishment' – the dramatic theme that links the newly adduced source to *Twelfth Night* – and 'compassion': the more a character deserves the former, the less deserving of the latter he appears to be. The opportunity to compare the treatment of Malvolio with its source is thus a precious instrument by which the audience may gain a superior understanding of the desirability of granting compassion compared to the attitude of other characters within the play.

Candelaio (The Candle-maker; 1582) is the only primarily literary work by philosopher and heretic Giordano Bruno (1548–1600). Its relationship with the subplot in *Twelfth Night* was pointed out by Hilary Gatti in a seminal article in 2012, and in a subsequent article I developed Gatti's argument by linking Shakespeare's use of Bruno's play to its political and religious background.[8] With Malvolio, Shakespeare gestures towards the rising figure of the Puritan, and Bruno was a harsh critic of the Calvinist faith, not only because of its doctrinal content but because of the destabilising effect of any religion that placed itself above the goals of political stability and peace.[9]

Bruno's play was published in Paris on the tenth anniversary of the St Bartholomew's Day massacre, and could be seen as an allegory of the all-round immorality of the Wars of Religion (possibly with the additional intent of exonerating his Valois patrons from the main responsibility for the 'furie française', as the massacre was sometimes called).[10] It presents a situation in which its three negative heroes Bonifacio, Bartolomeo and Manfurio are 'justly' punished for their trespasses, even while the self-appointed judges and executioners are themselves cheats and low-lives.[11] However, there are obvious differences between a comedy and a massacre. In *Candelaio*, after they have been cruelly and deceitfully humiliated, those who had threatened social cohesion are reintegrated into the community (even though the damage done to the negative heroes is never made good, and there are indications that they will continue to be cheated unbeknowst to them).

The divergence between Bruno's and Shakespeare's treatment of this theme is predicated precisely on this idea of the 'just' punishment of those who somehow trespass against the 'rules' of the community, with potentially dangerous consequences. While some degree of ambivalence is already present in Bruno through the dubious social status and morality of those meting out punishment, in *Candelaio* there is no real doubt that the trespassers have brought this punishment onto themselves.

There are at least two ways, besides his structuring of plot events, in which Bruno reiterates this point. *Candelaio* comes with a proliferation of paratexts, including an 'Argument and Arrangement of the Play' for the use of readers.[12] Bruno uses this opportunity to stress how Bonifacio had fallen victim to his own schemes. In doing so, he alludes to the myth of Actaeon, hinting that the victim had brought his misfortunes upon himself.[13] The second indication that the author justifies the punishment of the negative characters is the fact that he makes the main executor of the gulling plot an artist and gives him the name of 'Gioan Bernardo', an almost exact anagram of 'Giordano Bruno'.[14]

As we shall see below, both these semantic strategies, the Actaeon reference and the mirroring of names, are picked up by Shakespeare in *Twelfth Night*. However, Shakespeare weaves these elements into a plot that, when compared with the gulling of Bonifacio in *Candelaio*, reveals the opposite intent from Bruno's: that of complicating rather than directing our response.

In *Candelaio*, the punishment of Bonifacio makes sense from both a logical and a structural point of view: he has carried out certain actions and is punished for them. By contrast, in *Twelfth Night* Malvolio is attacked not for what he has done but for what he is. He is, indeed, a conceited spoilsport who fantasises about becoming a count, sleeping with Lady Olivia and 'gagging' and 'baffling' the comic characters. However, he is gratuitously deceived by those characters. Bonifacio is punished for and through his actions; Malvolio is punished for and through his thoughts. Bonifacio suffers mainly in material terms, while Malvolio is subjected to serious psychological mistreatment, making his punishment all the more unpalatable for the audience. In this way, Shakespeare deliberately problematises what in Bruno is a linear demonstration of cause and effect.

It is important to note that what we find in *Twelfth Night* is a 'problematisation': it is not a downright defence of Malvolio, any more than a downright attack on him. Jonathan Bate has pointed out that in Malvolio's exit cry, 'I'll be revenged on the whole pack of you' (V.i.365), the word 'pack' sets Malvolio up as a kind of Actaeon who has been attacked by hounds.[15] This effect has been prepared for earlier in the play, when Olivia's compassionate summing up of Malvolio's position – 'Poor fool, how they have *baffled* thee' (V.i.358) – unwittingly echoes the Steward's own uncharitable intents towards her uncle: 'I will *baffle* Sir Toby' (II.v.141–42). In the same way, the ploy to make Malvolio pass as mad mirrors his address to the night revellers: 'My masters, are you mad?' (II.iii.78). Thus the play does offer the possibility of seeing Malvolio as deservedly a 'hunter hunted' figure. Paradoxically, it does so in moments when he is theoretically in the right: when he is being commiserated with, and when he is using the voice of reason to counteract the rioters' unruly doings.

To complicate the use of the Actaeon metaphor even further, at the start of the play Count Orsino applies it to his love at first sight for Olivia: 'That instant was I turned into a hart, / And my desires, like fell and cruel hounds, / E'er since pursue me'.[16] Orsino is very distant from Malvolio in terms of social status and role in the community, but the two do mirror each other as would-be lovers of Olivia: the very aspect, in fact, that is one of the main charges against Malvolio. This startling connection between these two characters across the social gulf creates a paradoxical proximity that may challenge compassion rather than elicit it: how dare Malvolio appear in any way like Orsino? However, as we shall see below, the final action of the play vindicates this proximity when it is Orsino, the highest placed character in the play, who gives the order to 'pursue' Malvolio 'and entreat him to a peace' (V.i.367). In different ways throughout this comedy the play of similarities and differences forces us to reconsider our position as to who may or may not be deserving of our compassion.

Mirrorings and 'the whirligig of time'

The 'mirror' references to Actaeon, one placed at the beginning and one at the end of the play, are only one aspect of an extensive strategy of mirrorings in *Twelfth Night*.[17] On one level, this strategy invites us to spot the difference behind the similarity: two official suitors to Olivia – Orsino and Aguecheek; two objects of Olivia's love – Sebastian and Cesario; two priests – the real one who marries Olivia and Sebastian, and Feste disguised as 'Sir Topas', and so on. But, more to the point, it invites us to spot the similarity behind the difference. Ultimately this is a form of the 'identification' trope, similar to the challenge 'what would you think / To be thus used' that the character of Sir Thomas More deploys in the eponymous contemporary play in order to elicit compassion and curb violence.[18] As an artistic device rather than an explicit statement, this strategy challenges the withdrawal of compassion in a more obscure and, for that very reason, a more disquieting and powerful way.

One particularly insistent form of mirroring in *Twelfth Night* (which can now be linked back to Bruno's *Candelaio*) concerns anagrammatic names, most strikingly those of 'Olivia' and 'Viola'.[19] Again, there is some additional play with the positioning of these mirror elements, as Olivia's name is mentioned within twenty lines from the start of *Twelfth Night* (at I.i.18), while Viola's is withheld until fewer than 150 lines from the end, in the final scene of the play, when it is then repeated three times within the space of thirteen lines.[20] When the name is finally revealed, we are startled by the similarity between the name of the female protagonist and that of the lady ruler in the play. We might then also think back to a scene earlier in the play where another striking incident occurs involving a name: the notorious scene in which Malvolio desperately tries to make his own name fit the clues in the supposed love letter from Olivia.

The infamous acronym 'M.O.A.I.' that Malvolio tries to decipher in act II, scene v, to the merriment of his hidden tormentors, remains unexplained in the course of the play. In the final analysis, we are forced to accept as the only unequivocally correct explanation the one that Malvolio himself gives us: 'every one of these letters are in my name' (123–24). However, given the intense focus here on the letters in Malvolio's name, when we reach the final scene with its epiphanic revelation of the name 'Viola' we should realise not only how similar Viola's name is to Olivia's, but also, rather more startlingly, that 'every one of [the] letters' in these two names too is in Malvolio's name.

We could even apply the 'hunter hunted' equivalence directly to a reading of the riddle, in this way: the defining difference between the names Olivia and Viola on the one hand and that of Malvolio on the other is the initial M. There is only one other person in the play whose name begins with M (actually, with Ma): it is Maria, the author of the fake letter and thus principal instigator of Malvolio's torments. In fact, 'Mall', as in 'Mistress Mall's picture' (*Twelfth Night*, I.iii.106–7), was a common nickname for 'Mary'. In the acronym M.O.A.I., if we keep the initial M as the first letter, then read its mirror opposite I, followed by either O or A, as alternatives, what we have is either M(a)*IO or M(a)*IA. In most plays and situations this would be far-fetched. Here, it simply reproduces the onomastic parallelism and awareness of Italian masculine and feminine endings that is found, for instance, in 'Orsino' and 'Olivia'. Most importantly, it reinforces a fundamental thematic aspect, as once again the hunter turns into the hunted (and vice versa), the tormentor and the tormented coalesce.[21]

The idea of the constant alternation of positions or 'vicissitude' is a specific feature also of Bruno's philosophy. In *Candelaio* it surfaces explicitly in another of its paratexts:

> at whatever point we may be in this evening in which I wait, if the mutation is true, I who am in the night will move on into day, those who are in the day will move on into night; for everything that is, is here or is there, near or far, now or to come.[22]

In Shakespeare's play, in the final jibes against Malvolio (summarising a plot that mostly came from *Candelaio*) Feste arrives at a similar generalization: 'and thus the whirligig of time brings in his revenges' (V.i.364). And, true to form, the whirligig keeps spinning, as Malvolio's exit cry immediately picks up this mention of 'revenge'.[23]

Shakespeare's perception of the 'whirligig of time', which informs the structure and mood of *Twelfth Night*, responds to contemporary events whose presence in the play is enacted via his choice of sources. Shakespeare's intervention in the debate generated by these events consists in showing that compassion is not merely an emotion the lack of which leads to aberrations on a personal level: it is also the only logical reaction to history, and the most expedient choice in politics.

Anniversary Comedies

As already mentioned, *Candelaio* was published in Paris on the tenth anniversary of the St Bartholomew massacre, and contains more or less open references to this event. As Katherine Ibbett has argued for France, the language of compassion was restructured and intensified by a response to the Wars of Religion, becoming the 'affective undertow' of toleration.[24] While my argument is that Shakespeare too draws his compassionate imaginary from the French Wars of Religion, a little-discussed aspect of the Italian play that is the *main* source of *Twelfth Night* suggests that he was also pairing those wars and the ensuing refugee crisis with a mirror instance of European sectarian violence. In *Gli Ingannati* Lelia, the Viola equivalent, is separated from her brother Fabrizio not through a shipwreck but through its political equivalent: the 1527 Sack of Rome by the imperial troops of Charles V. Condemnation of this event surfaces in the play, not least in the heroine's fear that she may be 'damaged goods' because of having been held hostage by the Spaniards. The play features several derogatory comments against Spanish soldiers, who were a kind of occupying army in Italy.

The play's publication history and reception also appear significant in terms of anniversaries. *Gli Ingannati* was written and first performed at the start of the fifth year from the Sack of Rome, and first printed in the tenth anniversary year from this event (1532, o.s. 1531, and 1537 respectively). As it happens, these dates also correspond to the twentieth and twenty-fifth anniversaries of another large-scale atrocity: the 1512 Sack of Prato, whose horrors had led to the fall of the Florentine Republic. On that occasion, the Pope and the Emperor had formed an alliance to restore the Medici to power, and one might have reflected ruefully on the reversal that had seen the Emperor attack a Medici Pope fifteen years later in the Sack of Rome. With another turn of the wheel, sixty years almost to the day after the Prato atrocity, in Paris and in the rest of France thousands had once again been sacrificed to a common Papal, Imperial and Medici-Valois cause in the St Bartholomew massacre.

It is this 'whirligig of time' itself that is the most powerful source concept in *Twelfth Night*. The play's superabundance of mirrorings mimics what would have been evident to any contemporary observer of these horrors: history was seen as a constant series of mirror images of violence, starting with the dates of the 1527 attack on the Holy See of Catholicism and the 1572 massacre of a large Protestant community, the two events linked with the two main sources of *Twelfth Night*.

The Flemish Crisis

The earliest recorded performance of *Twelfth Night* took place on Candlemas Day (2nd February) 1602, the start of the thirtieth anniversary year from the St Bartholomew massacre. That month also saw the second anniversary of Bruno's burning by the Roman Inquisition, on 17 February 1600. The figure of Bruno looms behind the episode in which Feste disguised as a priest questions the imprisoned Malvolio on the doctrine of metempsychosis.[25] This rather odd dialogue brings to mind a certain former Dominican friar who was the scourge of Calvinists and rated the beliefs of the ancient Egyptians and Pythagoreans far above any modern organised religion.[26] Bruno's presence parallels the way in which he had 'participated' in the punishment in *Candelaio* in the guise of his alter ego Gioan Bernardo. If we see Feste 'as the character in *Twelfth Night* most closely associated with the playwright', this is another aspect that comes to Shakespeare directly from Bruno.[27]

The degree to which Malvolio himself should be considered a Puritan is a moot point. For the purposes of the present argument, what matters is that he functions as a religiously connotated Other – in the same way as Shylock in *The Merchant of Venice* and Don John in *Much Ado about Nothing* – and that he does so in a way that, in this case, references the Huguenot community of the French and Dutch refugees in London.

There are more than enough pointers in this direction. Maria calls the Steward 'a kind of Puritan' as well as 'Monsieur Malvolio' (II.iii.120–31).[28] And at act III, scene ii, lines 21–26, the exchange between Fabian and Sir Andrew on the latter's failure to outshine Cesario in Olivia's eyes is couched in terms that recall the Flemish need for military rescue, especially since they refer to a 'Dutchman's beard' and give Aguecheek another opportunity to express his gratuitous anti-Puritan stance, with an additional topical reference to the Netherlands:

FABIAN ... you are now sailed into the north of my lady's opinion, where you will hang like an icicle on a Dutchman's beard unless you do redeem it by some laudable attempt either of valour or policy.

SIR ANDREW An't be any way, it must be with valour, for policy I hate. I had as lief be a Brownist as a politician.

The references here are to 'the Dutch explorer Willem Barentsz, who became stranded in icefields off the island of Nova Zembla' in 1596–1597 and to 'the congregationalist followers of Robert Browne, who had been expelled to the Netherlands in 1581 for their uncompromising severity in matters of church ceremony and other vitriolic dissatisfactions with the established church'.[29] Feste's disguise as 'Sir Topas' may function in this way too. This assumed name alludes to the fact that topaz stones were supposed to cure madness, but a reference to 'Sir Priest' and 'Sir Knight' in *Twelfth Night* (III.iv.241) prepares us to see a link between this (fake) priest and Chaucer's 'Sir Topas', a knight of whom we are told:

> Iborne he was in farre countre
> In Flaundres, al beyonde the see
> At Poperynge in the place.[30]

Maria's otherwise inane observation that Feste could have played Sir Topas without a beard because Malvolio could not see him anyway could be linked to the 'Dutchman's beard' mentioned at act III, scene ii, line 23, thus reinforcing the Flemish allusion. Seemingly throw-away remarks in *Twelfth Night* turn into a whirligig of textual allusions. The play thus extends its allusive spectrum to the contemporary oscillation in English attitudes towards the beleaguered Flemish and French Protestants, whose numbers in London had soared from the mid-1580s because of the Spanish reconquest of the southern Netherlands and continued religious strife in France. Their large presence and the attendant economic problems put a serious strain on their English co-religionists' sympathy, and they were accused of various dishonest practices.[31]

The plight of the Huguenot immigrants in London is also the thinly disguised background for the riot scene from the Ill May Day of 1517 portrayed in the Hand-D fragment of *Sir Thomas More*.[32] Shakespeare is generally considered the author of this scene, which is part of a revision that is often situated close to 1600 – i.e. close to the presumed date of composition of *Twelfth Night*.[33] As for the date of the original *Sir Thomas More* play, critics are divided between a time near the specific episodes of anti-immigrant unrest that took place in 1593 and 1595, which would give it topical relevance, and stylistic and other evidence that links it to the turn of the century.[34] Given what we now know concerning the importance of certain anniversary years for *Twelfth Night*'s sources, and by extension possibly for Shakespeare's play itself, it is no longer necessary to choose between these two criteria, since the Huguenot plight would have had continued artistic, political and commercial relevance in 1597 or in 1602, i.e. in the twenty-fifth and thirtieth anniversaries of the St Bartholomew massacre.

The problematisation of Malvolio and the wealth of mirrorings and doublings in *Twelfth Night* are an appropriate artistic response to complex times characterised by reversals and mirror-opposite events: times when booksellers displayed only Bibles on St Bartholomew's Day in commemoration of the Paris massacre, while anti-Dutch and anti-French pamphlets were printed as a result of widespread resentment for the economic incentives offered to the refugees from such massacres – refugees whose Calvinist faith played a greater role in setting them apart than the common Protestantism did in uniting them with the original population; times when a play like *Sir Thomas More* opens with a scene that portrays the foreigners as obnoxious oppressors, and goes on five scenes later to castigate the anti-foreign rioters, denouncing their 'mountainish inhumanity';[35] a time, most disturbingly of all, when government-sponsored publications promising 'favour' and 'rest' to 'Poor strangers' were followed by official orders of expulsion.[36]

Critics have pointed out verbal echoes between the riot scene in *Sir Thomas More* and Malvolio's verbal attack on the night revellers in Olivia's house.[37] This is interesting not only in view of the common 'Huguenot' theme in both plays.[38] If, as has been remarked, 'More's speeches belong to a recognizable Shakespearian type' that includes other subduers of popular uproar such as Marullus in *Julius Caesar* and Menenius in *Coriolanus*, we must now add Malvolio to this company.[39] This is surprising only up to a point, in that it simply contributes a further ambiguity to those already present in the portrayal of these characters. As for Malvolio himself, his attitude here, of course, would have marked him as an outsider to the community of revellers, placing him beyond the scope of their compassion. The dilemma for the viewer is then whether they can and should extend their own compassionate boundaries to include the Steward – or indeed whether it makes sense for such boundaries to exist at all.

Compassion: From Social Luxury to Political Duty

Critics sometimes raise doubts over the possibility of using modern patterns of feelings as guidelines for the past.[40] Yet personal accounts by survivors of the St Bartholomew massacre, as discussed by Mark Greengrass, show remarkable similarities with reactions and behavioural patterns in the face of the persecution of Jews in the twentieth century both on the part of the persecuted and of the rest of the population, suggesting a degree of continuity.[41] In *Twelfth Night*, I suggest, the emotions Shakespeare draws on and scripts are immediately recognisable to the audience today: on the one hand, a sense of social and economic vulnerability; a feeling of hurt at a perceived unjust rebuke; on the other hand, the capacity to empathise and sympathise with these feelings, and to reach out to those experiencing them.

A peculiarity of Malvolio's case, compared with *Sir Thomas More*, is that he is not only the critic but also the victim of a riotous crowd. The parallel is illuminating when we reflect that what motivated the opposition to foreigners in London in the 1590s was mostly fear of an economic nature.[42] The same motivation is, ultimately, behind the 'eclipse' of compassion that can be observed in *Twelfth Night*.

Malvolio exposes the social and economic vulnerability of other members of Olivia's household, who therefore see him as a threat. It is Orsino and Olivia who pity and rescue him, while his tormentors are those who, like him, are dependent on their social superiors. This is shown clearly from Malvolio's first entrance in the scene that also introduces his nemesis, Feste the clown. It is worth taking a detailed look at this because it summarises the play's social microcosm.

At this point in the play, we do not know what the fool's name is. The only time that he is named is in act II, scene iv, lines 11–12, where he is described as 'Feste the jester ... a fool that the lady Olivia's father took much delight in.' His position is precarious: the master who delighted in him is dead; Olivia is in mourning for her brother: chances are that in her next household budget she will do away with him altogether. In his first few lines, in act I, scene v, lines 13–14, he reveals a sense of this: 'and those that are fools, let them use their talents'. Maria too points out Feste's vulnerability: 'to be turned away – is not that as good as a hanging to you?' (lines 15–16). In retaliation, Feste hints at a match between Maria and Sir Toby – that is a sore point with Maria: something that she would dearly love, but that at this stage is not really foreseeable. While the socially dependent characters may to a certain extent look out for one another, they are ready to lash out at any reference to their vulnerable status. Maria's evaluation of Feste's precarious position is immediately enacted as Olivia issues the order to get rid of him (line 33), and he indeed has to 'use [his] talents' to gain a reprieve. He succeeds by proving Olivia a fool, and is drawing a sigh of relief when Malvolio intervenes.

Malvolio's fault is that he is a 'yes-man' to those in power rather than one of the riotous 'pack': significantly, his first word in the play is 'Yes' (at I.v.65), though, again ominously, he has misunderstood Olivia's question: she says something positive about Feste, he replies as though she has said something negative. Malvolio turns Olivia's goodwill towards Feste into ill will ('Mal-volio'). We can imagine Feste's alarmed reaction: Malvolio risks undoing all the work he has just done to get back into Olivia's good graces.

Hence his snarling reply to Malvolio, which prophesies the trick they will later play on him: 'God send you, sir, a speedy infirmity for the better increasing your folly' (lines 67–68). In retort, Malvolio emphasises Feste's vulnerability, and undermines his professional credibility: 'I saw him put down the other day with an ordinary fool that has no more brain than a stone. Look you now, he's out of his guard already. Unless you laugh and minister occasion to him, he is gagged' (lines 72–75). This hurts: at the end of the play, in the 'whirligig of time' speech, Feste will throw these same words back into Malvolio's face.

Then something important happens. While most of the play problematises perceptions, here we are given one unambiguously positive example, with Olivia exercising her role as the just ruler who can afford to extend her help and sympathy in turn where it is needed most. First, she defends Feste against Malvolio: 'O, you are sick of self-love, Malvolio … There is no slander in an allowed fool, though he do nothing but rail' (lines 77–81). Here Malvolio must show his vulnerability too – he had not expected Olivia to turn against him, and certainly not with such a harsh rebuke. He is deeply hurt, and must have shown it – because with the same sentence Olivia turns to him and continues, in a gentler tone: '… nor no railing in a known discreet man, though he do nothing but reprove' (lines 81–82). This anticipates the last scene of the play, when the aristocratic characters acknowledge that Malvolio has been 'abused' and attempt to pacify him.[43] It also fulfils the conciliatory and impartial monarchical role that arguably both Bruno and Shakespeare saw as the only way out of the vicious circle of political and religious warfare.

Conclusion

As Malvolio storms off at the end of the play, the audience might realise that they have been tricked, morality-play fashion, into the wrong ethical response: they may have fallen into the Actaeon trap and allowed their sense of compassion, not to mention justice, to subside into the image of a hunter being deservedly hunted – the more readily so, in the case of the play's original audience, because of their social and economic fears. By contrast, the structural and intertextual references in *Twelfth Night* work towards identifying strife not as having a singular, linear trajectory involving specific sets of individuals, but as a circular and mirror-like process: in the light of which, the bestowing of compassion may be quite simply the most politically provident attitude.

Notes

1 The idiomatic phrase is found at act II, scene v, lines 8–10, where Sir Andrew Aguecheek responds to Sir Toby's assertion that they will fool Malvolio: 'An we do not, it is pity of our lives.' Shakespeare quotations in this chapter follow Stephen Greenblatt (gen. ed.), *The Norton Shakespeare* (New York: Norton, 1997).
2 Joan Coldwell, 'The Playgoer as Critic: Charles Lamb on Shakespeare's Characters', *Shakespeare Quarterly*, 26:2 (1975), 184–95 (p. 192). More recent critics sometimes concede that '[i]n Aristotelian terms, Malvolio might arguably have the necessary traits of a tragic hero'. Cf. Edward Cahill, 'The Problem of Malvolio', *College Literature*, 23:2 (1996), 62–82 (p. 79 n. 2).
3 Cf. Bridget Escolme, *Emotional Excess on the Shakespearean Stage: Passion's Slaves* (London: Bloomsbury, 2014), pp. 97–103 (esp. p. 102). A useful survey of critical discussions of Malvolio can be found in chapters 1 and 3 in Alison Findlay and Liz Oakley-Brown (eds.), *Twelfth Night: A Critical Reader* (London: Bloomsbury, 2014): R. S. White, 'The Critical Backstory', pp. 27–51, and William C. Carroll, 'The State of the Art', pp. 71–98.
4 Sabina Amambayeva, 'Laughter in *Twelfth Night* and Beyond: Affect and Genre in Early Modern Comedy', *Early Modern Literary Studies*, 17:2 (2014), 1–21 (p. 3).
5 Leo G. Salingar, 'The Design of *Twelfth Night*', *Shakespeare Quarterly*, 9:2 (Spring 1958), 117–39 (p. 135).
6 Accordingly, my chapter presents a rather harsher view of the below-stairs in Olivia's household than Robert J. Vrtis' 'small community' that 'embodies a celebration of shared emotion'. Cf. Vrtis, 'The Tempest Toss'd Ship: *Twelfth Night* and Emotional Communities in Early Modern London' in Brigitte Le Juez and Olga Springer (eds.), *Shipwreck and Island Motifs in Literature and the Arts* (Leiden: Brill, 2015), pp. 135–50 (p. 138), mentioned in Eric Langley's Chapter 10 in this volume.
7 In his diary entry dated 'Febr. 1601' (n.s. 1602), John Manningham describes *Twelfth Night* as 'most like and neere to that in Italian called Inganni' (cf. *The Norton Shakespeare*, p. 3334). In 1845, Joseph Hunter identified *Gli Ingannati* as the play that was actually closest to Shakespeare's plot – cf. Hunter, *New Illustrations of the Life, Studies, and Writings of Shakespeare* (London: Nichols, 1845), p. 393.
8 See Hilary Gatti, 'Giordano Bruno's *Candelaio* and Possible Echoes in Shakespeare and Ben Jonson', *Viator*, 43:2 (2012), 357–75; Elisabetta Tarantino, 'Bruno's *Candelaio*, Shakespeare and Ben Jonson: Building on Hilary Gatti's Work' in Martin McLaughlin, Ingrid D. Rowland and Elisabetta Tarantino (eds.), *Authority, Innovation and Early Modern Epistemology: Essays in Honour of Hilary Gatti* (London: Legenda, 2015), pp. 118–36. There are in fact several interconnected texts that contributed plot elements to *Twelfth Night*, such as the tale of 'Apollonius and Silla' in *Riche's Farewell to Military Profession* (1581), which ultimately derives from

Gli Ingannati. My discussion in this chapter both assumes and further strengthens the view that the latter play and Bruno's *Candelaio* provided the main source concept for Shakespeare's play. In 'Shakespeare and Religious War: New Developments on the Italian Sources of Twelfth Night', *Shakespeare Survey 72* (2019), 32–47, I additionally explore the relevance to *Twelfth Night*, and especially to the depiction of Sir Andrew Aguecheek, of Antonfrancesco Grazzini's *La Strega*, a play that has a number of points in common with *Candelaio*.

9 Gatti herself does not read the relationship between Shakespeare and Bruno in political or religious terms, her focus being on the moral corruption of the city. The latter aspect is certainly in evidence, alongside the socio-religious issue, in Ben Jonson's *Bartholomew Fair*, which advertises more obviously than *Twelfth Night* its connection with both *Candelaio* and the French historical background. I am grateful to Hilary Gatti for reading my work and offering helpful suggestions on these topics. I explore these issues further in 'History and Religion in Giordano Bruno's *Candelaio*' in Massimiliano Traversino Di Cristo (ed.), *Giordano Bruno: Law, Philosophy, and Theology in the Early Modern Era* (Paris: Garnier, 2021), pp. 335–54.

10 Responses to the St Bartholomew massacre in *tragedy* were of course not uncommon, including in England, starting with Christopher Marlowe's *The Massacre at Paris*. Robert White additionally discusses the massacre in relation to *Love's Labour's Lost*. White rejects Frances Yates' theory of the presence of Giordano Bruno in the latter play, but this should now be reviewed in the light of what is discussed in this article: cf. Robert White, 'The Cultural Impact of the Massacre of St Bartholomew's Day' in *Early Modern Civil Discourses*, ed. Jennifer Richards (Basingstoke: Palgrave Macmillan, 2003), pp. 183–99.

11 On the structural and semantic parallelism of the names 'Bonifacio' and 'Malvolio', see Gatti, 'Giordano Bruno's *Candelaio*', p. 366 and Tarantino, 'Bruno's *Candelaio*', p. 127. Besides containing the name 'Bartolomeo', the play makes explicit reference to the massacre in a monologue in act IV, scene v, in which Bonifacio complains about the fickleness of public opinion whereby an enterprise will be talked of as being by the 'Great Council of Paris' if it goes well or by the 'French fury' if it turns out badly. See Tarantino, 'Bruno's *Candelaio*', pp. 125–28.

12 There is no recorded early performance of *Candelaio*. For channels through which knowledge of *Candelaio* could have reached Shakespeare, see Gatti, 'Giordano Bruno's *Candelaio*', pp. 362–64.

13 'Consider then: it was his infatuation with Vittoria that first put him in the way of being deceived, and when he tried to enjoy her, he became deceived indeed; prefigured, in fact, by Actaeon, who went hunting for horned beasts and when he thought of enjoying Diana, was turned into a stag himself. So it is not surprising that this man was ripped and torn in pieces by these ruffianly hounds.' Quotations from *Candelaio* are from J. R. Hale's translation, included (with the slightly erroneous title of *The Candle Bearer*) in *The*

Genius of the Italian Theater, ed. Eric Bentley (New York: Mentor Books, 1964), pp. 194–314 (this quotation on p. 203). The Actaeon myth is a signature motif in Bruno's philosophical work, where, however, it is used as a positive epistemological metaphor; see n. 16 below.

14 Cf. Gatti, 'Giordano Bruno's *Candelaio*', pp. 361–62.
15 Jonathan Bate, *Shakespeare and Ovid* (Oxford: Clarendon, 1993), p. 147.
16 *Twelfth Night*, act I, scene i, lines 20–23. This identification of the subject's 'desires' with Actaeon's hounds is close to the way Bruno uses the metaphor in one of his Italian dialogues, printed in London in 1585, where the hounds represent his thoughts: 'The stag who sought to bend / His lightened step towards denser forest depths / His dogs devoured; they caught him in their trap. / The thoughts that I extend / Towards lofty prey recoil and deal me death, / Rending me in their fell and savage snap.' (Giordano Bruno, *On the Heroic Frenzies*, Italian text edited by Eugenio Canone, translation by Ingrid D. Rowland (Toronto University Press, 2013), p. 107.) This similarity is already noted in François Laroque, 'Le mythe d'Actéon dans *Twelfth Night*', *Etudes anglaises*, 48:4 (1995), 385–94 (p. 390).
17 On this aspect see Salingar, 'The Design of *Twelfth Night*'; Penny Gay, '*Twelfth Night*: "The Babbling Gossip of the Air"' in *A Companion to Shakespeare's Works: The Comedies*, ed. Richard Dutton and Jean E. Howard (Malden, MA: Blackwell, 2003), pp. 429–46; Keir Elam's introduction to his Arden edition of *Twelfth Night* (London: Cengage, 2008), pp. 1–53 (pp. 24–32); Marianne Novy, *Shakespeare and Outsiders* (Oxford University Press, 2013), ch. 2; Frances E. Dolan, *Twelfth Night: Language & Writing* (London: Bloomsbury, 2014).
18 *Sir Thomas More*, Add.II.D. 150–51. For the relevance of this passage see the section 'The Flemish Crisis' in this chapter.
19 Cynthia Lewis, '"A Fustian Riddle"?: Anagrammatic Names in *Twelfth Night*', *English Language Notes*, 22:4 (June 1985), pp. 32–37; Penny Gay, '*Twelfth Night*', pp. 435–36.
20 Anne Barton, *The Names of Comedy* (Oxford: Clarendon, 1990), pp. 137–39.
21 David Bevington has commented on the mirror structure of the acronym: see 'The Debate about Shakespeare and Religion' in *Shakespeare and Early Modern Religion*, ed. David Loewenstein and Michael Witmore (Cambridge University Press, 2015), pp. 23–39 (p. 27). See also Vincent F. Petronella, 'Anamorphic Naming in Shakespeare's *Twelfth Night*', *Names*, 35:3–4 (September–December 1987), 139–46 (p. 143).
22 'Letter to Morgana', p. 199 (adapted). On the possible parallel with *Hamlet*, and relevant critical bibliography, see Tarantino, 'Bruno's *Candelaio*', p. 121.
23 This point is made also in Karin S. Coddon, '"Slander in an allow'd fool": Twelfth Night's Crisis of the Aristocracy', *Studies in English Literature 1500–1900*, 33:2 (Spring 1993), 309–25 (p. 322).
24 Katherine Ibbett, *Compassion's Edge: Fellow-Feeling and Its Limits in Early Modern France* (Philadelphia: University of Pennsylvania Press, 2018), p. 5. See also my online exhibition in collaboration with the Shakespeare Birthplace

Trust for their *Shakespeare Connected* series: http://collections.shakespeare.org
.uk/exhibition/exhibition/shakespeare-connected-shakespeare-and-religious-
war (supported by the Museum University Partnership Initiative of the
National Co-ordinating Centre for Public Engagement; accessed November
2019). For other aspects of Shakespeare and the Wars of Religion, see chapter
2 in Richard Wilson, *Worldly Shakespeare: The Theatre of Our Good Will*
(Edinburgh: Edinburgh University Press, 2016), pp. 53–72.
25 On this passage, see Gatti, 'Giordano Bruno's *Candelaio*', pp. 367–68.
26 On references to the biblical Egyptian darkness as a metaphor for religious
blindness used by both Protestant and Catholic polemicists, see the introduction
to *Twelfth Night: A Critical Reader*, ed. Alison Findlay and Liz Oakley-
Brown, pp. 1–26 (pp. 17–18).
27 The quotation is from Cynthia Lewis, 'Whodunit? Plot, Plotting, and
Detection in *Twelfth Night*' in *Twelfth Night: New Critical Essays*, ed. James
Schiffer (London and New York: Routledge, 2011), pp. 258–72
(pp. 267–68).
28 I have restored the capital 'P' found in the First Folio.
29 I quote, respectively, from Keir Elam's notes to *Twelfth Night*, p. 264, and
David Bevington, 'The Debate about Shakespeare and Religion', p. 26.
30 *The Works of Geoffrey Chaucer* (London: William Bonahm, 1542), STC 5069,
fol. lxxviii^r, EEBO image 90. Around this time Shakespeare was engaging with
Chaucer in *Troilus and Cressida*.
31 On this issue, see, for instance, Eric Griffin, 'Shakespeare, Marlowe, and the
Stranger Crisis of the Early 1590s' in *Shakespeare and Immigration*, ed. Ruben
Espinosa and David Ruiter (Farnham: Ashgate, 2014), pp. 13–36 (esp. p. 19).
32 See the introduction to *Sir Thomas More*, ed. John Jowett, Arden Shakespeare
(London: Methuen, 2011), pp. 1–129 (esp. pp. 43–47).
33 Both plays are assigned to the indicative date of 1601 in Martin Wiggins, with
Catherine Richardson, *British Drama 1533–1642: A Catalogue*, vol. IV:
1598–1602 (Oxford University Press, 2014) (though Wiggins, p. 278, urges
caution on the identification of Shakespeare with Hand D).
34 Cf. Jowett's edition, p. 424.
35 Catherine Lisak points out that, when Olivia accuses Sir Toby of being 'Fit for
the mountains and barbarous caves' (*Twelfth Night*, IV.iv.44), '[t]he lesson
from *Sir Thomas More* seems to echo in her lines' (Catherine Lisak,
'Domesticating Strangeness in *Twelfth Night*', in *Twelfth Night: New
Critical Essays*, ed. Schiffer, pp. 167–83 [p. 181]). See Tarantino,
'Shakespeare and Religious War', for a discussion of how Grazzini's *La
Strega* helps explain this peculiar phrase in *Sir Thomas More*.
36 Cf. Griffin, 'Shakespeare, Marlowe, and the Stranger Crisis', pp. 25 and 30.
37 MacDonald P. Jackson, 'The Date and Authorship of Hand D's Contribution
to Sir Thomas More: Evidence from "Literature Online"', *Shakespeare Survey*
59 (2006), 69–78 (p. 76). See also E. A. J. Honigmann, 'Shakespeare, Sir
Thomas More and Asylum Seekers', *Shakespeare Survey* 57 (2004), 225–35.

38 Huguenot immigrants associated with Shakespeare are discussed in E. A. J. Honigmann, 'Shakespeare and London's Immigrant Community circa 1600' in *Elizabethan and Modern Studies Presented to Professor Willem Schrickx on the Occasion of His Retirement*, ed. J. P. Vander Motten (Ghent: Seminarie voor Engelse en Amerikaanse Literatuur, R.U.G., 1985), pp. 143–53. See also his 'Shakespeare, Sir Thomas More and Asylum Seekers', pp. 233–34.

39 The quotation is from Honigmann, 'Shakespeare, Sir Thomas More and Asylum Seekers', p. 228.

40 For a discussion of this issue, see the introductions to two recent collections of essays on this subject: *The Renaissance of Emotion*, eds. Richard Meek and Erin Sullivan (Manchester University Press, 2015) and *Shakespeare and Emotions*, ed. R. S. White, Mark Houlahan and Katrina O'Loughlin (Houndmills: Palgrave Macmillan, 2015).

41 Cf. Mark Greengrass, 'Hidden Transcripts: Secret Histories and Personal Testimonies of Religious Violence in the French Wars of Religion' in *The Massacre in History*, ed. Mark Levene and Penny Roberts (New York and Oxford: Berghahn, 1999), pp. 69–88 (p. 81), where the similarity is explicitly pointed out in one specific respect, but other incidents and reactions he describes could also serve as parallels.

42 See the letter of protest sent by Thomas Deloney to the French and Dutch Churches in London in 1595 (quoted in Jowett's edition of *Sir Thomas More*, p. 43).

43 Without referring to Shakespeare's plays, A. G. Dickens portrays the contrast between the attitudes of the lower and the higher classes towards the Huguenot refugees in very similar terms to those I have described in this scene. And he even recalls the 'Evil Mayday' of 1517 that is the subject of *Sir Thomas More*. (Cf. A. G. Dickens, 'The Elizabethans and St. Bartholomew' in *The Massacre of St. Bartholomew: Reappraisals and Documents*, ed. Alfred Soman (The Hague: Martinus Nijhoff, 1974), pp. 52–70.)

CHAPTER 10

Standing on a Beach
Shakespeare and the Sympathetic Imagination
Eric Langley

Shipwreck with Spectator

Men have pitty of those whom they see neere unto some great misfortune: As when they are ready to be buried in the waves of the sea by some accident of shipwracke; or of those who are to have a member cut off, or to receive some notable violence, yea or some indignity. Particularly men are toucht with pitty, when as they that are exposed to outrages, or endure great calamities, are their equalls in age, in humours, in exercise, or in breeding. For all these things make deepe impressions in the thought, that they are subject to the like miseries; wherefore they are moved to take compassion of their miseries.[1]

Discussing 'what things are worthy of pitty and compassion' in his *Tableau des passions humaines*, French theologian Nicolas Coeffeteau has recourse to an adapted Aristotelian conception of pathos (suffering) characterised by metaphors of emotional touch and mental plasticity; accordingly, Edward Grimeston's translation emphasises the importance of contact and proximity in the generation of sympathy, describing how 'those [piteous sights] which touch us so neere [produce] a feeling more violent', making 'deepe impressions' on the malleable and therefore moveable, easily 'wrought' affective and affected observer, pressing upon those who have, in John Donne's terms, a 'souple, and tractable, and ductile disposition'.[2] Pity, as described in the period's religious treatises and medical texts alike, is first and foremost a matter of tact, implicating the subject in emotional contracts predicated upon contact, where proximity of age, humours, or breeding, as Coeffeteau describes, help to ensure like-mindedness and thereby facilitate kindred feeling (of course, in Aristotle's influential formulation, pure pity – disentangled from his broader mixed category of *pathê* – entails a regulated proximity, circumventing terrifying immediacy).[3] Accordingly, including *convenientia* in his taxonomy of *The Order of Things*, Michel Foucault describes how sympathy facilitates resemblance, how subsequently 'resemblance imposes adjacencies', and therefore how adjacencies abet emotional transference: '[when things become] sufficiently close to one another to be in juxtaposition ... their edges touch, their fringes intermingle' and 'in this way, movement, influences, passions, and properties too, are communicated'.[4] Or, in Francis Bacon's sixteenth-century terms, 'thinges like and consenting in qualitie, [when] quartered together, spredde, multiplie and infect in similitude'.[5] Indeed, as Foucault cautions, 'sympathy is an instance of the *Same* so strong and so insistent ... [that] it has the dangerous power of *assimilating*, or rendering things identical to one another, of mingling them', and consequently, he concludes, 'of causing their individuality to disappear – and thus rendering them foreign to what they were before':

> Sympathy transforms. It alters, but in the direction of identity, so that if its power were not counterbalanced it would reduce the world to a point, to a homogeneous mass, to the featureless form of the Same: all its parts would hold together and communicate with one another without a break, with no distance between them.[6]

In short, the tactility and emotional kinesis at the heart of pathetic contact facilitates for both benevolent support – 'leane on me', as the period's Christian commentators insist – and yet, more disturbingly, contamination: 'quite literally, according to its etymology ("con": together; "tangere": to touch), *contagion* can put us in touch'.[7] This touch, as Donne warns, 'beget[s] ... a dangerous compassion, in spectators and hearers', moving them along new precipitous emotive 'incline[s]' and 'draw[ing] men ... to side', where they 'mingle themselves in [corrupted] impertinencies', losing their self-content.[8] Indeed, inheriting a natural philosophy informed by conceptions of humoral passibility and sensory impressionability, of planetary, ecological, emotional, and even imaginative influence and communication, the Renaissance subject – closely involved, tightly reticulated within the 'sympathetick Influence[s] of Nature' – understandably also has reactionary recourse to assertions of *antipathy*, which, as Foucault describes, would 'maintain ... the isolation of things and prevent ... their assimilation'.[9] As is often the case in Shakespeare, as Elisabetta Tarantino demonstrates in Chapter 9 in her discussion of *Twelfth Night*, compassion must be both 'evoked but also challenged'; indeed sometimes, sympathy needs to be denied.

Accordingly, in what follows, we will take just one of Coeffeteau's piteous spectacles, and return to a second Shakespearean scene of an observed shipwreck – after Tarantino's discussion of the Illyrian instance – and examine how early modern writers, and Shakespeare in particular, revisit this classically derived emblematic scenario as they assess the nature of compassionate contact in order to account for both the importance and cost of emotional interaction. This tableau of wreck and spectator – versions of which are found in Erasmus, Spenser, Sidney, Montaigne, Burton, and so on, but which I will demonstrate to have much older origins in the writing of Lucretius (c. 99–55 BCE) – offers an opportunity for both the articulation of sympathetic compassion and antipathetic dispassion.

Of course, in Shakespeare's words, as a 'vast tennis-court' in which humanity is 'the ball / For [Gods] to play upon', 'the liquid surge' of 'the wild and watery sea' with its 'ebb and flow', all 'puff'd up with winds [and] rag[ing]' with storms and tempests, provides a widely evoked and innately plural metaphor – 'the finny subject of the sea' is itself 'a theme as fluent as the sea' – connoting variously, a boundary-bursting 'sea of troubles'; the unpredictability of life or callousness of the deafly 'roar[ing]' gods; the irrational or contingent element; the unintelligibility of fate, 'fortune', or the natural order; signifying both remorseless constancy and vicissitudinous inconstancy; or, paradoxically, benevolent fortune and the 'boundless' fertility of a mutable world.[10] Equally, to 'suffer shipwreck' (*1HVI*, V.v.8) or to be sunk, to encounter mutiny or piracy, to be capsized, scuttled, or lost at sea, are all events that have similarly plural metaphoric possibilities, suggesting, for example, 'the collapse of the prevailing social order' or the insignificance of the individual; man's submission to irrationality or madness; the overwhelming impulses of 'HOT PASSION'; the vagaries of public 'OPINION [which toss man] up and downe'; his susceptibility to errant philosophical trajectories or impious inclinations; both 'a violent ecological encounter and harrowing theological risk'; financial ruin; inordinate grief; isolation; even, as Bruno has it, marriage, and so on.[11] But, crucially, the presence of a spectator more narrowly focuses our motif's metaphoric scope on what Steve Mentz has identified as 'the power of the philosophical mind, resting firm in the bedrock of reason', and therefore upon the empathetic tractility of the speculating subject, whose facility for selfless projection can be gauged according to their response to this frequently depicted tableaux.[12] Throughout the early modern period, poets and philosophers alike enquire, 'would we ... sit upon the quiet strand, / And thence behold the wracke like to ensue, / And pittie others, [while] we [were] secure on Land'?[13] The question – asked here by Bishop Joseph Hall in 1620 – of 'who [then] can pitty the ship-wracke of those Mariners, which will needs put forth, and hoise sailes in a tempest?' turns out to elicit an unexpectedly complex array of possible answers, and to generate yet more enquiries concerning the morality of disinterested witnessing, and the ethics of compassion.[14]

'Make a fair reckoning, and you find shipwreck everywhere': recurring from its classical inception, via early modern discussions of compassion, eighteenth-century conceptions of sentiment and the social contract, nineteenth-century models of elevated genius, to twentieth-century depictions of subjective estrangement (to name only a few instances of its appearance), the topos of shipwreck with spectator can, on the one hand, provide theologians with an emblem for laudable sympathetic vulnerability, and, on the other, provide philosophers with an opportunity to assess the reserve required to adopt a dispassionate rational stance.[15] In the broadest terms, each time the image occurs – be it in Nietzsche, Schopenhauer, or Kant – it provides insight into the extent to which vulnerability, affectivity, embeddedness, or interdependence is integrated into the substructure of the subject, allowing a quick historically localised assessment of the intensity of the individual's neurotic intractability or suppleness, their ipseic resistance or receptivity, their impulse towards incorporate un-dividuality or divided egoism. For example, Voltaire finds that the scene elicits engagement via 'curiosity', while, also in the 1750s, Rousseau complains that 'philosophy isolates [us]; because of it [we] say ... in secret, at the sight of a suffering man: Perish if you will, I am safe.'[16] Reason has 'fortifie[d]' and 'separate[d]' from 'all that bothers and afflicts him'. So 'philosophy', as Ann Hartle has concluded, may indeed 'begin ... with the pre-Socratics as the stance of the disinterested spectator', but this scene repeatedly demands that the spectator checks their ethical distancing, 'consider[ing] the distance [men] stand one to the other', testing the ligations and obligations of 'compassion ... fellow-feeling and sympathy' which should be as strong and taut as the 'strings of a viol' so that if we 'touch one ... the other trembles'; because, as any early modern essayist would rehearse, 'when my friend is under any affliction, my mind is troubled, and I feel that pain in my heart for him'.[17] Or, as one of Erasmus' speakers describes in his version of the scenario (identified as a source for Shakespeare's *Tempest*), 'my Flesh trembles to hear you relate [these calamities], as if I were in Danger myself.[18]

Knowing therefore that in order to be 'sensible in the feeling of a misfortune which befalls another, wee must have it as it were present before our eyes: for we are not moved with those miseries whose forme is remote from us', early modern writers repeatedly imagine this particularly contentious scene, as an opportunity to test sympathetic imagination's capacity to 'set before us as present, ... things [that are] farre off'; if 'every man by his contemplative and imaginarie presence is every where', it is compassionate contemplation in particular which demands an act of spatial foreshortening achieved via an affective telescoping which closes the speculative gap, putting the spectator dangerously close to the action, implicating the seeing subject in the scene's potentially terrifying immediacy, while consequently, and most importantly, disabusing any comforting fictions of autonomous isolation, hermetic monism, or quarantined self-sufficiency to which the early modern subject may aspire.[19] Marjorie Garber has identified a significant historical shift in the conception of compassion (*com*, together; *pati*, to suffer), demonstrating how the term's earlier usage to denote 'suffering with' becomes displaced by the more guarded 'suffering on behalf of'; and therefore it is by minding this delicately maintained gap – paying attention to early modern articulations of, variously, the need for emotional distancing or the virtue of pathos-induced proximity – that we can perhaps situate the Shakespearean subject somewhere on Garber's broad trajectory from the implicated involvement of a subject-*with*-another to the solipsistic displacement of a subject-guarded-*against*-another.[20] Similarly, the topos challenges each of Shakespeare's would-be compassionate observers to refute Lauren Berlant's twenty-first-century assertion that 'compassion is a term denoting privilege: the sufferer is *over there*'.[21]

Shipwreck with Spectators: Miranda and Lucretius

> Your honour [cannot] hear without pity. ... But at last, when ... the blackness of the sky could not be seen for the darkness of the air, when we expected nothing less than the splitting of sailes, breaking of shrouds, spending of masts, springing of planks – in a word the dreadful devouring of us all by some sea-swallowing whirlpool – we were most miraculously delivered.[22]

Looking out to sea at the 'direful spectacle of the wreck' in the opening scene of Shakespeare's *The Tempest*, Miranda's 'piteous heart' is 'touch'd [with] / The very virtue of compassion' (I.ii.14–27). As the 'mounting' sea mingles with the 'pour[ing]' skies, she suffers in sympathetic synergy with the 'poor' souls who perish in its wild waters: 'O! I have suffered', she exclaims, 'With those that I saw suffer' (3–9). Allowing herself empathetic engagement with the drowning sailors, Miranda is an involved and vulnerable spectator, alive to the invasive haptic 'touch' of sensitive contact as the mariners' cries 'knock / Against my very heart' (8–9). As the scene develops – 'O! I have suffered ...' – her 'O'pen compassionate receptivity – 'O, the cry ...' – becomes her emotional keynote – 'O woe the day! ...'. – punctuating her father's moving narrative – 'O the heavens ...' – with this reiterated 'O', the denotation of her ingenuous vulnerability, the sign of her 'passibility' – 'O, good sir ...' – as her knocked heart eventually begins to bleed: 'O, my heart bleeds ... O the heavens ...' (5–116).[23]

Exhibiting all the sensory receptivity of a co-suffering spectator, by responding so o-penly to those she 'heard cry' and 'saw'st sink' (32), Miranda demonstrates absolute attentive responsiveness to both the sinking boat and to her father's scene-setting narration; called to 'hear' and then 'hear a little further' (106–35), she 'opes [her] ear [to] obey and be attentive' (37–38). This insistence that she at*tends*, that she is tender or impressionably sensitive to Prospero's formative tale, shows Shakespeare engaged in a characteristic piece of half-homophonic, half-etymological word-play: as Bradin Cormack has demonstrated, Shakespeare's 'philological thinking [is] etymological when it serves him, but ... also looks to whatever acoustic forms are on hand', and here the playwright conflates *tender* and *attention*'s direct etymological sense (both from Lt. *tendĕre*, 'to stretch') with *tender*'s homophonic resonance of *tenerum* (Lt. 'delicate').[24] Through stretching her tenuous, intent attentions outwards both spatially towards the shipwreck and temporally via Prospero's account of his pitiable past, she is capable of both attentively *knowing further* and sympathetically coming to *know her father*, displaying both an empathetic ability to project towards the other, and a receptive ability to receive their pain. Caught up on this ebb and flow of tenderness, Miranda exemplifies an ideal condition of sympathetic receptivity – a humanist conflation of classical models of *communitas* with Christian conceptions of *caritas* and benevolence – and can therefore figure as the compassionate subject at its most generous and therefore at its most vulnerable.

And yet, as Susan Sontag has remarked in her discussion of the ethics of spectatorship, 'it is not always better to be moved'; although admirable in its intensity, there is a naivety in Miranda's compassion that could be tempered by Montaigne's more mature acceptance that 'no matter how great a man's wisdom, he can never grasp, through his judgement alone, the cause of another's grief in all its intensity'.[25] Terrifically open to the world's influences and influencies, Miranda is terrifyingly liable to drown in them, and her empathetic energies repeatedly lead her to emotive misconceptions that might make us fear that 'the more universally [her] sympathy is dispersed, the weaker it is'; her 'O ... O...' open assessment of others – 'O wonder! / How many goodly creatures are there here! How beauteous mankind is! / O …' (V.i.181–84) – is almost painfully guileless.[26] Watching the sinking ship, her unguarded empathy leads her to suppose it is a 'brave vessel / (Who had, no doubt, some noble creature in her)' (I.i.6–7), whereas Shakespeare has shown us – undermining her in advance – that it is full of 'drunk[en]' boatswains (56), cowardly mariners, and, for the most part, ignoble noblemen: it seems that 'pity', as Martha Nussbaum has suggested, can 'blind … us to [what] we can see before us or can easily imagine', and therefore, can 'distort … the world', into what Miranda mistakenly thinks to be a 'brave new world / That has such people in't' (184).[27]

In spatial terms, Miranda has not only come too close for her own objectivity, but so close as to obscure the integrity of the object, those hazily mis-seen subjects of her pity; Nussbaum would caution her that even 'in the temporary act of identification, one [should always remain] aware of one's own separateness from the sufferer', concluding that 'if one really had the experience of feeling the pain in one's own body, then one would precisely have failed to comprehend the pain of another *as other*'.[28] As the Introduction to this volume makes clear, the philosophy of compassion is frequently articulated in such spatial terms, right from its Stoic origins where it is the very impressionability of the subject – alive to an environment of impulse and the imprints of sensory and corpuscular interactivity – which prompts or necessitates a reactionary rational retreat from affective danger; always, compassionate experience demands we attend to this 'pathos of distance', which is invariably understood as a necessary dislocation with which to maintain 'the painful or dangerous, but exalted refinement … of difference'.[29] In brief, every philosophical approach to sympathy must negotiate what Hannah Arendt describes as the 'abysses of remoteness' between sufferer and viewer, either establishing a 'dialogue' between 'direct experience [which] establishes too close a contact [or retreating behind] mere knowledge [which] erects artificial barriers'.[30] As Sontag summarises, just as 'sight requires spatial distance', ethics too requires some spacing and therefore 'there's nothing wrong with standing back and thinking' while guarding against the 'kind of sentimentalism' that would offer 'knowledge [of the other only] at bargain prices – a semblance of knowledge, a semblance of wisdom'.[31]

Accordingly, around one thousand and sixty years before Miranda, a spectating precursor observed in the 'dredful swelling seas' another example – arguably the most influential, due to its polarising contentiousness – of our archetypal shipwreck scene; from his vantage point, the Epicurean Roman philosophical poet Lucretius looked out and thought ''tis pleasant, safely to behold from shore / The rowling Ship; and hear the Tempest roar'.³² Quickly, this extraordinarily unsympathetic assertion is qualified; it is 'not that anothers pain is our delight; / But pains unfelt produce the pleasing sight', just as "tis pleasant also to behold from far / The moving Legions mingled in the War.'³³ As far as is provable, this scene is the first section of Lucretius' controversial epic scientific poem *De rerum natura* (c. 50 BCE) to appear in English translation, as part of *Tottel's Miscellany* of 1557, and his cool detachment is clearly unpalatable even to its anonymous translator who inserts the placatory clause: 'and see with drede and depe dispaire, how shipmen are distrest'.³⁴ But any 'dispaire' the Lucretian observer may feel is explicitly not 'depe'; rather, the sanctity of the self-sufficient observer is preserved by their non-*part*icipatory, non-*part*aking stance: 'Our gladnes groweth to see their harmes, and yet to fele no *part*.'³⁵ Here, Lucretius promotes an intellectual dispassionate retreat by suggesting, in Dryden's later translation, that we should 'guide' our 'lab'ring steps ... / To Vertues heights, with wisdom well suppl'd, / And all the *Magazins* of Learning fortif'd.'³⁶ Secure in this armed emplacement of rationality, fortified in unempathetic immunity, we can 'look below on humane kind, / Bewilder'd in the Maze of Life, and blind'; as Hans Blumenberg describes, the scene literalises 'the relationship between philosophers and reality; it has to do with the advantage gained through Epicurus' philosophy, the possession of an inviolable, solid ground for one's view of the world'.³⁷ So while Miranda cries 'O ... poor souls' (I. i.8–9), and the Clown of Shakespeare's *The Winter's Tale*, watching a similar shipwreck scene, echoes her – 'O ... the poor souls!' (III.iii.90) – Dryden's Lucretius employs a far more abstracted metaphysical apostrophe: 'O wretched man! ... in what a mist of Life, / Inclos'd with dangers and with noisie strife, / He spends his little Span.'³⁸

The spatial dynamics of the two scenes are evidently antithetic, to the extent that Prospero's daughter appears to be offering a rebuke to the Epicurean philosopher: implicit in its lack of overt reference, but conspicuous in that the Lucretian scene had become so notorious (known to Shakespeare through his reading of Florio's Montaigne, an acknowledged influence on *The Tempest*, as well as to Giordano Bruno).³⁹ Of course, when topoi such as this are so often invoked they – in their intertextual play – come to acquire the enargeic efficacy characteristic of *ekphrasis*, which, as Quintilian's influential definition describes, allows the charge of pathos to 'penetrate the emotions' of the spectator by 'placing before the [ir] eyes' an otherwise inaccessible event, aiding *metathetic* transference.⁴⁰ Accordingly, it becomes commonplace to recount – as in Alexander

Browne's *Ars pictoria* and Shakespeare's *Lucrece* – how it is the 'sight of [a real or described] picture' that best moves 'the Mind of the beholder' to 'pitty, tears and sorrow', bringing the observer into emotional accord with the 'wretched image', 'shap[ing their] sorrow to [the depicted] woes' through the 'lend ... [and] borrow' of empathetic exchange, instigating immediate corporeal 'feeling' via the sympathetic imagination (*RL.*, 1492–1501; 1458).

Conversely, as Frederic M. Schroeder describes, against this *ekphrastic, metathetic* mode, Lucretius sets 'the Epicurean technique [of] *avocatio*, a system of training the imagination to avoid the seduction of passion and attain peace' by means of an 'affective displacement' with which 'we are delivered from passion and observe *apatheia*', the philosopher's goal; this technique requires the viewer not to avert their eyes, but to face the affective image, to observe the wreck and remain either unmoved or even repulsed.[41] Clearly, the spatial dynamic of Lucretius' scene – converting *ekphrasis* to this 'form of [distancing] architecture' – places Lucretius safely above and beyond harm, but I would like to adjust the received critical position on this episode, represented here by Phillip De Lacy, in one crucial respect:

> Distance really does make a difference ... between danger and safety .... Removal from the warring atoms, it seems, is as essential to our well-being as removal from the storm at sea [or] the battlefield.[42]

Of course, as De Lacy describes, for an Epicurean espousing *apathia*, 'the wrong way to look at the universe is ... to look on it not as something remote and indifferent, but as involving us in a way that makes us the helpless victims ... of cosmic powers', but Lucretius' construction of an artificial specular distance, holding the world at bay through occupation of the discrete position of observer, is, I would argue, a response to what he knows to be the impossibility of genuine isolation within an Epicurean atomist world: crucially, the scene does not speak of philosophic confidence – providing an opportunity to 'learn about atomic processes only to dismiss them' – but rather betrays the impossibility of that wishful position.[43] Lucretius' observer is – despite any attempt to deny it – embroiled among mutative vicissitudes (later adopted by Giordano Bruno from his reading of *De rerum natura*).

When Lucretius worries about being 'inclos'd with dangers and ... strife' or finding himself in the 'Maze [or] mist of life', his anxieties rationally stem from his conception of a world of radical sympathy, participation, and cross-contamination. For an Epicurean, the world is in a state of 'eternall mixture', where the 'first matter, ... the seeds of all', disseminates itself via flux, transmutation, and violent but formative interaction.[44] Atoms, the building blocks of all forms and forces, 'by impulsive force, / Or moving faculties, maintaine their course, / Wandring for ever in th'unbounded space', jostling and jarring in a lively, bustling interim.[45] 'When furious tempests drive [atoms] together', they ricochet away on new trajectories, or bind, hook, and combine in endless new permutations: 'armies of attoms sport ... in perpetuall skirmishies, / Here joine, there part, their motions never cease.'[46] Consequently, the dominant Lucretian metaphor for the 'secret tumults in ... matter' is that of 'flow', 'dissolve', and liquefaction, as he depicts the *pelagus materiae*, or 'ocean of matter', in its constant state of often invisible tempestuous interaction:

> There are some bodies eyes cannot discerne.
> The wind rufles the clouds, beats on the sands,
> Orewhelms tall ships.[47]

This atomic wind, 'which passes unseen through heaven, earth, and sea', knows no boundaries; elements mutate from air to liquid and back, boundaries break and reform, and all things, bar the smallest atoms, prove permeable to the 'passage' of 'perpetuall motion':

> Salt waves weare away
> The ragged cliffs, all this doth then declare
> That unseen bodies natures agents are.[48]

Solidity, undermined by the invisible vacuities or voids within every structure, is only ever temporary in a world where 'voices flie through the house, through walls of stone / And penetrating cold goes to the bone.'[49] And so, Lucretius' observer, even behind the stone battlements of his turret, is still saturated by the atomic ocean, which, no matter how far back from the sea he stands, 'through each porous passage penetrate[s]' as 'outward things themselves insinuate'.[50]

So although 'we perceive not how the wett comes in ... / For the moist humor in small attoms flies', if we stand on the shore by the 'sea side' our 'garments [do] grow moist', our 'corporiall natures shar[ing the] touches' of a material ocean that will not be kept at an observational remove: 'bodies ... can touch, and toucht againe can be'.[51] It seems therefore that the philosophical aspiration to refuse sympathetic involvement is in part an anxious response to an unavoidably inspirational atomic world; the Lucretian subject may be determined, but cannot be confident in defining their 'self-consciousness, over against the whirl of atoms'.[52] This, I would suggest, is why the poem – having celebrated the virtues of philosophical detachment – ends with its lengthy description of the Athenian plague in a tacit acknowledgement of the impossibility of hermetically sealed, quarantined, distanced subjectivity in a world of miasmic influence, porosity, and sympathetic contagion; ultimately, what aspires to be a poem espousing mental calm amongst the world's storm betrays itself at these crucial moments, conceding that even philosophers can catch the plague, and that the spectator of the shipwreck, seemingly stood safely on the shore, is actually wearing damp clothes, smelling of sea-spray, feeling saturated not separate.

Shipwreck < ... > Spectator: Montaigne and Prospero, Changing Places

> What is desired is a distance that won't destroy affect ('pathos of distance') ... a distance permeated, irrigated by tender feeling .... Here we'd rediscover the value ... of 'tact' ... : distance and respect.[53]

To this point then, we have two seemingly unsustainable models of shipwreck with spectator: on the one hand, Miranda, so tact-fully compassionate that she risks naivety, tactlessly projecting herself onto and over her environment, and Lucretius, whose estrangement proves to be a reactionary and arguably intrinsically untenable response to an overfamiliar world. Accordingly, Shakespeare deploys the scene elsewhere, offering alternative median positions and assessing their respective merits, and in each case we must, as Mentz suggests, touch the spectator's skin to discover to what extent they feel 'the wet shock of immersion' or have achieved 'the drying-out accomplished by intellectual understanding'.[54] Looking out on another chafing, raging ocean, and hearing 'the most piteous cry' of shipwrecked sailors, the rustic Clown of *The Winter's Tale* is also touched by compassion. As the yeasty frothing 'sea [becomes] the sky', he, like Miranda, suffers on behalf of the 'poor souls' whose ship is 'flap-dragon'd' by the waves (III.iii.84–98). But before we are tempted to assume that this innocent, receptive response simply equates to the naivety of a rural simpleton, his empathetic involvement snaps back via the distancing effect of dark humour: 'I would you had been by the ship side, to have help'd her; there your charity would have lack'd footing' (108–10). Here clownish literalism demonstrates the limits to idealised compassion: 'we are lucky boy' (125), and better off emoting with dry feet. As the equally naturally affiliated fishermen of *Pericles* prosaically describe, 'it griev'd my heart to hear what pitiful cries they made to us to help them', but 'well-a-day, we could scarce help ourselves', so while there is empathy at play, there is also self-preservation and a consequent retreat to the distance of reportage and safe spectatorship. Philosophy is brought down to earth.

Comparably, mediating between intellectual distance and embedded immediacy, while reading the shipwreck scene in his heavily annotated copy of *De rerum natura*, Michel de Montaigne admits 'in the middest of [his] compassion' the 'inward ... feele [of] a kinde of bitter-sweet pricking of malicious delight, to see others suffer', seemingly at once claiming to be innately compassionate, while subsequently out-doing even the dispassionate Epicurean.[55] Without justification or moral equivocation, Montaigne appropriates the Lucretian passage to illustrate his conception of man's plural, imperfect, and often contradictory nature:

> Our composition, both publike and private, is full of imperfection; yet is there nothing unserviceable ... ; nothing thereof hath beene insinuated in this huge universe, but holdeth some fit place therein. Our essence is simented with crased qualities; ambition, jealousie, envy, revenge, superstition, dispaire, lodge in us, with so naturall a possession, as their image is also discerned in beasts; yea, and cruelty, so unnaturall a vice.[56]

To deny the emotional and ethical eclecticism of our identities would be, Montaigne says, to 'ruine the fundamentall conditions of our life', and as such 'base' or 'faulty' vices are an integral part of the 'stitching up of our frame'.[57] On one level, he admits a Lucretian mood simply because he would not wish to deny this or any other influence, entertaining his isolationist inclinations as part and parcel of eclectic, accumulative identity. But furthermore, on a deeper structural level, his philosophical architecture – kinetic and inclusive, open to unexpected collision and influence, susceptible to creative drift and chance encounter – is intrinsically Lucretian, wilfully adrift in 'that general Ship-racke of the world, amidst so many changes and divers alterations'.[58] Indeed, the ever-present tension at the heart of Montaigne's 'strange dialectical [philosophical] proceedings' – where an early commitment to Stoic seclusion cohabits in each essay with later Epicurean insertions and swerves – is between a sceptic monism keen to particularise the subject (where doubt provides insulation against an uncertain world) and an atomist inclusivity which promotes participation (where radical catholicism admits every touch, *plaga*, or sympathy).

At one moment the 'crased', protean Montaigne declares himself to be 'wholie plunge[d]' in the world's frequencies, incapable therefore of 'the greatest indifference', but at another, feeling short of 'elbow-roome', he declares that 'the greatest thing of the world, is for a man to know how to be his owne', glad that 'our skin is ... sufficiently provided with hardnesse against the injuries of the wether', and relieved that he resides securely 'on the firm shore'.[59] Montaigne, in other words, is plurally positioned in our tableaux, by forever 'shift[ing and] chang[ing] places', 'pirouett[ing] ... trying out all positions', as Ibbett describes in her account of the multiple and complex 'structural ... organizational patterns' of Montaignean emotional responsivity: his philosophical methodology demands that he watches others as they watch the ship sink, assessing their position, wondering if he should be standing in their shoes; equally, he is often on the firm shore or up in his library-tower looking out from the 'immured cloister ... of Philosophie' or the 'store-house [of] our selves, ... wholy free ... hoard[ed]-up [in his] retreit and solitarinesse'.[60] But he is also present on the deck, wholly plunged, amidst and among, lost at sea, saturated by each sympathetic wave: arguably, he is even closer to the scene than the emotionally sympathetic Miranda, as he is thoroughly corporeally implicated. From the shore, he calmly pronounces that no 'communication of any strange thing may therein find place' in his sceptical hermetic 'selfe', which is all-in-all sufficient to 'keep it selfe companie'; but from the ship, he admits that 'contagion is [unavoidable] in a throng', as 'a man must imitate' everyone he encounters, warning that those 'that travel by sea, ... [should] take heede, that those which goe in the same ship, be not dissolute, blasphemers, and wicked', as no man can be free from the influence of an other.[61] More positively, the very form of his essays celebrate the ability of those 'active minds, and busie spirits [which] embrace all, [so] every where engage, and in all things passionate themselves'.[62]

Ultimately, like Lucretius, it often seems that the intensity of his occasionally professed desire to 'sequester ... himself from the concourse of people' comes from a more profound acceptance of isolationism's impossibility; once he admits that 'the popular conditions, ... are [already] in us', then to claim shoreline immunity is, he surely knows, as impossible as 'sequester[ing] himselfe from himselfe'.[63] Ultimately, Montaigne is drawn to a negotiated position where he is both out at sea and yet self-reliant – '*man ought to provide himselfe with munitions, that might float upon the water, and by swimming escape the danger of shipwracke with him*' – advising that 'you must no longer seeke, what the world saith of you, but [consider] how you must speake unto your selfe: withdraw your selfe into your selfe, if you can not governe your selfe': in other words, if there is fear of drowning, stay on the shore, while knowing that, as Judith Butler succinctly puts it, '[you]'re missing something'.[64] 'We are', as Butler and Montaigne both acknowledge, 'beings who are, of necessity, *exposed* to one another in our vulnerability', as 'if one were successful at walling oneself off from injury, one would become inhuman'.[65] From his mediated, or rather importantly unfixed, permanently impermanent, concordantly discordant position, he can both allow 'the rest [to] be our owne, yet not so combined and glued together, that [this com-/em-passionate intersubjectivity] may not be sundred'.[66]

As Arthur Kirsch has suggested, it is Prospero – the formerly immured philosopher who reconciles himself with his fallible nature and social responsibilities, receiving a more successful schooling in what Tarantino describes above as a 'masterclass' in tolerance – that Shakespeare stages a reconciliation between these 'oppos[ed positions of] compassion and detachment'.[67] The formerly self-determined 'schoolmaster' (I.ii.172), comparatively less capable of innocent empathy – 'so glad of this as they I cannot be, / Who surprised withal' (III.i.92) – is seemingly taught to integrate his daughter's tenderness into his resolved singularity; 'pity move[s this] father / To be inclin'd [her] way!' (I.ii.447–48). 'Becom[ing] tender', at the instigation of his 'tender heir' (Son. 1.4), and Ariel, his servant composed of 'tender air' (*Cym.*, V.iv.140), Prospero comes to allow 'a touch, a feeling / Of their afflictions', conceding 'kind[ness]' and kindred 'passions' with his fellow men (*Temp.*, V.i.18–24). Where initially, Miranda's calls for 'mercy' (437) were juxtaposed against Prospero's vengeful conception of the term – 'At this hour / Lies at mercy all mine enemies' (IV.i.262–63) – by act V, Prospero arrives at the Montaignean realisation that 'the rarer action is / In virtue than in vengeance' (V.i.27–28). Advocating the mollification of this overly severe, vengeful recluse, the play tempers his temper with the temperate warmth of compassion, and finds the common ground – a kind of applied, politically and socially applicable philosophy predicated on the acceptance of the common condition – between our two polarised spectator positions.

But, in conclusion, perhaps Shakespeare's most complex version of the topos appears only by omission. It is in *Lear*, the most tonally Lucretian of all Shakespearean dramas, where, 'made tame to fortune's blows', the subject becomes 'pregnant to good pity' (IV.iv.221–23). As the 'contentious storm / Invades us to the skin' (III.iv.6–7), and sympathetically manifests as 'this tempest in my mind' (12), the 'not ague-proof' subject (IV.vi.105) becomes 'minded like the weather' (III.

i.2), until 'expose[d enough] to feel what wretches feel' (I.iv.33–34). Somewhere between the naivety of 'O you kind gods!' (IV.vii.13) and the cynicism of 'O cruel! O you gods!' (III.vii.70), comes the realisation that the 'the heavens [will] touch ... us not with pity' (V.iii.232–33), and 'Heaven's vault should [but actually will not] crack' (V.iii.260); yet nonetheless 'nothing *will* come of nothing' (I.i.90, emphasis added), and although the gods may withhold their pity, this world of atomic 'fall, and cease' (V.iii.265) is not without compassion, not without affect, not without natural sympathy. Lucretius offers us a world in which while gods may have none, nature has absolute sympathy: indeed, only by seeing how disinterested the gods are in us – we are flies and tennis balls in their games – can humanity come to an appreciation of its place in the natural condition. Within this system, Shakespeare advocates pity as a poor but necessary human substitute for the divine compassion we lack (an emotion tested to its breaking point, yet never fully suppressed, as Toria Johnson describes in her contribution to this collection): neither Christ-like sufferance nor inhumane distancing last the course of this play.

Gloucester is not, in truth, on a cliff top, and does not in fact look out to sea; he is neither within sound of its 'murmuring surge' (IV.vi.20), nor can he see Edgar's illusory 'tall anchoring bark' (18), but he is the recipient of a surprisingly cruel pity, made the 'patient' (IV.v.177) to a precariously violent 'cure' (IV.iv.34). Edgar's sympathy for his father may be manifested in a form of sadistic kindness as he 'trifle[s] thus with [Gloucester's] despair' (33–34), but this is emphatically no illusory 'miracle' (vi.56); Gloucester, staring blindly out to sea, sees no evidence of a sympathetic god, but what we see, from our vantage point, is just enough pity to keep the play's vision of humanity humane: our 'tears begin to take his part' (III.vi.59), as, made tender to and by suffering, we participate in Gloucester's pain. This is perhaps the tenderest of Shakespeare's plays because the cost of pity, the pain of pity's bruise, is incrementally and haptically felt: 'Why, this would make man a man of salt / To use his eyes for garden water-pots' (IV.vi.195–96). By its conclusion, touched, beaten, tenderised, we 'should ev'n die with pity / To see another thus' (IV.vii. 52–53): compassion really is co-sufferance and, as physician James Hart cautions, 'tender bod[ies should be prepared, made] apt to receive evil impressions' in a play where even 'cadent tears [would] fret channels in [our tender] cheeks' (I.iv.285).[68] Saturated in an atomic thunderstorm, *Lear* enforces immediate tactile compassion, right on the skin of its subjected subjects, until we 'see it feelingly' (IV.vi.145): this is no brave new world, but it is full of real natural sympathies, which, 'when the rain came to wet [us]', made us sneeze (100–4). Storm-soaked, stood out on Dover beach, Shakespeare's Lucretian subjects come alive to the cost of empassioned, atomised, influent existence, arriving at their hard-earned compassionate maturity.

Notes

1. Nicolas Coeffeteau, *A Table of Humane Passions* (1620), trans. Edward Grimeston (London, 1621), p. 369.
2. Coeffeteau, *Humane Passions*, p. 365; 368; John Donne, 'Sermon 8' in *Fifty Sermons* (London, 1649), pp. 59–66, p. 63. Fear and pity, Aristotle explains, 'put the disasters before our eyes, and make them seem close to us' (*Rhetorica*, trans. W. Rhys Roberts, in *The Basic Works of Aristotle*, ed. Richard McKeon [New York: Random House, 2001], pp. 1317–1451, 1386^{b}1–5).
3. See David Konstan, *Pity Transformed* (London: Duckworth, 2001), p. 4.
4. Michel Foucault, *The Order of Things: An Archaeology of the Human Sciences*, trans. Alan Sheridan (London: Routledge, 2005), p. 20.
5. Francis Bacon, *Essayes* (London, 1597), p. 25.
6. Foucault, *Order of Things*, pp. 26–27.
7. John Boys, *An Exposition of the Festivall Epistles and Gospels used in our English Liturgie* (London, 1615), p. 100.
8. John Donne, 'Sermon XXXVI. Preached upon Whitsunday', in *LXXX Sermons* (London, 1640), p. 353.
9. Leonard Willan, *The Exact Politician; Or, Compleat Statesman* (London, 1670), p. 123; Foucault, *Order of Things*, p. 27.
10. All Shakespearean quotations from *The Riverside Shakespeare*, gen. ed. G. Blakemore Evans, 2nd ed. (Boston: Houghton Mifflin, 1997), *Per.*, II. i.60–61; *TA*, IV.iii.442; *Err.*, II.i.21; *LLL*, IV.iii.216; *Shr.*, I.ii.202; *HV*, III. vii.36; *Per.*, II.i.48; *Ham.*, III.i.59; *Temp.*, I.i.18; *1HVI*, V.i.50; *R&J*., II. ii.133. All further quotations to be cited in parentheses within the text. On the ocean topos, see Philip Steinberg, *The Social Construction of the Ocean* (Cambridge University Press, 2001), and Bernhard Klein and Gesa Mackenthun (eds.), *Sea Changes: Historicizing the Ocean* (London: Taylor and Francis, 2004).
11. Carl Thompson, introduction to *Shipwreck in Art and Literature: Images and Interpretations from Antiquity to the Present Day*, ed. Carl Thompson (London, 2013), pp. 1–26, 7; Henry Peacham, '*nec igne, nec unda* [emblem of MANLIE CONSTANCIE]', in *Minerva Britanna* (London, 1612), p. 158. Giordano Bruno, *Cause, Principle and Unity: And Essays on Magic*, Cambridge Texts in the History of Philosophy, ed. Richard J. Blackwell and Robert de Lucca (Cambridge University Press, 1998), p. 73. On Peacham's emblem, see Robert J. Vrtis, 'The Tempest Toss'd Ship: *Twelfth Night* and Emotional Communities in Early Modern London' in Brigitte Le Juez and Olga Springer

(eds.), *Shipwreck and Island Motifs in Literature and the Arts* (Leiden: Brill, 2015), pp. 135–50; Steve Mentz, *Shipwreck Modernity: Ecologies of Globalization, 1550–1719* (Minneapolis: University of Minnesota Press, 2015), p. xxxi. Mentz's discussion of the 'microgenre of shipwreck' presents the scene as 'an ecological parable', thinking of how 'representations of shipwreck [figure] as literary responses to the disruptive new world of global connectedness' (pp. xix–xxvii).

12 Steve Mentz, *At the Bottom of Shakespeare's Ocean* (London: Bloomsbury, 2009), p. 21. On the shipwreck motif in literature and art, see Thompson (ed.) *Shipwreck in Art and Literature*; James V. Morrison, *Shipwrecked: Disaster and Transformation in Homer, Shakespeare, Defoe, and the Modern World* (Ann Arbor: University of Michigan Press, 2014).

13 Francis Hubert, *The Historie of Edward the Second* (London, 1629), p. 125.

14 Joseph Hall, *Contemplations, the fifth volume* (London, 1620), p. 385.

15 Petronius, *The Satyricon*, trans. Michael Heseltine (London: Heinemann, 1913), pp. 115–16. On Petronius, see Catherine Connors, *Petronius the Poet: Verse and Literary Tradition in the Satyricon* (Cambridge University Press, 1998), pp. 78ff; for detailed discussion of the shipwreck scene's full historical lineage, see Hans Blumenberg, *Shipwreck with Spectator: Paradigm of a Metaphor for Existence* (Cambridge, MA: MIT Press, 1997).

16 Voltaire, *Philosophical Dictionary, pt. II* in *The Works of Voltaire*, vol. IV, trans. William F. Fleming (New York: E. R. DuMont, 1901), 'Curiosity'; Jean-Jacques Rousseau, *The First and Second Discourses*, trans. Roger and Judith R. Masters (New York: Columbia University Press, 1964), p. 132; see Blumenberg, *Shipwreck with Spectator*, p. 38, and Ann Hartle, *Death and the Disinterested Spectator: An Enquiry into the Nature of Philosophy* (Albany: State University of New York Press, 1986), p. 191.

17 Hartle, *Death and the Disinterested Spectator*, p. 204; E. G., *A Discourse of Friendship* (London, 1676), pp. 42, 108.

18 Desiderius Erasmus, 'The Shipwreck [Naufragium]' in *The Colloquies*, trans. N. Bailey, vol. 1 (London, 1878), p. 275.

19 Coeffeteau, pp. 370–71; John Welles, *The Soules Progresse to the Celestiall Canaan, or Heavenly Jerusalem by way of godly meditation, and holy contemplation* (London, 1639), p. 21.

20 Marjorie Garber, 'Compassion' in Lauren Berlant (ed.), *Compassion: The Culture and Politics of an Emotion* (New York: Routledge, 2004), pp. 15–27.

21 Lauren Berlant, 'Compassion (and Withholding)' in Berlant (ed.), *Compassion*, pp. 1–13, 4.

22 Captain Wright, *Robert Dudley's Voyage to the West Indies (1595)*, in *The Tempest: Sources and Contexts*, ed. Peter Hulme and William H. Sherman (New York: W. W. Norton, 2004), pp. 105–6.

23 On 'passibility' see Thomas Blount, *Glossographia* (London, 1661); Timothy J. Reiss, *Mirages of the Selfe: Patterns of Personhood in Ancient and Early Modern Europe* (Stanford University Press, 2003), p. 96.

24 Bradin Cormack, 'Tender Distance: Latinity and Desire in Shakespeare's Sonnets' in Michael Schoenfeldt (ed.), *A Companion to Shakespeare's Sonnets* (Oxford: Blackwell, 2007), pp. 242–60, 242.
25 Susan Sontag, *Regarding the Pain of Others* (London: Hamish Hamilton, 2003), p. 91; Michel de Montaigne, *Essays*, trans. John Florio (London, 1613), p. 772.
26 Montaigne, *Essays*, p. 975.
27 Martha C. Nussbaum, *Upheavals of Thought: The Intelligence of Emotions* (Cambridge University Press, 2001), p. 43.
28 Nussbaum, *Upheavals*, p. 35.
29 Jean-Michel Rabaté, *The Pathos of Distance: Affects of the Moderns* (London: Bloomsbury, 2016), p. 8.
30 Hannah Arendt, 'Understanding and Politics', in *Essays in Understanding, 1930–1954*, ed. Jerome Kohn (New York: Schocken Books, 1994), pp. 307–27, 323.
31 Sontag, *Regarding*, pp. 105–6; 24. Katherine Ibbett similarly concludes by advocating a 'tactful proximity [which would] allow us to respond to another's separateness, and to measure the distance between us even as we look across it', in *Compassion's Edge: Fellow Feeling and Its Limits in Early Modern France* (Philadelphia: University of Pennsylvania Press, 2018), p. 226.
32 Anon., 'The felicitie of a minde imbracing virtue, that beholdeth the wretched desires of the worlde', in various, *Songes and Sonettes, written by the right honorable Lorde Henry Haward late Earle of Surrey, and other[s]* [or; *Tottel's Miscellany*] (London, 1557), fol. 65–66, 65; Lucretius, 'The beginning of the Second Book [of *De rerum natura*]', trans. John Dryden [?], in various, *Miscellany Poems,* coll. John Dryden (London, 1692), pp. 56–59, 56.
33 Lucretius, 'The beginning,' 1692, p. 56.
34 *Tottel's Miscellany*, fol. 65. See Stuart Gillespie, 'Lucretius in the English Renaissance' in Stuart Gillespie and Philip Hardie (eds.), *The Cambridge Companion to Lucretius* (Cambridge University Press, 2007), pp. 242–53.
35 *Tottel's Miscellany*, fol. 65, emphasis added.
36 Lucretius, *De rerum natura*, p. 56.
37 Blumenberg, *Shipwreck with Spectator*, p. 26.
38 Lucretius, *De rerum natura*, p. 57.
39 See R. Allen Shoaf, *Lucretius and Shakespeare on the Nature of Things* (Cambridge University Press, 2014); Gillespie, 'Lucretius in the English Renaissance'; L. C. Martin, 'Shakespeare, Lucretius, and the Commonplaces', *Review of English Studies*, 21 (1945), 174–82; George Depue Hadzsits, *Lucretius and His Influence* (London: G.G. Harrap & Co., 1935); Eric Langley, 'The Path to Which Wild Error Leads: A Lucretian Comedy of Errors', *Textual Practice*, 28 (2014), 161–87; Jacques Lezra, *Unspeakable Subjects: The Genealogy of the Event in Early Modern Europe* (Stanford University Press, 1997).
40 Quintilian, *Institutio oratoria*, trans. H. E. Butler (Cambridge, MA: Harvard University Press, 1982), 8.3.67; 9.2.40–41. See Ruth Webb, *Ekphrasis*,

Imagination, and Persuasion in Ancient Rhetorical Theory and Practice (Farnham; Burlington: Ashgate, 2009), esp. pp. 87–130.

41 Frederic M. Schroeder, 'Philodemus: Avocatio and the Pathos of Distance in Lucretius and Vergil' in David Armstrong et al. (eds.), *Vergil, Philodemus, and the Augustans* (Austin: University of Texas Press, 2004), pp. 139–56, 139–40.
42 Schroeder, 'Philodemus', p. 147; Phillip De Lacy, 'Distant Views: The Imagery of Lucretius 2' in Monica R. Gale (ed.), *Oxford Readings in Classical Studies: Lucretius* (Oxford University Press, 2007), pp. 146–57, 149.
43 De Lacy, 'Distant Views', p. 149.
44 Lucretius, *De rerum natura*, trans. Lucy Hutchinson, ed. Hugh de Quehen (Ann Arbor: University of Michigan Press, 1996), I.248; I.51–52.
45 Lucretius, *De rerum natura*, II.61–63.
46 Lucretius, I.774; II.115–17.
47 Lucretius, II.125; I.173; I.222; I.277–79.
48 Lucretius, I.284–85; I.362; II.311; I.334–35.
49 Lucretius, I.360–61.
50 Lucretius, II.392; II.431.
51 Lucretius, II.338; I.314–15; I.308–15.
52 *OED*, 'inspire, v.', I.1.a: 'To breathe or blow upon or into'. Blumenberg, *Shipwreck with Spectator*, p. 26.
53 Roland Barthes, *How to Live Together: Novelistic Simulations of Some Everyday Spaces* (New York: Columbia University Press, 2013), p. 132.
54 Mentz, *Shipwreck Modernity*, p. xxxii.
55 Montaigne, *Essays*, p. 443.
56 Montaigne, p. 443.
57 Montaigne, pp. 443–44.
58 Montaigne, p. 444.
59 Montaigne, pp. 122, 118, 121, 253, 444.
60 Montaigne, pp. 118–20; Ibbett, *Compassion's Edge*, pp. 55–56.
61 Montaigne, pp. 118, 120. On the importance of conversation and communication, which 'naturally test ... and break ... down [any] illusory ideas of self-sufficiency', in Montaigne's 'ethics of yielding', see David Quint, *Montaigne and the Quality of Mercy: Ethical and Political Themes in the Essais* (Princeton University Press, 1998), pp. 102, 111.
62 Montaigne, *Essays*, p. 121.
63 Montaigne, p.119.
64 Montaigne, pp. 120, 124; Judith Butler, *Precarious Life: The Powers of Mourning and Violence* (London: Verso, 2004), p. 23.
65 Butler, *Precarious Life*, p. 31, 103.
66 Montaigne, *Essays*, p. 121.
67 Arthur Kirsch, 'Virtue, Vice, and Compassion in Montaigne and *The Tempest*' in Harold Bloom (ed.), *William Shakespeare: Romances* (New York: Bloomsbury, 2011), pp. 71–86, 78.
68 James Hart, *Klinic; Or, the Diet of the Diseased* (London, 1633), p. 354.

PART VI
Giving

CHAPTER 11

'To Feel What Wretches Feel'
Reformation and the Re-naming of English Compassion
Toria Johnson

'In worse case then ever'

In an extensive physical description of London's suburbs, John Stow's *Survay of London* (1598) also included this insight into the city's compassionate decline:

> But now wee see the thing in worse case then ever … as in other places of the Suburbes, some of them like Midsommer Pageants, with Towers, Turrets and Chimney tops, not so much for use, or profites, as for shew and pleasure, bewraying the vanitie of many mens mindes, *much vnlike to y*ᵉ *disposition of the ancient Citizens, who delighted in the building of Hospitalles, and Almes houses for the poore* and therein both imployed their wits, and spent their wealthes *in preferment of the common commoditie of this our Citie.*[1]

Stow places his own London on a timeline of dwindling compassion, citing a diminishing interest in the 'common commoditie' and highlighting, in its place, a growing emphasis on personal interests: vanity, profit, show and pleasure. He reaches back to a time when the physical landscape reflected a more positive emotional landscape, with 'Hospitalles' and 'Almes houses' standing as a material reminder of the community's emotional and financial investment in the well-being of its citizens. Stow describes *his* London as a place stripped of these physical and emotional structures of compassion. Just a few years earlier, in the 1593 *Christ's Teares Over Jerusalem*, Thomas Nashe offered another, more lurid vision of London's heartlessness, this time looking to the Protestant Reformation as the cause of this emotional decline. He begins with an apparent reference

---

[*] I am grateful to Alex Davis, Rebecca Tomlin, Kristine Steenbergh, Katherine Ibbett and Alexander Thom for their comments on earlier drafts of this chapter. Additional thanks are due to Katherine Ibbett, whose term 'misfirings' has been very helpful in thinking about pity.

to the Protestant belief that salvation was 'wholly a matter of God's impenetrable decision, made without regard to the efforts of humans':

> Those Preachers please best which can fit vs with a cheap Religion, that preach Faith, & *all Faith, and no Good-works* ... Ministers and Pastors ... tis you that haue brought downe the price of Religion.[2]

Nashe is wary of this 'cheap Religion', not just because it has 'brought down the price of Religion' more generally, but because he sees it as a worryingly appealing doctrine, the message peddled by 'Those Preachers [who] *please best*' (my emphasis). Like Stow, Nashe also looks backwards with a certain amount of nostalgia:

> It were to bee wished that order were taken vp amongst you, which was obserued in S. Augustines time: For then it was the custom, that the poore should begg of none but the Preacher or Minister, and if he had not to giue them, they should exclaime and cry out of him, for not more effectually moouing and crying out to the people for them. Had euery one of you, all the poore of your Parishes hanging about your doores, and ready to rent your garments off your backes, and teare out your throats for bread euery time you stird abroad, you would bestirre you in exhortation to charity and good workes, and make your selues hoarse, in crying out against couetise and hardnesse of heart. *London, thy heart is the hart of couetousnes, all charitie and compassion is cleane banished out of thee*: except thou amendest, Ierusalem, Sodome, and Thou shalt sit downe and weepe together.[3]

If the passage does reveal a certain wistfulness, it is a yearning for a medieval model: 'It were to bee wished', he writes, 'that order were taken vp amongst you, which was obserued in S. Augustines time'. Nonetheless, the argument is somewhat more practical than pure: to Nashe, the 'order' of St Augustine's time is precisely that: more *orderly*. Nashe's stated preference is that the poor 'should begg of none but the Preacher or Minister'; the Preacher or Minister, in turn, should either alleviate the plight of the poor directly, or become their advocate. The Preacher or Minister of Nashe's imagination thus fulfils a crucial mediating role, keeping 'the people' from 'the poor' – or perhaps more importantly, keeping the poor away from the people. As in the Stow passage, the individual is ideologically set apart from his community in 'couetise and hardnesse of heart', but Nashe importantly adds this idea of an ever-encroaching, physical threat of a growing collective of misery.

As Rebecca Tomlin discusses in the next chapter, the uncomfortable physical proximity of the poor was also identified by Philip Stubbes ten years earlier, in 1583. In the quotation Tomlin cites, Stubbes speaks, with a clear discomfort, of the poor and diseased 'hanging upon the sleve[s]' of passersby, 'and craving of releéfe'.[4] Both Stubbes and Nashe introduce a vivid physicality to their accounts, particularly imagining the invasion of personal boundaries: Stubbes's '*hanging upon* [the] *sleve*' suggests a kind of physical burden; Nashe offers a more violent vision of a group 'ready to rent your garments off your backes, and teare out your throats for bread'. These accounts, while ostensibly about the plight of the poor, in fact more effectively emphasise the impact on those who encounter them. As Tomlin puts it, 'the "great pity" that Stubbes evokes seems to be directed more towards the man who is unable to go about his business without being hindered by beggars, than towards those suffering individuals'.[5] The same might be said of Nashe's yearning for an earlier, more orderly model. Nevertheless, Nashe seems also to criticise that the threat of emotional and physical confrontation has failed to prompt an outpouring of Christian charity: the plight of the poor reflects more on those who witness or encounter it. As in Stow, something vital has been lost: 'London, thy heart is the hart of couetousnes, *all charitie and compassion is cleane banished out of thee*'.

What is striking about these passages is that while Nashe and Stow both agree that something important has been lost, both struggle to name exactly what it is that is absent: Stow calls it an interest in 'the common commoditie'; for Nashe, it is 'charitie and compassion' that has been banished. Elsewhere Nashe deploys yet another word – pity – to bemoan the damage: 'No where is pitty, no where is pitty', he writes, 'our House must needs be left desolate vnto vs.'[6] In this chapter, I will argue that Nashe and Stow are identifying the perceived weakening of compassionate culture in post-Reformation London: they are reacting to the loss of a structure for mediating this type of emotional exchange. This new instability is also, I think, bound up in this problem of language, this difficulty in defining compassion in a shifting religious landscape.[7] I argue that the upheaval expressed by Nashe and Stow is a consequence of the Reformation shift away from medieval structures surrounding *charity* – grounded as they were in clear church doctrine – and the subsequent rise of concepts more commonly associated with interpersonal connection, like pity, fellowship and compassion. To demonstrate this, I will begin with the treatment of these concepts in a pre-Reformation morality play, *Everyman*, before moving on to their post-Reformation revision in Shakespeare's *King Lear*. These texts both stage explicit calls for compassion. In *Everyman*, the response to that call follows the guidelines of medieval charity doctrine, but Shakespeare's characters are not afforded that structure. Read together, these plays reveal that changing the way subjects talk and think about compassion ultimately changes the way they perceive compassion in their surroundings.

Views of Charity and Compassion in *Everyman*

As the institution responsible for charitable doctrine, the medieval Church positioned itself as the community hub for the kind of action Stow and Nashe might have associated with compassion – namely, provisions for the poor and the giving of alms. The conceptual and religious significance of charity in medieval England can hardly be understated: it was, as John Colet preached in a sermon at St Paul's, 'the roote of all spirituall lyfe'.[8] Contemporary religious writing and practice conceived of charity primarily as a virtue performed in the image, and service, of God. Although the language associated with charity often appears to mimic that used to describe human sociability – as in Aquinas's description of charity as 'a *friendship* of man and God' – charity is at the same time obviously not a social virtue.[9] 'Man's charity is with God and ... *not with creatures of flesh*', Aquinas writes; 'Therefore, charity *is not friendship.*'[10] This type of language – blurry as it is – makes it easy to see how charitable doctrine might have influenced one's understanding of his/her social relationships, even as doctrinal writing attempted to position charity well above earthly sociability. The Church did, after all, acknowledge charitable love amongst men, if only as a by-product of an overarching love of God. 'It would be wrong', Aquinas writes, 'for a man to love his neighbour *as if he were his principal end in life*, but not if he loves him *for God's sake*, which is charity's way.'[11] The love for God – as demonstrated through charitable work – may have clarified and structured one's human relationships, but not as an end in itself. The 'end' remained, as ever, one's relationship with God.

The most obvious practical application of charitable doctrine was a certain form of giving, directed towards the poor. This is one of the easiest types of medieval charity to track: in wills, in payments or bequests made in exchange for intercessory prayers, and in the repeated emphasis, both in theological writing and in contemporary drama, on the significance of 'good works'. Understanding the importance of charity and good works was a vital component of one's faith, as Thomas Lupset wrote in a manual concerning 'the waye of dyenge well': 'faithe can not be *perfect*', he asserted, 'onles there be good workes'.[12] Good works were not just the key to perfect faith, however; they were also the key to salvation. As Lupset reminds his readers, Christ 'commaundeth almes dedes, sayinge, that who so ever helpeth not a pore man in his nede, he wil not helpe him not yet knowe him at the fearefull day of dome'.[13] The inevitability of judgement made the preoccupation with 'dying well', as one critic has noted, an 'obsession' that placed charity at the centre of medieval life.[14] Claiming itself as the overseeing structure of charitable action – which expanded to include various penitential practices such as confession, penance and repentance – the Church effectively became the earthly mediator and guarantor of personal salvation.[15] In this way, as Eamon Duffy has argued, the Church successfully coupled 'anxiety over the brevity and uncertainty of life to the practical need for good works, to ensure a blissful hereafter'.[16] Medieval charity is a form of compassion that is indivisible from its religious origins.

This is precisely the message depicted in the 1518 morality drama *Everyman*. An English reworking of an earlier Dutch play, *Elckerlijc*, *Everyman* tracks the progress of the eponymous character towards death and judgement. The revisions made to the original European text, as one critic has noted, reflect a specifically English emphasis on charity: the English author, 'eager to explore the relationship between good deeds and salvation', made substantial additions to the existing exchange between the character 'Good Deeds' and the play's hero, Everyman.[17] Good Deeds becomes a central figure in the play's clearly outlined process of preparing for a good death. The necessity of judgement, however, in this play is not so much about the failure to attend to the poor as it is a failure to cultivate a robust relationship with God. The God of *Everyman* complains that men show a lack of love (or fear) of Him: 'They fear not my righteousness', God observes, 'My law.... They forget clean' (ll. 28–30). Later, this complaint is reformulated with a specific view to mankind's charitable failures: 'Charity they do all clean forget' (l. 51).

The correlation between a contented God and mankind's undertaking of charitable work is almost entirely symbolised by the character Good Deeds, who, as Everyman himself notes, is the only character capable of offering him the support he needs. Nonetheless, Good Deeds is the last person to whom Everyman makes an appeal. Rather than diminishing the character's importance, her late appearance helps to clarify the play's stance on alternate forms of compassion, such as human pity, and their utility.[18] Here, Everyman summarises the first half of the play's action, detailing his repeated appeals for support, their subsequent denial and the plight that drives the piece – the prospect of an unsupported progress to judgement. He laments:

> EVERYMAN:
> Oh, to whom shall I make my moan
> For to go with me in that heavy journey?
> First Fellowship said he would with me go –
> His words were very pleasant and gay –
> But afterward he left me alone.
> Then spake I to my kinsmen, all in despair,
> And also they gave me words fair.
> They lacked no fair speaking,

> But all forsook me in the ending.
> Then went I to my Goods, that I loved best,
> In hope to have comfort, but there had I least;
> For my Goods sharply did me tell
> That he bringeth many into hell.
> ...
> Of whom shall I now counsel take?
> I think that I shall never speed
> Till that I go to my Good Deeds.
> But, alas, she is so weak
> That she can neither go ne speak.
>
> (ll. 463–83)

The speech emphasises the impact of earthly behaviour, while simultaneously downplaying the long-term value of earthly living. Everyman is abandoned by the trappings of his earthly life – human fellowship, material goods – and his only hope of redemption is the record of the charitable action done in God's service, as embodied by Good Deeds. Good Deeds is the only character Everyman petitions who shows him any good will, although as Everyman notes in this speech, she is initially unable to help him towards judgement. She is, nonetheless, also the only character to show a sincere willingness to go: 'I *would* full fain' (l. 498, my emphasis).

By contrast, Everyman offers a cynical view of pity as cruel, empty and seductive: what he describes is an earthly, empty form of human compassion that is ultimately both fleeting and unhelpful. Fellowship, Kindred and Cousin are all disappointments, he tells us, but what's particularly striking is Everyman's sense that this constitutes a betrayal. 'He left me alone', he reports of Fellowship; 'All forsook me in the ending.' What exacerbates this sense of emotional abandonment is the turnaround in the rhetoric, notable in Everyman's admission that Fellowship's 'words were very pleasant and gay' and the kinsmen 'lacked no fair speaking'. Indeed, Fellowship's language in his initial encounter with the downtrodden Everyman does speak to the comfort of human compassion, pity and fellow-feeling. 'Sir why lookest thou so *piteously?*' Fellowship cries, 'If anything be amiss, I pray thee me say, that I may help to remedy' (ll. 206–9). 'Sir, I *must* needs know your heaviness', he argues, claiming he has 'pity to see [Everyman] in any distress' (ll. 216–17). The exchange shows us the positive qualities we might want to associate with pity: the outpouring of human compassion as an instinctive reflex, and the creation of an instant and formidable bond. Fellowship imagines that he is also implicated in Everyman's suffering, that they are joined by one's offer of pity to another. The apparent strength and conviction of Fellowship's compassionate reaction is alluring: it imagines a sort of comfort and salvation inherent in human community. The original promise of this reaction only strengthens the blow of Fellowship's ultimate abandonment when Everyman explains his predicament:

> That is matter indeed! Promise is duty,
> But … it should be to my pain;
> Also it maketh me afeard, certain.
> (ll. 248–51)

The immediacy of the retreat reinforces the blow, making Fellowship's offer of emotional connection look unreliable, insubstantial and ultimately undesirable. Moreover, it demonstrates how the promise of pity invariably produces a worrying type of personal vulnerability: Everyman is made emotionally vulnerable by his desire to receive Fellowship's pity. This is a play that clearly believes and shows, in excruciating detail, that pity and compassion are in fact not as similar to charity as they may first appear. In articulating the difference between them, the play also highlights something threatening or potentially dangerous in compassion's appeal. *Everyman* goes to great lengths to show that the feelings of earthly solidarity produced by these expressions of human compassion are not only unstable and unreliable, but ultimately, inevitably, also useless.

Charity, by contrast, in this play is a stable and well-supported path, easily navigated by the willing. There is a moment of outreach to the unseen poor, in which Everyman promises: 'In alms, half my goods … In the way of charity with good intent' (ll. 699–700), but the bulk of the play's redemption narrative focuses on Everyman's completion of a series of penitential practices, mediated by the doctrinal figure of 'Knowledge', and the priest-like figure of 'Confession'. Knowledge's doctrinal role is confirmed with her announcement that she will lead Everyman to Confession. Confession, who 'is in good conceit with God almighty' (l. 544) goes on to oversee Everyman's penance. The procedure is heavily laden with the trappings of religious practice: hoping that Confession will 'Wash from me the spots and vices clean, / That on me no sin may be seen' (ll. 546–47), Everyman announces that he 'come[s] with Knowledge for [his] redemption, / [and] Repent[s] with heart and full contrition' (ll. 548–49). It is also only through this interaction with Confession, and completion of the penance, that Everyman ultimately restores Good Deeds, reiterating the point that one's 'good deeds' ultimately fall under the jurisdiction and supervision of the Church. Because Everyman has come with Knowledge, Confession promises the 'precious jewel ... / Called penance' (ll. 556–57), and finally assures Everyman 'ye will saved be' (l. 569). The play could not be clearer in setting out the path to redemption and Heaven; it could not offer a more explicit vision of the Church's central role in this process.

'Let us consider one another': Reforming Charity

The ideas that I have traced in *Everyman* – the idea of pity as an earthly, fleeting feeling, the promise underpinning charity and the support offered by Church infrastructure in practicing charity – these are all themes common to the morality genre. The wayward king featured in an early morality play, *The Pride of Life*, for example, is instructed to 'do dedis of charite' in order 'To savy thi soul fre sor'; this is imagined as part of a larger commitment to 'lernen Cristis lor'.[19] *The Interlude of Youth* stages Charity as a distinct character who announces that 'There may no man saved be / Without the help of me', further asserting the more active, mediating role in the process of salvation.[20] This system of charity imposes certain guidelines and expectations, making one man's compassionate response just one part of a bigger campaign to protect his own soul after death; Joel Rosenthal has called this system 'the purchase of paradise'.[21] This is a compassionate model that is undeniably implicated in the possibility or promise of eternal suffering.

We might distil the English Reformation to this very issue. Protestants 'believed that God's reward was a pure gift', made without consideration for one's earthly behaviour, whereas Catholics 'believed that, in one way or another, God did reward the human effort of works in the world'.[22] The interconnectivity of values like charity, pity and fellowship changed radically during the Reformation, as Protestants sought to create a 'new relationship between faith and works', and to demonstrate, as another critic has argued, 'that their faith and social vision could be put into practice, creating *a more truly Christian community*'.[23] Although the religious shifts that occurred during this period were anything but clean and complete – as Tomlin details in her account of sixteenth-century alms petitioning in London – this point of theological disagreement became a major pressure point with equally significant emotional ramifications.

Protestant writing increased the emphasis on the plight of the poor, the intensity and cause of their suffering and the need for action. Poverty, in this way, became politicised: the continued suffering of the poor was displayed in close focus as evidence of the ineffectuality of Catholic,

Church-sponsored charity, and of the need to dismantle it. But it was not the case that Protestant thinkers objected to the term 'charity' itself. Rather, Reformers sought to redefine the concept, reimagining it as a practice in which obligations were formed on the basis of the shared connection between one person and another. 'Why shoulde wee thinke scorne to receive them into our houses', Samuel Bird asked, in a sermon advocating compassion for those unfortunates 'whom God has placed with us *in the same house of the world.*'[24] Protestant authors saw charity as an expression of common humanity, rather than a penitential process: as Stephen Bateman defines the term in a volume titled *A Christall Glass for Christian Reformation*: 'Let us be rooted in charitie, that is, *let us consider one another.*'[25] This shift in vision removes the immediate 'carrot' of salvation earned through works, but in other ways it increases the importance and intimacy of earthly action, making the actions more specifically an exchange between humans.

The Protestant assault on a charity that imagines the clergy as intermediaries between the people and God is evident, for example, in the Ten Articles, issued in 1536 as guide for religious practice. The document acknowledges the virtue of some charitable principles, noting that 'it is a very good and charitable deed to pray for souls departed, and ... also to cause other[s] to pray for them in masses and exequies, and to give alms to other[s] to pray for them', but denies that these practices might provide some added eternal benefit.[26] The piece goes on to instruct that these 'abuses', which 'make men believe that through the bishop of Rome's pardons souls might clearly be delivered out of Purgatory', must 'clearly be put away'.[27] This kind of attack continued with the Chantries Act of 1547, under Edward VI, which disassembled 'trentals, chantries, and other provisions' on the grounds that they cultivated 'superstition and errors' about the possibility of investing in one's own immortal soul. The Act declares that this money will instead be distributed by the Crown, for 'good and godly uses', which included 'the education of youth in virtue and godliness' and 'better provision for the poor and needy'.[28]

While these changes retain the crucial deference to God – these things are done in His name – it also represents a major realignment in priorities, redirecting funds to the living suffering and thereby refocusing the social priority on a problem that was suddenly too pressing and close to go unnoticed. Reformers sought to make charitable work a public, social project. As one critic puts it, 'Men's aspirations underwent a notable metamorphosis in the century following the English Reformation, an almost complete absorption with secular needs and a stalwart concern for the visible needs of the society marking this transformation.'[29] That said, it seems that the shift in approach had significant behavioural and emotional ramifications: the increased emphasis on earthly suffering and the demand for its address closed the distance between the dispenser and the recipient of charity. Rather than being channelled through a mediating figure, the suffering of the poor became everyone's intimate, immediate problem.

In principle, these changes sound well intentioned and appealing, an attempt to rebuild charity as a form of pure compassion. Nonetheless, there is ample evidence – even beyond the opinions offered by the likes of Stow and Nashe – that these changes were experienced as a reduction in human compassion. Several critics have interpreted post-Reformation organisational changes as a cold, institutional, more *anonymous* approach to helping the needy.[30] Ian Archer, for example, has characterised Protestant charity as 'increasingly discriminating, channelled through institutional forms like the parish and the hospital, and subject to lay control'.[31] Speaking of more intimate forms of face-to-face giving, he writes: 'We know that in the long run it declined, but we have little sense of the chronology of decline or its significance.'[32] These interpretations suggest that reforms were perceived as removing a 'human' element of charity. These accusations were also levelled at the time. Stephen Gardiner, for instance, was unrestrained in his critique of Protestant minister Thomas Mowntayne: 'Ser, you have made a greate speke; for wheras yow have set upe one begarlye howse, yow have pulde down an [hundred] prynsly howses for yt; puttynge owte godly, lernyd, and devoyte men that sarvyd god daye and nyghte, and thruste yn ther plase a sort of scurvye and lowsye boyes.'[33] The sense of reduction is plain, as is the feeling of forced interaction with something worse: the 'scurvye and lowsye' replacements are 'thruste' into place, changing the very landscape of compassion.

By denying the possibility of attaining salvation through earthly works, Protestant Reformers forever changed the English conception of charity. This may, as Reformers claimed, have reduced corruption, certainly the types of 'abuses' against faithful parishioners outlined in texts like the Ten Articles, or the Chantries Act. While Tomlin has traced the continued practice of almsgiving in parish churches, on another scale these reforms also destabilised the formal, fundamental institutions through which feelings of pity and compassion might otherwise have been channelled. The Protestant emphasis on the plight of the poor and their need for relief may have made the case for reform a convincing one, but it also made the business of compassion seem all the more urgent: stripped of the guidance of priests and the processes of salvation, people became suddenly confronted with compassion as an organising principle for human interaction. In this way, works of fellowship – in which pity and its notions of mutual bonds, shared suffering and human vulnerability feature prominently – become intensely intimate, no longer clearly motivated by the possibility of self-service, and no longer explicitly overseen by a regulating superstructure. Without the more formal structures surrounding medieval charity, we are left with pity, compassion and fellowship: the very instincts so routinely depicted as seductive and unstable in morality plays like *Everyman*. Both the action of morality drama and the regulatory elements of charitable doctrine suggest a certain longing for guidance and stability in social relationships, a desire to identify and organise one's obligations. What, then, are the consequences of using pity as a guiding principle? This is the question of Shakespeare's *King Lear*: a post-Reformation play about a pre-Christian world, a new morality play for a new era of emotional regulation.

Re-forming the Morality Play: *King Lear*

There are many reasons to think about *King Lear* in the context of the medieval morality play. Shakespeare's piece tracks Lear's progression towards his death, the work traces his growth as a character, and he is the point around which all of the play's action turns. With the arguable exception of Gloucester, Lear is also the only character that has any real development, the only character that changes significantly (for the better) over the course of the play. Like Everyman, Lear finds himself abandoned by those who have been most vocal in their support and affection, and his ultimate salvation comes from the character that he initially rejects.[34] As in the morality tradition, *Lear* ends with the death of its title character, a fate that arrives just as he has recognised his transgressions and expressed the appropriate remorse. For these and other reasons, critics have long viewed *King Lear* as one of the strongest early modern examples of a reworked morality, a work that, as Michael O'Connell has argued, is 'as conscious of [the] morality tradition as *Hamlet* is of the contemporary theatre world'.[35] *Lear* also shares the morality genre's interest in social and emotional obligations, but for Shakespeare, this ultimately returns to ideas about pity – something that, in *Lear*, is both desperately valued and devastatingly unreliable.

If *King Lear*, as one critic has commented, is a play that takes as its premise 'the desperate need which human beings have for each other', then it is also a piece that seems determined to see that need remain unfulfilled.[36] Notions of human obligation (and their subsequent denial) are intensified by the family dynamics at work in the play, and the expectation of, and desire for, certain types of social bonds (father and daughter, master and servant, king and subject) emerge early in the opening scene. The exchange between Cordelia and her father ultimately expels Cordelia from one such bond, as Lear disowns her:

> Here I disclaim all my paternal care,
> Propinquity and property of blood,
> And as a stranger to my heart and me
> Hold thee, from this, for ever. The barbarous Scythian,
> Or he that makes his generation messes
> To gorge his appetite, shall to my bosom
> Be as well neighbour'd, pitied, and relieved,
> As thou my sometime daughter.[37]

Lear's invocation of pity alongside neighbourly behaviour and relief suggests, on some level, the doctrinal practice of almsgiving, of 'loving thy neighbour' as commanded in Matthew 22:39. Nonetheless, Lear frames his comment in more secular terms, referencing the paternal blood bond he shares with Cordelia and severing it on the grounds that her actions place her alongside another 'barbarous' race. The accusation relies heavily on notions of *kind*: for Lear, Cordelia's actions reveal her as not of the same 'kind', not capable (or worthy) of the compassionate terms of the family community. Lear's apparent disbelief and upset at this turn – his bewildered, 'So young and *untender?*' (I.i.107, my emphasis) – suggests that the speech is invested in an emotionally charged, punning exploration of kind/kindness: Lear's use of the word 'untender' to mean 'unkind' is also the first documented use in English.[38] There is an underlying expectation that this brand of emotional tenderness is a condition of *kind*ness. Cordelia's perceived emotional misstep – her perceived failure to act compassionately – has in turn rendered her unfit for the pity of others. This turn, of course, also acts as an early indication that pity is not functioning well in the play: Cordelia is arguably the hero, the most virtuous and loving. Her almost immediate emotional alienation, therefore, seemingly confirms the characters' inability to dispense pity in a reliable and reasonable way.

The play's depiction of pity as a specifically human emotion is further developed in the storm scenes, in which the marooned Lear is subjected to the unpitying forces of nature. Here, the absence of pity from the storm itself is accepted, expected, and again on the grounds that the emotion is a marker of *kind*-ness. The Fool observes that 'here's a night pities neither wise men nor fools' (III.ii.12–13), just as Lear admits 'I tax not you, you elements, with *unkindness*' (III.ii.16, my emphasis). The storm is cruel, but cannot be expected to recognise human vulnerability, or to offer pity in the face of it: it behaves in accordance to its own kind. Gloucester's reaction to Lear's expulsion onto the heath reaffirms the connection between pity and humanity, while demonstrating that the reflex is still not functioning as expected. Gloucester complains:

> Alack, alack, Edmund, I like not this unnatural dealing. When I desired their leave that I might pity him, they took from me the use of mine own house; charged me on pain of their perpetual displeasure neither to speak of him, entreat for him, or any way sustain him. (III.iii.1–6)

This is more than a personal failure to offer pity, on the part of Regan and Goneril; it also represents a structured attempt to curtail *any* pity for Lear whatsoever. Shakespeare in this respect produces an inverted morality play: the structure imposed in *Lear* is one of non-feeling; Regan and Goneril impose an order that actively blocks the compassion that Gloucester strains to offer. Gloucester's condemnation of this 'unnatural' response further envisions pity as a human response. However, while Gloucester and others seem convinced that pity should organise their interactions, and while they insist that the failure to offer pity signals a sort of deviant humanity, the play insists on staging these pitiful misfirings, these moments in which the compassionate response fails to materialise.

In many ways, the storm distils the play's exploration of pity, highlighting both its appeal and its shortcomings. Lear's immediate care for Kent and the Fool during the storm, his desire to secure their shelter: these are perhaps Lear's first true moments of consideration for others. Here we get his first recognition of suffering on a larger level, and his first acknowledgement of his own obligation to act in the interest of others:

> Poor naked wretches, whereso'er you are,
> That bide the pelting of this pitiless storm,
> How shall your houseless heads and unfed sides,
> Your looped and windowed raggedness, defend you
> From seasons such as these? *O, I have ta'en*
> *Too little care of this*. Take physic, pomp,
> Expose thyself to feel what wretches feel,
> That thou mayst shake the superflux to them
> And show the heavens more just.
> (III.iv.28–36, my emphasis)

Debora Shuger has argued that this passage is an epiphany of Christian *caritas* for Lear, calling it an expression of 'the social teachings of the medieval church'.[39] And indeed, Lear touches upon many of the major elements of Christian charity: the need to provide shelter and food to the poor speaks to the practice of almsgiving, as does the suggestion of offering up the 'superflux' – the surplus wealth in aid of the poor; the invocation of the heavens in this instance might also be a reference to the divine underpinnings of charitable doctrine. These arguments might be more persuasive if the play acknowledged any sort of social structure, but in fact there is not much society in *Lear* beyond the immediate community of Lear's family and followers. Therefore, if this is the moment in which Lear recognises the importance of pity, of acting in the interest of men, then it comes too late to be of any use. At this point Lear is weak, old, impoverished – one in need of help rather than one able to offer it. He is arguably only able to express pity here because he himself has been confronted, forced 'to feel what wretches feel'. Perhaps for this reason, Jonathan Dollimore has identified the pity in *Lear* as 'precious yet ineffectual', a thing that stands, rather uselessly, in the absence of the pre-existing structures that I have identified elsewhere.[40] The ineffectuality of Lear's pity here, combined with the improbability that a king would ever, under normal circumstances, be reduced to this level, leads Dollimore to conclude this of the play's message: 'in a world where pity is the prerequisite for compassionate action, where a king has to share the suffering of his subjects in order to "care", the majority will remain poor, naked and wretched'.[41] Lear's vision of a compassionate kingdom, therefore, is exactly what the play lacks in practice; the lack of a structured system that ensures or demands compassionate action creates the opportunity for the suffering Lear imagines in his subjects (and endures himself). The charitable works that Lear references have no obvious place in his world: the play's action denies a culture of their practice. Instead, this world has only vague notions of pity and emotional obligation, which in practice are revealed as unstable and unreliable.

In spite of the apparently pity-hostile environment in *Lear*, the emotion is seemingly impervious to complete suppression: the play allows the emotion to function just well enough to demonstrate its continued appeal. When Cordelia returns to assist her father, it is because her husband 'My mourning and important tears hath pitied' (IV.iv.26). Edgar, as Poor Tom, offers Gloucester anonymous assistance after describing himself as

> A most poor man, made tame to fortune's blows;
> Who, by the art of known and feeling sorrows,
> Am pregnant to good pity.
>
> (IV.vi.217–19)

Edgar suggests that his susceptibility to pity has evolved from earthly experience, rather than religious instruction: his experience of personal vulnerability has bred a desire to assist those falling victim to their own. These examples prove that pity exists in the play, but they also suggest that it floats around untethered: the resulting impression is that the emotion is ineffectual without the accompanying support of an institutional structure. The characters, however, seem either unaware of this or unwilling to accept it. Nonetheless, with these successful moments of pity, the play demonstrates a crucial difference between what pity *should* be – what we want to believe it can be – and what it is in practice. In this way *King Lear* juxtaposes the hope and impulse for pity with the emotion's capacity to fail (or the human capacity to mismanage it).

As Eric Langley argues in Chapter 10 of this volume, in *King Lear*, 'Shakespeare advocates pity as a poor but necessary human substitute for the divine compassion we lack'. Shakespeare's play may well be taking aim at a poorly functioning replacement for an earlier model of compassion that has been lost. Still there is, I think, more than just emotional scepticism at the heart of *Lear*. While the play demonstrates the essential fallibility of an emotion dependent on shared human goodness, it also acknowledges the persistent attractiveness of pity. The play laments something that has been lost, but it also acknowledges that there is perhaps no way of regaining it in its original form: the play accepts the instinct to seek some – or any – alternative. Ultimately, *Lear* reflects a vision of early modern humanity that is emotionally untethered: desperately in need of pity, desperately wanting to offer it, and nevertheless wholly unsure how to manage it, or how to make it efficacious. By placing his characters in the familiar structure of the morality play, Shakespeare shows us people being confronted by similar emotions in new, more intimate ways. Nashe's description in particular calls to mind the vision we are presented in *Lear*: a horrifying and extreme depiction of blood, death and emotional suffering that is left unchecked, and remains both amplified and close. At the same time, the play reflects the sense of longing and regret implicit in Stow, a felt loss of security that casts a different light on one of Cordelia's final comments, to Edmund: 'We are not the first / Who with best meaning have incurred the worst' (5.3.3–4).

Notes

1 John Stow, *A survay of London* (London, 1598), sig. Aa1r, my emphasis.
2 James Simpson, *Burning to Read: English Fundamentalism and Its Reformation Opponents* (Cambridge, MA: Harvard University Press, 2007), p. 2; Thomas Nashe, *Christs Teares over Jerusalem* (London, 1613), sig. O3r.

3 Nashe, *Christs Teares*, sig. O3v, my emphasis.
4 Phillip Stubbes, *The second part of the anatomie of abuses* (1583), sig. G1v, quoted in Tomlin, Chapter 12 in this volume.
5 Chapter 12.
6 Nashe, *Christs Teares*, sig. O3v.
7 Steven Mullaney has also recently argued that the Protestant Reformation had a profound effect on the English emotional landscape during this period. 'The generation that was born Elizabethan', he writes, 'did not know what to believe, whether in terms of their own faith or the spiritual identities of those around them, and they also, perhaps even as a consequence, did not know what or how to *feel.*' See *The Reformation of Emotions in the Age of Shakespeare* (University of Chicago Press, 2015), p. 16.
8 John Colet, *The sermon of doctor Colete, made to the convocacion at Paulis* (London, 1530), sig. B3r. Colet was the Dean of St Paul's and Henry VIII's chaplain. This pre-Reformation sermon, originally delivered in 1511, criticised the English clergy heavily on the grounds of secularism and encouraged immediate reform from within.
9 St Thomas Aquinas, *Summa Theologiae*, ed. Thomas Gilby and Thomas C. O'Brien (London: Eyre and Spottiswoode, 1964–76), at II-II, q. 23, a. 1.
10 Aquinas, *Summa*, my emphasis.
11 Aquinas, *Summa*, II-II, q. 25, a. 1, ad 3, my emphasis. C. S. Lewis makes a similar distinction, identifying charity as 'that Love which is God itself', something quite different from 'the human activities called "loves"'. C. S. Lewis, *The Four Loves* (London: Fount, 1960), p. 115.
12 Thomas Lupset, *A compendious and a very fruteful treatyse, teachynge the waye of dyenge well* (London, 1534), sig. B4v. Lupset, a Catholic, was a friend of Thomas More and was a part of John Colet's household; he died in 1530.
13 Lupset, *A compendious*, sig. C2v.
14 Susan Brigden, 'Religion and Social Obligation in Early Sixteenth-Century London', *Past & Present*, 103 (1984), 67–112, p. 84.
15 Christopher Daniel, *Death and Burial in Medieval England, 1066–1550* (London: Routledge, 1997), p. 1.
16 Eamon Duffy, *The Stripping of the Altars* (New Haven, CT: Yale University Press, 1992), p. 308.
17 Andrew Hadfield, 'The Summoning of *Everyman*' in Thomas Betteridge and Greg Walker (eds.), *The Oxford Handbook of Tudor Drama* (Oxford University Press, 2012), pp. 93–108, p. 93.
18 That 'Good Deeds' is presented as a female character is perhaps surprising when read alongside comparable works, such as *The Interlude of Youth*, which typically render 'Charity' as male. *Everyman* does not offer any comment on the gender of Good Deeds, but it is nonetheless worth noting that the play includes a strikingly large number of female roles. Two of these roles in particular – 'Good Deeds' and her sister 'Knowledge' – are central to the play's overarching project of Everyman's salvation. For more on this, see

Douglas Bruster, 'Women and the English Morality Play', *Medieval Feminist Forum*, 45 (2009), 57–67.
19 *The Pride of Life* in Osborn Waterhouse (ed.), *The Non-Cycle Mystery Plays*, (London: Kegan Paul, 1909), pp. 88–104, quoted here at l. 403, l. 406 and l. 404, respectively.
20 *The Interlude of Youth* in Ian Lancashire (ed.), *Two Tudor Interludes* (Manchester University Press, 1980), pp. 98–152, ll. 8–9.
21 Joel T. Rosenthal, *The Purchase of Paradise* (London: Routledge & Kegan Paul, 1972).
22 Simpson, *Burning to Read*, p. 2.
23 Felicity Heal, *Hospitality in Early Modern England* (London: Clarendon Press, 1990), p. 122; quote from Marjorie Keniston McIntosh, *Controlling Misbehavior in England, 1370–1600* (Cambridge University Press, 1998), p. 203, my emphasis. For more on the transition between medieval and Renaissance thoughts on charity, see also John Bossy, *Christianity in the West, 1400–1700* (Oxford University Press, 1985); Susan Brigden, 'Religion and Social Obligation'; W. K. Jordan, *The Charities of London: 1480–1660* (London: George Allen & Unwin Ltd., 1960); and W. K. Jordan, *Philanthropy in England, 1480–1660: A Study of the Changing Pattern of English Social Aspirations* (Westport, CT: Greenwood Press, 1978).
24 Samuel Bird, *Three Sermons, or Homelies to Moove Compassion towards the Poore* (London, 1596), no folio, my emphasis.
25 Stephen Batman, *A Christall Glass for Christian Reformation* (London, 1569), sig. D3v, my emphasis.
26 *English Historical Documents* V, ed. C. H. Williams (London: Eyre & Spottiswoode, 1967), pp. 804–5.
27 *Historical Documents*, p. 805.
28 *Historical Documents*, p. 775.
29 Jordan, *The Charities of London*, p. 9.
30 See Felicity Heal, *Hospitality in Early Modern England*; and Ian W. Archer, 'The Charity of Early Modern Londoners', *Transactions of the Royal Historical Society*, 12 (2002), 223–44.
31 Archer, 'Charity', p. 224.
32 Archer, p. 242.
33 *Narratives of the Days of the Reformation*, ed. J. G. Nichols (Camden Society, O.S., LXXVII, 1859), pp. 182.
34 The structural similarities between *King Lear* and *Everyman* are outlined in detail in Michael O'Connell, '*King Lear* and the Summons of Death' in Curtis Perry and John Watkins (eds.), *Shakespeare and the Middle Ages* (Oxford University Press, 2009), pp. 199–216, especially at p. 210.
35 O'Connell, '*King Lear*', p. 203. A number of critics have made associations between Shakespeare's work and the medieval morality play. See, for instance, John Wasson, 'The Morality Play: Ancestor of Elizabethan Drama?', *Comparative Drama*, 13 (1979), 210–21; Robert Potter, *The English Morality Play: Origins, History and Influence of a Dramatic Tradition*

(London: Routledge & Kegan Paul, 1975); Curtis Perry and John Watkins, introduction to *Shakespeare and the Middle Ages*, pp. 1–20; and Maynard Mack, *King Lear in Our Time* (Berkeley: University of California Press, 1965).
36 Sears Jayne, 'Charity in *King Lear*', *Shakespeare Quarterly*, 15 (1964), 277–88, p. 277.
37 William Shakespeare, *King Lear*, ed. R. A. Foakes (London: Thomson Learning, 1997). All subsequent references to *King Lear* will be from this edition, and provided parenthetically.
38 *OED*, 'untender, *adj.*', 1: 'Not tender in dealing with others; ungentle, unkind'.
39 Debora K. Shuger, 'Subversive Fathers and Suffering Subjects: Shakespeare and Christianity' in Donna B. Hamilton and Richard Strier (eds.), *Religion, Literature, and Politics in Post-Reformation England, 1540–1688* (Cambridge University Press, 1996), pp. 46–69, p. 53.
40 For this treatment of *King Lear*, see Jonathan Dollimore, *Radical Tragedy*, 2nd ed. (London: Harvester Wheatsheaf, 1989), esp. pp. 189–203, here at p. 193. Philip Brockbank similarly identifies pity as an important feature of the play, but has a more positive reading of it, arguing that the 'access of pity' is depicted as 'a condition for the renewal of human life' (p. 133). See Philip Brockbank, 'Upon Such Sacrifices', *Proceedings of the British Academy*, 62 (1976), 109–34.
41 Dollimore, *Radical Tragedy*, p. 191.

CHAPTER 12

Alms Petitions and Compassion in Sixteenth-Century London

Rebecca Tomlin

'Is it not great pity', Philip Stubbes complained in 1583, 'when a man can passe no waie almost neither citie nor country, but shall have both halt, blind, lame, old aged, sicke, sore & diseased hanging upon his sleve, and craving of reléefe?'[1] Despite the polemical purpose of his tract, which was intended to shame the authorities into action against widespread begging, Stubbes' 'great pity' seems to be directed more towards the man who is unable to go about his business without being hindered by beggars than towards those suffering individuals. Using examples taken from the churchwardens' Memoranda of St Botolph's, Aldgate, this chapter discusses some of the ways in which a subgroup of beggars, those equipped with alms-gathering licences, tried to shape the parishioner from a passerby into an almsgiver. Unlike those who solicited Stubbes, those who petitioned for relief in church were authorised to collect alms, but like them, they too aimed to materialise compassion into coins in the collecting bowl.

Thomas Wilson, in his *Christian Dictionary* (1612), defined compassion as 'a disposition or affection, prone to pitty others, so much as neede is'.[2] The qualification here is important; Wilson bounds pity for others within the limits of need. The licences discussed here construct a donor who restrains his or her compassion with reason, to give 'so much as neede is', but 'neede' is not an absolute. Rather, the greater the loss, the more deserving of alms the victim is seen to be, as licences gesture towards some kind of restitution of the pre-existing social order, rather than evoking

---

[*] This research was funded under the European Union's Seventh Framework Programme (FP7/2007-2013)/ERC grant agreement no 617849, as part of *Crossroads of Knowledge in Early Modern England: The Place of Literature* research project at the University of Cambridge. Early versions of this chapter were presented at *Compassion in Early Modern Culture*, VU University, Amsterdam and *Addressing Authority* at Birkbeck, London and my thanks go to Kristine Steenbergh and Brodie Waddell who organised these events. I also thank Ceri Sullivan, Lizzie Swann and Rachel Holmes for their assistance in preparing this chapter. Any mistakes are, of course, my own.

compassion for destitution. As Stubbes suggests, compassion towards early modern beggars was often framed in terms that define them in opposition to the settled and prosperous but the licences show that the boundaries between alms-seeker and almsgiver were often precarious and overwhelmed in a moment of disaster. Notwithstanding the devastating consequences for individuals and communities of the calamities that left them destitute, distress is effaced in the homogenised language of the collections, which try to move donors by focusing on the economic consequences of disasters rather than emotive descriptions of physical or emotional suffering. In contrast to the depersonalised and unemotional language of the petitions for strangers, a sense of social solidarity is operative when the parish gathered for local causes; compassion seems to be more readily available when it is closer to home and directed towards neighbours rather than strangers.

Collecting at St Botolph's

St Botolph's, Aldgate was located just outside the city gates on the main road that connected London to Essex and East Anglia.[3] The church served a large and poor extramural parish extending north and east around the Tower of London and, dealing with both its own poor and the beggars passing through, was an important part of the daily life of the church as recorded by Thomas Harridance, the church clerk.[4] Unlike the common beggar in the street, about whom Stubbes complains, the petitioner who collected at St Botolph's usually carried a 'protection', often called a Letter Patent or 'bill' in the Memoranda, which was his or her license to beg.[5] Parishioners hearing the stories of alms collectors read aloud before the collection were invited to make judgements about the petitioner and whether they merited relief, a process often described in the bills as exercising their 'charitable benevolence'.

The (approximately) three hundred alms collections recorded in the Churchwardens' Memoranda of St Botolph's between c.1580 and 1600 illustrate some of the ways in which compassion was conceived of, and exercised, in early modern London.[6] The largest two groupings, which relate to fires (around forty-two cases) and maimed soldiers and mariners (around seventy cases), are the focus of the discussions in this chapter. Other collections are for local institutions, including the prisoners at the Marshalsea and King's Bench gaols; for national projects such as re-edifying harbours; and for some thirty cases of mariners, traders and Christian clerics held prisoner 'by the Turke' or captured by pirates or

Dunkirk raiders.[7] The social status of those who gathered at St Botolph's varied widely, from the humblest former soldiers and mariners to collectors for Lawrence Palliologo, the former Archbishop of Cyprus.[8] Occasionally collections were made without an official bill, usually by the personal recommendation of the preacher, the curate or another leading member of the parish, on behalf of incapacitated local people, poor scholars or clergymen without a living. In 1589, for example, a collection was gathered for William Camp, a scholar at St John's, Cambridge, at the request of Mr Scott, a regular preacher at the church.[9]

Collections under official bills were authorised by powerful people including the Queen, her Privy Council, the Lord High Admiral, the Lord Mayor and the Bishop of London. The official licensing process points towards a growing concern about the indigent poor. This has been related variously to the impact of the dissolution of the monasteries and other pre-Reformation charitable institutions and to large-scale economic movements such as enclosure and the movement of people away from the land; and connected to more immediate political events such as the wars on the Continent and the disbanding of Essex's fleet following the Azores expedition.[10] An alms collection at St Botolph's enacted a number of social relationships: religious solidarity, neighbourly charity, compliance with national authorities, or any combination of these, and despite the theoretically reduced role for the Church in mediating relationships with the poor post-Reformation described by Toria Johnson in the previous chapter, the parish church remained a site for the exercise of charitable giving. The discussion that follows focuses mainly on the theological reasons for almsgiving because its evidence is taken largely from church collections, but spiritual motivations for giving were intertwined with ideas of economic and social solidarity that complicated the urge to fulfil a religious duty by giving to the poor.

The Memoranda do not describe in detail many of the daily activities to which they refer, and collections, like most of the church's rituals, are assumed to be familiar to the reader. Some of the bills indicate that they were intended to be read out loud by the Minister during the collection, but Nashe's complaint about preachers, cited by Johnson, raises the question of how effective they were. It is unlikely that the collectors' own voices were heard in the church, although there are occasional mentions of petitioners collecting on their own behalf outside the church after the service. Many of the collections were made by agents or delegates, but even where petitioners appeared in person, what survives is the official documentation, rather than the direct unmediated account of their misfortune. Although they often give the beguiling impression of being immediate accounts of disaster and woe, the stories of the collectors are mediated by several layers of authority, translated into the versions told in the official letters patent and then extracted for the record made by the clerk of St Botolph's. Several of the Memoranda books open with an ambitious claim to omniscience: 'Heare after is Speacefyed and Then regestered all Suche thinges as is done in the churche', but despite this claim the material recorded in the books is, of course, partial and selective, shaped to fit the needs of those who kept them.[11] The Memoranda do not form a continuous narrative in themselves but are the records of a series of moments and events arranged in chronological order without any narrative shaping to smooth out elisions, omissions or discontinuities. As material objects, in their claimed omniscience, the Memoranda perform the churchwardens' adherence to rules, recording their compliance and justifying any deviance. They are less records of compassion than documentation of surveillance and control of the space of the church, and the people who use it; nonetheless, they can also be read for the material traces of the ephemeral emotions, processes and actions elicited and framed by compassion.

The Reformation and Giving to the Poor

Collecting alms at St Botolph's was at once a quotidian activity and a potentially problematic one. The alms petition, and giving alms generally, is a nexus at which Reformed theology, tradition and social necessity met, and as the Reformation progressed, parishes within the London diocese, like St Botolph's, were closely watched for compliance with liturgical changes.[12] The parish collection for the poor was an element of the pre-Reformation liturgy carried forward into the new, and while everyone knew they were supposed to put their penny in the poor box, it was not always theologically clear why they were doing it, and as Toria Johnson discusses, there was a pervasive sense of the city's 'compassionate decline'.[13] Even where the Reformation was enthusiastically embraced, 'some fragments of the old world', as Diarmaid MacCulloch observes, 'took their cue from the survival in modified form of the liturgical year, adopted new guises and found a home within the reformed Protestant parish' – among these was the collection for the poor during service.[14] The shift that Johnson identifies, from medieval charity grounded in Church doctrine towards post-Reformation concepts rooted in interpersonal connections like fellowship and compassion, seems to have sometimes aroused anxiety and confusion.

While they rarely refer to the physical process of collecting, the Memoranda do make careful and detailed notes about other aspects of charitable collections: who made them, on whose behalf, who they were authorised by, and how much was collected. While part of a general increase in record-keeping of all kinds in the period, this performative documentation is perhaps a response to changing official understanding of almsgiving that made it an activity where uncertainty, and consequently anxiety, about the reformed theology may have arisen.[15] Prior to the Reformation, collections paid for masses to be said on behalf of the souls of the dead and giving to the poor sped one's own soul through Purgatory. Pre-Reformation churches and liturgy were expensive, and required fundraising among the congregation, who believed that their donations benefited their immortal souls.[16] Reformed theology discarded the notion of Purgatory and denied the efficacy of salvation by good works, replacing it with the doctrine of salvation by faith alone. Nevertheless, as Eamon Duffy comments, the church collection represented 'at least one element of continuity with Catholic belief and practice' and giving alms to the poor remained a Christian duty.[17] Christopher Haigh, who describes the church-goers of England in the late sixteenth century as 'de-catholicized but un-protestantized', points to the persistence among the population of the belief that salvation might be bought by good works, despite the austerity of Protestant teaching on the reliance on faith alone.[18] There is, of course, no way of knowing how many of the parishioners of St Botolph's donated alms in the secret hope of securing their own salvation.

The homily *Of Almes Deedes* (1563) deals extensively with the spiritual reasons for giving to the poor and needy, countering arguments that sins are cleansed by the giving of alms and presenting the Reformed view that the giver of alms instead shows that God's grace is present and working through him.[19] The need for this detailed discussion indicates that, at least early in Elizabeth's reign, the church authorities were unsure that parishioners understood why they should give alms and that confusion about the precise purpose of their charity probably persisted even among reformed congregations. Stephen Bateman, who was associated with the parish and was close to the formative discussions of Anglican theology, adapted pre-Reformation doctrine to Anglican theology in his statement that 'suche as say that workes onely iustifieth from sinne' are incorrect and 'although workes are nedefull and necessary, yet beyng without faith, hope, & charitie, nothing at all auayleth'.[20] For Calvinists, visible good works were a means of distinguishing the elect from the reprobate, and, as Ian Archer observes, 'it is one of the paradoxes of Calvinism that while denying that good works were efficacious in achieving salvation, its adherents were nevertheless urged to perform them'.[21] This lack of clarity about why anyone should give alms had to be overcome by the alms collector; if prosperity was a sign of God's favour to the elect, it was an easy step to interpret poverty and misfortune as a sign of error or God's displeasure. Part of the task of the alms petition was to convince the hearer that the recipient was worthy of God's grace as it operated through the giver.

Despite the nuances of theological interpretation, almsgiving was a Christian duty that transcended confessional difference, and the discourse around begging framed the relationships between giver and receiver, deserving and undeserving. It recognised that the alms donor and the recipient were mutually dependent, and that the giving and receiving of alms was a reciprocal arrangement since the donor required the existence of the beggar in order to fulfil the spiritual obligation to give alms. Giving to the poor was everyone's duty, even those who were poor themselves, as Thomas Harman acknowledged in his *Caveat for Commen Cursetors* (1567).[22] Despite his unremitting hostility to the vagrant poor, Harman quotes scripture and St Augustine to argue that even the poorest, who have nothing more to offer than a cup of cold water, have a duty to give.[23] Charity is described in the meagre terms of the widow's mite in the Bible, argues Harman, to show that even the poorest can partake in the spiritual blessings that it offers. This did not, of course, excuse the rich from giving more than just bread and water, in accordance with their greater wealth. Conversely, the rich also had an obligation to accept even the smallest offerings of the poor, so that they, too, could benefit from the spiritual exercise of giving. When the story of an alms-seeker was heard in St Botolph's, it was aimed not only at the wealthiest members of the congregation, but also towards all parishioners who sought an opportunity to give alms for their own spiritual welfare.

While they were encouraged for spiritual reasons to be charitable, donors had a social duty to ensure that they gave only to those who begged because they were incapable of earning their own living, and not out of 'idleness'.[24] The funeral sermon preached for Lord Russell in 1614 praised his investigative visits to the poor; 'neyther did he look only on their want and misery, but he looked into it', visiting their homes and enquiring about their own attempts to mitigate their situation.[25] Russell's discriminate giving is held up by the sermon as exemplary; would that all noblemen, like Russell 'readily afford them the bowels of compassion, whom now they passe by with scorne and contempt'.[26] Notwithstanding the promise of the homily *Of Almes Deedes*, and the assurances of preachers, that God would ensure that those who gave alms would not be left in poverty, the congregation of St Botolph's seem to have understood that a certain amount of pragmatic judgement was to be exercised by the charitably inclined. The cautionary story of Dorothy Hobson, a widow who had 'falen into Extreame povertie much want and distrese' despite formerly being 'of good welth whereby she maynteyned her selfe and famely in good sorte' was heard in St Botolph's in 1590.[27] 'Trowbled and afflicted in mynd and concience' Hobson had given away or sold her property to give to the poor 'thinking there by to merritt some love and mercye of god'; in her attempt to self-fashion through self-abnegation, 'she sowght to destroye her self'. Hobson's generosity appears to have been motivated by her own troubled conscience and an attempt to win God's favour, rather than compassion for the poor. Perhaps this is why the congregation did not appear to feel much sympathy for her and why she received just 2 shillings 8d, one of the smallest collections recorded in the Memoranda. 'The bowels of compassion' were to be exercised with discretion and judgement, as Harman argued, and as the examples of Dorothy Hobson and Lord Russell demonstrated.

Judgement and the Maimed Soldier

Although giving to the poor was a religious obligation that St Botolph's facilitated, the wardens and clerk had a duty to ensure that only genuine and deserving cases were allowed to collect alms, and that the church was not a site where the parishioners were defrauded. There was also concern that the parish's own poor, of which there were many, should not lose out to wandering strangers. On the one hand, the beggar functioned as an avatar of Christ, towards whom mercy and compassion should be directed and, in a tradition stretching back to the Greeks, was often depicted as a wise man able to critique society from his position as an outsider.[28] On the other hand, a petitioner hoping to collect at St Botolph's had to counter a discourse in popular literature and drama of the period in which the beggar was portrayed as a fraud and a cheat, preying on the settled citizen.[29]

The tension between the duty to give to the poor and the suspicion that all beggars were frauds and cheats, 'undeserving' of charity, is clear in texts like Harman's *Caveat*, which warns against the various false and cheating beggars that it claims are roaming the countryside and exploiting and frightening law-abiding people. The vagabond former soldier, whose identity could slip easily from maimed serviceman to dishonest rogue, was a figure of particular concern.[30] The idea that a man claiming to be a former soldier could not be trusted became fixed in official language as Elizabethan statute and proclamations, ever more vehemently, denounced beggars, and especially those allegedly masquerading as counterfeit soldiers or 'rufflars' through the 1580s and 1590s when plague, famine and the wars on the Continent drove many into beggary. A 1591 proclamation declared that the 'great multitude' of beggars 'wandring abroad' who claimed to be former soldiers were frauds and deserters: 'whereof the most part pretend, that they have served in the warres of late on the other side of the Seas, though in trueth it is knowen, that very mane of them, either have not served at all, or have not bene licenced to depart from the places of their service, as they ought to have beene, but have runne away from their service.'[31] Similar proclamations were made in 1592 and 1594.[32]

By the time that Middleton and Dekker staged *The Roaring Girl* (1611), which features the 'rufflars' Tearcat and Trapdoor, the counterfeit soldier had become a comic figure but, as Linda Woodbridge notes, laughter can mask oppression and 'pieces couched as comic warnings occurred in periods of deep public anxiety [which] suggests serious purposes underneath the laughter'.[33] Tearcat and Trapdoor are based on characters in Harman's *Caveat* and other rogue literature, and in their encounter with the gentlemen of the play, they first elicit sympathy and a few coins with their tales of arduous and exotic travel in service of the Queen, and their consequent injuries. By making dupes of the gentlemen who believe their lies, however, Tearcat and Trapdoor subvert the deferential relationship that was implicit in any early modern patronage or gift-giving.[34] The play's heroine Moll sees through the deceit and restores the appropriate reciprocity between beggar and giver by making Tearcat enter into a 'canting' competition with her for the amusement of the gentlemen. By 'singing for his supper' he earns the reward of a tip from Moll's gentlemen friends, who can go on their way without loss of face. A parishioner at St Botolph's might also have been a reader of rogue literature or have seen characters like Tearcat and Moll in action on stage; in varying modes, the possibility of being made to look a fool by those to whom you offered compassion was made uncomfortably real.

Alongside the popular 'rogue literature' of Harman and others and theatrical depictions of devious beggars, Protestant writers attempted to encourage compassion and to counter hostility towards beggars. The parable of Dives and Lazarus, which told of a rich man's lack of compassion towards the poor man at his gate, was used in Foxe's *Acts and*

Monuments to frame the contemporary story of the dissolute Christopher Landesdale.[35] In writings by other reformists, including Stephen Bateman, Anthony Gilby and Philip Stubbes, the rich man without compassion appears as a recurring literary and theological trope: 'The rich man signifieth a proude man, covetous, such a one as careth for no poore man, but for such as hym lyketh (to many such are not good in a common wealth): the poore man signifieth the povertie generall, whose petitions of such are not heard, nor once relieved', wrote Bateman.[36] Philip Stubbes, despite his concern about all forms of performance and their potential for hypocrisy, is less sceptical about the honesty of the poor than Harman. While agreeing that 'stout, strong, lustie, couragious, and valiant beggers' who are able to work should do so, as far as the 'halt, lame, impotent, decrepite, blind, sicke, sore, infirme, and diseased, or aged and the like' are concerned, 'everie Christian man is bound in conscience to reléeve' them.[37] In what could be read as a riposte to Harman, who claimed to be a Justice of the Peace, he complains that the poor are driven from parish to parish like flocks of sheep and comments on the cruelty of requiring those who are clearly in need to obtain a license to beg:

> Here they dare not tarrie for this Justice, nor there for that Justice, here for this man, nor there for that man, without a licence or a pasport, wheras a man would thinke their old age, their hoare haires, their blindnesse, lamenesse, and other infirmities shoulde bee pasports good inough for them to go abrod withal if they cannot get reléefe at home.[38]

Even as he acknowledges that the 'licence or pasport' is a vital document for the wandering beggar, which distinguishes him from the unlicensed rogue, Stubbes deplores the way in which bureaucratic paperwork is regarded by the Justices as better evidence than the compassion evoked by visible physical disability.

In spite of a discourse that classified many beggars, especially former soldiers, as frauds, the Memoranda show that many were able to persuade the wardens and clerk of St Botolph's of the truth of their stories. The Memoranda carefully record the petitions that were heard, providing evidence, should it be required, that the churchwardens had not been easily duped by any passing rogue and that they had carefully policed access to their parishioners. Around seventy injured soldiers or mariners were allowed to collect between 1580 and 1600, by some way the largest number for any type of petitioner. Before 1589, this kind of collection was infrequent and raised modest amounts for local men who were blind or otherwise incapacitated by their injuries, and who may well have been known to the parishioners, their need confirmed by communal memory and local knowledge. A discernible shift occurs during 1589 when many more former soldiers and mariners begin to appear in the Memoranda, the majority between March 1590 and October 1592.[39] This coincided with a severe outbreak of plague, which meant that the parish was barely able to deal with its own poor, and began to turn some petitioners away without allowing them to collect, on the basis that the parish's resources were already stretched. Typically, those travelling soldiers and mariners who were allowed to collect carried the Queen's Letter Patent and are described as 'maymed'; they had often been offered an alms room at one of the great cathedrals, which was not yet available, or to which they had to travel. John William, for example, is described as a poor and maimed soldier with a wife and children, who lost a leg and his right arm during service in the Low Countries. William had been allocated an alms room at Worcester Cathedral but was fourth in line for the next vacancy, and so in the meantime was allowed to beg for relief.[40] William's license allows him a degree of compulsion in collecting alms; he is permitted to 'demand and collect' alms, 'praieng and Requiring' assistance from those who could offer it. In none of these cases was a collection made without the appropriate licence – William's missing arm and leg may have confirmed the validity of his paperwork but they were not in themselves adequate testimony to enable him to receive official assistance.

One of the evidential limitations of the Memoranda that claim to record 'all thinges done in the church' is their lack of information about absence. We have no way of knowing how many petitioners were turned away from St Botolph's for lack of proper documents, or because the churchwardens suspected they were frauds; the Memoranda rarely include references to the things not done. Informal help may have been given to impoverished people without licences but not recorded, because the purpose of the Memoranda is to demonstrate compliance. Even with the partial and limited account given by the Memoranda, we can understand, however, that questions of truth and fraud were evaluated on a regular basis. How to distinguish between an alms-seeker who deserved relief and a 'counterfeit' must have been a question that the churchwardens of St Botolph's asked themselves almost daily. The popular discourse around begging showed that the decision about whether or not to give alms to a maimed man claiming to be a former soldier required judgement and discrimination; compassion, as Thomas Wilson noted, was an emotion to be exercised within limits.

Fires and the Pitiless Language of Alms Petitions

After collections for maimed soldiers and mariners, the next largest group in the Memoranda consists of forty-two collections relating to fires, some made on behalf of individuals, others for towns so devastated that the community was left unable to relieve those affected from its own resources. Two contrasting accounts of a devastating fire at Tiverton show that alms collectors were less concerned to arouse compassion for the emotional consequences of the fire than to seek restoration of the social order disrupted by sudden economic catastrophe. *The True lamentable discourse of the burning of Teverton* (1598) is a pamphlet that describes in dramatic detail a fire that started in a frying pan and proceeded to destroy the prosperous market town and kill fifty people:

> Most dreadful was the noise which was then heard in every corner and street of the Towne, women piteously screaking, maidens bitterly crying, and children roaring out of measure, the mother running to save her children, the husband for the wife, neighbor calling for neighbor, friend, for friend, while they were beaten out of the town with raging flames of fire.

In a lengthy description over several sides of broadsheet, it vividly and pitifully describes the after-effects of the fire:

> the residue of the wofull people remaining yet alive being overburdened with exordinerie sorrow, runs up and downe the fields like distraught and frantick men ... moreover they are so greatly distressed for lack of food, that they seem to each man's sight more like Spirits and Ghosts then living creatures.[41]

The pamphlet presents the disaster that hit Tiverton as God's punishment of the town for its lack of charity, specifically its 'small regard of the poore, which were dayly seene to dye and perish in their streetes for lacke of reliefe' and warns the wealthy merchants of London and other towns to 'learne by her calamitie to loke unto thy selfe'. Highly emotive descriptions are used throughout to prompt compassion in the reader, and to underline the moral lessons that the pamphlet presents about charity.

In comparison, the language used by the Memoranda to describe the same fire is moderate and reserved, stating, rather flatly, that the people of the town:

> were greatly hindered by fire whereby four hundred dwelling houses within the said town were utterly consumed and burnt, and the moveables, writings & plate, money, goods, ware and other merchandizes within the same were destroyed to the value of 150,000 pounds besides fifty persons burnt to death.[42]

The emotional language of lamentation, fear and pity that we find in the pamphlet is entirely absent from the collection bill. The descriptive element is limited to the value of the goods and other assets that have been lost, with the deaths of fifty people mentioned almost as an afterthought. Nowhere does it mention the terrible emotional and social consequences for the townsfolk of losing everything they possessed, so vividly conveyed in the pamphlet. This absence of emotion is typical of the alms bills, which are largely composed of standardised, generic phrases. Fires are typically 'extreme and sudayne', houses and goods have been 'burnt, wasted and consumed', or simply 'burnt with fire'. Of all the fire petitions, only the collection for Blythburgh hints at a divine cause: 'by the vissitatio'of god in the nyght season there was destroyed by fire'.[43] Petitions describe the 'extreame empoverishinge and utter undoing of the Sayd Inhabitaunts there poor wife and Children for ever' in Beccles; the 'grete henderance losses & utter undoing of many' in Blythburgh; similarly, the people of Wandsworth were suffering 'there great hinderance and utter undoinges'.[44] At Bottisford there was 'utter undoing and decay'; at Stratford-upon-Avon the 'greate hinderance & utter undoing of many people' and the people of Uttoxeter were similarly 'utterly undon or Hindred by misfortune'.[45] A rhetoric of economic disaster is deployed, in which the phrases 'great hindrance', 'extreme impoverishing' and 'utter undoing' appear repeatedly. As Ian Archer has observed, early modern charity was often an opportunity to control those requesting assistance, and this coercive aspect of charity is echoed in the constrained generic form and language of the bills themselves in which individual narratives of disaster are moulded into standardised forms.[46]

Even when they deal with potentially exciting stories about pirates or fires, the petitions remain focused on material need and affect is elicited by the 'absolute undoing' both financially and socially, a source of anxiety in a society that, by and large, believed in fixed social hierarchies. Sudden and unexpected misfortune, the petitions show, could befall anyone at any time, resulting in a catastrophic fall in economic and social status. In this language of absolutes, to be 'utterly undone' is to be financially ruined; the phrase also carries an active sense of reversal, 'un-doing' what had been done, the loss of fortunes that had been built, of prosperity that had been achieved or inherited. Connecting the word's material and social meanings, 'undoing' in the sense of 'unfastening and opening' (as in to 'undo' a parcel) relates to the releasing of bonds, ties or fastenings. 'Undoing', then, is also suggestive of the loosening of the social bonds and ties that bind communities together. The opposite of 'undoing' in the sense that it is used in the petitions is not relief, then, but restoration or even making again. If pity, as Johnson argues, is an 'untethered emotion', the unpitying petitions offer a mechanism for refastening the structures of community that is grounded in economic reality rather than affect. The language of the bill offers not only the relief of absolute poverty but also the hope of some restoration of the correct social order, and economic distinction which was obliterated by disaster; the undoing, or reversal, of the 'undoing' is the unspoken objective of the petitions.

Where prosperity may have been regarded as a sign of providential reward for good character, paradoxically in the petitions, great loss is not interpreted as a punishment, or as a sign of God's displeasure.[47] In this, the petitions differ from the pamphlets and ballads, which as we have seen in the case of *The True lamentable discourse*, often took a highly moralised stance towards the disastrous stories they retold. Even though, as the Memoranda witness, the indigenous and wandering poor sometimes lay dying in the streets of St Botolph's parish, the greater the previous wealth of the applicant, and accordingly, the larger the size of their loss, the more the rhetoric suggests that they deserve the charitable benevolence of the congregation.[48] The Lord Mayor's order for a collection for several merchants ruined in a fire at New Fish Street Hill states that it will 'be ratably distributed by me and my bretheren the aldermen according to everie mens losses', that is, proportionately or pro rata to what they had started with, and not according to their absolute need.[49] In a culture where social status was largely fixed, the previously well-to-do were able to call on communal support in a way that the roaming bands of 'sturdy beggars' could not. The New Fish Street Hill merchants obtained the support of powerful members of London's civic elite, and 'honnest and Discrete inhabitanntes' of the ward were nominated to visit every parishioner in person, along with the petitioners, and 'to do there best indevors by all the good means the can to pswade everie suche inhabitaunnt to yeald there liberall and charitable benovelence'.[50] While the rhetoric of the petition draws on notions of neighbourly charity, the Lord Mayor and Aldermen had a clear interest in persuading the affluent people of London to contribute towards supporting their peers, as a form of mutual insurance should they require such help themselves one day. The effectiveness of their rhetoric can be measured by the amount that was collected at St Botolph's for the New Fish Street Hill merchants, an exceptional £5.19.½. As a comparison, the next largest collection recorded is 33 shillings gathered towards a national collection for Gregory Pormorte of Hull, another formerly rich merchant, and only fourteen collections in the period covered by the Memoranda exceeded 20 shillings. Obligations of neighbourhood, combined with the pressure of a personal visit from the senior members of the parish, were clearly an effective strategy for ensuring 'liberall and charitable benovelence'; we can only speculate as to how voluntary this charitable compassion really was.

Conclusion

The Memoranda of St Botolph's record some of the earliest collection petitions, and subsequently their use continued to grow so that, writing in 1661, Samuel Pepys recorded that he was experiencing an early form of compassion fatigue: 'To church; where we observe the trade of briefs [petitions] is come now up to so constant a course every Sunday, that we resolve to give no more to them.'[51] As with any archival source, much remains unspoken in the St Botolph's Memoranda; nevertheless, they provide some insights into compassion in sixteenth-century London. Compassion was an emotion that was regulated by the giver's judgement about the merit of the petitioner and the truth of his or her story. Conflicting imperatives operated through religious, literary and other popular discourses not only to encourage charitable compassion but also to ensure that it was exercised only towards the appropriate recipients for the sanctioned reasons. Petitioners had therefore to counter anxiety about the truthfulness of their stories or, more generally, about the social and theological necessity of almsgiving. Cash provided the material expression of the desire to relieve poverty, and this practical enactment of compassion was encouraged not by emotive descriptions of physical or emotional suffering, but by a focus on the economic consequences of disasters.

Notes

1 Philip Stubbes, *The second part of the anatomie of abuses* (1583), sig. G1v.
2 Thomas Wilson, *A Christian Dictionarie* (1612), p. 215.
3 There were a number of churches dedicated to St Botolph in London; all references in this chapter are to St Botolph's, Aldgate.
4 A. G. B. Atkinson, *St Botolph, Aldgate: The Story of a City Parish* (London: Grant Richards, 1898); Thomas Rogers Forbes, *Chronicle from Aldgate: Life and Death in Shakespeare's London* (New Haven: Yale University Press, 1971); Malcolm Johnson, *Outside the Gate: St Botolph's and Aldgate 950–1994* (London: Stepney Books, 1994); Martha Carlin, 'Historical Gazetteer of London before the Great Fire. St Botolph Aldgate: Minories, east side; the

Abbey of St. Clare; Holy Trinity Minories', ed. by Derek Keene (unpublished, IHR BL.533/Sbo).
5 Wyndham A. Bewes, *Church Briefs or Royal Warrants for Collection for Charitable Briefs* (1896); Mark Harris, '"Inky Blots and Rotten Parchment Bonds": London, Charity Briefs and the Guildhall Library', *Historical Research*, 66:159 (1993), 98–110.
6 London Metropolitan Archives P69/BOT2/A/019/MS 09234/001-007. There are 304 entries described as collections between 22 December 1583 and 20 April 1600. The number is given as 'approximately 300' because, for example, the sequence of four collections in autumn 1598 to raise funds to build a new gallery in the church should perhaps be counted as one. Alternatively, on some Sundays a number of separate claimants seem to have had the collection divided between them and this could be counted as a single or multiple collection. Similarly, the number of collections for each cause is not precise, because in some cases the cause of an individual's disability is unclear or there are a number of contributing factors.
7 Roslyn L. Knutson, 'Elizabethan Documents, Captivity Narratives and the Market for Foreign History Plays', *English Literary Renaissance*, 26:1 (1996), 75–110; Daniel J. Vitkus, *Piracy, Slavery and Redemption* (New York: Columbia University Press, 2001); Linda Colley, *Captives: Britain, Empire and the World* (London: Jonathan Cape, 2002).
8 9234/5/1 fol.245v. While a number of petitioners are described as having previously been of sufficient, or even great wealth, none is an aristocrat.
9 9234/2/1 fol.100r.
10 John F. Pound, *Poverty and Vagrancy in Tudor England* (London: Longman, 1971); J. Thomas Kelly, *Thorns on the Tudor Rose: Monks, Vagabonds and Sturdy Beggars* (Jackson: University Press of Mississippi, 1977); A. L. Beier, *The Problem of the Poor in Tudor and Stuart England* (London: Taylor and Francis, 1983) and *Masterless Men: The Vagrancy Problem in England 1560–1640* (London: Methuen, 1985); Paul Slack, *Poverty and Policy in Tudor and Stuart England* (London: Longman, 1988), *The English Poor Law 1531–1782* (London: Macmillan, 1990) and *From Reformation to Improvement: Public Welfare in Early Modern England* (Oxford: Clarendon Press, 1998); Steve Hindle, *The State and Social Change in Early Modern England* (Basingstoke: Palgrave, 2000); Patricia Fumerton, *Unsettled: The Culture of Mobility and the Working Poor in Early Modern England* (University of Chicago Press, 2006).
11 9234/1/2 fol.1r.
12 Christopher Haigh, *English Reformations: Religion, Politics, and Society under the Tudors* (Oxford: Clarendon Press, 1993) and *The Plain Man's Pathways to Heaven: Kinds of Christianity in Post-Reformation England, 1570–1640* (Oxford University Press, 2007); Katherine L. French, Gary G. Gibbs and Beat Kümin (eds.), *The Parish in English Life* (Manchester University Press, 1997); N. J. G. Pounds, *A History of the English Parish: The Culture of Religion from Augustine to Victoria* (Cambridge University Press, 2000); Diarmaid MacCulloch, *The*

Later Reformation in England, 1547–1603 (New York: St. Martin's Press, 2001); Eamon Duffy, *The Stripping of the Altars: Traditional Religion in England, 1400–1580* (New Haven: Yale University Press, 2005); Alec Ryrie, *Being Protestant in Reformation Britain* (Oxford University Press, 2013).

13 Johnson, Chapter 11 in this volume.
14 MacCulloch, *The Later Reformation*, p. 116.
15 Adam Fox, 'Custom, Memory and the Authority of Writing' in Paul Griffiths, Adam Fox and Steve Hindle (eds.), *The Experience of Authority in Early Modern England* (Basingstoke: Palgrave Macmillan, 1996); James Daybell and Peter Hinds (eds.), *Material Readings of Early Modern Culture: Texts and Social Practices, 1580–1730* (Basingstoke: Palgrave Macmillan, 2010); Andrew Gordon, *Writing Early Modern London: Memory, Text and Community* (Basingstoke: Palgrave Macmillan, 2013).
16 Eamon Duffy, *The Voices of Morebath: Reformation and Rebellion in an English Village* (New Haven and London: Yale University Press, 2001).
17 Duffy, *Stripping of the Altars*, p. 505.
18 Haigh, *English Reformations*, p. 290.
19 John Jewel, *Certain sermons or homilies appointed to be read in churches* (1563), p. 172.
20 Stephen Bateman, *A christall glasse of christian reformation* (1569), sig. D1v. There were several Batman/Bateman families in the parish of St Botolph's, and Bateman preached in the church several times between January and March 1583/84. The sermon on 5 January 1583/4 was his 'newe yeares gift' to the parish. 9234/1/2 fol.8v.
21 Ian W. Archer, 'The Charity of Early Modern Londoners', *Transactions of the Royal Historical Society (Sixth Series)*, 12 (2002), 223–44.
22 Thomas Harman, *A Caveat for Commen Cursetors* (1567); see also John Awdelay, *The fraternitye of uacabondes* (1575).
23 In this case, Harman does not seem to be equating his own work with the humble gift, but this was a trope often found in dedications where the author was angling for patronage. For further discussion of this point, see Michael Saenger, *The Commodification of Textual Engagements in the English Renaissance* (Aldershot: Ashgate, 2006).
24 Ryrie argues that idleness and hypocrisy were the two defining vices, fear of which shaped early modern British Protestantism; *Being Protestant*, p. 4.
25 William Walker, *A Sermon preached at the funerals of the Right Honourable William, Lord Russel* (1614), p. 48.
26 Walker, *A Sermon*, p. 49.
27 9234/2/1 fol.52r; 9234/2/1 fol.113v.
28 See, for example, Anthony Gilby, *A pleasaunt dialogue, betweene a souldoir of Barwicke, and an English chaplain* (1581) or George Peele, *The Old Wives Tale* (1595).
29 Arthur F. Kinney, *Rogues, Vagabonds and Sturdy Beggars* (Amherst: University of Massachusetts Press, 1990); William C. Carroll, *Fat King, Lean Beggar: Representations of Poverty in the Age of Shakespeare* (Ithaca: Cornell University

Press, 1996); Linda Woodbridge, *Vagrancy, Homelessness, and English Renaissance Literature* (Urbana: University of Illinois Press, 2001); Paula Pugliatti, *Beggary and Theatre in Early Modern England* (Aldershot: Ashgate, 2003); Craig Dionne and Steve Mentz (eds.), *Rogues in Early Modern English Culture* (Ann Arbor: University of Michigan Press, 2004); Tom Nichols, *The Art of Poverty in Sixteenth Century Beggar Imagery* (Manchester University Press, 2007); Kevin A. Quarmby, *The Disguised Ruler in Shakespeare and His Contemporaries* (Farnham: Ashgate, 2012); Robert Henke, *Poverty and Charity in Early Modern Theater and Performance* (University of Iowa Press, 2015).

30 Linda Bradley Salamon, 'Vagabond Veterans: The Roguish Company of Martin Guerre and *Henry V*' in Dionne and Mentz (eds.), *Rogues*.

31 *The Queenes ... wandring abroad of a great multitude of her people* (1591).

32 *Wheras ... there are diuers persons pretending* (1592); *A proclamation for suppressing of the multitude of idle vagabonds* (1594).

33 Thomas Middleton and Thomas Dekker, *The Roaring Girl* (1611); Woodbridge, *Vagrancy*, p. 20.

34 Natalie Zemon Davies, *The Gift in Sixteenth Century France* (Oxford University Press, 2000); Ilana Krausman Ben-Amos, *The Culture of Giving: Informal Support and Gift-Exchange in Early Modern England* (Cambridge University Press, 2008).

35 John Foxe, *The Actes and Monuments* (1583), vol. 12, p. 2128. Online at *The Unabridged Acts and Monuments Online* (Sheffield: HRI Online Publications, 2011), www.johnfoxe.org.

36 Bateman, *Christall Glasse*, sig. H4r.

37 Stubbes, *Anatomie of Abuses*, sig. F8r–v.

38 Stubbes, *Anatomie of Abuses*, sig. G1v.

39 Memoranda covering the period 14 December 1592 to 8 September 1593 are missing, possibly because record-keeping broke down in the plague years, although this seems unlikely as the clerk survived and the registers were maintained for the same period. After the resumption of the records, there is a marked decrease in the number of collections recorded for former soldiers and mariners.

40 9234/3 fol.21r.

41 Anon., *The True lamentable discourse of the burning of Teverton* (1598), sig. B2r. See also John Morgan, 'The Representation and Experience of English Urban Fire Disasters, c.1580–1640', *Historical Research*, 89 (2016), 268–93.

42 9234/5/2 fol.179r.

43 9234/2/1 fol.21r.

44 9234/2/1 fol.8r; 9234/2/1 fol.21r; 9234/4 fol.151r.

45 9234/4 fol.151v; 9234/6 fol.5v; 9234/7 fol.60r.

46 Archer, 'The Charity of Early Modern Londoners'.

47 The Protestant approach to wealth is a much-debated matter and detailed discussion of it is outside the scope of this study. Ryrie, however, offers the following summary: 'being rich was not itself an obstacle to salvation. What mattered was how you went about it. Protestants' theology of justification

made this possible; their commitment to the social hierarchy and their need for friends in high places made it prudent. And so wealthy Protestants could, quite literally, have the best of both worlds.' Ryrie, *Being Protestant*, p. 453.
48 On poverty in the parish, besides the parish histories listed above, see also Lena Cowen Orlin, 'Temporary Lives in London Lodgings', *Huntington Library Quarterly*, 71:1 (2008), 219–42.
49 9234/2/1 fol.2r.
50 9234/2/1 fol.2v.
51 *The Diary of Samuel Pepys*, vol. II, ed. Robert Latham and William Matthews Berkeley: University of California Press, 1971), p. 128.

PART VII
Racialising

CHAPTER 13

Pity and Empire in the Brevísima relación de la destrucción de las Indias *(1552)*

Matthew Goldmark

In his famous condemnation of sixteenth-century Spanish conquest, the *Brevísima relación de la destrucción de las Indias* (1552), the Dominican friar Bartolomé de las Casas describes Spaniards' violent attacks on defenceless indigenous populations across the so-called New World. His text maps an aggressive itinerary of conquest where locations shift, but events remain the same: Spanish soldiers enter into dense and idyllic indigenous settlements and leave these polities in ruins. The term 'destruction' in the text's title emphasises the sociopolitical consequences of such violence; in the sixteenth century, '*destruir*' was to eliminate populations and unfound polities.[1] However, the violence recorded in the *Brevísima relación* not only indicates how horrific Spanish violence destroys established social structures. As Las Casas's text shows, violence undermines the religious justifications for Spanish presence in the New World, as identified in Pope Alexander VI's *Inter Caetera* (1493). This papal bull entrusted the Spanish Crown with the moral duty to teach indigenous subjects the Catholic faith and good customs.[2] Against the religious authority and proper practices assumed in this donation, Spanish violence shows these religious representatives to behave in opposition to such Christian ideals.

These bad practices of political, social and religious destruction do not name only acts of violence, but also improper affects. Las Casas's text describes Spanish soldiers in the New World who kill and terrorise indigenous populations without the compassion or pity (*sin piedad*) that define Christians as such. In contrast, indigenous subjects plead for the mercy (*misericordia*) that they are due, given their unwarranted subjection. A lack of pity casts Spaniards, and not indigenous subjects, as deviants bereft of the feelings that would foster the development of a transatlantic Christian empire.

I argue that in the *Brevísima relación*, affect justifies action; it is feeling for indigenous suffering that obliges the text's royal recipient Philip II to stop the violent destruction perpetrated by his unmanaged vassals in the

New World. While scholars have mined the juridical, classical and religious source base that Las Casas employs in the *Brevísima relación*, few have placed emotion at the centre of this intellectual inquiry.[3] In one of the few articles dedicated to affect in the *Brevísima relación*, Barbara Simerka argues that readers have underemphasised empathy in order to show the intellectual genealogy that undergirds Las Casas's arguments.[4] However, I argue that emotion – specifically pity – is essential to the *Brevísima relación*'s defence of indigenous peoples and, as important, to its creation of an transatlantic imperial relationship between 'Indians' and the Crown.

In the next chapter, John D. Staines also studies the power of feeling to spur one to act. He emphasises that compassion requires one both to bear witness and to intervene to stop the suffering of another. However, while Staines considers the forms of compassion that produce equality between the witness and sufferer, Las Casas's text reveals a distinctly *imperial* permutation of compassion that incorporates the 'Indian' into empire. In the *Brevísima relación*, pity identifies a hierarchical relation that obliges intervention from a powerful imperial witness-authority. The text does not only command its reader to empathise *with* an indigenous subject. He must feel *for* a subordinate and intervene. Thus, the affective imperative created by pity is not one of contemplation of an equal, but rather a call to action for an Other whose relation to empire remains undetermined.

In Spain's early modern religious and juridical contexts, a suffering recipient of pity was designated a 'miserable'. Often this miserable person found her- or himself in a pitiable circumstance due to the absence of paternal protection; thus, the term often identified particular bodies: the destitute, women, children and the elderly.[5] Given this paternal frame, it is no surprise that miserables feature prominently in the *Brevísima relación*, a text that describes the frequent absence of patriarchal guardians. Soldiers separate men from women and children, kill resistant male subjects and create a set of miserable gendered and impotent human spoils of war. However, misery also provides vocabulary to justify intervention. This articulation of destruction as an undoing of patriarchal power emphasises that indigenous peoples need a new male guardian.[6] Pity hails the royal patriarch and requires that he protect the 'miserable Indian' from his violent vassals. Misery thus solidifies a paternal relation of pity and creates an obligation of feeling to intervene.

By studying pity in the *Brevísima relación*, this chapter demonstrates how feeling produces an imperial relation that reverberates across the Atlantic and draws indigenous people into the Spanish empire. While studies of affect in recent years have turned to empire and indigeneity, they often emphasise colonisation by Northern European powers during and after the Enlightenment. Such studies have made great strides in showing how affective ties enabled the creation and management of imperial hierarchies.[7] However, a study of pity in the *Brevísima relación* brings this conversation on affect and imperialism to the early modern period and presents a deeper genealogy for the function of such imperial affects as they tie European and non-European subjects together. In the case of the *Brevísima relación*, pity designates proper and improper relations that, according to the text, should guide the practice of empire. Though Spanish soldiers violate the dictates of Christian feeling, pity puts empire together in a determined relation with Spanish actors. Pity draws 'Indians' into an imperial order that, for these authors, feels right.

To See Is to Pity

The *Brevísima relación* emerges out of the contentious sixteenth-century Spanish Atlantic, where friars, academics and courtiers debated the religious and legal justifications of conquest. At the time of the composition of the *Brevísima relación*, Las Casas's efforts at reform focused on the *encomienda*, an evangelical-labor system that entrusted indigenous wards to a Spanish guardian, an *encomendero*, who received indigenous labor in recompense for his work at evangelisation. In practice, however, the system served as a de facto institution of indigenous slavery. In 1542, Las Casas presented a tract on the injustices of this system, an early version of what would become the *Brevísima relación*, to the Council of the Indies in Seville.[8] His presentation led to the institution of the New Laws, a legal decree that provided for the abolishment of such practices of indigenous slavery and to the prohibition of the perpetual transmission of encomiendas. Resistance to these laws was ferocious. They were not put into practice in the Viceroyalty of New Spain, and encomenderos in the Viceroyalty of Peru assassinated the Viceroy Blasco Núñez Vela in response to his attempts to institute the laws. Parts of the New Laws were repealed in 1545. The reaction to the New Laws demonstrated the danger that unchecked vassals posed to the authority of the Spanish Crown, a threat that the *Brevísima relación* emphasises. The text highlights how the appropriative acts of conquistadors undermine the Crown's transatlantic authority when vassals establish de facto fiefdoms in the New World and seek to 'rise to a high status incommensurate with their rightful place'.[9] By usurping authority of the royal patriarch, undeserving subordinates threaten social order and royal right. A 1545 letter composed by the *visitador* of New Spain, Tello de Sandoval, confirms this warning. Sandoval's missive notes that many indigenous subjects believed the encomenderos to be kings.[10]

At the opening of his text, Las Casas presents the New World as a Christian paradise soon deformed by the acts of Spanish soldiers.[11] Las Casas notes that the island of Hispaniola was once 'fertile and fortunate' and filled with measured peoples. They are, according to the text, 'simple, without evil intent nor duplicity'; they are the 'most humble, patient, pacific and calm' peoples in the world. In a use of religious hyperbole, the text envisions indigenous peoples' simple lifestyle as an evocation of the 'Desert Fathers'.[12] In contrast, Spaniards arrive 'like wolves, tigers, and the cruelest lions who have not eaten for days' to destroy 'these gentle lambs, imbued by their Creator with the above listed qualities'.[13] By presenting indigenous peoples as Christian paragons and Spanish soldiers as diabolical aggressors, Las Casas inverts expected religious character and bestows indigenous peoples with Christian attributes.

This reversal of Christian character will in turn undermine the assumed alignment between religious and geopolitical origin and particular passions. As Anthony Pagden notes in his reading of Spanish disputes over indigenous rights, Las Casas writes in another text, the *Apologética historia sumaria*, that barbarism identifies populations overtaken by passions. In that text, Las Casas writes that it is the Spaniards in the Indies who, 'in the cruel acts they have carried out against [the Indians] have exceeded all the barbarians and anyone, in short, whose behavior is marred by the sin of *ferocitas*'.[14] Likewise, in the case of the *Brevísima relación* improper acts blur the lines between Christian dictates and unchristian passions, making the Spaniard, and not the 'pacific' indigenous subject, barbarous. The perversion of Christian order takes place in the manifestation of the Spaniard's presentation of improper feeling.

However, the vassal's actions are not his alone. When the *Brevísima relación* hails its royal audience with descriptions of vassals in the New World, these scenes implicate centralised authority as well. Philip II must take responsibility for the mismanaged and dangerously autonomous subjects who are under his jurisdiction. The text thus empowers as it critiques the royal figurehead through the insinuation that he has neglected his authority. As Patricio Boyer notes, the *Brevísima relación*'s introduction evokes Aristotelian philosophy's rule of natural right and Christian allegory to reaffirm royal authority,[15] since, Las Casas states, Kings remains without error 'as long as they have the information that will prevent it'.[16] And Las

Casas's text will ensure that such information is laid before this figure's eyes. The text's 'Prologue ... to the Prince' opens: 'Divine Providence has ordered that the world, for the governance and function of the human race, be formed into kingdoms and peoples, and that these shall be ruled by kings who are (as Homer names them) fathers and shepherds to their people and are, accordingly, the noblest and most virtuous of beings'.[17] With classical and Christian precedent, Las Casas establishes order under a royal patriarch defined by his inclination to justice. This statement conveys a royal authority's responsibility for the body politic; as the noblest member, father and pastor, he is accountable for the actions of his children and flock. While Philip II may have overlooked the actions of his vassals in the New World, the *Brevísima relación* promises to bring them to his attention and thus ensure their correction.

According to the *Brevísima relación*, royal inaction can only be attributed to oversight. While Las Casas had documented these destructive acts of violence in 1542, his 'Prologue' notes that New World violence could only have continued if, 'perhaps, Your Highness had not read that account or had forgotten it'.[18] This statement implies that the royal interlocutor had lost sight of his vassals' actions documented in this earlier presentation and thus overlooked the threat they pose to his own political power and Christian authority. However, the text does note in a summary of the New World's discovery and the acts that have proceeded since them that these events are so fantastic and immeasurable that they may 'not be believable to those who have not seen them' and become 'clouded' over and even 'forgotten'.[19] To that end, Las Casas reiterates the need to bring the atrocities of the New World to light via the language of vision. Only by making them visible to the royal interlocutor will this authority be compelled to stop the violent acts of his vassals in the New World.

For scholars of colonial writing, the visual terms of Las Casas's argument align with the generic expectations of the relación, a form that communicated an author's personal experience to an authoritative interlocutor.[20] Such texts derive their truth function from phenomenological experience; the author of the relación transmits scenes at which he himself has been present. However, while experience determines the reliability of a text's contents, the relación requires that this experience transfer and be held true by a distant recipient – in this case, a royal figurehead at an Atlantic remove from the narrated events. To accomplish this goal, Las Casas's appeal seeks to make visible the unseen. It must create presence in the space of absence and transmit the violence of conquest.[21] In accordance with the generic demands of the relación, the authorial voice repeats the assertions that 'I saw', 'other things I saw' and similar phrases that authorise the text's contents. The rhetorical impact of these horrific scenes of violence depends upon the ability of the seen to carry affective force to another's eyes.

This visual presentation of violence in the *Brevísima relación* dovetails with Aristotle's formulation of an intimate tie linking pity, vision and politics. For Aristotle, according to David Konstan, the persuasive force of pity depends upon making 'the catastrophe (*pathos*) seem both underserved and immediate (literally, "apparent to the eyes")'.[22] Staines's study of pity in Aristotle also notes that vision ensures rhetorical force and that the object must remain in view, lest the rhetorician lose his audience. In a gloss of Aristotle, he writes, '[T]he effect of sympathy, of imagining the other's suffering as my own, fades when it is not an object in my direct view, which is why an orator's performance must make the evil vivid and directly present to the imagination of the audience.'[23] As Las Casas states in the *Brevísima relación*, should events be clouded over and forgotten, they will continue unabated. The truth function of sight in the *relación* thus aligns with pity's affective power; seeing suffering will move the recipient-witness to pity, believe and act.

Thus, in the case of the *Brevísima relación*, Las Casas intertwines the rhetoric of pity with that of the visual. In a section on Santa María, the *Brevísima relación* describes one 'tyrannical' Spaniard who, along with many soldiers acted 'without fear of God or compassion (*compasión*) for the human race'. This group 'ravaged, killed and committed acts without pity (*impiedades*)'.[24] He defies the Christian compassion and respect for God as if he would go unseen and unpunished. In a similar case that occurs in Granada, the text reports that Spaniards have 'destroyed without pity or respect for God or King'.[25] Again, this accusation of pitilessness emphasises religious and political irreverence.

In turn, though Spaniards refuse to perform pity, the text has indigenous subjects appeal to the rules of Christian feeling via this same language. For instance, a scene from New Spain places the call for pity in the mouths of indigenous subjects who find themselves trapped in unmerited violence. There, 'many Indians covered in blood who had hidden and sought shelter under the bodies of the dead, since there were so many, went crying and pleading for mercy (*misericordia*) before the Spaniards so as to not be killed. There was, however, no mercy or compassion (*misericordia ni compasión*) from [the Spaniards]. As soon as they emerged, they were cut to pieces.'[26] When indigenous subjects seek compassion from Spanish soldiers, they do not receive it; instead, their pleas are met with violence. The cry emerges from the border between life and death, redemption and damnation. These indigenous subjects reach out from beneath the bodies of the dead and make a claim on Christian ideals. Their plea for pity is at once a call for life and, implicitly, baptism, rebirth and salvation. Spaniards respond, however, with violence and pitilessness. Only the royal reader can answer this call for pity with the proper Christian response and draw the suffering indigenous person into the Christian and imperial body politic.[27] Once the Prince has viewed the nefarious acts of his vassals in the New World, he will be moved to pity its indigenous victims and, in turn, to bring an end to this violence.

Misery Makes the Indian

Violence in the *Brevísima relación* is decidedly patriarchal. Many of the acts that open the text emphasise affronts against paternal authorities in the Americas, themselves. Early sections focus on the assassination of male leaders – indigenous lords and their male subjects. As Las Casas summarises: 'All who could long for, desire, or think of freedom or escape from the torments they suffered, that is, the natural lords and men (since war leaves only women and children), were subject to harsh, amoral, and brutal servitude, far worse than any animal.'[28] Tyrannical violence committed against masculine, agential subjects leads to gendered consequences. The deaths of these men leave behind women and children who are consigned to servitude due to their assumed impotence. In fact, in one passage, Las Casas writes of indigenous men who 'hid … their wives and children' along with foodstuffs.[29] These male authorities move their impotent charges from encroaching Spaniards. Like inanimate possessions, women and children require male authority to protect and ensure their survival.

In scenes of violence against women, Las Casas shows that pity has a gendered formation. That is, Las Casas's text frequently codes scenes of violence against unsheltered women, children and the elderly as particularly merciless and enabled by the absence of men. In New Spain, he notes that Spanish soldiers 'entered into towns and left no children, elderly, or women, whether pregnant or with newborns, whom they did not tear apart at the stomach and hack to pieces'.[30] In Hispaniola, Spaniards 'distribute youths, women, and children' upon the death of these impotent subjects' male protectors.[31] In turn, 'Christians take the wives and children of the Indians to serve themselves and misuse them (*usar mal dellos*)'.[32] Like the inverted affective state that defines pitilessness, Spanish soldiers act in violation of expected patriarchal Christian dictates. They 'misuse' women and children, and do not respect a proper role as patriarchal defenders.

The text's emphasis on suffering women and children dovetails with classical and religious formulations of pity. According to Kostan's study of biblical and classical sources, 'the defeated and defenceless were always potential objects of pity, but women and children, along with the aged, were deemed to be especially deserving of it because they were considered weak by nature'.[33] Without men, such "weak" women stand no chance against violent Spaniards and become undisputed objects of pity. This association of women and children with pity appears in the *Brevísima relación* in a familiar maternal script. Throughout the text, Spanish soldiers destroy a universalised tie between mother and child by killing both at the moment of nursing. As Simerka notes, 'In order to evoke the sympathy of the reader, Las Casas employs a particular form of pathetic representation that is also seen in the Cervantes' *Numancia* play: violent aggression interfering with the process of a mother nursing her offspring.'[34] Las Casas's text records how soldiers would 'take infants by the legs from the breasts of their mothers and smash the children's heads against rocks'.[35] In another scene, Las Casas's text describes mothers who are unable to feed their children, given the scarcity of food. On the brink of starvation, these mothers lose breast milk and, in turn, their children.[36]

Beyond this first maternal trope, the suffering of mother and child echoes a primal Christian scene of compassion and pity: Mary's despair over the body of Christ. According to Sarah McNamer, this meditative tableau forged Christian community through a shared emotional script replete with gendered connotations. However, while McNamer writes that this 'emotional regime' created a Christian community of the feminine, given that it evoked the Marian example, the *Brevísima relación* employs pity as a masculine call to action for a feminised, imperial Other – one that evokes a hierarchical and racialised script predicated on the trope of the 'miserable Indian'.[37] Pity for this imperial subject demands that a royal official intervene in the place of absent (indigenous) fathers and bad Spanish surrogates.

In its manifold descriptions of Spanish violence, the *Brevísima relación* condemns 'those who call themselves Christians' for inhibiting the spread of the faith. The text notes that without evangelisation, indigenous populations, named 'those miserable peoples (*miserandas naciones*)', are condemned to death and damnation.[38] The term 'miserable' as a descriptor merits pause given that this term gathers different types of subjects under a single identity label. In the *Brevísima relación*, miserable identifies both indigenous peoples but also Spanish ones when it turns to the matter of a religious state. The difference is a matter of culpability. For instance, in a section on the Kingdom of Yucatán, the text argues that the 'bad works' of Spanish soldiers have undone the successful inroads of illumination and salvation, leaving indigenous populations in 'the darkness of ignorance, and misery (*miseria*)'.[39] However, while such indigenous misery designates the failures of evangelisation, the term also identifies nominally Christian subjects (i.e. Spaniards) marked by sin. According to the precedent established by Saint Isidore (and reiterated by the Spanish jurist Juan López de Palacios Rubios), 'miserable' could identify all sinners.[40] In fact, Sebastián de Covarrubias's definition of the term 'miserable' in 1611 could cast the Indies as a landscape of misery, since his definition gathers together the unfortunate and the greedy, he who does not deserve misery and he who brings it upon himself.[41] For this reason, it is fitting that Las Casas calls a Spaniard a 'miserable man' (*mísero hombre*) after this soldier destroys an entire indigenous community.[42]

However, while that Spanish subject creates his own miserable status through sin, the *Brevísima relación* insists that Spaniards impose and maintain indigenous misery. Indigenous subjects are miserable 'due to the unforgivable behavior and absolute wickedness of those Spaniards'.[43] To that end, indigenous misery in the *Brevísima relación* points to an outside source: Spanish violence. It is this lack of culpability that ensures pity for the Indian; this sad New World subject does not merit his or her current fortunes. In contrast, Las Casas emphasises that indigenous subjects are blameless for and in their misery. He excises any trace of bellicosity or duplicity in his descriptions of their character. They are 'gentle, meek, and docile'.[44] They are 'of utmost obedience to their lords and to the Christians whom they serve'.[45] By assigning culpability to Spaniards, Las Casas's text poses indigenous misery as an undeserved state. These are, he writes, 'miserable peoples (*gentes míseras*), though innocent'.[46]

Though Spaniards in part cause indigenous misery, they are also charged with its resolution. Misery indeed authorises Spanish intervention. In a study of the 'Indian's miserable condition' in the seventeenth-century Spanish Atlantic, Paulino Castañeda Delgado notes that judicial authorities justified intercession on the behalf of a 'miserable Indian' by looking to Old Testament sources, wherein miserable designated a subject in need and in merit of divine protection.[47] The juridical application of this term also pulled from Alfonso X's *Siete Partidas* (thirteenth century), the primary foundation of family law in the Indies. There, miserable designated subjects who by right of their 'unsheltered' status (*desemparados*) deserved just hearing from the courts and, in case of no other recourse, the direct shelter of the king.[48] While as noted above miserables could include all sinners, Bianca Premo has noted that the term accrued particular strength for those subjects 'who had somehow come loose from the natural order of generational or gender relations'.[49] Thus to be identified as miserable implied the absence of patriarchal protection and the need for a paternal surrogate. Along these lines, Castañeda Delgado noted that the category was especially applied to orphans, wives with 'useless' husbands and new converts.[50] The miserable subjects of the *Brevísima relación*, women and children bereft of their husbands and torn from an organised social structure, align with these subject positions. However, these subjects and their present circumstances are created by Spaniards, themselves.

The Paradox of Imperial Pity

The *Brevísima relación* is not the only text from the period that identifies indigenous subjects as miserables. A letter composed by Dominican friars on Hispaniola that is considered a direct source for the *Brevísima relación* employs the term 'miserable' to describe indigenous populations bereft of Christianity. This 'Carta que escribieron varios padres de la órden de Santo Domingo, residentes en la isla Española a Mr. de Xevres' (1516) decries the fate of many 'miserable souls (*miserables ánimas*)' sent to hell due to the sins of the Spanish encomenderos and conquistadors.[51] In scenes almost identical to those employed in the *Brevísima relación*, the letter describes the violent separation of families, the robbery of infants from mothers and the elimination of masculine protectors. However, despite these similarities, the term 'miserable' does not appear with frequency in the letter as a justification for Spanish intervention. Instead, it serves as a designation of indigenous subjects' religious state and evinces the evangelical failures of the Spanish mission.[52]

In contrast, a petition composed by Las Casas and Antonio de Valdivieso, bishop of Nicaragua, employs the term 'miserable' with frequency. Transcribed by Carlos Sempat Assadourian, the 'Petitión y requerimiento de los obispos de Guatemala, Chiapa y Nicaragua' (1545) asserts the need for religious officials to protect the 'miserable populations (*miserandas naciones*)' of the New World. Misery, in the case of this petition, intersects religious and juridical oversight in cases of violence. The text presents an explicit definition of the miserable person as 'he who cannot defend his own concerns nor seek justice due to his poverty, pusillanimity, knowledge, experience, fear, or any other weakness'.[53] In this definition, misery is not explained by religious state alone, but rather appears in the attribution of impotence before the law. While this powerlessness can result from a number of factors, the petition presents the now-familiar insistence that misery is not an inherent quality of indigenous populations, but rather one maintained by Spanish violence. These are a 'most miserable, oppressed, injured, distraught, and unprotected people', it notes, because of the 'injustices that they suffer'.[54] While for the petition the guardian of the miserable is the Church, an important departure from the royal appeal made in the Brevísima relación, both texts establish that the knowledge of misery demands intervention by a witness in an advantageous position.[55] In that regard, the petition presents a theory of affect that the Brevísima relación seeks to put into practice: seeing and feeling pity for the miserable will move the viewer to action.[56]

The petition asserts that the sight of misery carries an affective imperative; misery 'moves those men who take pity (*se compadezcan*) on others'.[57] Later, the text specifies that pity and intervention are Christian duties. It is here that imperial hierarchies of difference between Spaniard and indigenous enter into question, since it states that 'Christians have the greatest obligation, both natural and divine, to work with all of their ability to save [the miserable Indians] and to defend them. [Christians] must do for [the Indians] what they would wish another to feel obligated to do if [these Christians] were in the same sad and despondent state.'[58] In *feeling* the obligation to act, Christians are asked to imagine 'Indians' as if they could be Christians, as if they could be the same as themselves. This is the central question of compassion whereby there is a potential alignment, where one must work to stop another's suffering as if it could be his or her own. However, feeling for the miserable Indian puts a paradoxical limit on sameness. To defend this imperial Other, one must be in better fortunes and capable of action on behalf of the powerless.

The paradox of pity in the Brevísima relación therefore turns upon the simultaneous attribution and dissolution of sameness based on misery. When the text demands pity for the 'miserable Indian', it first constitutes these objects of pity as recognisable, similar subjects. (According to Konstan, he who pities must be able to see himself in a parallel condition.)[59] However, the royal recipient of the Brevísima relación must simultaneously view the difference of hierarchy to assure intervention. Pity both affirms indigenous similarity and dissolves this similarity into difference when it demands intervention for an indigenous subject marked by misery.

The pity that indigenous peoples arouse enforces a group identity that is defined by subservience, regardless of gender or patriarchal hierarchy internal to their own communities. The petition, for instance, places all indigenous peoples under the rubric of the miserable, 'lords great and small as well as their vassals, without excepting anyone'; all are miserables in need of 'shelter, defence, and protection'.[60] In its justification of intervention, the petition makes misery constituent of all indigenous populations. The *Brevísima relación* evokes a similar formulation when it rouses its royal interlocutor to action. Indigenous subjects – including men – fall to Spanish violence. In the process, they are cast as impotent and helpless. For instance, when he writes of peoples on the island of Hispaniola, Las Casas writes that indigenous peoples could offer little resistance since their weapons were like those of children playing at jousting.[61] Despite the text's affirmation of indigenous peoples' patriarchal organisation, the comparison between men and children imposes an infantilising designation that awards indigenous peoples paternal defence. The attribution of misery extends beyond temporal age and gender. Instead, misery creates a collective whereby pity is bestowed on a population of the powerless.

An attention to pity shows how early modern empire, just as those empires consolidated in later centuries, engaged affect to imagine and structure hierarchies of difference. The *Brevísima relación* rejects perverse ties made in violence and pitilessness and, instead, offers proper emotional bonds based on pity that entitle indigenous subjects to Christian relationships with imperial power.[62] Thus, a study of pity in the *Brevísima relación* shows that multiple affective bonds defined imperial structures in the early modern period. In turn, each affective relation enabled distinct formulations and revisions of imperial regimes, just as they created the subjects within them. Pity and compassion flowed across the Atlantic, wove and unravelled imperial relations and showed just how far early modern affects – and their consequences – could travel.

Notes

1 José Miguel Martínez Torrejón, 'Notas complementarias' in Bartolomé de las Casas, *Brevísima relación de la destruición de las Indias*, ed. Martínez Torrejón (Madrid: Real Academia Española, 2013), p. 221.
2 Cited in Monique Alaperrine-Bouyer, *La educación de las élites indígenas en el Perú colonial* (Lima: Institut français d'études andines, 2007), p. 13. The language of 'good customs' was reiterated in Charles V's edicts of 1540 and 1563. Alcira Dueñas, *Indians and Mestizos in the 'Lettered City': Reshaping Justice, Social Hierarchy, and Political Culture in Colonial Peru* (Boulder: University Press of Colorado, 2010), p. 27.

3 Bianca Premo and Rebecca Earle have called for a greater emphasis on affect in their studies of colonial bureaucracy. See Bianca Premo, 'Familiar: Thinking Beyond Lineage and across Race in Spanish Atlantic Family History', *The William and Mary Quarterly*, 70:2 (2013), 295–316; and Rebecca Earle, 'Letters and Love in Colonial Spanish America', *The Americas*, 62:1 (2005), 17–46.

4 Barbara Simerka, 'The Role of Empathy in Reading, Interpreting, and Teaching Las Casas's *Brevísima relación de la destrucción de las Indias*' in Isabel Jaen and Julien Jacques Simon (eds.), *Cognitive Approaches to Early Modern Spanish Literature* (New York: Oxford University Press, 2016), pp. 202–18.

5 See Victor M. Uribe-Uran, *Fatal Love: Spousal Killers, Law, and Punishment in the Late Colonial Spanish Atlantic* (Stanford: Stanford University Press, 2016); Caroline Cunill, 'El indio miserable: nacimiento de la teoría legal en la América colonial del siglo XVI', *Cuadernos inter.c.a.mbio*, 8:9 (2011), 229–48; Premo, *Children of the Father King: Youth, Authority, and Legal Minority in Colonial Lima* (Chapel Hill: University of North Carolina Press, 2005); Carlos Sempat Assadourian, 'Fray Bartolomé de las Casas obispo: la condición miserable de las naciones indianas y el derecho de la iglesia (un escrito de 1545', *Allpanchis*, 35/36 (1990), 29–104; Paulino Castañeda Delgado, 'La condición miserable del indio y sus privilegios', *Anuario de Estudios Americanos*, 28 (1971), 245–335.

6 Moreover, depictions of patriarchal social organisation in the *Brevísima relación* implicitly combat the attribution of 'natural slavery' to indigenous peoples by humanist philosopher and imperial chronicler Juan Inés de Sepúlveda at the Valladolid debates (1550–1551). Las Casas countered Sepúlveda's position by arguing that indigenous subjects did not fall into the category of the 'natural slave' and that the papal donation could only authorise conversion, and did not provide a legal right to Spanish sovereignty. See Rolena Adorno, *The Polemics of Possession* (New Haven: Yale University Press, 2007), pp. 61–98; Anthony Pagden, *The Fall of Natural Man: The American Indian and the Origins of Comparative Ethnology* (New York: Cambridge University Press, 1982), pp. 109–45; Kenneth J. Pennington, 'Bartolomé de Las Casas and the Tradition of Medieval Law', *Church History*, 39:2 (1970), 149–61; Henry Raup Wagner and Helen Rand Parish, *The Life and Writings of Bartolomé de las Casas* (Albuquerque: University of New Mexico Press, 1967).

7 See, for instance, Ann Laura Stoler, *Carnal Knowledge and Imperial Power: Race and the Intimate in Colonial Rule* (Berkeley: University of California Press, 2002); Elizabeth A. Povinelli, *The Empire of Love: Toward a Theory of Intimacy, Genealogy, and Carnality* (Durham: Duke University Press, 2006).

8 A summary of this presentation is recorded in Alonso de Santa Cruz's *Crónica del Emperador Carlos V*. See Patricio Boyer, 'Framing the Visual Tableaux in the *Brevísima relación de la destruición de las Indias*', *Colonial Latin American Review*, 18:3 (2009), 365–82; Martínez Torrejón (ed.), *Brevísima relación*, p. 130.

9 Bartolomé de las Casas, *Brevísima relación de la destruición de las Indias*, ed. Martínez Torrejón (Madrid: Real Academia Española, 2013), p. 15. Unless otherwise noted, all translations are my own from Spanish originals.
10 Quoted in Cunill, 'El indio miserable', p. 235.
11 It is important to note that the *Brevísima relación* presents a strategic flattening of indigenous populations in order to appeal to the royal interlocutor. Las Casas' wider production provides a complex vision of indigenous populations in the Americas. See, among other texts, Adorno, *Polemics of Possession*.
12 Adorno, *Polemics of Possession*, p. 12.
13 Las Casas, *Brevísima relación*, p. 13.
14 Quoted in Pagden, *The Fall of Natural Man*, p. 126.
15 Boyer, 'Framing the Visual Tableaux', p. 373.
16 Las Casas, *Brevísima relación*, p. 7.
17 Las Casas, p. 7.
18 Las Casas, p. 9.
19 Las Casas, p. 5.
20 See Roberto González Echevarría, *Myth and Archive: A Theory of Latin American Narrative* (Durham: Duke University Press, 1998); Adorno, 'The Discursive Encounter of Spain and America: The Authority of Eyewitness Testimony in the Writing of History', *The William and Mary Quarterly*, 49:2 (1992), 210–28; and Walter Mignolo, 'Cartas, crónicas y relaciones del descubrimiento y la conquista' in Luis Iñigo Madrigal (ed.), *Historia de la literature hispanoamericana, época colonial* (Madrid: Cátedra, 1982), vol. I, pp. 57–116.
21 Boyer, 'Framing the Visual Tableaux', p. 366.
22 David Konstan, *Pity Transformed* (London: Duckworth 2001), p. 132.
23 John Staines, 'Compassion in the Public Sphere of Milton and King Charles' in Gail Kern Paster, Katherine Rowe and Mary Floyd-Wilson (eds.), *Reading the Early Modern Passions: Essays in the Cultural History of Emotion* (Philadelphia: University of Pennsylvania Press, 2004), pp. 89–110 (p. 98).
24 Las Casas, *Brevísima relación*.
25 Las Casas, p. 106.
26 Las Casas, p. 42.
27 Las Casas, p. 9.
28 Las Casas, pp. 14–15.
29 Las Casas, p. 16.
30 Las Casas, pp. 16–17.
31 Las Casas, p. 23.
32 Las Casas, p. 16.
33 Konstan, *Pity Transformed*, p. 17.
34 Simerka, *Discourses of Empire: Counter-Epic Literature in Early Modern Spain* (University Park: Pennsylvania State University Press, 2003), p. 31.
35 Las Casas, *Brevísima relación*, p. 17.
36 Las Casas, p. 24.

37 Sarah McNamer, *Affective Meditation and the Invention of Medieval Compassion* (Philadelphia: University of Pennsylvania Press, 2010), p. 7.
38 Las Casas, *Brevísima relación*, p. 14.
39 Las Casas, p. 68.
40 Castañeda Delgado, 'La condición miserable', p. 246.
41 Sebastían de Covarrubias, *Tesoro de la lengua castellana, o española* (Madrid: Luis Sanchez, 1611), p. 551.
42 Las Casas, *Brevísima relación*, p. 34.
43 Las Casas, p. 68.
44 Las Casas, p. 8.
45 Las Casas, p. 11.
46 Las Casas, p. 107.
47 Castañeda Delgado, 'La condición miserable', pp. 248–49.
48 Premo, *Father King*, pp. 30–31.
49 Premo, p. 26
50 Castañeda Delgado, 'La condición miserable', pp. 250–58.
51 'Carta que escribieron varios padres de la órden de Santo Domingo, residentes en la isla Española a Mr. de Xevres', in Luis Torres de Mendoza (ed.), *Colección de documentos inéditos relativos al descubrimiento, conquista y organización de las antiguas posesiones españolas de América y Oceanía sacados de los Archivos del Reino y muy especialmente del de Indias* (Madrid: Frias y compañia, 1867), vol. 7, pp. 397–430 (p. 398).
52 The other instance condemns the unjust distribution of 'miserable Indians (*miserables indios*)' for the accumulation of wealth rather than evangelisation. 'Carta', p. 421.
53 Quoted in Assadourian, 'Fray Bartolomé de las Casas obispo: La naturaleza miserable de las naciones indianas y el derecho de la iglesia. Un escrito de 1545', *Historia Mexicana*, 40:3 (1991), 387–451.
54 Unlike the *Brevísima relación*, this petition makes explicit the authority of religious intercessors, stating, 'for being miserable persons, we come to the conclusion that the concerns and protection of these people remit to ecclesiastical jurisdiction'. Assadourian, 'Fray Bartolomé de las Casas obispo', pp. 441–42.
55 Assadourian posits that this strict application of ecclesiastical authority over the 'miserable' does not extend throughout Las Casas's body of work. 'Fray Bartolomé de las Casas obispo', (1990, 1991).
56 In his description of the relation between mercy and vision, Staines cites the Catholic bishop Nicolas Coeffeteau, who writes in 1621 that passionate mercy 'gives us a commendable feeling' that moves us to action when 'our eyes are spectators'. 'Compassion', pp. 98–99.
57 Quoted in Assadourian (1991), 'Fray Bartolomé de las Casas obispo', p. 440.
58 Quoted in Assadourian (1991), p. 441.
59 Konstan, *Pity Transformed*, p. 50.
60 Quoted in Assadourian (1991), 'Fray Bartolomé de las Casas obispo', p. 440.
61 Las Casas, *Brevísima relación*, p. 16.

62 Pity, however, will not only be a means of subjugation and control. In the seventeenth century, the position of the 'miserable Indian' would extend to all indigenous subjects and become a site of possibility. (Cunill notes that a legal inscription of the *'indio'* as a miserable subject first appears in 1563.) Premo writes that although the status of 'miserable' and the establishment of 'Indians as minors' insinuated a subordinate position for indigenous subjects in an empire structured by the hierarchies of patriarchy and the rhetoric of kinship, it also provided a particular recourse for the navigation of legal arenas. Cunill, 'El indio miserable', p. 231. Premo, *Father King*, pp. 32–34.

CHAPTER 14

'Our Black Hero'
Compassion for Friends and Others in Aphra Behn's Oroonoko

John D. Staines

In seventeenth-century European thought, compassion is the feeling of the self being drawn out to join with others in community. Tragic pity, suffering for the misfortunes of others, is the fullest literary model of that passion. *Passion* itself, as Erich Auerbach has shown, is rooted in suffering, and the seventeenth-century elevation of passion to sublime love develops from centuries of Christian meditations on the meaning of Christ's suffering (*passio*) and the mystical experience of divine love.[1] Compassion is suffering together, sharing a feeling that ennobles the one who suffers it. It is both passive, something a spectator experiences, as when watching a play, but also an action and spur to action. It is intimate, an imagined connection with other people's bodies and feelings, with their embodied passions and sufferings.

Repeatedly, early modern writers shock their audiences with the most extreme experiences of that paradoxically intimate and communal suffering. Performing his final sermon, 'Death's Duel', John Donne, emaciated and hoarse from the ravages of cancer, directs the congregation's gaze: 'There now hangs that sacred body upon the cross, rebaptized in his own tears and sweat, and embalmed in his own blood alive. There are those bowels of compassion, which are so conspicuous, so manifested, as that you may see them through his wounds.'[2] The physicality of Donne's image, the bowels of compassion, points to a strong passion seizing body and soul. Donne borrows the image from Scripture (Luke 1:78, Phil. 1:8, Phil. 2:1, 1 John 3:17), and it allows him to emphasise the corporeal nature of the Son and his passion. Sharing body, sharing bowels, sharing compassion – for Donne, that is the nature of the Christian community. His final staging of the compassionate bowels revisits images he meditated upon during his illness seven years earlier. A church bell tolling for the dead calls to all. 'No man is an island, entire of itself; every man is a piece of the continent, a part of the main.... Another man may be sick too, and sick to death, and this affliction may lie in his bowels, as gold in a mine, and be of no use to him; but this bell, that tells me of his affliction, digs out and applies that gold to me.'[3] Compassion for the suffering of others reminds us all that we are part of a larger community. The bowels tie humans together in the flesh, and imagining those bowels digs into the body to forge an affective community with others.[4]

Donne's lessons in fellow-feeling take place in a society encountering a larger global world of different humans, even as its own Christian community was tearing itself apart in religious civil war. Aphra Behn's *Oroonoko; or, The Royal Slave* comes at the end of a century of those conflicts. It is a tale of pity for the sufferings of a fallen king, in a direct line from the martyred King Charles I to the soon-to-be deposed James II.[5] It tells that tale, though, through a figure of difference, an African transported across the Atlantic to South America. Although the novel's attitude towards slavery is complicated, its pathos makes readers feel compassion for an injustice committed against a noble human.[6] Behn's narrative stands at the start of the creation of the modern novel, a new genre that justified itself as a means of educating readers in sentiment and sympathy.[7] Yet Behn's decision to end her story by torturing and dismembering her hero is, by the standards of later novels, shockingly indecorous as it forces readers to confront his body in a final scene of compassion.[8] Although Richard Kroll makes a strong case that Behn's primary intention in *Oroonoko* was likely to give political advice to James II through a neoclassical work of rhetoric, he does not account for the place of *pathos* in its rhetoric.[9] The appeal to compassion is central to her text, as it is central to neoclassical discussions of rhetoric and poetics. *Oroonoko*'s pathos helped it continue to have influence long after its political interventions had passed into obscurity and irrelevance. Its shared suffering endured.

As Katherine Ibbett has shown, Corneille and other neoclassical critics pushed Aristotle by thinking more deeply about how the audience shares in the suffering presented on stage, seeing compassion not as a narrow and self-involved passion, but as a communal experience that brings the individual self out into imaginative emotional contact with a larger world.[10] A socially mixed audience joins in fellow-feeling with characters who are in many ways quite unlike them. Dryden adapts *The Poetics*' account of the tragic passions: 'The end of Tragedies or serious Playes, says *Aristotle*, is to beget admiration, compassion, or concernment.'[11] His gloss not only makes Aristotle's comments on wonder more central to the process of catharsis, as in French neoclassical commentaries;[12] it implies a change in emphasis from the usual translation of 'pity and fear'.[13]

Compassion implies a sharing of feeling, and likewise *concernment* implies a care for the well-being of the other lacking in *fear*, which suggests avoiding one's own danger more than caring for someone else's. In the *Rhetoric*, Aristotle defines fear as 'the imagination of a future destructive or painful evil', and he suggests that fear or dread in particular can work against pity: 'for the dreadful is something different from the pitiable and capable of expelling pity . . . ; for people no longer pity when something dreadful is near themselves'.[14] Fear works against pity in a way that concernment might not. Moreover, Dryden's reformulation of the terms from 'pity and fear' to 'compassion and concernment' suggests greater intimacy with the characters on stage. Corneille urges such intimacy in his *Discours de la tragédie*: 'It is thus a great advantage, for exciting commiseration, that there be close kinship and ties of love or friendship between the persecutor and the persecuted, the pursuer and the pursued, the one who causes suffering and the one who suffers'.[15] Ibbett sees here 'a real change in the notion of how we relate to a tragic figure, who is no longer an exemplar or a warning, but our friend'.[16] She notes that in the Greek, the pitier and the pitied remain distinct so that the one who pities does not participate in the experience of the sufferer, but in seventeenth-century transformations of tragic pity into commiseration and compassion, the two merge in fellow-feeling.[17]

Oroonoko has such scenes of commiseration with kin, lovers and friends, though it uses the language of the passions sparingly. *Pity* appears twice, once when Aboan is courting Onahal (pity for a suffering lover) and a second when Behn sees Oroonoko after he has been whipped (pity for tragic suffering). *Compassion* appears just once, in Oroonoko's speech to the African slaves when he tells them that honour spurs men to acts of virtue like compassion. *Commiseration* and *sympathy* do not appear at all, nor does *tragedy* or *tragic*. Tragedy instead is signalled by the words *suffering* and *sacrifice*. The words that occur most often to express fellow-feeling are *friend* and *friendship*. The difficulties in *Oroonoko* of forging and maintaining true bonds of friendship across barriers of culture, class, race and status complicate Corneille's observation that commiseration is heightened when there are close bonds between those who suffer and those who inflict the pain. Behn creates a character whose social, political and racial identity pushes at the limits of compassion and shared humanity, his history never quite shattering those categories of difference. In that failure lies the meaning of his tragic suffering and sacrifice.

Compassion and Fear for Friends and Other Humans

The suffering of a tragic hero can serve to forge a social and political connection, and compassion is potentially radical in that it can build new ties as much as reinforce existing ones.[18] But such sacrificial violence is also terrifying.[19] The terror of the blood sacrifice in the sixteenth and seventeenth centuries confronts Europeans not only on a mimetic stage but in historical confrontations with others in the Americas and in their own communities. To justify his campaign, Cortés provides an account of Aztec religious sacrifice: '[They] sometimes sacrifice their own persons, some cutting their tongues, others their ears, while there are some who stab their bodies with knives. All the blood which flows from them they offer to those idols, sprinkling it in all parts of the temple, or sometimes throwing it into the air or performing many other ceremonies, so that nothing is begun without sacrifice having first been made.' The horror begins with the blood that the worshippers shed from their own bodies, offering their own blood up as scapegoats for the community. When that fails, they substitute living bodies: 'they open their chests while they are still alive and take out their hearts and entrails and burn them before the idols, offering the smoke as sacrifice. Some of us have seen this, and they say it is the most terrible and frightful thing they have ever witnessed'.[20] The Christian witnesses respond with fear, and it is important for Cortés's argument that he include their responses. It is impossible to feel pity for such inhumane creatures, just fear, and that terror provides the religious justification for his conquest of Mexico. He will substitute saints for their pagan idols, and Christ's blood sacrifice for the blood of their bodies. Writing in response, as Matthew Goldmark has shown in the previous chapter, Las Casas will flip Cortés around by showing the Christians shedding sacrificial human blood: 'They erected certain Gallowses, that were broad but so low, that the tormented creatures might touch the ground with their feet, upon every one of which they would hang thirteen persons, blasphemously affirming that they did it in honour of our Redeemer and his Apostles, and then putting fire under them, they burnt the poor wretches alive.'[21] That gruesome and blasphemous parody of a Catholic ritual turns the Spanish into the bloody idolators.

Behn will put multiple versions of such torments in the final pages of her romance, her hero subject to three separate scenes of torture that reveal the English merchant colonisers as barbarians in need, as Elliott Visconsi suggests, of absolute monarchy to control their passions.[22] Readers are drawn to feel compassion for a character whose body is marked as racially different, and Behn repeatedly presents Oroonoko and his black body to her white English reading public as a friend, yet a problematical one. At times, Oroonoko's friendly relationship with the narrator represents an ideal version of the public sphere in the world of letters envisioned by Habermas as a first stage in the political public sphere.[23] Oroonoko, free in mind if not in legal status, exercises his reason and passion with Behn, who shares her entertaining stories of the ancient Romans and nuns and tries, unsuccessfully, to teach him the Christian faith. He prefers the company of women to that of the colony's men, who seem to do nothing but drink when they gather together. '[W]e had all the Liberty of Speech with him, especially my self, whom he call'd his *Great Mistress*', Behn claims, this little salon serving as a place of freedom for woman and slave (p. 41).[24] Yet that he calls her *Mistress*, the name for the slave owner's wife, while she calls him by his slave name *Caesar* reminds us of the social divide. Indeed, the colonists only want her to entertain Oroonoko because they fear Imoinda's pregnancy will provoke him to rebel: 'I was oblig'd, by some Persons, who fear'd a Mutiny . . . to discourse with *Caesar*, and to give him all the Satisfaction I possibly cou'd' (p. 41). Her friendship is a tool for the colonisers, as is their fear, which works against her compassion. Compassion creates community, while fear breaks those bonds by making a person focus narrowly on the danger to oneself.

Even in this limited public sphere, Oroonoko remains the intellectually curious one befitting that social ideal. The English are no longer on friendly terms with the Indians, but Oroonoko insists on visiting them and taking his friend or Great Mistress there. The Indians see them approach and treat the African and European visitors as the barbarian others: 'So advancing to him, some of 'em gave him their Hands, and cry'd, *Amora Tiguamy*, which is as much as, *How do* you, or *Welcome Friend*; and all, with one din, began to gabble to him, and ask'd, If we had Sense, and Wit? If we cou'd talk of affairs of Life, and War, as they cou'd do?' (p. 49). The Indians offer friendship, calling Oroonoko and his companions friends. The narrator says they 'gabble', though ironically what she perceives as 'gabble' are questions whether the strangers have 'Sense and Wit', whether the whites are barbarians, the word *barbarian* being rooted etymologically in *balbus*, stammering, babbling, gabbling (see *OED*). Despite these difficulties, Oroonoko's special character manages to create a community of communication and friendship.

At this point, Behn encounters the terrifying spectacle of a sacrificial blood ritual: 'But so frightful a Vision it was to see 'em no Fancy can create; no such Dreams can represent so dreadful a Spectacle. For my part I took 'em for Hobgoblins, or Fiends, rather than Men; but however their Shapes appear'd, their Souls were very Humane and Noble ...' (p. 50). The narrator's fear of whether these warriors are human parallels the Indians asking whether the white and black strangers have wit, intelligence, and language. What is 'humane' shape? These warriors have marked themselves as different by their ritual dismemberments. She describes how 'some wanted their Noses, some their Lips, some both Noses and Lips, some their Ears, and other Cut through each Cheek, with long Slashes, through which their Teeth appear'd; they had other several formidable Wounds and Scars, or rather Dismemberings; ... They cry'd, *Amora Tigame* to us, at our entrance, and were pleas'd we said as much to 'em' (p. 50). They appear not quite human, yet they cry out 'Welcome friend' and are pleased that the strangers call them friend in return. This is a curious allegory of the difficulties of intercultural exchange. The dismembered face has changed the appearance of humanity into something unfamiliar; the estranged face then cries out as a friend and is recognised by the others as a friend. Like all differences in the other, the face disfigured by an alien cultural practice has the potential to create fear and disrupt compassion and fellow-feeling, yet communication and friendship are possible despite the difficulty of translation. *Tigame* can be taken as friend.

It is Oroonoko who sets out to understand the rituals of dismemberment and by understanding them bridge the alienation produced by the disfigurement. He learns about their leadership ritual where the candidates prove their worth by sacrificing parts of their faces. The narrator observes, 'And 'tis by a passive Valour they shew and prove their Activity; a sort of Courage too Brutal to be applauded by our Black Hero; nevertheless he express'd his Esteem of 'em' (p. 50). Oroonoko uses his reason to judge that custom as 'Brutal' while also understanding its purposes and respecting the virtue it shows.

At this moment, Behn calls Oroonoko 'our Black Hero'. *Our* joins him to her community, while *Black* is a reminder of his distance from it. *Hero* sets him up as a man to be esteemed by that community. In yet another irony, four paragraphs later, 'our Black Hero' rebels against the white English. When word comes of his revolt, the narrator tells us that she, with the other women, flees the plantation, 'possess'd with extream Fear ... that he wou'd come down and Cut all our Throats' (p. 57). As Aristotle would have predicted, she can feel no compassion when in the throes of fear, imagining Oroonoko slitting her throat.

The epithet 'our Black Hero' points to the challenge the European encounter with the American and African other posed to a politics and ethics rooted in compassion. Feeling compassion for Oroonoko, so distinct in identity from his English audience, tests the self-reflexive link between compassion and the self. How much compassion can one feel in the face of differences in race, class and social status? Racial difference, Ayanna Thompson has shown, is marked in such texts by who can be tortured and who commits torture; torture constructs racial difference.[25] I want to follow Thompson by looking at how compassion for the victim unsettles those differences as they are being socially constructed.

'My dear friends and fellow-sufferers'

Behn opens *Oroonoko* with an account of the Indians of Surinam, drawn largely from the idealised accounts of writers like Montaigne. These are people who have no word for liar, who grieve for the death of the Governor when he said he would visit them one day and did not come as promised. The English do not 'dar[e] to command 'em; but on the contrary, caress 'em with all the brotherly and friendly Affection in the World' (p. 8). It is only at the end of her description of them that Behn makes it clear this is not a disinterested friendship born of admiration for their nobility: 'So they being, on all Occasions, very useful to us, we find it absolutely necessary to caress 'em as Friends, and not to treat 'em as Slaves; nor dare we do other, their Numbers so far surpassing ours in that *Continent*' (p. 11). Usefulness and fear are the grounds of this friendship more than the noble virtues the Indians embody. Although that friendly 'caress' seems like a sincere expression of love the first time she says it, when the narrator repeats the word, the cynical pretense of that friendship becomes obvious. Friendship is a colonial strategy, not a virtue that develops community and justice.

By contrast, the word *friend* is often in the mouth of Oroonoko, addressed with sincerity to free Africans, enslaved Africans, Europeans, and Indians. It is an important part of his *ethos*, and it is not only a rhetorical device for him but a genuine expression of communal fellow-feeling. Oroonoko, pleased with the intelligence and character of his new owner Trefry, 'put himself wholly into the Hands of his new Friend' (p. 35). Whether Oroonoko or the narrator is calling him 'Friend' here is ambiguous, but certainly Oroonoko in his free mind sees Trefry as friend, even though the rest of the tragedy shows the complete inability of a slave owner's friendship to effect justice. European friendship has been shown corrupt from the moment the slave trader betrayed his friendly hospitality and slapped Oroonoko and his friends in chains. The English are the only ones who pretend friendship, abusing the word *friend* and the feelings it evokes for unjust ends. As Aristotle explains, friendship is tied to justice:

> For in every community there seems to be some sort of justice, and some type of friendship also . . . . And the extent of their community is the extent of their friendship, since it is also the extent of the justice found there. The proverb 'What friends have is common' is correct, since friendship involves community.[26]

Community marks the boundaries of friendship and justice, and vice versa. These affective bonds unite people in a community of fellow-feeling, one that depends upon truthful use of language. Outside those boundaries, friendship and justice break down.

Compassion can create a new community of justice, though seventeenth-century writers recognised that building politics around such passions presents dangers.[27] Victoria Kahn has shown how the pathos of romance allowed writers to explore the affective ties of political communities at a time when traditional sources of political authority were proving inadequate.[28] Behn's romance belongs to that debate over the place of passions in forging political bonds. On one hand, Behn shows excessive passions linked to tyranny. Oroonoko's grandfather is an impotent old man who is nonetheless controlled by his passions. A tyrant, he seizes his grandson's lover Imoinda for his own. Although what he does is legal – Behn takes pains to explain the laws and customs the king follows – the reader feels the injustice of his actions, perhaps a warning to James II about the dangers of testing the limits of royal authority. On the other hand, Behn imagines a royalist community of compassion of the sort created by Charles's *Eikon Basilike*. The king's supposed meditations on the rebellion against him represent him as a man of deep feeling who pities his misguided people: 'I thanke God, I never found but My pity was above My anger; nor have My passions ever so prevailed against Me, as to exclude My most compassionate prayers for them, whom devout errours more than their own malice have betrayed to a most religious Rebellion.'[29] His compassion for his people, despite their errors, unites the royalist nation to him: 'upon whom I look, as Christ did sometime over *Jerusalem*, as objects of my prayers and teares, with compassionate griefe'.[30] Charles and Christ feel pity for their people and in turn are to be pitied. The text creates a royalist Christian community out of compassion for the martyr who felt compassion for them. Moreover, the royalists claim that the tragedy speaks beyond the particularities of culture. 'See here, what would make Indians weep', one writes.[31] Oroonoko likewise 'had heard of the late Civil Wars in *England* and the deplorable Death of our great Monarch; and wou'd discourse of it with all the Sense, and Abhorrence of the Injustice imaginable' (p. 13). Oroonoko's correct thoughts and feelings about the death of the king mark him as not just human but specifically noble in education and nature. He is a prince, and thinks and feels like one.

Oroonoko's nobility is even marked upon his racialised body, marking him as prince and African doubly different from the narrator and reader:

> He came into the Room, and address'd himself to me, and some other Women, with the best Grace in the World. He was pretty tall, but of a Shape the most exact that can be fancy'd. The most famous Statuary cou'd not form the Figure of a Man more admirably turn'd from Head to Foot. His Face was not of that brown, rusty Black which most of that Nation are, but a perfect Ebony, or polish'd Jett. His Eyes were the most awful that cou'd be seen, and very piercing; the White of 'em being like Snow, as were his Teeth. His Nose was rising and *Roman,* instead of *African* and flat. His Mouth, the finest shap'd that cou'd be seen; far from those great turn'd Lips, which are so natural to the rest of the *Negroes.* The whole Proportion and Air of his Face was so noble, and exactly form'd, that, bating his Colour, there cou'd be nothing in Nature more beautiful, agreeable and handsome. There was no one Grace wanting, that bears the Standard of true Beauty. (p. 13)

Behn posits a natural nobility that is simultaneously a cultivated nobility, an innate grace but one also, like his long hair pulled 'down to his Shoulders, by Aids of Art' (pp. 13–14), developed by careful training. That tension between the natural and artificial is captured in the phrase 'true Standard of Beauty'. Oroonoko's lips, like his Roman nose, are 'the finest shap'd that cou'd be seen', formed to European standards, yet his skin is not, as might be expected according to later racist standards of beauty, light but 'perfect Ebony, or polish'd Jett', in contrast to the perfect snow white of his eyes and teeth. That perfection sets him apart from his fellow Africans as it does from the common English: absolute black and white, absolute perfection and absolute difference. As an African prince, he is in essence in his own category of identity. Behn is constantly negotiating with her English audience's racial prejudices, their vulgar opinions about others. In one sentence, she is saying that 'bating his Colour, there cou'd be nothing in Nature more beautiful, agreeable and handsome', and in the next insisting, 'There was no one Grace wanting, that bears the Standard of true Beauty'. Just a few paragraphs earlier, she was describing the King of Coramantien's 'many beautiful *Black*-Wives; for most certainly, there are Beauties that can charm of that Colour' (p. 11), and Imoinda herself charms all the men of the plantation, regardless of their colour. Difference creates beauty but also stands in the way of judging it clearly.

Immediately after telling of the reunion of the African lovers, at the height of the romance plot, Behn says, in a curious aside, 'I had forgot to tell you, that those who are Nobly born of that Country, are so delicately Cut and Rac'd all over the fore-part of the Trunk of their Bodies, that it looks as if it were Japan'd' (p. 40). Beauty and nobility are literally 'carv'd in fine Flowers and Birds all over [Imoinda's] Body', just as the Indian warriors carve their honour upon their disfigured faces (p. 40). Behn compares this culturally alien practice to japanning, the East Asian lacquering process that was an important part of the luxury trade.[32] It is significant, though, that Behn draws attention to these distinctive markings of nobility only now at this moment of great romantic pathos. She reminds her English readers that they are feeling compassion for a noble human being that has become a commodity for sale like a decorated japanned box. They feel compassion for people whose bodies differ from them in colour and ornamentation, feelings created despite the differences. These feelings are opposed to the economic forces that are commodifying those distinctive bodies. That the English will one day whip scars upon Oroonoko's body sits in the background.

In the end, the developing institutions of racialised slavery frustrate these ties of fellow-feeling. Behn notes that the plantation laborers are divided between the permanently enslaved Africans and the white '*Slaves* for Four Years, that Inhabited among the *Negro* Houses' who 'were a sort of Spys upon *Caesar*' (pp. 51–52). They are all fellow slaves and neighbours, yet their status is creating a firm divide between them, the white slaves more loyal to their white masters than to their fellow slaves who are black. 'Our Black Hero' waits until those white slaves are drunk on their Sunday 'Day of Debauch' to gather the enslaved Africans, addressing them as '*my dear Friends and Fellow-sufferers*' (p. 52). Oroonoko himself fully recognises the racial divide created by enslavement. Describing all their undeserved miseries, he imagines into being an African community of fellow-feeling that spurs them to revolt. His speech develops his *ethos* as a friend in compassion and honour, concluding '*That Honour was the First Principle in Nature, that was to be Obey'd; but as no Man wou'd pretend to that, without all the Acts of Vertue, Compassion, Charity, Love, Justice and Reason*' (p. 53). Honour is the spur to acts of virtue, including acts of compassion. Compassion is an action in Oroonoko's ethics. It is not enough to feel but to act. By contrast, the narrator Behn flees the revolt in fear, marking the limit to her compassion. In any case, she repeatedly fails to translate her feelings of compassion into acts of compassion – even as the reader is drawn to sympathise with the revolt. The fellowship of the slaves, however, does fail as the bulk of the enslaved Africans do not share Oroonoko's honour. In that way, the slaves resemble most of the English. Oroonoko condemns them to slavery, and on similar grounds the English are condemned, for failure to hold to word, to keep to bonds honestly.

Oroonoko, African man of honour, believes he has reached an agreement with Deputy Governor Byam to surrender, but the Englishman deceives him and has him whipped. The narrator and Oroonoko have briefly engaged in a literary public sphere, yet that world fails since the Christians cannot keep their word. Communication of ideas and feelings depends upon holding to conventional and truthful meanings of words. Without sharing the meaning of words, there can be no sharing of feeling and no friendship or justice. She insists, 'We said all things to him, that Trouble, Pitty, and Good Nature cou'd suggest' (p. 58). Once again, her pity and friendship come down largely to the words she says, albeit joined to some acts of compassion for the wounded body. Oddly, though, they only put him in the 'healing Bath' and call the 'Chirurgeon to anoint him with healing Balm' (p. 59) *after* they interview him and get him to accept their protest of innocence and give a promise not to seek revenge or commit suicide (p. 58). The acts of compassion seem less driven by love or honour, as Oroonoko would have them, than by a transactional promise. And he does promise forgiveness and is 'anointed', with the suggestion of sacred kingship. Only Byam fails to earn his forgiveness. Charles I, incidentally, forgave all his enemies in *Eikon Basilike*, so there is a limit to Oroonoko's Christ-like, Charles-like passion.

Oroonoko tries to frame his revenge as a tragic sacrifice. Behn comments, 'he first resolv'd on a Deed, that (however Horrid it at first appear'd to us all) when we had heard his Reasons, we thought it Brave and Just' (p. 60). The sacrifice begins with tender descriptions of 'the Passion and Languishment of a dying Lover' (p. 60) before moving to the horror of the blood sacrifice:

> ... the Lovely, Young, and Ador'd Victim lays her self down, before the Sacrificer; while he, with a Hand resolv'd, and a Heart breaking within, gave the Fatal Stroke; first, cutting her Throat, and then severing her yet Smiling Face from that Delicate Body, pregnant as it was with Fruits of tend'rest Love. (p. 61)

The strange synecdoche of the face for the head heightens the horror of this ritual sacrifice. She becomes his idol, and he lies there looking at her face in compassion. That is when the ritual goes wrong. Oroonoko is so overwhelmed with the passions produced by his sacrifice of his love that after covering the body with leaves and flowers, he cannot part from her face, which 'he left yet bare to look on' (p. 61). Unable to move, he wastes away until Byam's search party is drawn to the 'Loathsom' stink (p. 62), the rot an emblem of the corruption of Surinam and what it has done to the man of honour and his passionate love. About to be captured, Oroonoko then performs a tragic parody of the Indian warriors' honour ritual:

> *Look ye, ye faithless Crew*, said he, *'tis not Life I seek, nor am I afraid of Dying*; and, at that Word, cut a piece of Flesh from his own Throat, and threw it at 'em, ... At that, he rip'd up his own Belly; and took his Bowels and pull'd 'em out, with what Strength he cou'd . . . (pp. 62–63)

Oroonoko proves his strength and honour like the Indian warriors and marks himself again as different. Once more we look upon the bowels of compassion, these fleshly markers of humanity.[33] They 'sew'd up his Belly', and his ravaged body becomes an emblem of mortality, as in Donne's sermon: 'We ran all to see him; and, if before we thought him so beautiful a Sight, he was now so alter'd, that his Face was like a Death's Head black'd over; nothing but Teeth, and Eyeholes: For some Days we suffer'd no body to speak to him, but caused Cordials to be poured down his Throat, which sustained his Life' (p. 63). Behn's compassion here in pouring medicine down the throat that he himself had torn open perversely saves him from a quick death.

Behn ends *Oroonoko* with the gruesome description of the torture and dismemberment of the hero's body as Oroonoko's white friends once again fail to protect him. As the executioner hacks off the parts of his body, he smokes a tobacco pipe in silence: '[They] first cut off his Members, and threw them into the Fire; after that, with an ill-favoured Knife, they cut his Ears, and his Nose, and burn'd them; he still Smoak'd on, as if nothing had touch'd him; then they hack'd off one of his Arms, and still he bore up, and held his Pipe' (p. 64). The effect in the end evokes both compassion and admiration, with Oroonoko's princely pride standing above the 'inhumane' justices and the 'rude and wild . . . Rabble' (p. 64). Sounding (surprisingly) a bit like Milton attacking the crowd at the end of *Eikonoklastes*, Behn presents a horrifying image of the modern political economy, where once the ties of compassion and honour are broken, the wild passions of the crowd and the self-interested greed of the merchants dominate.

It is important to remember that in Foucault's account of the premodern scaffold, the state depends upon the consent of the spectators to complete and ratify the meaning of the justice put on display.[34] If the spectators do not agree with the meaning of the execution, the ritual fails and transforms from a display of justice into an unjust sacrifice. The public execution was an assertion of state power that also marked the moment when it was most vulnerable to criticism and resistance born of sudden and often unforeseen affects spreading contagiously through the crowd. This is why the early print market was filled with so many competing accounts of events performed on the scaffold.[35] The public response to King Charles's 'tragic scaffold' (to borrow Marvell's phrase), where pity and fear turned in the king's favour against the display of republican justice, is certainly in the background of Oroonoko's death. Compassion for the scaffold's victim does important political work.

Standing in for the compassionate readers are two women witnesses, the narrator's mother and sister, evoking the women at Golgotha, with the irony that Behn criticises the Christianity of the English in Surinam. Their compassion is largely ineffectual in that they were 'not suffer'd to save him' (p. 64), yet these female witnesses make possible the telling of his story. The world of romance, represented by the tragic love story of Oroonoko and Imoinda, is the world of pathos and compassion, one that makes space for women's passions. With women mostly driven out, the all-male world of the novel's end is without pity and honour. Such a masculine public sphere is all commerce and power, with no communal feeling. In such a world, the foreign other is reduced to instruments of economic interests, the slave's body just a commodity. Yet the reader, who 'partakes of the victim's distress by becoming a cosufferer', experiences feelings that challenge that economy.[36] That tragic compassion is heightened, as Corneille understood, by the ties of love and friendship between Behn and Oroonoko, by how she and, by extension, her readers are implicated in our friend's torments. Paradoxically, however, even as the institutions of racialised slavery corrupt and render impotent bonds of friendship, the text forges ties of compassion between readers and 'our Black Hero'.

Oroonoko's Afterlife among Friends and Fellow Sufferers

Behn's *Oroonoko* is a tragedy of the failure of compassionate friendship to bridge the divides of race, culture and class, yet it expresses, at best, ambivalent feelings about the institution of slavery. That ambivalence remained part of its eighteenth-century legacy, particularly after it moved to the stage in Thomas Southerne's 1695 adaptation.[37] Nonetheless, the text's affective power would gradually erase the ambivalence so that during the course of the century, the legend of Oroonoko would become an argument for abolition. In 1749, famously, a real African prince, freed from his own enslavement, attended a production of the play commissioned for him, and audiences cried to see him weeping as he watched a version of his own experience. The play was still not opposed to slavery, since one could weep for the injustices committed against the prince without necessarily sympathizing with abolition. Yet the pathos made it possible for abolitionists to appropriate the play for their cause, culminating in John Ferriar's 1788 adaptation of the Oroonoko legend as *The Prince of Angola*, a play fully committed to unveiling the injustice of the slave trade. Oroonoko's status as the sentimental hero, and the reader's compassion for him, made this rewriting possible. Compassion involves recognising the human in the other, and its force gives the text its persuasive power. Moreover, as this story involves feeling not for the weak but for the strong and honourable, its compassion differs from the pity generated by Las Casas for the 'patient, meek and peaceful' Indians.[38] Indeed, that has been my experience teaching *Oroonoko* for the past decade in New York City classrooms where the majority of students are African American and Latino, many of whom can trace their family ancestry to the West Indian plantations. Despite the alienating racist assumptions Behn makes when addressing her white English audience and their vulgar opinions, my students identify with 'our Black Hero', not just with Oroonoko's sufferings but his honour, feeling compassion and indignation for the injustice of his tragedy. Behn makes possible a fellow-feeling that her own narrator was unable to maintain.

Notes

1 Erich Auerbach, '*Passio* as Passion', Martin Elsky (ed. and trans.), *Criticism*, 43 (2001), 285–308, trans. of 'Passio als Leidenschaft', *PMLA*, 56 (1941), 1179–96.
2 Donne, 'Death's Duel', in John Carey (ed.) *Major Works* (Oxford University Press, 1990), p. 416. See David Hillman, 'Visceral Knowledge: Shakespeare, Skepticism, and the Interior of the Early Modern Body' in Hillman and Carla Mazzio (eds.), *The Body in Parts: Fantasies of Corporeality in Early Modern Europe* (New York and London: Routledge, 1997), pp. 81–105.

3 Donne, *Devotions upon Emergent Occasions*, in *Works*, p. 345.
4 On the imagination in meditative and poetic texts, see John D. Lyons, *Before Imagination: Embodied Thought from Montaigne to Rousseau* (Stanford University Press, 2005).
5 Anita Pacheco, 'Royalism and Honor in Aphra Behn's *Oroonoko*', *SEL*, 34 (1994), 491–506; Richard Kroll, '"Tales of Love and Gallantry": The Politics of *Oroonoko*', *Huntington Library Quarterly*, 67 (2004), 573–605.
6 On *Oroonoko* as an American text on slavery and racial identity, see William C. Spengemann, 'The Earliest American Novel: Aphra Behn's *Oroonoko*', *Nineteenth-Century Fiction*, 38 (1984), 384–414. Much subsequent criticism has been especially attuned to the intersections of race and gender in the novel. For example, Laura Brown, 'The Romance of Empire and the Trade in Slaves' in Brown and Felicity Nussbaum (eds.), *The New Eighteenth Century* (New York and London: Methuen, 1987), pp. 41–61; Margaret Ferguson, 'Juggling the Categories of Race, Class, and Gender: Aphra Behn's *Oroonoko*' in Janet Todd (ed.), *Aphra Behn: New Casebooks* (Basingstoke: Macmillan, 1999), pp. 209–33; Stephanie Athey and Daniel Cooper Alarcón, '*Oroonoko*'s Gendered Economies of Honor/Horror: Reframing Colonial Discourse Studies in the Americas' in Michael Moon and Cathy N. Davidson (eds.), *Subjects and Citizens: Nation, Race, and Gender from 'Oroonoko' to Anita Hill* (Durham and London: Duke UP, 1995), pp. 27–55.
7 On how eighteenth-century revaluation of the sentiments legitimised the novel as an education in the emotions, see John Mullan, *Sentiment and Sociability: The Language of Feeling in the Eighteenth Century* (Oxford: Clarendon, 1988). Martha Nussbaum's defences of reading literature are related, as in *Upheavals of Thought: The Intelligence of Emotions* (Cambridge University Press, 2001).
8 Arguing for the importance of spectacle to Behn's narrative, a technique acquired from her experience as a dramatist, Marta Figlerowicz complicates the history of the novel, reminding us of its relationship to theatrical representation. '"Frightful Spectacles of a Mangled King": Aphra Behn's *Oroonoko* and Narration through Theater', *New Literary History*, 39 (Spring 2008), 321–34.
9 Kroll, '"Tales"'.
10 Katherine Ibbett, 'Pity, Compassion, Commiseration: Theories of Theatrical Relatedness', *Seventeenth-Century French Studies*, 30 (2008), 196–208.
11 'An Essay of Dramatick Poesie', in Samuel Holt Monk et al. (eds.), *The Works of John Dryden*, vol. 17 (Berkeley and Los Angeles: University of California Press, 1971), p. 35.
12 John D. Lyons, *Kingdom of Disorder: The Theory of Tragedy in Classical France* (West Lafayette, IN: Purdue University Press, 1999).
13 On the connections between pity and fear, see Kathy Eden, *Poetic and Legal Fiction in the Aristotelian Tradition* (Princeton: Princeton University Press, 1986), pp. 55–58.

14 Aristotle, *On Rhetoric: A Theory of Civic Discourse*, trans. George A. Kennedy (Oxford: Oxford University Press, 1991), 1382a, p. 139; 1386b, p. 154.
15 Pierre Corneille, *Discours de la tragédie, et des moyens de la traiter, selon le vraisemblable ou le nécessaire* in *Œuvres complètes*, ed. Georges Couton (Paris: Gallimard, 1987), p. 151, my translation.
16 Ibbett, 'Compassion', p. 205.
17 Ibbett, 'Compassion', pp. 206–7, citing David Konstan, *Pity Transformed* (London: Duckworth, 2001), p. 60, who charts the origins of *compassio* in the writings of the early Church Fathers, who were responding to classical writings on pity.
18 See Terry Eagleton, *Sweet Violence: The Idea of the Tragic* (Oxford: Blackwell, 2003).
19 René Girard describes the mimetic process whereby the scapegoat is both similar to and separate from the community that sacrifices it and the sacrificial crisis that results when those distinctions break down. *Violence and the Sacred*, trans. Patrick Gregory (Baltimore: Johns Hopkins University Press, 1977).
20 Hernán Cortés, *Letters from Mexico*, trans. Anthony Pagden, rev. ed. (New Haven and London: Yale University Press, 2001), p. 35.
21 Bartolomé de las Casas, *Tears of the Indians: Being an Historical and true Account of the Cruel Massacres and Slaughters of above Twenty Millions of innocent People*, trans. John Phillips (London, 1656), p. 9.
22 Elliott Visconsi, *Lines of Equity: Literature and the Origins of Law in Later Stuart England* (Ithaca, NY, and London: Cornell University Press, 2008), p. 163.
23 Jürgen Habermas, *The Structural Transformation of the Public Sphere: An Inquiry into a Category of Bourgeois Society*, trans. Thomas Burger (Cambridge, MA: MIT Press, 1989). See also Joan B. Landes's complication of the model in her study of *Women and the Public Sphere in the Age of the French Revolution* (Ithaca, NY: Cornell University Press, 1988).
24 Citations, which will appear in the text, are to *Oroonoko*, ed. Joanna Lipking (New York: Norton, 1997).
25 Ayanna Thompson, *Performing Race and Torture on the Early Modern Stage* (New York: Routledge, 2008).
26 Aristotle, *Nicomachean Ethics*, trans. Terence Irwin (Indianapolis, IN: Hackett, 1985), 1159b, p. 224.
27 I have explored some of these problems in 'Compassion in the Public Sphere of Milton and King Charles' in Gail Kern Paster, Katherine Rowe and Mary Floyd Wilson (eds.), *Reading the Early Modern Passions* (Philadelphia: University of Pennsylvania Press, 2004), pp. 89–110, and *The Tragic Histories of Mary Queen of Scots 1560–1690: Rhetoric, Passions, and Political Literature* (Farnham and Burlington, VT: Ashgate, 2009).
28 See 'Reinventing Romance, or the Surprising Effects of Sympathy', *Renaissance Quarterly*, 55 (2002), 625–61; '"The Duty to Love": Passion and Obligation in Early Modern Political Theory', *Representations*, 68

(1999), 84–107; *Wayward Contracts: The Crisis of Political Obligation in England, 1640–1674* (Princeton: Princeton University Press, 2004).
29 *Eikon Basilike, The Povrtraictvre of His Sacred Maiestie in His Solitvdes and Svfferings*, 1st ed., 2nd issue (London, 1648), p. 123.
30 *Eikon Basilike*, pp. 227–28.
31 *The Famous Tragedie of King Charles I* ([London], 1649), p. 42, Early English Books Online, eebo.chadwyck.com.
32 George Parker and John Stalker's *Treatise of japaning and varnishing* was first published in Oxford in 1688, the same year as *Oroonoko*, suggesting the contemporary vogue for the Japanese lacquer.
33 On the pain of anger experienced in the bowels, see Kristine Steenbergh, 'Green Wounds: Pain, Anger, and Revenge in Early Modern Culture' in Jan Frans van Dijkhuizen and Karl A. E. Enenkel (eds.), *The Sense of Suffering: Constructions of Physical Pain in Early Modern Culture* (Leiden and Boston: Brill, 2009), pp. 165–87.
34 Michel Foucault, *Discipline and Punish: The Birth of the Prison*, trans. Alan Sheridan, 2nd ed. (New York: Vintage-Random House, 1991), especially pp. 59–60. Thomas Laqueur demonstrates the crowd's power in 'Crowds, Carnival, and the State in English Executions, 1604–1868' in A. L. Beier, David Cannadine and James M. Rosenheim (eds.), *The First Modern Society* (Cambridge University Press, 1989), pp. 305–44.
35 See, for example, Peter Lake with Michael Questier, *The Antichrist's Lewd Hat: Protestants, Papists, and Players in Post-Reformation England* (New Haven and London: Yale University Press, 2002).
36 Ramesh Mallipeddi, 'Spectacle, Spectatorship, and Sympathy in Aphra Behn's *Oroonoko*', *Eighteenth-Century Studies*, 45 (2012), 475–96 (p. 489). Mallipeddi does overstate his case when he argues that Behn 'revises this traditional framework encompassing suffering, public spectacle, and punishment' since the scaffold had often been presented in such emotional ways, not merely in matter-of-fact ways, as he claims (p. 489). Such accounts are prevalent in Las Casas, Montaigne, Foxe and the English Jesuit writing, to name a few.
37 My brief overview of eighteenth-century *Oroonoko* adaptations derives from Jane Spencer, *Aphra Behn's Afterlife* (Oxford University Press, 2000), pp. 223–64. See also Brycchan Carey, 'To Force a Tear: British Abolitionism and the Eighteenth-Century London Stage' in Stephen Ahern (ed.), *Affect and Abolition in the Anglo-Atlantic, 1770–1830* (Farnham and Burlington, VT: Ashgate, 2013), pp. 111–17. On Southerne, see Thompson, *Performing Race*, pp. 51–74.
38 Las Casas, *Tears*, p. 2.

PART VIII
Contemporary Compassions

CHAPTER 15

Contemporary Compassions
Interrelating in the Anthropocene

Kristine Steenbergh

In the Introduction to this volume, we suggested that a richer engagement with the early modern period might bring us to a more complex understanding of compassion's operations today. The preceding chapters explored the extent to which early modern compassion is shaped by the radical fault lines of the Reformation as well as the sliding scales of difference and alterity informed by colonial encounters in Asia and the Americas. In other words, this volume foregrounded how notions of singularity and alterity shaped early modern thinking about compassion, and how the emotion is a situated practice shaped by the religious battles of the Reformation. Compassion was a complex and contested emotion, in England, on the Continent, and in colonial contexts. As Bruce Smith puts it in the opening chapter of this volume, the ethics of compassion in early modern culture was 'rife with conflict'. If the experience of compassion was viewed as a means to strengthen a sense of solidarity within a community, it also raises questions about the bounds of that community and the grounds upon which compassion is extended to others. Questions on how to cultivate compassion, with whom to have compassion and whom to exclude, and how to put the feeling into practice abound in early modern texts.

As a touchstone in their exploration of early modern compassion, many of the contributors to this volume cite Steven Mullaney's description of the English Reformation as a radical fault line in the cultural history of emotions, as 'an undoubted climacteric – something fundamental had been loosened, broken, and reset'.[1] Mullaney argues that because the Protestant church had eradicated traditional emotional practices, the English in the long aftermath of the Reformation not only did not know what to believe, they also did not know what or how to feel.[2] The Elizabethan theatre functioned as a laboratory in which new affective vocabularies and gestures were tried out – it provided a space to 'plumb and sound out the gaps that had been opened up in the Elizabethan social body as a consequence of the English Reformation'.[3]

Like the Reformation, the Anthropocene invites a rethinking of our ideologies, values and practices. The realisation of humankind's impact on the earth's ecosystems shapes a need for new worldviews that are less anthropocentric and more attuned to the interconnections between different life forms on our planet. If early modern inflections of compassion were shaped by the need for new emotional practices after the radical break of the Reformation, thinking about the role of compassion today retraces similar fault lines but is also shaped by the pressures of the Anthropocene. This volume has traced a prehistory of today's social fractures around the question of religion and identity. These questions, however, are interconnected with the pressing issue of ecological crisis that risks causing even greater social fractures. The question of compassion with refugees, for example, which Bruce Smith and Richard Meek address in this volume, receives new urgency due to the impact of climate change on global patterns of migration. Whereas early modern writings on compassion struggled with questions of difference and alterity in the context of colonial encounters in Asia and America, contemporary theorists, faced with the need for new and less anthropocentric models of interrelatedness, expand such questions of alterity and compassion to the affective relations between human and non-human others.

In the work of Donna Haraway, Deborah Bird Rose and Thom van Dooren, compassion is envisaged as central to posthuman affective relations. It is inflected less as modern hierarchical notions of 'pity' and is more similar to early modern definitions of compassion in its literal sense of 'suffering-with'. Like early modern authors, these scholars ask which practices can be used to cultivate an attentiveness and openness to the other, which they view as a prerequisite for the experience of this mode of compassion.

Practising Compassion in the Anthropocene

Paul Crutzen and Eugene Stoermer proposed naming our current geological epoch the Anthropocene, after humankind's transformative impact on the planet. They argued that the major, still growing and long-lasting impacts of human life on the earth and atmosphere necessitate this emphasis on the central role of humankind in the current and future state of our planet.[4] With the realisation of this immense and destructive human impact, this new geological epoch functions as a fault line. In the words of Christophe Bonneuil and Jean-Baptiste Fressoz, 'the Anthropocene is an event, a point of bifurcation in the history of the Earth, life, and humans. It overturns our representations of the world.'[5] The reality of humans' destructive impact on the earth's systems not only impresses the necessity to rethink our economical, legal, social, cultural, political, religious paradigms, it also stimulates a radical rethinking of humankind's relations with other species – it calls for a mode of thinking non-anthropocentrically about human relations to non-human others.[6] Within the environmental humanities, this rethinking of human/non-human relations takes shape in metaphors of entanglement, sympoiesis and intra-action. 'The ecological thought', as ecocritic Timothy Morton puts it, 'imagines interconnectedness.'[7]

Recent work in literary studies has explored the role of affect and emotions in the Anthropocene. Nicola Merola, for example, considers environmental melancholy as the primary affect governing the Anthropocene. Lesley Head argues that grief must become part of our politics in facing ecological crisis, for only by acknowledging grief over the extinction of non-human others and the loss of ecological variety is hope and action possible. Ashlee Cunsolo and Karen Landman similarly find hope at the heart of ecological loss and grief.[8] Next to rituals and modes of expressing grief and mourning in confronting the ecological reality of the Anthropocene, compassion is often evoked as one of the emotional practices that can contribute to an ethics of multispecies living. Indeed, the ecologist Marc Bekoff has argued that we should undertake a transition from the Anthropocene, the era defined by humankind's destructive impact on our planet, to the 'Compassionocene, an era defined by our compassion for other animals'.[9] Even if scholars are aware of the danger that compassion can function as a sentimental and hierarchical gesture in response to the suffering of non-human others, they nevertheless urge that we stay with the trouble and explore the potential of compassion.

As in early modern debates about compassion, the pressing question of who is included and who is excluded in practices of compassion figures prominently in thinking about interrelations in the Anthropocene. Lauren Berlant's axiom that 'there is nothing simple about compassion apart from the desire to be taken as simple', reverberates strongly in the Anthropocene.[10] In an era in which humankind inflicts immense suffering on the species with which we cohabit the earth – from cows slaughtered for food to marine species on the verge of extinction – what role can compassion possibly play in multispecies ethics? The question of what could constitute sympathetic agency when confronted with suffering remains as knotty in the face of our current systemic crisis as it was in the context of 1980s compassionate conservatism. Compassion in Berlant's view cannot be considered an ethical emotion *an sich* – indeed, individual deeds of compassion run the risk of becoming sentimental alibis for structural injustice. Anna Tsing has warned that the compassion with domestic animals fostered in households in the United States has a colonising effect that may lead to the elimination of humans and non-humans considered as 'other'.

> U.S. publics learn to imagine themselves as compassionate, moral people because they love their children and their pets. They learn that this love makes them 'good people' – unlike terrorists, who only hate. [...] Other peoples, and other species, are judged by their ability to live up to U.S. standards of domestic intimacy. If they are properly engaged with family love, they may deserve to live. Others risk becoming 'collateral damage' in U.S. projects to improve the world; to eliminate them may be unfortunate but not 'inhumane'.[11]

Here, as in many early modern texts, the question of community, alterity and difference is central to the problematisation of the ethics of compassion. The danger in mimetic sympathy is that, based in a sense of similarity between sufferer and sympathiser, it excludes those who are experienced as dissimilar. Bruce Smith explored how certain categories of people were not considered worthy of compassion in early modern England – the homeless, people who refuse to work, veterans, foreigners. With a number of other contributors, he stresses that 'compassion for religious differences was in shorter and shorter supply' during the course of the early modern period in England.[12] As in Tsing's example, the question of whether a person is able to experience compassion with others was sometimes pivotal in mechanisms of in- and exclusion. Richard Meek discussed how in Edwin Sandys' metaphor of the common body, those who are unable to feel sympathy with other members of that body are considered 'dead and rotten' without hope for salvation. In my own chapter, Robert Bolton thought that an inability to experience compassion is a clear sign of being outside God's grace. Similarly, Tsing argues that the capacity to feel compassion as dictated by discourses of domestic intimacy in the United States serves as a litmus test for a neocolonial and potentially destructive distinction between self and other.

Although the complex social emotion of compassion comes with many problems attached, several scholars do see a role for compassion in multispecies ethics. Alexis Shotwell recognises that as embodied beings, we cannot live without inflicting suffering: 'we live in this world thoroughly connected with all of the suffering that individualist practices of purity attempt to manage'.[13] In her view, however, the impurity of ethical practices is not a reason to turn away from them altogether. Rather, the entanglement with distant suffering others calls for an ethical practice that is not based in an idea of personal purity, but is more consonant with the complexity of our world. As Donna Haraway puts it, 'Like it or not, we are in the string-figure game of caring for and with precarious worldlings made terribly more precarious by fossil-burning man.'[14] Recognising that canonical ethical theories often assume a moral agent who is not relationally implicated with others, Shotwell, drawing on Haraway, shapes an impure ethics based in relationality and connectivity: 'rather, we might craft affective, cognitive, and embodied ethical responses to the complex and unequal multispecies ecologies in which we live'.[15]

What, then, is the role of compassion in these affective, cognitive and embodied responses to multispecies entanglement? Anna Tsing advocates a kind of multispecies love that is based in attention to and immersion in the other. In 'Arts of Inclusion, or How to Love a Mushroom', she proposes that in times of extinction, even 'slight acquaintance can make the difference between preservation and callous disregard'. She proposes a new model at the intersection of the natural sciences and the humanities, the key characteristic of which is multi-species love. This cultural study of science does not merely critique, but 'encourages a new, passionate immersion in the lives of the nonhuman subjects being studied'.[16] For Donna Haraway, the Anthropocene calls for an awareness of participating in a common becoming between humans and other species. It 'requires making oddkin; that is, we require each other in unexpected collaborations and combinations [...]. We become-with each other or not at all'.[17] In her work, this kind of entanglement and becoming-with each other is not thought in terms of sympathy between microcosm and macrocosm evocative of early modern humoral ecology. Rather, it evokes the early modern practice of softening and opening the bowels of compassion in becoming receptive to the suffering of others.

This 'curious practice' of openness to the other, a capacity to respond that Haraway terms 'response-ability', is also a practice of staying present with the pain of others. As she noted in *When Species Meet*, 'this unnameable being/becoming with in copresence [...] is about suffering and expressive, relational vitality, in all the vulnerable mortality of both'.[18] The relation expressed here is not a one-sided, hierarchical relation in which the human does the pitying and 'the sufferer is over there', as Berlant had it. Indeed, Haraway fine-tunes her concept of becoming-with by contrasting it to the role of pity in Derrida's thinking on human–animal relations. 'The question of suffering led Derrida to the virtue of pity, and that is not a small thing', she writes. 'But how much more promise is in the questions, Can animals play? Or work? And even, can I learn to play with this cat?'[19] More than in pity, Haraway is interested in interrelating with non-human others, in becoming in a co-presence of suffering and play.

Even though the literal word 'compassion' does not figure often in her texts, her notion of 'staying with the trouble' resonates with the early modern definition of compassion as 'suffering together with another, participation in suffering'.[20] Haraway views grief as a path to understanding our entangled shared living and dying. She writes: 'human beings must grieve *with*, because we are in and of this fabric of undoing'.[21] Unlike many forms of early modern fellow-feeling, her inflection of multispecies compassion is non-mimetic: it does not involve taking the place of the suffering other or feeling their pain. Unlike Aristotelian pity, which requires a certain level of similarity between the pitier and the pitied, this compassion-in-relating is attentive to difference. Its practice is based in modes of attention to otherness, rather than in similitude. In other words, the experience of compassion does not cancel out the difference between human and non-human other but cultivates attention to the strangeness of becoming-with in relation.

Taking laboratory animals as her case study, Haraway argues that staying with the complexities of animal testing does not mean that we should no longer do this this kind of research or engage in unequal instrumental relationships with non-human others. But it does mean 'learning to live and think in practical opening to shared pain and mortality'. What does that mean in practice? Haraway writes that she does not think 'we will ever have a general principle for what sharing suffering means, but it has to be material, practical, and consequential, the sort of engagement that keeps the inequality from becoming commonsensical or taken as obviously okay'. By learning to share other animals' pain non-mimetically, humans' 'capacity to respond may yet be recognised and nourished on this earth'.[22] Like early modern compassion, this feeling comes into being in careful everyday practices of relating to others. Just as the seventeenth-century clergyman Edward Topsell urged his congregation to soften their bowels of compassion by regularly visiting the poor, Haraway embeds the experience of compassion in everyday relationships to non-human others.[23] In this sense, the role of compassion in her work resembles also the notion of being 'exposed to one another in vulnerability' that Eric Langley (Chapter 10) finds in early modern texts. The essence of affective relating in posthuman ethics, as Elisabeth Arnould-Bloomfield puts it, is this 'commitment to paying attention and remaining open to the fundamental heterogeneity of other and self in relationship'.[24]

For Deborah Bird Rose and Thom van Dooren, this mode of attention takes the shape of witnessing and participation. Like softening the bowels in the early modern period, the development of an attitude of attentiveness requires practice.[25] The environmental humanities in their view could develop practices to give shape to such a multispecies ethics:

> From this grounding in an attentiveness to ethos, we understand ethics as an openness to others in the material reality of their own lives: noisy, fleshy, exuberant creatures with their multitude of interdependencies and precarities, their great range of calls, their care and their abundance along with their suffering and grief. Within entangled worlds of mutual becoming, attentiveness is necessarily a complex mode of participation.[26]

Rose and Van Dooren intertwine their argument on attentiveness to other species' suffering and grief with careful observations of albatross and mistletoe, shaping an ethics-in-practice as they write. Language – careful factual descriptions as well as fictional stories – is elemental in this mode of attention to the non-human other. Haraway cites the science fiction author Ursula K. Le Guin to conjure up a future in which humankind has learned to listen to other species attentively. Careful observation of plants and lichen (itself an organism living in symbiosis) leads to an understanding of their languages: '"Do you realize", the phytolinguist will say to the aesthetic critic, "that [once upon a time] they couldn't even read Eggplant?" And they will smile at our ignorance, as they pick up their rucksacks and hike on up to read the newly deciphered lyrics of the lichen on the north face of Pike's Peak.'[27] For Haraway, one of the practices that shapes attentiveness to the other is the reading and writing of fiction. Stories about companion species can help shape attentiveness to their suffering. She views her pigeon tales in *Staying with the Trouble* as strengthening response-abilities: stories exercise a muscle of knowledge critical for caring about flourishing, which enhances our ability to stay attuned to the complexities of ecological crisis.[28] Similarly, in the fictional 'Camille Stories' that close *Staying with the Trouble*, Haraway imagines that storytelling is found to be the most powerful practice for 'nurturing compassion and becoming-with-each other'.[29]

If early modern compassion is often based in the desire to feel another's pain as one's own, suffering-with in the Anthropocene is non-mimetic.

Not grounded in a desire to absorb another's pain mimetically, this mode of compassion pays careful attention to difference. It does not seek to colonise but aims to cultivate a sense of interrelatedness and responsiveness through a practice of careful listening. In its emphasis on the need for attentive and careful everyday practices to shape new modes of interrelating, the radical awareness of the Anthropocene stimulates a search for new practices of compassion similar to that of the early modern period – evoking similar questions of belonging and exclusion, identity and alterity while inflecting them in new ways.

Notes

1. Steven Mullaney quoting Peter Marshall, *The Reformation of Emotions in the Age of Shakespeare* (University of Chicago Press, 2015), p. 12.
2. Mullaney, *Reformations*, p. 16.
3. Mullaney, p. 46.
4. P. J. Crutzen and E. F. Stoermer, 'The "Anthropocene"', *Global Change Newsletter*, 41 (2000), 17–18.
5. Christophe Bonneuil and Jean-Baptiste Fressoz, *The Shock of the Anthropocene: Earth, History, and Us* (London: Verso, 2016), e-book, p. 52.
6. Jan Zalasiewicz, Mark Williams and Colin N. Waters, 'Anthropocene' in Joni Adamson, William A. Gleason and David N. Pellow (eds.), *Keywords for Environmental Studies* (New York University Press, 2016), p. 14.
7. Timothy Morton, *Ecological Thought* (Cambridge, MA: Harvard University Press, 2012), p. 15.
8. Nicole M. Merola, 'Materializing a Geotraumatic and Melancholy Anthropocene: Jeannette Winterson's *The Stone Gods*', *Minnesota Review*, 83 (2014), 123; Lesley Head, *Hope and Grief in the Anthropocene: Reconceptualising Human-Nature Relations* (London: Routledge, 2016), p. 4; Ashlee Cunsolo and Karen Landman, *Mourning Nature: Hope at the Heart of Ecological Loss and Grief* (Montreal and Kingston: McGill-Queen's University Press, 2017).
9. Mark Bekoff, introduction to Marc Bekoff and Jessica Pierce (eds.), *The Animals' Agenda: Freedom, Compassion, and Coexistence in the Human Age* (Boston: Beacon Press, 2017), p. 9.
10. Lauren Berlant, *Compassion: The Culture and Politics of an Emotion* (New York: Routledge, 2004), p. 7.
11. Anna Tsing, 'Unruly Edges: Mushrooms as Companion Species', *Environmental Humanities*, 1 (2012), 151.
12. See also Richard Meek, Chapter 5, and Katherine Ibbett's Chapter 2 in this volume. Similarly, Skarga's 'economy of mercy' in the Polish-Lithuanian commonwealth excluded certain religious others; see Clarinda Calma and Jolanta Rzegocka's Chapter 7.

13 Alexis Shotwell, *Against Purity: Living Ethically in Compromised Times* (Minneapolis and London: University of Minnesota Press, 2017), p. 135. In this paragraph, I mainly draw on chapter 4, 'Consuming Suffering', pp. 107–35.
14 Donna Haraway, *Staying with the Trouble: Making Kin in the Chthulucene* (Durham and London: Duke University Press, 2016), p. 55. Alison Searle in this volume refers to thieves' realisation that they are implicated in 'networks of living concern' – a phrase that evokes a similar attention to entanglement and accompanying urge to care for those with whom we are entangled.
15 Shotwell, *Against Purity*, p. 126.
16 Anna Tsing, 'Arts of Inclusion, or How to Love a Mushroom', *Manoa*, 22:2 (2010), 201 and 192.
17 Haraway, *Staying with Trouble*, p. 4.
18 Donna Haraway, *When Species Meet* (Minneapolis and London: University of Minnesota Press, 2008), p. 311.
19 Haraway, *When Species Meet*, p. 22.
20 *OED*, 'compassion, *n.*', 1.
21 Haraway, *Staying with the Trouble*, 39.
22 Haraway, 'Sharing Suffering: Instrumental Relations between Laboratory Animals and Their People' in *When Species Meet*, pp. 83, 77 and 84, respectively.
23 See Chapter 6 this volume.
24 Elisabeth Arnould-Bloomfield, 'Posthuman Compassions', *PMLA*, 130:5 (2015), 1474.
25 See Chapter 6 in this volume.
26 Deborah Bird Rose and Thom van Dooren, 'Encountering a More-Than-Human World: Ethos and the Arts of Witness' in Ursula Heise, Jon Christensen and Michelle Niemann (eds.), *The Routledge Companion to the Environmental Humanities* (London: Routledge, 2017), p. 124.
27 Ursula K. Le Guin, quoted in Haraway, *Staying with the Trouble*, p. 57.
28 Haraway, *Staying with the Trouble*, p. 29.
29 Haraway, *Staying with the Trouble*, p. 150.

Index

alms, 12, 17, 33, 166, 169, 222, 225, 227–8, 230–1, 237–50
anger, 2, 30, 49, 280
Anthropocene, 293–300
Aquinas, Thomas, 10, 222
Arendt, Hannah, 2, 203
Aristotle, 3–6, 11, 27, 30, 44, 88, 109, 144, 147, 197, 262, 274–5, 278, 280
   Poetics, 27, 44, 146, 274
   Rhetoric, 275
Averell, William, *A mervailous combat of contrarieties*, 106, 110, 118
Aylett, Robert (poet), 133

Bacon, Francis, 28, 36, 40, 89, 198
becoming-with, 297–9
Becon, Thomas (clergyman), 121–2, 126, 132
Bedel, Henry (clergyman), 131
beggars, 17, 31, 33, 159–74, 221, 237–8, 242–7, 249
Behn, Aphra, *Oroonoko*, 18, 273–86
Bellarmine, Robert, 14, 45, 50–4, 56
Berlant, Lauren, 1–2, 6, 134, 201, 295, 297
Bolton, Robert (clergyman), 107, 132, 296
bowels, 4, 15, 30, 47, 75–6, 123, 126–34, 242–3, 273–4, 276, 284, 297–9
Bright, Timothy, *Treatise of Melancholy*, 105
Browne, Thomas, *Religio Medici*, 82, 91, 95
Bruno, Giordano, 51, 187, 191, 199, 204–5
   Candelaio, 181–5, 187
Burton, Robert, 199
   Anatomy of Melancholy, 73, 93–4
Butler, Judith, 210
Byrd, William, 37–8

Calvin, John, 33, 73, 75–6
Calvinism, 46, 73, 83, 181, 187, 189, 241
captives, 148, 150–2
care, 92, 109–10, 231–2, 275, 299
   medical, 36, 82, 84–95
   self-care, 46, 50, 76, 83

charity, 6–8, 17, 26, 36, 52–4, 69, 82, 121–3, 125–6, 128–9, 132–4, 143, 159, 164, 167–8, 173, 221–9, 231–2, 239–43, 247–50 (*see also* alms)
Charles I, King of England, 28, 142, 160, 162, 274, 280, 283, 285
Christ, suffering of, 5–6, 30, 37, 103–4, 122–4, 264, 273
church, building, 27, 36–9
   St Botolph's, London, 17, 237–50
   St Mary's, Oxford, 30
   St Paul's, London, 38, 222
Church, early, 4
Cicero, Marcus Tullius, 4, 25, 29, 41, 86–9, 91
Civil Wars, England, 159–60, 274, 281
clemency, 4, 9–10, 47, 67, 146
clementia. See clemency
Coeffeteau, Nicolas, 2, 89, 197–8
commiseration, 9, 36, 92, 105, 111–12, 146–8, 152, 183, 275
compassion
   across religious difference, 33–5, 152, 189
   bowels of. *See* bowels
   classical views of, 3–4, 6, 25, 29, 65, 243, 275
   contemporary views of, 1–2, 84, 293–300
   critiques of, 1–2, 64, 67
   definitions of, 1, 3–4, 6, 8–11, 146, 294, 298
   early Christian views of, 4–5
   eighteenth-century views of, 2–3, 18, 113
   historical cognates of, 2–6, 8–11, 15, 26–7, 103, 105, 146, 148, 179
   medieval views of, 5–7, 11, 17, 121, 123–4, 222–3
   neo-Stoic views of, 45, 64, 67–8, 72, 76
   phenomenology of, 12, 126–30
   withholding of, 38, 211, 262
consolation, 14–15, 63–77, 83, 85, 87, 95
contagion, emotional, 4, 11, 16–17, 44, 67, 71–2, 106, 114, 123–4, 160, 170–2, 174, 198, 207, 285

302

Index

Cortés, Hernán, 276
Coryate, Thomas, 37–8

Day, Angel, *The English Secretorie*, 63
Dekker, Thomas, 244
Delaurenti, Béatrice, 11
Descartes, René, 44, 47, 53
difference
  human-animal, 55, 294, 298–9
  racialised, 267–8, 274, 278–9, 281–2, 293
  religious, 242, 293, 296
Digby, Kenelm, 64, 82, 92
Diggers. *See* Protestant dissenters
Dijkhuizen, Jan Frans van, 5, 77
disaster, response to, 17, 52, 238
doctors, 14, 71, 83–95
Donne, John, 37, 77
  Death's Duel, 273–4
  Sermons, 30, 33, 36, 75–6, 197–8, 273, 284
Dooren, Thom van, 294, 299
Dryden, John, 204, 274–5

eleos, 3–6, 9
Elizabeth I, Queen of England, 28, 31, 36, 106, 108, 241
Elyot, Thomas, 88
emotions. *See* anger; compassion; contagion, emotional; *eleos*; fear; laughter; *misericordia*; mourning; *oiktos*; sympathy; terror
Empire, Ottoman, 150–1, 165
Empire, Spanish, 257–8
entrails. *See* bowels
Erasmus, Desiderius, 25, 65–8, 71, 84, 86, 199–200
ethos, 14, 27–40, 63–9, 74, 279, 282, 299
Everyman, 17, 223–6, 229
execution, public, 172, 285

fear, 3, 10, 30, 37, 44–5, 88, 90, 118, 150, 166, 190–1, 209, 223, 248, 262, 266, 274–9, 283, 285
Florio, John, 10, 204
Foucault, Michel, 50, 197–8, 285
friendship, 14, 18, 68, 82–90, 92, 94–5, 222, 275–80, 283, 285
funeral, 64, 68, 72, 74, 242

Galen, theories of, 39, 71, 94, 105, 110, 114
Gospels, 4, 45, 127
  John, 37, 64, 74–6, 83, 273
  Luke, 30, 273
  Marc, 25
  Matthew, 103, 111, 230
Gregory, John, 95
guts. *See* bowels

Habermas, Jürgen, 277
Hall, Joseph (bishop), 90, 199
Haraway, Donna, 294, 297–9
heroism, 46, 48
hierarchy, social, 18, 108, 110, 165–6, 248, 258, 264, 267, 297
Hippocrates, 87, 95
Hobbes, Thomas, 9, 44
Holland, Henry (clergyman), 113–14, 116, 130
hospitals, 36, 47, 52, 122, 219
humanism, 72, 83
Hume, David, 2

Ibbett, Katherine, 8, 186, 209, 274–5
iconoclasm, 7
illness, 4, 7–8, 33, 36, 47, 51, 56, 84–95, 110, 237, 245, 273
imagination, 1, 9, 15, 44, 47, 55, 95, 104–5, 107, 112–14, 116–17, 123–4, 130, 160, 172, 198, 200, 203, 205, 232, 262, 267, 273–4
Ingannati, Gli, 181, 186

James I, King of England, 51
James II, King of England, 274, 280
James, William (clergyman), 108–12, 115–16
Jesuits, 16, 34, 45, 51–2, 54–6, 141–52
Job, 30, 54, 63, 114, 130
Joubert, Laurent, 84–6
judgement, 4, 53, 56, 66, 144, 223–4, 238, 243

Kahn, Victoria, 280
Kant, Immanuel, 4, 200
Konstan, David, 3, 9, 262, 267

La Primaudaye, Pierre de, 90, 129
Las Casas, Bartolomé de, *Brevísima relación de la destrucción de las Indias*, 17, 257–68, 276, 286
laughter, 94, 117, 180, 191, 244
laws, regulating compassion, 31, 160
Le Moyne, Pierre, 14, 45, 54–7
letters, 63–6, 83, 185, 260, 266
London, 6, 12, 17, 31–2, 36, 38–9, 113, 116, 125, 160–3, 166, 187–8, 190, 219–22, 226, 237–50
Lucretius, 16–17, 181, 199, 209, 211
  De rerum natura, 203–7

MacCulloch, Diarmaid, 240
Mandeville, Bernard de, 94–5
Mary, mother of Christ, 5, 74, 264
Master of Alkmaar, 7
maternity, 5, 72, 129, 264

Matt, Susan, 8
McNamer, Sarah, 9, 264
medicine, 14, 84, 87–9, 91, 93–5, 284
mercy, 2, 4, 7–11, 15, 30–1, 33, 36, 47, 52,
  67–8, 82, 127, 129, 131, 133, 142–4, 146,
  148, 160, 162, 210, 243, 257, 262
Middleton, Thomas, 244
Milton, John, 34, 77, 284
misericordia, 3–5, 10, 67, 146–7, 257, 262
Montaigne, Michel de, 91, 181, 199, 202, 204,
  208–10, 279
mourning, 14, 63–4, 68–76
Muggletonians. *See* Protestant dissenters
Mullaney, Steven, 29, 38, 122, 293
multispecies ethics, 295–6, 299
music, responses to, 12, 33, 37–8, 90

Nashe, Thomas, 219–22, 228, 233, 239
neighbour, compassion for, 6, 8, 47, 52–4, 56,
  67, 126, 144, 160, 169, 222, 230, 238–9,
  249
neo-Stoicism, 6, 73, 83
Nussbaum, Martha, 203

oiktos, 3

pain, 2–3, 5, 11, 15, 44, 71, 124, 128, 130, 200,
  202–3, 211, 275, 297–9
pamphlets, 31, 189, 247–9
parrhesia (frank speech), 87–8
Pascal, Blaise, 50, 55
Paul, St, 29, 33, 37, 73, 103, 107, 145
pedagogy, 54
Perkins, William, 33, 130
petitioners, 163, 238–9, 243, 245–6, 249–50
Petrarch, Francesco, 64–5, 77, 86
Petrarchism, 179
Pigman, George, 63–4
playbills, 145–6, 148–51
Plutarch, 30, 86–8
Poland-Lithuania, Commonwealth of, 16,
  141–52
Pontanus, Jacobus, 146
poverty, responses to, 49, 51–2, 161, 226, 242,
  249–50
Prime, John (clergyman), 103–5
Protestant dissenters, 28, 34–5, 109, 132, 187
Puritan. *See* Protestant dissenters

Quakers. *See* Protestant dissenters
Quintilian, 67, 91, 204

Ranters. *See* Protestant dissenters
refugees, 31, 33, 142, 179, 187, 189, 294
republics, 35, 141, 144

Roach, Joseph, 39
Rose, Deborah Bird, 294, 299
Rousseau, Jean-Jacques, 2–3, 200

Sack of Rome, 186
Sales, Saint François de, 14, 45–51, 54, 57
salvation, 7, 29, 48–9, 51, 53, 57, 73,
  132, 220, 222–3, 225–9, 241–2, 263,
  265, 296
Sandys, Edwin (Archbishop of York), 107–8,
  296
Sarbievius, Matthias Casimirus (Sarbiewski),
  145–8
Scaliger, Joseph Justus, 146
Scaliger, Julius Caesar, 68
Scheer, Monique, 12, 108, 125, 132–3
Senault, Jean-François, 160
Seneca, Lucius Annaeus, 4, 67, 88, 93
sermons, 6–7, 12, 14–15, 30, 33, 36–7,
  64, 73–5, 103–18, 122–3, 125,
  127–8, 131, 143–4, 222, 227, 242,
  273, 284
Shakespeare, William, 32, 199
  As You Like It, 41
  Coriolanus, 106
  Henry VI, Part One, 33, 38
  King Lear, 17, 63, 210–12, 229–33
  Pericles, 207
  The Rape of Lucrece, 205
  Richard II, 38
  Richard III, 33
  Romeo and Juliet, 15, 114–16
  Sir Thomas More (contribution to), 15, 28,
    31–2, 116–17
  The Tempest, 28, 200–3, 210
  Titus Andronicus, 33, 38
  Twelfth Night, 16, 37, 179–96
  The Winter's Tale, 204, 207
shipwreck, 16, 39–40, 163, 179, 181, 186,
  197–212
Shirley, James, 16, 141–2, 159–74
Shotwell, Alexis, 296–7
sickness. *See* illness
Skarga, Piotr (Jesuit preacher), 142–3
slavery, 4, 18, 112, 259, 273–86
Smith, Adam, 18, 113
Smith, Henry (clergyman), 121–2, 131
Sontag, Susan, 202–3
Sorbière, Samuel, 94
Spenser, Edmund, 199
  Daphnaïda, 14, 64, 68–73
Stoicism, 28, 73, 83
Stow, John, 219–22, 228, 233
strangers, 28, 31–2, 37, 116, 144, 189, 230, 238,
  243, 277–8

sympathy, 2–4, 6, 9, 15, 26, 63, 65, 69–70, 77, 92, 95, 103–18, 123, 130, 146, 148, 151, 167, 188, 191, 197–212, 243–4, 262, 264, 274–5, 296–7

tact, 84, 197, 207, 211
Taylor, Charles, 159, 169
tears, 40, 45, 51–2, 65, 71, 74–7, 83, 205, 211, 232, 273
Terpstra, Nicholas, 159
terror, 44, 147–8, 152, 276 (*see also* fear)
theatre (building), 2, 12, 15–16, 27, 36–40, 160–2
Topsell, Edward (clergyman), 131, 298
translation, 11, 197, 274, 278
Trent, 57
Tsing, Anna, 296–7

vagrancy, 159–62, 166–7, 169, 242 (*see also* beggars)
Vives, Juan Luis, 53, 84, 90

vulnerability, 14, 17, 64, 76, 83, 86–8, 180, 189–91, 200, 202, 210, 225, 229, 231, 233, 298

Wars of Religion, France, 8, 46, 111, 182, 186
Warsaw Confederation, 142, 145, 172
wealth, 49, 52, 161, 163, 165–6, 169, 231, 242, 249
Wessel, Susan, 4–5, 126
Williams, Raymond, 27–8
Wilson, Thomas, 65–6, 92, 237, 246
witnessing, 40, 124, 200, 221, 258, 262, 267, 276, 285, 299
women, as readers, 46–7, 49–50
Wright, Thomas, *The Passions of the Minde in Generall*, 10, 29–30, 32–4, 37, 39, 117–18

Yamamoto-Wilson, John, 127–8

CPSIA information can be obtained
at www.ICGtesting.com
Printed in the USA
LVHW080921030821
694401LV00004B/328